CONTRIBUTORS TO VOLUME 2

J. Stacy Adams

Vernon L. Allen

Albert Bandura

Leonard Berkowitz

Keith E. Davis

Jonathan L. Freedman

L. Richard Hoffman

Edward E. Jones

John Schopler

David O. Sears

ADVANCES IN
Experimental
Social Psychology

EDITED BY

Leonard Berkowitz
DEPARTMENT OF PSYCHOLOGY
UNIVERSITY OF WISCONSIN
MADISON, WISCONSIN

VOLUME 2

 ACADEMIC PRESS   New York and London   1965

ACADEMIC PRESS INC.
111 Fifth Avenue, New York, New York 10003

United Kingdom Edition published by
ACADEMIC PRESS INC. (LONDON) LTD.
Berkeley Square House, London W.1

LIBRARY OF CONGRESS CATALOG CARD NUMBER: **64-23452**

Third Printing, 1968

PRINTED IN THE UNITED STATES OF AMERICA

CONTRIBUTORS

Number in parentheses indicate the pages on which the authors' contributions begin.

J. STACY ADAMS, *Behavioral Research Service, General Electric Company, Crotonville, New York (267)*

VERNON L. ALLEN, *Department of Psychology, University of Wisconsin, Madison, Wisconsin (133)*

ALBERT BANDURA, *Department of Psychology, Stanford University, Stanford, California (1)*

LEONARD BERKOWITZ, *Department of Psychology, University of Wisconsin, Madison, Wisconsin (301)*

KEITH E. DAVIS, *Department of Psychology, University of Colorado, Boulder, Colorado (219)*

JONATHAN L. FREEDMAN, *Department of Psychology, Stanford University, Stanford, California (57)*

L. RICHARD HOFFMAN, *Graduate School of Business, University of Chicago, Chicago, Illinois (99)*

EDWARD E. JONES, *Department of Psychology, Duke University, Durham, North Carolina (219)*

JOHN SCHOPLER, *Department of Psychology, University of North Carolina, Chapel Hill, North Carolina (177)*

DAVID O. SEARS, *Department of Psychology, University of California, Los Angeles, California (57)*

v

PREFACE

The appearance of this second volume of the *Advances in Experimental Social Psychology* a year after the publication of Volume 1 is a testimony to the vitality and breadth of the field. There clearly is no shortage of problems to be investigated or research areas to be reviewed. Social psychologists continue to be active both in conducting research and in formulating new theoretical generalizations. We will try to reflect the most important developments in these endeavors as this serial publication continues.

The contents of this volume provide a clear illustration of social psychology's impressive breadth of interests. All of the papers, of course, deal with reactions to stimuli associated with other people, but there may be many different kinds of reactions and there is a great variety of social stimuli. Bandura concentrates on imitative responses and discusses various theoretical interpretations of imitation, while Berkowitz places considerable emphasis upon the role of externally based stimuli in evoking aggressive behavior. Social psychology has long been concerned with social influence processes. In accord with this continuing interest, Allen provides a comprehensive review of situational factors governing conformity and Schopler presents an analysis of the construct of "social power" as it has been employed in influence research. How the individual will behave in response to social stimuli often depends upon his particular motives operating at the time. Contemporary social psychology gives considerable attention to cognitive motives, such as for dissonance reduction. Adams extends dissonance theory to cover exchange conceptions of interpersonal relations and especially worker productivity. Freedman and Sears argue, on the other hand, that people are often not as defensive in responding to information opposing their beliefs as this type of theorizing has generally assumed. To round out this summary, one of social psychology's oldest concerns is with the productivity and behavior of small groups. Hoffman reviews much of the current literature in this area and reports the findings of a comprehensive research program. Person perception is one of the newer fields within the discipline; Jones and Davis offer a valuable analysis of the attribution process in person perception.

Because of the great number of possible topics, the selection of any particular area for review is all too susceptible to the Editor's biases and prejudices. He welcomes any and all proposals. Readers are invited to suggest ideas for the forthcoming volumes.

Now let me take advantage of the Editorial Chair to ride one of my favorite hobbyhorses. There are at least two prejudices that the Editor is not prepared to surrender. These have to do with the nature of social psychology and the preferred method of investigation. With regard to the first of these matters, it has always been difficult to define the boundaries and scope of social psychology. Shortly after World War II, when the first interdisciplinary training programs in this field were being established, social psychology was generally regarded as an amalgam of psychology and sociology, and yet somewhat outside of psychology. One advocate of these interdisciplinary programs said psychology was concerned with "within-the-skin" processes, while social psychology dealt with what went on "between skins." Such a distinction obviously does not apply to the theoretical formulations of interest to most *psychological* social psychologists today. Many psychological social psychologists clearly are psychologists first of all. They make inferences regarding internal events and, as is readily apparent from the two volumes of this publication, often do so employing the constructs, assumptions, and wisdom of general psychology. Instead of being different from other psychological fields, psychological social psychology typically brings them all together, taking the knowledge and concepts of all areas as well as providing knowledge and concepts of its own, in attempting to account for social behavior.

I do not claim that every social psychologist must be a general psychologist. The discipline as a whole undoubtedly benefits from having researchers and theoreticians who think primarily in terms of "between skins" constructs. The *Advances* will always have room for their formulations (as can be seen, for example, in Gamson's chapter on coalitions in Volume 1). Nevertheless, the Editor is convinced that psychological social psychologists can serve a very important function in integrating material from the various components of general psychology—and from sociology as well. They are *social* psychologists because they then relate this integration to social phenomena, and not because they disregard the contributions of other psychological areas. I hope to promote this vital integrative task in the pages of this serial publication.

LEONARD BERKOWITZ

November, 1965

CONTENTS

Vicarious Processes: A Case of No-Trial Learning

Albert Bandura

Selective Exposure

Jonathan L. Freedman and David O. Sears

Group Problem Solving

L. Richard Hoffman

Situational Factors in Conformity

Vernon L. Allen

Social Power

John Schopler

From Acts to Dispositions
The Attribution Process in Person Perception

Edward E. Jones and Keith E. Davis

Inequity in Social Exchange

J. Stacy Adams

The Concept of Aggressive Drive: Some Additional Considerations

Leonard Berkowitz

VICARIOUS PROCESSES: A CASE OF NO-TRIAL LEARNING[1]

Albert Bandura

DEPARTMENT OF PSYCHOLOGY
STANFORD UNIVERSITY
STANFORD, CALIFORNIA

Research and theoretical interpretations of learning processes have focused almost exclusively on a single mode of response acquistion which is exemplified by the operant or instrumental conditioning paradigm. In this procedure the organism is impelled, in one way or another, to perform responses under specific stimulus conditions and, through differential reinforcement of spontaneously emitted variations in behavior, new response patterns are developed or existing repertoires are brought under new discriminative stimulus control. It is generally assumed that the principles

[1] Work on this manuscript was facilitated by Research Grant M-5162 from the National Institutes of Health, United States Public Health Service.

1

governing the latter mode of response acquisition account also for social learning phenomena occurring under naturalistic conditions.

The continued adherence to a relatively narrow range of learning principles and procedures stems primarily from the fact that certain critical conditions that obtain in real-life situations are rarely, if ever, reproduced in laboratory studies of learning. Thus, in laboratory investigations experimenters arrange comparatively benign environments in which errors will not produce fatal consequences for the organism. By contrast, naturalistic environs are loaded with potentially lethal consequences that unmercifully befall those who happen to perform hazardous errors. For this reason, it would be exceedingly injudicious to rely primarily upon trial-and-error and successive approximations methods in teaching children to swim, adolescents to drive automobiles, or adults to master complex occupational and social tasks. If rodents and pigeons toiling in Skinner boxes and various mazes could likewise get electrocuted, dismembered, or extensively bruised for errors that inevitably occur during early phases of learning, it is a reasonably safe prediction that few of these venturesome subjects would ever survive the shaping process. Apart from the questions of efficiency (Bandura and McDonald, 1963) and survival, it is doubtful if many classes of responses would ever be acquired if social training proceeded solely by the method of approximations through differential reinforcement of emitted responses (Bandura, 1962).

It is evident from informal observation that vicarious-learning experiences and response-guidance procedures involving both symbolic and live models are utilized extensively in social learning to short-circuit the acquisition process, and to prevent one-trial extinction of the organism in potentially hazardous situations. Although historically, learning by vicarious experience has been generally labeled "imitation," in the contemporary literature essentially the same phenomena are subsumed under other terms such as "observational learning," "copying," "social facilitation," "vicarious learning," "contagion," "identification," and "role-playing." The diversity in constructs reflects the arbitrary distinctions between vicarious learning events that have been proposed, at one time or another, based on the types of response classes modified (Lazowick, 1955; Osgood et al., 1957), the antecedent variables supposedly governing the occurrence of matching responses (Parsons and Shils, 1951), the fidelity with which modeling stimuli are reproduced (N. E. Miller and Dollard, 1941; Riopelle, 1960), the specificity and generality of observational learning (Parsons and Shils, 1951), and in terms of whether matching responses are performed in the presence or absence of the model (Mowrer, 1950). While it is possible to draw distinctions between descriptive terms based on certain stimulus, mediating, or terminal-response variables, one might question whether it is advantageous to do so, since essentially the same learning process is involved regardless of the content and generality of what is learned, the models from whom the response patterns are acquired, and the stimulus situations in which the relevant behavior is subsequently performed. Therefore, the terms imitative, observational, and vicarious learning will be employed interchangeably to refer to behavioral modifications resulting from exposure to modeling stimuli.

For the purposes of the present discussion, a vicarious learning event is defined as one in which new responses are acquired or the characteristics of existing response repertoires are modified as a function of observing the behavior of others and its reinforcing consequences, without the modeled responses being overtly performed by the viewer during the exposure period. In demonstrating vicarious learning phenomena, it is therefore necessary to employ a nonresponse acquisition procedure in which a subject simply observes a model's behavior, but otherwise performs no overt instrumental responses, nor is administered any reinforcing stimuli during the period of acquisition. Any learning that occurs under these limiting conditions is purely on an observational or covert basis. This mode of response acquisition is accordingly designated as no-trial learning, since the observer does not engage in any *overt responding trials* although, as will be shown later, he may require multiple *observational trials* in order to reproduce the modeled stimuli accurately. Moreover, the development of mediational responses, in the form of imaginal and implicit verbal representations of the perceived stimulus events, may play a critical role in the vicarious learning process.

I. Theories of Response Acquisition through Observation

The concept of imitation in psychological theory has an extended history dating back to Morgan (1896), Tarde (1903), and MacDougall (1908), who regarded imitativeness as an innate propensity. These early instinctive interpretations of the imitative process not only impeded empirical investigations of probable controlling variables, but due to the vehement reaction against the instinct doctrine, even the phenomena subsumed under the concept were, until recent years, either widely ignored or repudiated.

A. ASSOCIATIVE AND CLASSICAL CONDITIONING THEORIES

As the instinct doctrine fell into disrepute, a number of psychologists, notably Humphrey (1921), Allport (1924), and Holt (1931), attempted to account for imitative behavior in terms of associative or Pavlovian conditioning principles. According to Holt's conceptualization, for example, when an adult copies a response made by a child, the latter tends to repeat the same behavior, and, as this circular associative sequence continues, the adult's matching behavior becomes an increasingly effective stimulus for the child's response. If, during this spontaneous mutual imitation, the adult performs a response that is novel for the child, the latter will copy it. Piaget (1951) is a more recent exponent of essentially the same point of view, according to which the imitator's response serves initially as the stimulus for the model in alternating imitative sequences. Allport similarly presented imitative responses as instances of classical conditioning of verbalizations, motoric responses, or emotions to matching social stimuli with which they have been contiguously associated.

Although the associative theories account adequately for the imitator's repetition of his own behavior, they fail to explain the psychological mechanisms governing the emergence of *novel* responses during the model-observer interaction sequence. Moreover demonstrations of observational learning in animals and humans do not ordinarily commence with a model's matching a semi-irrelevant response of the learner. Thus, in utilizing modeling procedures to teach a mynah bird to talk, the trainer does not engage initially in circular crowing behavior; instead, he begins by emitting verbal responses that he wishes to transmit, but which clearly do not exist in integrated form in the bird's vocal repertoire.

B. INSTRUMENTAL CONDITIONING THEORIES

As theoretical explanations of learning shifted the emphasis from classical conditioning to instrumental learning based on rewarding and punishing response consequences, theories of imitation similarly assumed that the occurrence of observational learning is contingent upon the administration of reinforcing stimuli either to the model or to the observer. This point of view was most clearly expounded by Miller and Dollard (1941) in the classic publication, *Social Learning and Imitation*. According to this theory, the necessary conditions for learning through imitation include a motivated subject who is positively reinforced for matching the correct responses of a model during a series of initially random, trial-and-error responses.

The experiments conducted by Miller and Dollard involved a series of two-choice discrimination problems, in each of which a trained leader responded to environmental stimuli that were concealed from the subject; consequently, he was totally dependent upon the cues provided by the leader's behavior. The model's choices were consistently rewarded and the observing subject was similarly reinforced whenever he matched the choice responses of the imitatee. This form of imitation was labeled by the authors "matched-dependent behavior" because the subjects relied on the leader for relevant cues and matched his responses. Based on this paradigm, it was shown that both rats and children readily learn to follow their respective models, and generalize imitative responses to new stimulus situations, new models, and different motivational states.

While these experiments have been widely accepted as demonstrations of learning by imitation, they in fact represent only the special case of discrimination place-learning, in which the behavior of others provides discriminative stimuli for responses that already exist in the subject's behavior repertoire. Indeed, had the relevant environmental cues been made more distinctive, the behavior of the models would have been quite irrelevant and perhaps even a hindrance in the acquisition process. By contrast, most forms of imitation involve *response* rather than *place* learning, in which subjects combine behavioral elements into relatively complex novel responses solely by observing the performance of social models, without any opportunity to perform the model's behavior in the exposure setting and without any reinforcers administered either to the models or to the observers (Bandura, 1965a). In the latter instance, modeling cues constitute an indispensable aspect of the learning process. Moreover, since the S-R reinforcement paradigm for observational learning requires the subject to perform the imitative response before he can learn it, the theory propounded by Miller and Dollard evidentially accounts more adequately for the emission of previously learned matching responses than for their acquisition. Continuing with our example of language learning, in order for our mynah bird to learn the words *social psychology* imitatively it would first have to emit the words *social psychology* in the course of random vocalization, match them accidentally with the trainer's verbal responses, and secure a positive reinforcement. It is evident from the foregoing discussion that the conditions assumed by Miller and Dollard to be necessary for learning by imitation place severe limitations on the types of behavioral changes that can be attributed to the influence of social models.

The operant-reinforcement analysis of imitative behavior (Baer and Sherman, 1964; Skinner, 1953, 1957) is in many respects similar to one originally advanced by Miller and Dollard. According to the former interpretation, if matching responses are positively reinforced and divergent responses are either nonrewarded or punished, the model's behavior comes to serve as discriminative stimuli for reinforcement. Given an adequate reinforcement history for behavioral reproduction of modeling stimuli, matching responses per se may gradually acquire secondary reinforcing properties. After a generalized imitative repertoire has been developed on the basis of consistent rewarding consequences in a variety of situations, the individual will tend to display a high incidence of precisely imitative behavior which, due to its acquired reward value, may be maintained at least temporarily in the absence of externally administered reinforcers.

Reinforcement control of generalized imitation is well illustrated in a recent study conducted by Baer and Sherman (1964). Three imitative responses (head nodding, mouthing, and novel verbalizations) were strongly established in young children by social reinforcement from a puppet who had instructed the subjects to match his modeling behavior. After a stable rate of imitative responding had been achieved, the puppet displayed nonreinforced bar-pressing interspersed among the other three matching responses, which were maintained in the children on a continuous schedule of reinforcement. Under these conditions, the subjects showed an increase in imitative bar-pressing behavior over their operant levels. In order to further demonstrate the dependence of generalized imitative bar-pressing on direct reinforcement of other matching responses either social reinforcers were no longer presented following imitative head nodding, mouthing, and verbalization, or the puppet ceased to exhibit these responses. Both the extinction and the time-out from modeling procedures resulted in decreased imitative bar-pressing. Moreover, reinstatement of the other three modeling cues and reinforcement of the corresponding matching responses produced increased imitative bar-pressing behavior.

It should be noted that, like the Miller and Dollard theory, the operant-reinforcement interpretation of modeling processes accounts satisfactorily for the discriminative and reinforcing stimulus control of previously learned matching responses, but it throws no light on the variables governing the acquisition of novel responses through observation. Such responses are learned during the period of exposure to modeling stimuli prior to the operation of the reinforcement practices. Indeed, had the children in the experiment cited above been tested for imitative learning immediately following demonstration of the four critical responses, it is a safe prediction that they could have reproduced the modeled repertoire without undergoing any imitation contingent reinforcement. In evaluating the role of reinforcement in modeling processes, it is therefore important to distinguish *acquisition* from *performance*.

Numerous investigations, differing considerably in the choice of reinforcing stimuli, types of matching responses, and age status of the subjects, have shown that the presentation of imitation-contingent positive or negative reinforcers either to the model (Bandura, 1965; Bandura *et al.*, 1963c; Kanfer, 1965; Walters *et al.*, 1963; Walters and Parke, 1964) or to the subject (Kanareff and Lanzetta, 1960a,b; Lanzetta and Kanareff, 1959; Metz, 1964; Schein, 1954) have a facilitative or a suppressive effect on the subject's subsequent performance of matching responses. However, results from a recent experiment (Bandura, 1965b) lend support to the theory that the *acquisition* of matching responses results primarily from stimulus contiguity and associated symbolic processes, whereas reinforcing consequences to the model or to the observer have a major influence on the *performance* of imitatively learned responses.

In the above study, children observed a film-mediated model who exhibited a sequence of novel physical and verbal aggressive responses. In one treatment condition the model was severely punished following the

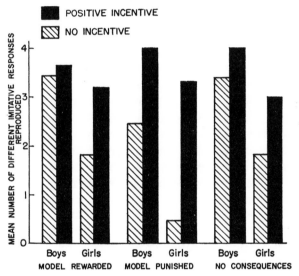

FIG. 1. Mean number of different matching responses reproduced by subjects as a function of incentive conditions and the model's reinforcement contingencies. (Adapted from Bandura, 1965b.)

display of aggressive behavior; in the second, the model was generously rewarded with delectable treats and lavish praise; the third condition presented no response consequences to the model. A postexposure performance test of imitation revealed that the reinforcement contingencies applied to the model's responses resulted in differential degrees of matching behavior. Relative to subjects in the model-punished condition, children in the model-rewarded and the no-consequence groups spontaneously performed a significantly greater variety of imitative responses. Moreover, boys reproduced substantially more of the model's behavioral repertoire than girls, the differences being particularly marked in the model-punished treatment (Fig. 1).

Following the performance test, children in all three groups were offered highly attractive incentives contingent upon their reproducing the model's responses, so as to activate into performance what the children had acquired through observation. Although learning must necessarily be inferred from performance, it was assumed that the responses reproduced under positive incentive conditions would provide a relatively accurate index of acquisition.

As shown in Fig. 1, the introduction of positive incentives completely wiped out the previously observed performance differences, revealing an equivalent amount of learning among children in the model-rewarded, model-punished, and the no-consequences conditions. Similarly, the initially large sex difference was substantially reduced.

While there is ample evidence that reinforcing stimuli can significantly alter the probability of future occurrence of preceding matching responses, consequent events can hardly serve as a necessary precondition for their acquisition. However, under conditions where reinforcers are repeatedly administered to a model as he displays an ongoing series of responses, observation of reinforcing consequences occurring early in the sequence might be expected to increase the vigilance of the observer toward subsequently modeled behavior. The anticipation of positive reinforcement for reproducing matching responses by the observer may therefore, indirectly influence the course of vicarious learning by enhancing and focusing the subject's observing responses.

C. SENSORY FEEDBACK THEORY

Mowrer's proprioceptive feedback theory of imitation (1960) similarly highlights the role of reinforcement but, unlike the preceding approaches which reduce imitation to a special case of instrumental learning, Mowrer emphasizes the classical conditioning of positive and negative emotions to matching response-correlated stimuli. Mowrer distinguishes two forms of imitative learning in terms of whether the observer is reinforced directly or vicariously. In the former case, the model performs a response and at the same time rewards the observer. Through the repeated contiguous association of the model's behavior with rewarding experiences, these responses gradually take on positive value for the observer. On the basis of stimulus generalization, the observer can later produce self-rewarding feedback experiences, simply by reproducing as closely as possible the model's positively valenced behavior.

In the second or "empathetic" form of imitative learning, the model not only exhibits the responses but also experiences the reinforcing consequences. It is assumed that the observer, in turn, experiences empathetically the sensory concomitants of the model's behavior, and also intuits his satisfactions or discomforts. As a result of this higher-order vicarious conditioning, the observer will be predisposed to reproduce the matching responses for the attendant positive sensory feedback.

There is considerable research evidence that imitative behavior is enhanced by increasing the rewarding qualities of a model (Bandura and Huston, 1961; Grusec, 1965; Grusec and Mischel, 1965; Hanlon, 1964; Henker, 1964; Mussen and Parker, 1965), and by positive reinforcers administered to a model (Bandura, 1965b; Bandura *et al.,* 1963c; Walters *et al.,* 1963). Although the sensory feedback conception of imitation does not require a response to be performed before it can be learned, it nevertheless fails to explain the acquisition of matching responses when reinforcers are not dispensed either to the model or to observers.

There is some reason to believe that the acquisition, integration, facilitation, and inhibition of responses are in large part centrally, rather than peripherally, mediated. For example, preliminary findings from curare-conditioning experiments—in which animals are skeletally immobilized during aversive conditioning or extinction—demonstrate that conditioned emotional responses can be readily acquired and extinguished independently of skeletal responding and its correlated proprioceptive feedback (Black, 1958; Black *et al.,* 1962). Moreover discriminative classical conditioning, established under curare, can subsequently control discriminative instrumental avoidance responses in the normal state (Leaf, 1964; Solomon and Turner, 1962). Although the mediators of this discriminative transfer have not been identified, the data bring into question theories of learning that rely heavily upon differential proprioceptive cues as explanatory factors.

A peripheral feedback theory would also require highly differential proprioceptive cues to be associated with practically identical overt response patterns. It is more likely that proprioceptive stimulation arising from hitting responses directed toward parents and toward peers may differ little, if at all; nevertheless, physically aggressive responses toward parents are generally strongly inhibited, whereas physical aggression toward peers is much more readily expressed (Bandura, 1960; Bandura and Walters, 1959). One could therefore predict more accurately the expression or inhibition of aggression from knowledge of the stimulus context (e.g., church, athletic gymnasium), the object (e.g, parent, priest, policeman, or peer), and other cues that signify predictable reinforcement contingencies, than from any direct assessment of the type of sensory feedback correlated with the agent's aggressive responses. Thus, in most social interaction sequences, proprioceptive cues constitute only a small portion of the total stimulus complexes. It is therefore necessary to take account also of external stimulus elements and their cognitive correlates, which probably serve as important discriminative stimuli in the regulation of both matching and nonimitative behavior.

It is also evident that rapid selection of responses from among a varied array of alternatives cannot be governed by proprioceptive feedback since relatively few responses could be activated, even incipiently, during characteristically brief pre-decision periods (N. E. Miller, 1964). In recognizing this problem, Mowrer (1960) has conjectured that the initial scanning and selection of responses may occur primarily at the symbolic rather than at the action level.

In this same connection, behavior is influenced by models even when the responses in question do not generate cues possessing motivational properties. This is best exemplified by studies of observational learning of perceptual-motor tasks from filmed demonstration (Sheffield and Maccoby, 1961) that do not contain positive or aversive stimuli essential for the classical conditioning of emotional responses. Mowrer has, of course, pointed out that sensory experiences not only classically condition positive or negative emotions, but also produce conditioned sensation or images. In most cases of observational learning, such perceptual or imaginal responses may be the only important mediating processes. Mowrer's sensory-feedback theory of imitation may therefore be primarily relevant to instances in which the modeled responses incur relatively potent reinforcing consequences capable of endowing response-correlated stimuli with motivational properties.

D. STIMULUS CONTIGUITY AND MEDIATIONAL THEORIES

Recent theoretical analyses of observational learning (Bandura, 1962; Sheffield, 1961) place primary emphasis on the role of stimulus contiguity and associated cognitive response-stimulus events in the acquisition process. According to contiguity theory, during the period of exposure modeling stimuli elicit in observing subjects configurations and sequences of sensory experiences which, on the basis of past associations, become centrally integrated and structured into perceptual responses.

There is some research evidence in the sensory conditioning literature (Conant, 1964; Leuba, 1940; Naruse and Abonai, 1953) that, as a function of contiguous stimulation, an antecedent stimulus can acquire the capacity to elicit imaginal representations of associated stimulus events even though they are no longer physically present. These findings indicate that imaginal responses are conditionable, and presumably extinguishable, as are overt classes of behavior. It is therefore reasonable to suppose that, in the course of observation, transitory sensory and perceptual phenomena are converted to retrievable images of the modeled sequences of behavior. Indeed, a reader could readily elicit, through verbal self-instruction, vivid imagery of the stylistic social responses, physical attributes, role behaviors, and skilled performances of close acquaintances, instructors, entertainers, and a host of other models either encountered in actual social situations or provided in audiovisual displays.

In addition to the acquisition of imaginal responses, once verbal labels have become attached to objective stimuli, the observer acquires, during the period of exposure, verbal equivalents of the model's behavior. Recent modeling experiments (Bandura, 1965b; Bandura *et al.*, 1963c), for example, revealed that children who had observed a model exhibit novel patterns of aggressive responses subsequently described the entire sequence of aggressive acts with considerable accuracy. The above findings thus provide some basis for assuming that symbolic or representational responses in the form of images and verbal associates of the model's behavior constitute the important residues of observational experiences.

The discussion has so far been concerned with the process whereby different forms of representational responses are acquired on the basis of observation. A mediational theory must also account for the nature of the linkage between cognitive representation, on the one hand, and behavioral reproduction, on the other. There is ample evidence (Dollard and Miller, 1950; Mowrer, 1960; Staats and Staats, 1963) that implicit responses provide cues which can serve as discriminative stimuli for directing and controlling instrumental responses in the same way as environmental events. It is likewise assumed that symbolic matching responses possess cue-producing properties that are capable of eliciting, some time after observation, overt responses corresponding to those that were modeled. However, it should be noted here that although the stimuli generated by symbolic behavior can become discriminative for overt action, it does not mean that the observer will necessarily be able to execute skillfully the matching patterns of behavior. This issue will be discussed later.

In order to test the proposition, advanced in the above theory, that symbolization facilitates vicarious learning, a modeling study was conducted (Bandura *et al.,* 1965a) in which symbolic responses were directly manipulated. During the response-acquisition phase of the experiment, children observed a film-mediated adult model exhibit an extended sequence of relatively novel responses, projected on a lenscreen in a television console. The following three conditions of observation were employed. In the *facilitative symbolization* condition, subjects verbalized the modeling stimuli as they were presented on the lenscreen. The purpose of the concurrent verbalization was to enhance the development of imaginal and verbal associates for the model's behavior. Children in the *passive observation* group were instructed simply to observe the film carefully. A third experimental treatment was designed to counteract the establishment of representational responses by having subjects produce interfering verbal responses throughout the period of exposure. In the latter *competing symbolization* condition, subjects were instructed to count rapidly while attending closely to the film.

The degree of observational learning may also be partly governed by incentive-related sets which exert selective control over the type, intensity, and frequency of observing responses. It is likewise entirely possible that different symbolization instructions could create in observers differential anticipations as to whether or not they might later be called upon to demonstrate what they had learned from the filmed presentation. Such self-induced sets, if operative, might affect attentive behavior and thus confound the effects of symbolization processes. Hence, in the present study half of the subjects in each of the three observational treatments were assigned to a positive incentive-set condition. These children were informed that following the movie, they would be asked to reproduce the model's responses and given candy treats for each behavioral element performed correctly. The remaining subjects, assigned to the no-incentive nonperformance condition, were told that immediately after viewing the film they would return to their classroom, thus providing them with little or no incentive to learn the model's repertoire.

An incentive set may influence the amount of behavioral reproduction by either (1) augmenting and channeling the observing responses during acquisition, or (2) actuating deliberate, implicit rehearsal of matching responses immediately after exposure. Since the present experiment was primarily concerned with issues of response acquisition, and the occurrence of differential anticipatory rehearsal would obscure results, children in all groups were assigned the task of counting out loud during the brief period intervening between the end of the movie and reproduction. By this procedure, interpolated activities were held constant for all groups and facilitative symbolic rehearsal was prevented.

In the test for acquisition, children in all treatment conditions were offered candy reinforcers and social rewards for each matching response that they reproduced correctly.

Table I presents the mean number of matching responses achieved by children in the various treatment conditions. In each incentive condition for both boys and girls, the mean reproduction scores attained by the active symbolizers exceeds the corresponding means for the passive observers who, in turn, show a higher level of acquisition than subjects in the competing symbolization treatment. Analysis of variance of these data reveals that symbolization is a highly significant source of variance. Further comparisons of pairs of means indicate that subjects who generated verbal equivalents of the modeling stimuli during presentation subsequently reproduced significantly more matching responses than children who either observed passively or engaged in competing symbolization. The latter two groups also differ significantly. However, observational learning was not influenced by incentive set, nor were there any significant interaction effects.

Although the results of the present study provide confirmatory evidence for the facilitative role of symbolization in observational learning, alternative interpretations of these findings might be examined. It is conceivable that the method utilized for preventing the acquisition of representational responses may have interfered with observation of the pertinent

TABLE I

MEAN NUMBER OF MATCHING RESPONSES REPRODUCED AS A FUNCTION
OF SYMBOLIZATION AND INCENTIVE CONDITIONS

	Observational conditions		
Incentive set	Facilitative symbolization	Passive observation	Competing symbolization
No incentive set			
Boys	16.8	14.5	11.5
Girls	17.5	13.2	6.0
Total	17.2	13.8	8.7
Incentive set			
Boys	16.2	15.3	13.0
Girls	14.8	11.7	9.8
Total	15.5	13.5	11.4

stimuli. Considering, however, that the modeling stimuli were projected on a large television screen directly in front of the subject, seated in a dark room, it is improbable that, under such conditions of highly focused attention, concurrent competing verbalization could appreciably reduce the occurrence of observing responses. Indeed, the marked external control of observing responses in all likelihood accounts for the absence of a significant incentive effect on the acquisition of matching behavior.

In situations where a person is exposed to multiple models exhibiting diverse patterns of behavior, knowledge of the reinforcement contingencies associated with the corresponding response patterns, and anticipation of positive or negative reinforcement for subsequent reproduction may exert selective control over the nature and frequency of attending responses.

The effects of incentive set on observational learning would, therefore, be most clearly elucidated by a comparative study involving (a) highly focused observation of a single sequence of modeling stimuli, (b) controlled exposure to multiple .models requiring selective attentiveness to the different cues presented simultaneously, and (c) self-selection of frequency and duration of exposure to specific types of models. The latter condition, which corresponds most closely to observational learning in naturalistic situations, would probably maximize the influence of reinforcement-oriented set.

Simultaneous competing verbalizations during observation of pictorial displays would not be expected to interfere too extensively with the development of visual imagery, particularly when the modeling stimuli are highly salient, as in the present experiment. It would therefore be of considerable theoretical significance to determine whether any matching responses could be reproduced if, in addition to preventing the development of verbal associates, visual imaginal responses were likewise precluded masked, or obliterated. Such imagery interference procedures would provide the most decisive evidence as to whether representational mediators are necessary for the achievement of delayed, behavioral reproduction.

II. Behavioral Effects of Exposure to Modeling Stimuli

Results of numerous investigations (Bandura, 1962, 1965a; Bandura and Walters, 1963a) reveal that observation of models' responses and their reinforcing consequences may have several different behavioral effects, some of which have been mentioned earlier. As shown in preceding sections, an observer may acquire topographically novel responses that did not previously exist in his behavioral repertoire. Second, observation of response consequences to the model may produce incremental or decremental changes in existing classes of behavior by modifying the strength of inhibitory responses. Third, observation of another person's behavior may facilitate the occurrence of previously learned but non-inhibited responses through the stimulus enhancement and discriminative functions of modeling cues. In the following sections some of the variables controlling these diverse behavioral outcomes and associated mediating processes will be discussed at length.

A. MODELING EFFECTS

In order to demonstrate experimentally the acquisition of new response patterns through observation, it is necessary for a model to exhibit highly novel responses, and the observer must later reproduce them in a substantially identical form. Any behavior that has a very low or zero probability of occurrence given the appropriate stimulus conditions fulfills the criterion of a novel response.

The basic components that enter into the development of more complex integrated units of behavior are usually present in subjects' behavioral repertoires as products either of maturation or of prior observational learning and instrumental conditioning. Thus, while most of the elements in activities that are typically modeled in imitation experiments have undoubtedly been previously learned, the particular pattern of components in each response may be unique. For example, children can manipulate objects, sit on them, and punch them, and they can produce vocal responses, but the likelihood that a young child would spontaneously place a Bobo doll on its side, sit on it, punch it in the nose, and remark "Pow . . . boom . . . boom" is exceedingly remote (Bandura, 1965b; Bandura *et al.*, 1961). It is likewise highly improbable that children who possess even an extensive linguistic repertoire would ever emit verbal responses such as "weto-smacko" or "lickit-stickit" (Bandura *et al.*, 1963b) in the absence of exposure to a model who exhibited these unique word combinations.

In addition to response formation, acquisition outcomes are revealed when existing integrated patterns of behavior are brought under new stimulus control as a function of observational experiences.

The social transmission of novel responses is demonstrated in a series of experiments (Bandura *et al.*, 1961, 1963a) in which nursery-school children observed adults exhibit unusual forms of physical and verbal aggression, while other groups witnessed nonaggressive models, or had no exposure to any social cues. In a post-exposure test for imitative learning, children who had observed the aggressive models displayed a large number of precisely matching aggressive responses (Fig. 2), whereas such patterns of behavior rarely occurred in either the nonaggressive-model condition or the control group. Additional evidence of modeling effects is provided by experiments employing similar classes of responses (Bandura, 1965b; Hicks, 1965) as well as considerably more complicated patterns and sequences of behavior (Bandura *et al.*, 1965; Bandura *et al.*, 1963b; D. Ross, 1962). At an even higher level of complexity, it has been shown that children can acquire contingencies for self-reinforcement and self-evaluative responses (Bandura and Kupers, 1964; Bandura and Whalen, 1965), judgmental orientations (Bandura and McDonald, 1963), self-imposed delay-of-reward patterns (Bandura and Mischel, 1965), self-directed aversive behavior (Mischel and Grusec, 1965), linguistic structures (Bierman, 1965), and distinctive phonetic variation in verbal behavior (Hanlon, 1964), as a function of brief exposure to the behavior of models. Moreover, responses acquired observationally may be retained over an extended period of time (i.e., six months) even though there is little or no occasion to perform the novel patterns of behavior during the interval (Hicks, 1965).

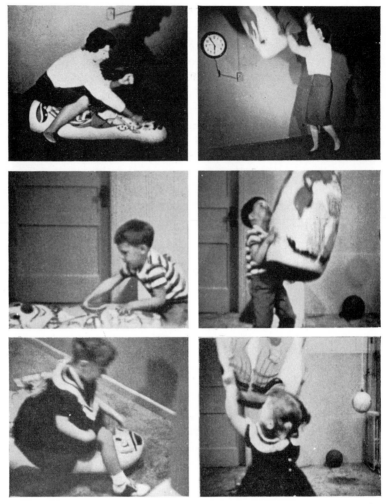

Fig. 2. Photographs of children spontaneously reproducing the behavior exhibited by an aggressive model. (Adapted from Bandura, 1962.)

Considering that the subjects in the experiments cited above had no opportunities to practice the models' responses during the acquisition stage, the process of combining and chaining matching responses must be primarily achieved through central integrative mechanisms.

There have been numerous experiments of observational learning in infrahuman species dating back to the early studies of Thorndike (1898) and Watson (1908). These initial investigations, which were conducted at a time when instinctive interpretations of imitation were in vogue, summarily dismissed the existence of observational learning

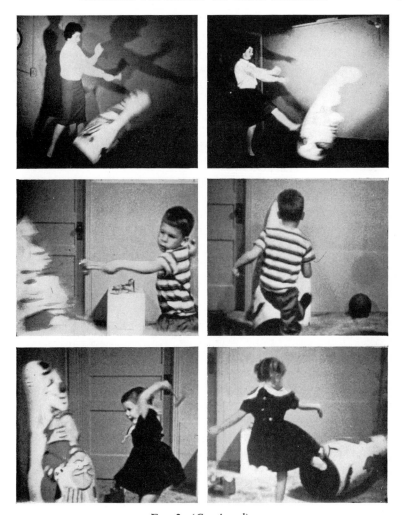

FIG. 2. (Continued)

on the basis of disappointing results from a few animals tested under weak incentives and conditions that failed to ensure adequate observation of the demonstrator's performance. Subsequent studies conducted under more favorable experimental conditions have generally shown that primates can learn to solve manipulative problems (Hayes and Hayes, 1952a; Warden et al., 1940; Warden and Jackson, 1935), and animals of lower order can acquire discriminations (Bayroff and Lard, 1944; Church, 1957; Miller and Dollard, 1941; Solomon and Coles, 1954) and master relatively complex tasks (Herbert and Harsh, 1944) more rapidly through observation than the original models achieved by trial and error. Moreover, the results of several experiments (Darby and Riopelle, 1959, Herbert and Harsh, 1944) show that the increments in performance resulting from observation are not attributable to the fact that the model's demonstration may have simply enhanced the relevant aspects of the stimulus situation.

The animal experiments, with few exceptions, have involved relatively simple responses that were reproduced either simultaneously or immediately after demonstration. Although relevant comparative data are lacking, it is highly probable that, unlike humans who are capable of acquiring observationally and retaining large, integrated units of behavior, lower species would display a limited capacity for delayed reproduction of modeling stimuli due to sensory-motor deficiencies. Delayed imitation also requires some capacity for symbolization, since the absent modeling stimuli must be retained in representational form. As might be expected, the most striking evidence of observational response learning in animals comes from naturalistic studies of both immediate and delayed imitation of human responses by primates reared in human families (Hayes and Hayes, 1952a, 1952b; Kellogg and Kellogg, 1933). Field studies of primate social behavior (Imanishi, 1957; Kawamura, 1963) likewise provide dramatic illustrations of the manner in which idiosyncratic patterns of behavior can be acquired and transmitted to other members of the subculture through observation.

The available cross-species data thus suggest that the rate and level of observational learning will be governed by the extent to which subjects possess the requisite *sensory capacities* for accurate receptivity of modeling stimuli, the *motor capabilities* necessary for precise behavioral reproduction, and the *capacity for representational mediation and covert rehearsal* which is crucial for successful acquisition and long-term retention of extended, complex sequences of behavior.

Although the findings from studies with humans lend support to a stimulus contiguity theory of observational learning, the fact that the majority of subjects fail to reproduce the entire repertoire of behavior exhibited by the model indicates that contiguity of sensory stimulation is a necessary but not a sufficient condition for imitative response acquisition.

Exposing a person to a complex sequence of modeling stimuli is no guarantee that he will attend closely to the cues, that he will necessarily select from a total stimulus complex only the most relevant stimuli, or that he will even perceive accurately the cues to which his attention is directed. Motivational conditions, prior training in discriminative observation, and the presence of incentive-oriented sets may be influential in channeling, augmenting, or reducing observing responses. Indeed, the wide individual differences frequently noted in the classes of matching responses that are acquired and reproduced by viewers are probably attributable to differences in these types of subject variables.

Procedures that alter the affective valence (Grusec and Mischel, 1965) and that enhance the distinctiveness (Sheffield and Maccoby, 1961) of modeling stimuli have also been shown to affect the degree of observational learning.

In addition to attention-directing variables and factors influencing rehearsal processes, stimulus input conditions (i.e., the rate, number, distribution, and complexity of modeling stimuli presented to viewers) will regulate acquisition outcomes to some extent. The observer's capacity to process information sets definite limits on the number of modeling cues that can be acquired during a single exposure. Therefore, if modeling stimuli are presented at a rate or level of complexity that exceeds the viewer's receptive capabilities, imitation will necessarily be limited and fragmentary. Under such conditions repeated presentations of the modeling stimuli would be required in order to produce complete and precise response matching. The acquisition of matching responses through observation of lengthy sequences of behavior, and their retention, are also likely to be governed by traditional principles of associative learning such as frequency and recency, serial organization, and multiple sources of associative interference (McGuire, 1961).

Finally, the availability of necessary component responses in the observer's behavioral repertoire will partly determine the rate and level of observational learning. Responses of higher-order complexity are produced by combinations of previously learned components which may, in themselves, represent relatively intricate compounds. Therefore, a person who lacks some of the necessary behavioral elements will, in all probability, display only partial reproduction of the model's behavior, even though the corresponding representational responses have been established. If, on the other hand, the relevant components are already present in the observer's repertoire, he is likely to perform well integrated matching responses following several demonstrations. It is perhaps for this reason that young children, who have greater motor than verbal development, could reproduce a substantially higher percentage (67%) of imitative motor responses (Bandura, 1965b) than matching verbalizations (20%). A similar pattern of differential imitation was obtained in a previous experiment (Bandura and Huston, 1961) in which preschool children served as subjects.

It is evident from the foregoing discussion that an observer does not function as a passive video-tape recorder that registers indiscriminately and stores cognitive representations of all modeling stimuli encountered in everyday life. Motivational and other attention-directing variables, associative and rehearsal processes, and numerous other factors facilitate or impede observational learning.

B. INHIBITORY AND DISINHIBITORY EFFECTS

In addition to the transmission of novel responses, exposure to the behavior of others may strengthen or weaken observer's inhibitions of existing behavioral repertoires. The occurrence of *inhibitory effects* is indicated when, as a function of observing aversive response consequences to a model, observers exhibit either decrements in the same class of behavior or a general reduction of responsivity. In the experiment to which reference was made earlier (Bandura, 1965b), for example, children who had observed a model's aggressive behavior severely punished performed significantly fewer matching responses than subjects who observed the same behavior either rewarded or associated with no evident consequences. Indeed, the vicarious punishment produced virtually complete suppression of imitative aggression in girls, whose inhibitions over physical forms of aggression are relatively strong to begin with. The inhibited responses were, however, restored to the level of the model-rewarded and no-consequences treatments when the children were offered, under highly permissive conditions, positive reinforcers contingent upon the performance of matching responses.

The findings of a related experiment (Bandura *et al.*, 1963c) reveal that the effects of punishment administered to a model may be quite selective. Whereas the frequency of emission of matching aggressive responses by observers was significantly reduced as a function of witnessing such responses negatively reinforced, other classes of aggressive behavior were essentially unaffected. It might be supposed that more severe intensities of aversive consequences to the model, and longer durations of exposure to the punishment condition, might result in more generalized suppression of responsivity in observing subjects.

The studies referred to above demonstrate the inhibitory effects of observed, negative consequences to a model on the aggressive behavior of viewers. Walters and his associates (Walters *et al.*, 1963; Walters and Parke, 1964) have likewise shown that witnessing a peer model undergo punishment for engaging in prohibited play activities increased observers' resistance to deviation in a similar temptation situation.

In the foregoing experiments the negative reinforcers were administered to the performing model by an external social agent. A highly important but less well understood reinforcement phenomenon characteristic of humans is evident in situations in which a person imposes a particular response-reinforcement contingency upon his own behavior, and self-administers reinforcers which are under his own control on occasions when he attains or surpasses the self-prescribed standards of behavior. Results of investigations concerned with self-reinforcing processes provide some evidence (Bandura and Kupers, 1964; Bandura and Whalen, 1965) that discriminative patterns of inhibition of self-rewarding behavior can be acquired without the mediation of direct reinforcement, through observation of achievement-contingent rewards and punishments *self-administered* by a model.

Partial or complete inhibition of social responses, established through previous modeling or aversive conditioning, may also be reduced on the basis of observational experience. Such *disinhibitory effects* are evident when observers display increments in socially disapproved behavior as a function of viewing a model either rewarded or experiencing no adverse consequences for performing the prohibited responses.

The reduction of inhibitions through modeling has been demonstrated most clearly in studies of aggression involving intense physical forms such as kicking, striking with mallets, and other pain-producing responses that are likely to be inhibited in viewers as a result of past social training. In a series of experiments Bandura *et al.,* (1961, 1963a) found that children who had observed adult models behaving in a highly aggressive manner subsequently displayed twice as much nonimitative aggression as subjects who either witnessed inhibited adults or had no exposure to social cues (Fig. 3). Numerous other laboratory investigations (Larder, 1962; Lövaas, 1961; Mussen and Rutherford, 1961; Siegel, 1956), differing considerably in choice of both aggressive stimuli and dependent measures, have consistently shown that observation of models displaying aggressive behavior with no untoward consequences increased the incidence of aggressive responses in viewers. Moreover, Walters and Llewellyn Thomas (1963) have demonstrated that the disinhibitory effect of exposure to aggressive models, as measured in terms of subjects' increased willingness to administer painful electric shocks to another person, occurs among adolescents and adults as well.

1. Vicarious Participation in Aggression and Cathartic Processes

According to the widely accepted catharsis hypothesis, vicarious participation in aggressive activities presumably reduces hostile impulses and thereby decreases the probability of subsequent aggressive behavior. The largely negative experimental findings (Bandura and Walters, 1963b; Berkowitz, 1962), however, have led some writers to propose a revision of the original formulation (Buss, 1961; Feshbach, 1961, 1964). They contend that the cathartic or drive-reducing function of aggressive model-

ALBERT BANDURA

ing stimuli obtains only under certain, specified conditions. Witnessing the behavior of aggressive models supposedly produces decrements in subsequent aggression when the observer has been aggressively aroused at the time of exposure. If, on the other hand, the aggressive drive has not been activated during the period of vicarious participation, such exposure augments ensuing aggressive responses. The revised catharsis theory thus presupposes that the functional properties of modeling stimuli can be radically altered by transitory emotional states of the observer.

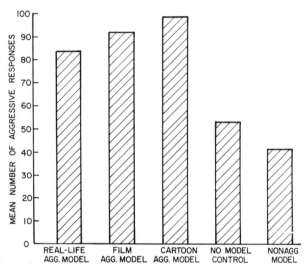

Fig. 3. Mean frequency of aggressive responses performed by control children and by those exposed to aggressive and inhibited models. (Adapted from Bandura, 1963.)

A recent investigation by Hartmann (1965), employing an experimental design in which pre-exposure level of instigation to aggression and types of aggressive cues were both varied, provides data that help to clarify the nature of the relationship between arousal and response to modeled aggression.

An aggressive response sequence generally contains two important stimulus events, i.e., the instrumental aggressive response of the agent, and the pain cues exhibited by the object of the attack. Although a number of investigators have reported changes in subjects' aggressive behavior after viewing film clips depicting fight sequences, no attempt has been made to determine whether the depicted instrumental aggression or the pain cues are primarily responsible for the obtained differences.

It is apparent from the findings of experiments employing inanimate targets such as plastic dolls that observation of instrumental aggression in the absence of pain cues can produce substantial increases in aggressive behavior. The important question, therefore, is whether expressive pain reactions augment or counteract the effects af aggressive displays.

According to the theory of aggression proposed by Sears *et al.* (1957), signs of pain and injury resulting from a child's aggressive behavior occur sufficiently often in conjunction with the removal of his frustrations to have acquired secondary reinforcing properties. Pain cues could, therefore, serve as positive reinforcers to enhance aggressiveness. On the other hand, it would be predicted on the basis of the principle of stimulus generalization that a victim's pain reactions will tend to elicit conditioned emotional responses in the observer and thus lead to aggression inhibition. The problem of determining the functional value of witnessed pain cues is further complicated if conditions of anger arousal affect their reinforcing and anxiety-eliciting properties.

The study conducted by Hartmann objectively assessed the independent and interactive effects of anger instigation, aggressive displays, and pain cues on subsequent interpersonal punitiveness. In the first phase of the experiment, adolescent delinquent boys overheard an anonymous partner (actually a tape-recording) make evaluative statements about their performance on an ego-involving task. The boys in the *aggression-arousal* condition were subjected to a number of unwarranted and disparaging criticisms by the "partner"; in contrast, subjects assigned to the *nonarousal* condition received essentially neutral comments.

Following the experimentally induced arousal the subjects were further subdivided into one of three conditions. In each condition a film was shown which portrayed two adolescent boys shooting baskets on a basketball court. In the *control* film the boys engage in an active but cooperative basketball game, whereas in the other two films the boys get into an argument that develops into a fist fight. The *pain-cues* film focuses almost exclusively on the victim's pain reactions as he is vigorously pummeled and kicked by his opponent. The *instrumental-aggression* film, on the other hand, focuses on the aggressors' responses including angry facial expressions, foot thrusts, flying fists, and aggressive verbalizations.

After exposure to the film sequences the subjects were asked to assist the experimenter in a study ostensibly of the effects of performance feedback on learning rate. The aggression performance task, which was patterned after the device originally designed by Buss (1961), contained a panel with ten shock switches arranged in increasing intensity, and lights that signaled right or wrong responses presumably made by the subject's "partner" in the adjacent room. After the boys sampled several of the

shock intensities to apprise them of the magnitude of aversive stimulation
associated with the different switches, the subjects were asked to administer
the pain-producing shocks to their partner whenever he made an error
on the learning task. They were free, however, to vary the intensity
and duration of shock administration. During the series of learning trials,
the subjects' panel signaled a number of errors according to a prearranged
program controlled by the experimenter, and the length and intensities
of shocks inflicted upon the partner were recorded.

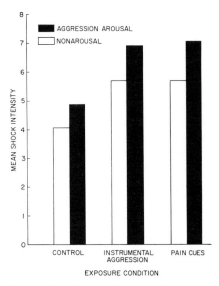

FIG. 4. Mean shock intensities administered by aroused and nonaroused subjects after observing either instrumental aggression, pain cues, or a nonaggressive
control film. (Adapted from Hartmann, 1965.)

The results of this experiment, based on several indices of punitiveness, are contrary to the catharsis hypothesis, but entirely consistent with
social-learning theory. Subjects who had observed either the aggressive
acts or the pain cues selected significantly higher shock levels, both under
aroused and nonaroused conditions, than subjects who watched the control
film (Fig. 4). Moreover, angered viewers behaved more aggressively than
nonangered observers following exposure to the aggressive film sequences,
a finding that is directly counter to prediction from a catharsis hypothesis.
Prior arousal also produced an increase in aggression in control subjects,
but not of statistically significant magnitude. The latter finding provides
additional suggestive evidence for the influential role of the aggressive

stimulus value of the target person and modeling cues in determining aggressive modes of response to emotional arousal (Bandura and Walters, 1963a; Berkowitz, 1964; Schachter and Singer, 1962).

In the present experiment, the initially offensive behavior of the "partner" was not only anger-provoking, but also served to increase his aggressive cue value. According to a recent theory proposed by Berkowitz (1964), the effects of pictorially modeled aggression are a joint function of the observer's level of internal arousal and the target person's cue properties which are treated as eliciting stimuli analogous to the ethological concept of "releaser." Under low arousal a powerful releaser is presumed to be necessary to elicit aggressive responses, whereas a relatively weak external stimulus will suffice under high instigation to aggression. The importance of external stimuli in governing the effects of exposure to film-mediated models is clearly demonstrated in a series of experiments by Berkowitz (Berkowitz, 1965; Berkowitz and Geen, 1965; Geen and Berkowitz, 1965) in which the aggressive cue value of the target person was varied by assigning him either an aggressive vocational label (e.g., boxer, speech major) or the first name of the aggressive film model. The findings reveal that witnessing assaultive behavior significantly increased viewers' aggressiveness only when they were aroused and provided a target possessing cue properties. The fact, however, that modeling augmented the intensity of punitive behavior in Hartmann's study in nonaroused subjects toward a considerate target suggests that the generality of Berkowitz's findings may be primarily confined to highly socialized college samples.

Although subjects in the instrumental-aggression and pain-cues conditions administered virtually identical intensities of pain-producing responses, the latter two groups displayed differential patterns of punitive behavior based on the shock-level $\times$ duration index (Fig. 5).

Aroused subjects in the instrumental-aggression and the control groups did not differ from their nonangered counterparts in overall level of aggressiveness. On the other hand, nonaroused subjects who had observed the suffering victim subsequently exhibited a relatively low degree of pain-producing behavior, and did not differ significantly in this respect from the controls. In marked contrast, angered viewers became extremely punitive as a function of witnessing another person beaten severely.

In a study of cathartic effects through vicarious experience, Feshbach (1961) found that adults who had been initially subjected to critical remarks and then had viewed a prize fight sequence, produced fewer aggressive responses to a word association test and questionnaire than insulted subjects who had watched a film depicting the consequences of the spread of rumors. No significant differences were obtained, however, between groups of subjects exposed to the aggressive film or to the rumor movie under nonaroused conditions. While these findings are frequently cited as evidence for the cathartic reduction of aggression, alternative interpretations should be considered, particularly in view of the fact that some of the findings are inconsistent with both the catharsis hypothesis and the results of numerous investigations published in recent years.

Considering that exposure to aggressive stimuli has generally been shown to increase aggressive behavior in young children (Bandura *et al.,* 1961, 1963a; Larder, 1962; Lövaas, 1961; Mussen and Rutherford, 1961),

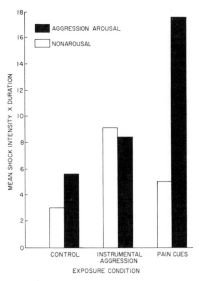

FIG. 5. Mean pain-producing responses (shock level × duration) displayed by aroused and nonaroused subjects after observing either instrumental aggression, pain cues, or a nonaggressive control film. (Adapted from Hartmann, 1965.)

adolescents (Hartmann, 1965; Walters and Llewellyn Thomas, 1963), and adults (Walters and Llewellyn Thomas, 1963), the failure to obtain an enhancement effect of an aggressive film under *nonaroused* conditions in Feshbach's experiments suggests that either the dependent measure has serious limitations, or the content of the control film did not provide a sufficiently neutral stimulus. The interpretation of the difference obtained between subjects in the *aroused* condition is similarly complicated by the fact that the control movie, which was concerned with the negative effects of rumors, may have been somewhat anger-provoking to the viewers.

The experiments cited above have, almost without exception, employed measures of overt physical aggression. In contrast, verbal responses to questionnaires or word association tests, and measures obtained from ratings of attitudes toward psychological experiments and toward the experimenter, are not only somewhat ambiguous indices of aggressive behavior, but also subject to social desirability response sets which may seriously affect results (Bandura and Walters, 1963b).

It is also by no means clear whether decrements in aggression, when they occur under certain circumstances as a function of witnessing physical violence, reflect a genuine drive-reduction process, the effects of an inhibitory process generated by displays of violence and its injurious consequences, or some other mechanism (Berkowitz, 1962; Berkowitz and Rawlings, 1963). A study of vicarious reduction of hostility by Rosenbaum and deCharms (1960), for example, demonstrated that insulted subjects who heard a third person reply to the original aggressor later evaluated the aggressor less negatively. This outcome, however, is certainly not attributable to a reduction of hostility, since, as the authors point out, the replies rarely contained any aggressive verbalizations.

The growing body of research provides considerable evidence that vicarious participation in aggressive activities can be highly effective in modifying observers' aggressive behavior, but not in the direction predicted by the catharsis hypothesis. These findings are perhaps not too surprising. It is highly improbable that even advocates of vicarious drive reduction would recommend community programs in which sexually aroused adolescents are shown libidinous movies at drive-in theatres as a means of reducing sexual behavior; famished persons are presented displays of gourmands dining on culinary treats in order to alleviate hunger pangs; and assaultive gangs are regularly shown films of assailants flogging their antagonists in an attempt to diminish aggressive behavior. Such procedures would undoubtedly have strong instigative rather than reductive consequences.

The persistence of the belief in cathartic energy discharges through vicarious participation despite substantial, negative experimental findings, is probably supported by frequent subjectively experienced "tension" reduction following exposure to aggressive content provided in films, televised programs, and other audiovisual displays. There is no disputing the fact that a person who is in a state of heightened emotionality resulting from stressful and frustrating everyday events is apt to undergo some reduction in general arousal level as a function of observing aggressive performances. While such an outcome is generally interpreted as evidence of vicarious reduction in "pent-up" affects and impulses, a more plausible alternative explanation is in terms of stimulus-change processes.

After a person has been insulted, unjustly criticized, or otherwise thwarted, the resultant emotional arousal is typically revivified and even augmented on later occasions through symbolic reinstatement of the anger-provoking incidents. Thus, by brooding over the ill treatment and possible negative consequences of disturbing episodes, intense feelings can be reinstated long after the initial reactions to the situation have subsided. The persistence of elevated arousal, according to this social-learning view, is attributable to self-generated stimulation rather than to the existence of an undischarged reservoir of "aggressive drive." If the person should become immersed in new activities that supersede the preoccupying, internal eliciting stimuli, a noticeable degree of "tension" reduction will, in all likelihood, take place. On the supposition that the diminution of emotional arousal is a consequence of *attentional shifts* rather than a cathartic effect of having experienced aggression vicariously, one would expect aroused subjects to experience equally salutary effects from getting involved in an absorbing book, a movie, a stage play, or a televised program containing few, if any, aggressive stimuli. In order to test predictions derived from the *stimulus-change* and the *energy-discharge* conceptualizations of emotional "cathartic" effects, a study is planned in which decrements in physiological arousal will be compared in angered subjects who are exposed to movies either depicting aggression, with equally absorbing but nonaggressive content, or are presented no pictorial stimuli. The results of this experiment should throw some light on the influence of aggressive stimulus events and attentional shifts to nonaggressive competing stimuli in reducing viewers' pre-existing levels of emotional arousal.

2. Modification of Resistance to Deviation Through Modeling

The preceding discussion has been specifically concerned with changes in the incidence of aggressive responses resulting from observation of the behavior of aggressive models and its response consequences. Inhibitory and disinhibitory effects, however, are not confined to aggression. The frequency of other socially disapproved classes of behavior has likewise been experimentally modified through witnessing models violating prohibitions.

Studies by Grosser et al. (1951) and by S. A. Ross (1962), for example, have demonstrated that exposure to transgressors increases the probability that the observer will likewise deviate. On the other hand, conforming models tend to strengthen the observer's self-controlling responses, and thereby reduce conflictive behavior in temptation situations (Ross, 1962). Blake and his associates (Blake, 1958) have conducted investigations of some of the conditions determining the influence of noncompliant and conforming models on observers' inhibitions in prohibition situations. In one study, Freed et al. (1955) found that, although exposure to a noncompliant model lowered students' resistance to deviation, transgressions occurred most frequently if the restriction was weak and the model violated the prohibitory signs, whereas the combination of a strong restriction and a conforming model produced the lowest incidence of deviation. A second experiment (Kimbrell and Blake, 1958) demonstrated that the efficacy of modeling cues for modifying inhibitions varies with the observer's level of instigation to transgression. That is, under extreme provocation, subjects disregarded both the imposed restriction and the conforming model. However, under conditions where the instigation was not so strong as to force deviation, students who observed a conforming model displayed more compliant behavior than subjects who witnessed a model violate the prohibition.

In the studies referred to above, the probability of deviation was significantly altered simply as a result of witnessing the model's behavior. Inhibitory and disinhibitory effects can be greatly influenced by observation of rewarding and punishing consequences associated with deviant responses. For example, in experiments cited earlier (Walters et al., 1963; Walters and Parke, 1964) children who observed a peer model either being rewarded or experiencing no evident consequences for performing a prohibited act were more likely to deviate than children who witnessed the model being punished for engaging in the same behavior.

In naturalistic situations the observer often actually witnesses the rewards or punishments immediately following the model's transgressions. At other times, however, he can only infer probable consequences from discriminative symbols and attributes of the model that tend to be correlated with differential reinforcements. The manner in which distinctive modeling cues signifying likely reinforcing outcomes may increase a model's effectiveness in reducing inhibitions is illustrated in an experiment conducted by Lefkowitz et al. (1955). Traffic signal violations by a high-status person attired in a freshly pressed suit, shined shoes, white shirt and tie produced a higher pedestrian violation rate than the same transgression performed by the same model dressed in soiled, patched trousers, scuffed shoes, and a blue denim shirt. The differential reduction in restraints noted in the latter experiment is probably attributable to the fact that transgressions by persons who occupy a high position in a prestige hierarchy are likely to be punished less frequently and less severely than those performed by low-status transgressors. The differential leniency is apt to apply to the imitator as well, provided that the matching behavior is performed in the presence of the deviating model.

Other discriminative properties of the model, such as age, sex, socioeconomic status, social power, ethnic background, and intellectual and vocational status, which are associated with predictable contingencies of reinforcement, may likewise influence the extent to which prohibited acts will be imitated.

3. Conceptualization of "Vicarious Reinforcement"

A number of the studies discussed in preceding sections provide evidence of vicarious reinforcement effects, as shown by the fact that the behavior of observers is modified as a function of witnessing reinforcing stimuli administered to performers. Indeed, systematic investigations of the relative efficacy of vicarious and direct reinforcement reveal that the changes exhibited by observers are of the same magnitude (Kanfer and Marston, 1963) or, under certain conditions, may even exceed those achieved by reinforced performers (Berger, 1961). Moreover, vicarious reinforcement processes are governed by variables such as the percentage (Kanfer, 1965; Marston and Kanfer, 1963), intermittency (Rosenbaum and Bruning, 1961), and magnitude (Bruning, 1965) of reinforcement in essentially the same manner as when they are applied directly to a performing subject.

While the efficacy of vicarious reinforcement procedures is well established, the response changes exhibited by observers may be interpreted in several ways. One possible explanation is in terms of the discriminative function of reinforcing stimuli presented to the model. Response consequences experienced by another person undoubtedly convey information to the observer about the probable reinforcement contingencies associated with particular performances in similar situations. Knowledge concerning the types of responses that are likely to meet with approval or disapproval can later serve as discriminative stimuli in facilitating and inhibiting overt behavior. The information gained from witnessed consequent events may be particularly influential in regulating behavior under conditions where there is considerable ambiguity as to what constitutes permissible or punishable actions.

In most investigations of vicarious reinforcement the model merely performs a prearranged sequence of responses in the absence of any discriminative environmental cues. In many situations, however, the model responds differentially to certain salient or ambiguous cues within a total stimulus complex. Under these circumstances, observation of the pattern of reinforcement associated with the model's responses helps to direct the observer's attention to the critical environmental stimuli which would be difficult to distinguish without the observed informative feedback. The observer's responses may thus become conditioned not only to the model's responses, but also to the relevant environmental stimuli. The resultant discrimination learning can later facilitate the performance of matching responses by the observer in the presence of cues to which the model previously had been responding (Church, 1957; McDavid, 1962).

Observation of reinforcing stimuli presented to a model and his concomitant affective reactions may also have important motivational effects on the observer. The mere sight of highly valenced reinforcers can produce anticipatory arousal which, in turn, will affect the level of imitative performance. Thus, for example, witnessing a performer rewarded with a succulent beefsteak for executing a given sequence of responses will convey the same amount of information about the probable reinforcement contingencies to a famished and to a satiated observer, but their subsequent imitative performances will, in all likelihood, differ radically because of the differential effects of deprivation state on the activating power of the anticipated incentive. Similarly, variations in the magnitude of observed reinforcers, while providing equivalent information about the permissibility of matching responses, have different motivational effects on observers (Bruning, 1965). As in the case of direct reinforcement, incentive-produced motivation in observers is most likely to affect the speed, intensity, and persistence with which matching responses are executed.

A vicarious reinforcement event not only provides (1) information concerning probable reinforcement contingencies, (2) knowledge about the controlling environmental stimuli, and (3) displays of incentives possessing activating properties, but it also includes affective expressions of the rewarded or punished performer. As will be shown later, the pleasure and pain cues emitted by a model generally elicit corresponding affective responses in the viewer. These vicariously aroused emotional responses can readily become conditioned, through repeated contiguous association, either to the modeled responses themselves, or to environmental stimuli (Bandura and Rosenthal, 1965; Berger, 1962) that are regularly correlated with the performer's affective reactions. As a consequence, the subsequent initiation of matching responses by the observer or the occurrence of the correlated environmental stimuli is likely to generate some degree of emotional reactivity. It is therefore possible that the facilitative or suppressive effects of observing the affective consequences accruing to a performer are partly mediated by the arousal of vicariously acquired emotional responses.

In similar manner, witnessing the nonoccurrence of anticipated aversive consequences to a model can extinguish in the observer previously established conditioned emotional responses (Bandura and Rosenthal, 1965). It is informative to note in this connection that, when socially disapproved behavior exhibited by a model is followed by neither reward nor punishment, the incidence of matching deviant behavior is comparable to that produced by observation of rewarding consequences (Bandura, 1965b; Walters and Parke, 1964). These data suggest that nonreaction to formerly prohibited activities takes on, through contrast, positive qualities. Similar contrast-of-reinforcement effects have been demonstrated in studies of direct reinforcement (Buchwald, 1959a,b; Crandall, 1963; Crandall *et al.*, 1964) in which nonreward following punishment had functioned analogously to a positive reinforcer, whereas the occurrence of nonreward subsequent to a series of rewards had functioned as a negative reinforcer. In fact, even a weak, positive reinforcer, when contrasted with more rewarding prior events, may acquire negative reinforcing value (Buchwald, 1960).

The incremental changes produced in observers by the omission of anticipated punishment of the model may, of course, be attributed to several factors that are difficult to separate. In addition to weakening inhibitions through vicarious extinction, nonreactions also have informative value concerning the permissibility of the modeled responses.

C. RESPONSE FACILITATING EFFECTS

The behavior of models often serves merely as discriminative stimuli for the observer in facilitating the occurrence of previously learned responses in the same general class. Response facilitating effects are distinguished from disinhibition and modeling by the fact that, in the former case, no new responses are acquired, and disinhibitory processes are not involved since the exhibited responses have rarely, if ever, incurred punishment. A familiar example of this type of outcome is provided in situations where a person gazes intently skyward and most passers-by respond in a similar manner.

In laboratory experiments with humans, a wide variety of socially approved behaviors, such as volunteering services or monetary contributions (Blake *et al.,* 1955; Rosenbaum, 1956; Rosenbaum and Blake, 1955; Schachter and Hall, 1952), pledging oneself to a course of action (Blake *et al.*, 1956; Helson *et al.*, 1956), and preferences for certain types of foods (Duncker, 1938) and pictorial items (Gelfand, 1962), have been readily induced by the presentation of actual or symbolic modeling stimuli. Some of the most influential theoretical formulations of imitative processes (Miller and Dollard, 1941; Skinner, 1953) have, in fact, been almost exclusively concerned with the discriminative function of social cues. In the prototypic experiment the model's responses serve as the occasion upon which another organism is likely to be reinforced for displaying the corresponding patterns of behavior. After a period of exposure to differential reinforcement, imitative tendencies become strongly established; conversely, by reversing the social contingencies so that matching responses are never reinforced but nonmatching behavior is consistently rewarded, imitativeness is reduced to a very low or zero level (Miller and Dollard, 1941).

Ethologists provide extensive documentation of the response facilitating function of social cues in birds, fish, and mammals (Hall, 1963; Thorpe, 1956). Typically, the sight of certain responses performed by an animal elicits a similar or identical pattern of behavior in other members of the same species. This process is generally referred to as "social facilitation" or "behavioral contagion" when it is presumably determined by prior discriminative reinforcements, and "mimesis" when corresponding unconditioned response patterns are supposedly instinctively aroused.

As Hinde (1953) points out, the occurrence of matching behavior in animals is often erroneously attributed to mimetic processes. In the first place, what appears to be mimetic behavior may, in fact, involve response patterns that have been established through prior social learning. Even in cases where matching behavior is clearly instinctive, it is frequently difficult to determine whether social cues constitute the critical eliciting stimuli. Readily discriminable "sign stimuli" (Tinbergen, 1951) or "releasers" (Thorpe, 1956) in the form of color displays, preparatory movement sequences, postural cues, and specific vocalizations frequently serve as unconditional stimuli for complete patterns of instinctive behavior in other members of the species. Therefore, when appropriate releasing stimuli are displayed by a model during the performance of a given activity, the corresponding responses on the part of observing animals may be primarily controlled by releasing stimuli, rather than the model's behavioral cues. Thus, for example, the white tail feathers of a bird flying upward can function as flight-eliciting stimuli for other members of a flock (Armstrong, 1942). A suitably feathered but non-flying artificial model might likewise succeed in getting a flock of birds airborne.

Pseudo-mimesis is also evident in instances where the model's behavior directs the observer's attention to environmental stimuli which, in turn, elicit similar innate response patterns. Satiated chickens, for example, will begin to eat at the sight of other birds feeding (Katz and Révész, 1921). It is entirely possible that in such cases modeling cues primarily serve an *orienting function,* whereas the consummatory responses of the sociable chicks are reinstated and maintained by the grain to which their attention has been redirected. The fact that the stimulus complex to which observing animals are responding frequently contains, in addition to social cues, releasing stimuli and other controlling environmental events complicates the identification and analysis of genuine mimetic phenomena.

The behavior of a model may not only function as a discriminative stimulus for a similar response, but it also serves to direct the observer's attention to the particular stimulus objects manipulated by the performer (Crawford and Spence, 1939). As a consequence, the observer may subsequently utilize the same objects to a greater extent, though not necessarily in an imitative way. In one modeling experiment, for example, the model pummelled a plastic doll with a mallet. Children who had observed this aggressive act later displayed significantly more behavior in which they pounded a peg board with the mallet than both control subjects and those who had viewed a nonaggressive model (Bandura, 1962). *Stimulus enhancement effects* are distinguished from social facilitation in that the observer's behavior in the former case may bear little or no resemblance to the model's activities.

III. Vicarious Classical Conditioning

The investigations reviewed in the preceding sections have been essentially confined to the social transmission of instrumental classes of responses as a function of exposure to real-life or symbolic models. Vicarious classical or respondent conditioning, on the other hand, has received surprisingly little experimental attention, despite ample evidence from informal observation that emotional responses are frequently acquired through observation of the pain and fear reactions exhibited by other persons exposed to aversive stimuli. Indeed, most persons exhibiting snake phobias have never had any direct aversive experiences with reptiles, and similarly, children often acquire, on the basis of exposure to modeled stimulus correlations, intense emotional attitudes toward members of unpopular minority groups or nationalities with whom they have little or no personal contact. Positive incentive learning may likewise occur on a vicarious basis by observing others experiencing positive reinforcement in contiguous association with discriminative stimuli.

A. VICARIOUS EMOTIONAL AROUSAL

One of the earliest studies of vicarious affective arousal was reported by Dysinger and Ruckmick (1933), who measured the autonomic responses of children and adults to movie scenes depicting dangerous situations and romantic-erotic displays. A more recent demonstration of vicarious emotional instigation through filmed stimulation is provided in a series of experiments by Lazarus and his associates (1962). Continuous recordings of subjects' autonomic responses were obtained while they viewed a film portraying a primitive ritual of an Australian tribe in which a pubertal native boy underwent a crude genital operation. The college students displayed heightened autonomic responsivity while witnessing the genital subincision scenes, the reactions being particularly marked when the operation was accompanied by sobs and other pain cues on the part of the young initiate. Both the deletion of the vocal pain cues and the provision of sound-track commentaries that minimized the aversiveness of the depicted operation significantly reduced the subjects' level of emotional arousal, whereas commentaries highlighting the suffering and hazards of such operations enhanced observers' physiological arousal (Speisman *et al.*, 1964).

In an erudite analysis of vicarious processes, Berger (1962) restricts the phenomenon of vicarious instigation to situations in which an observer responds emotionally to a performer's presumed affective experiences. Since the emotional state of another person is not directly observable, its presence, quality, and intensity are typically inferred from stimuli impinging upon the performer and behavioral cues indicative of emotional arousal. As Berger points out, a person may be vicariously instigated on the basis of erroneous inferences primarily from stimulus events, as in the case of a mother who responds fearfully at seeing her child fall even though the child is, in fact, unhurt and undisturbed. Similarly, a bystander may react apprehensively to hearing a sudden, loud scream although, unknown to him, the distressing vocalizations are simulated as part of a game.

Berger has reasoned that a loud scream which elicits a fear response from the observer may represent a case of pseudovicarious instigation, since the vocal cue may serve merely as a conditioned fear stimulus independent of the performer's unconditioned emotional response or stimulus situation. The basis for this distinction is debatable, since expressive cues are the observable indicants of a performer's assumed emotional state and, as will be shown later, it is precisely because such social cues have acquired emotion-provoking properties that an observer can be at all vicariously aroused by the experiences of another person. There are, however, instances in which covariations in the emotional responses of observers and performers do not necessarily involve vicarious-instigation processes. Once a given environmental stimulus has acquired strong eliciting potency for an observer, his emotional responses are likely to be evoked directly by the nonsocial conditioned stimulus, regardless of the behavior of others. Thus, for example, individuals will experience fear upon hearing the sound of a fire alarm in the building in which they are working, although, due to common conditioning histories, each person may be responding similarly, but independently, to the same nonsocial cues. Under these circumstances it is exceedingly difficult to establish precisely the stimulus sources of the observer's emotional state since the behavior of others, depending on its character, undoubtedly augments or reduces the effects of environmental eliciting stimuli. The most convincing demonstration of vicarious instigation is, therefore, provided under condi-

tions where the observer's emotional responses are elicited entirely by
the performer's affective expressions, because the latter's evocative stimuli
either are unobservable to, or of neutral valence for, the observing subject.
Social cues signifying affective arousal can acquire emotion-provoking properties through essentially the same process of classical conditioning that is involved in the establishment of positive or negative valences
to nonsocial environmental stimuli. That is, if affective responses of others
have been repeatedly followed by emotional experiences on the part of
observers themselves, the affective social cues alone gradually acquire
the power to instigate emotional reactions in observers. The clearest
demonstrations of vicarious arousal are furnished by laboratory studies
with infrahuman subjects in which the requisite social and temporal contingencies are instituted.

In testing the conditioning interpretation of the development of
"sympathetic" responses, for example, Church (1959) either subjected
groups of rats to paired aversive consequences, unpaired consequences,
or assigned them to a control condition in which no aversive stimuli
were presented. In the paired-consequences condition, animals were
administered brief shocks after another rat had been shocked for thirty
seconds, with the aversive stimulation to both animals being terminated
simultaneously. Animals in the unpaired-consequences condition received
the same number of brief shocks, but these were not temporally associated
with painful stimulation to another rat. Following the emotional conditioning phase of the experiment, decrements in the animals' rate of bar-
pressing for food, which served as the index of vicarious fear arousal,
were measured in response to the pain reactions of another rat that
was continuously shocked in an adjacent cage. Animals that had previously
experienced paired consequences were markedly affected by the
pain responses of another rat, the control group showed little empathetic
responsivity, and animals whose past aversive experiences were unassociated with the pain responses of another member of their species showed
an effect intermediate between the two groups.

The manner in which vicariously instigated emotions may motivate
avoidance responses is illustrated in experiments by R. E. Miller *et al.*
(1962, 1963) employing a cooperative, avoidance-conditioning procedure.
Rhesus monkeys were first trained to avoid an electric shock by pressing
a bar whenever a stimulus light appeared. Following the avoidance training, the animals were seated in different rooms, with the bar removed
from the chair of one monkey and the stimulus light from the other.
Thus, the animal having access to the conditioned stimulus had to communicate by means of affective cues to his partner, equipped with the response
bar, who could then perform the appropriate instrumental response that

would enable both animals to avoid aversive stimulation. Distress cues exhibited by the stimulus monkeys in anticipation of shock were highly effective in eliciting fear in their observing companions as reflected in rapid performance of discriminated avoidance responses. Moreover, mere exposure to a monkey reacting in an apprehensive or fearful manner could reinstate avoidance responses in the observer after they had been extinguished to a zero level (R. E. Miller *et al.* 1959).

B. Vicarious Classical Conditioning

The foregoing studies identify the contingencies under which emotional responses of a model, as conveyed through auditory cues, facial expressions, and postural manifestations, acquire the capacity to arouse empathetic emotional responses in observers. In the case of vicarious classical conditioning, the observers' vicariously elicited emotional responses become conditioned, through contiguous association, to formerly neutral stimuli. One of the earliest laboratory investigations of this process was reported by Kriazhev (1934), who conditioned one animal in each of seven pairs of dogs to stimuli presented in conjunction with food or electric shock, while the other member of the pair merely witnessed the procedure. The observing dogs rapidly developed salivary responses to the signal for food, and conditioned agitation and respiratory changes to that for shock. However, this brief report does not contain sufficient information on the details of the experimental procedure to determine whether the observers' reactions to the conditioned stimulus were tested in the absence of the models.

In laboratory investigations of vicarious classical conditioning in humans (Barnett and Benedetti, 1960; Berger, 1962) one person, the performer or model, typically undergoes an aversive conditioning procedure in which a formerly neutral stimulus is presented, and shortly thereafter the model displays pain cues and other emotional reactions supposedly in response to an unconditioned aversive stimulus. If an observer witnesses the model undergoing this conditioning procedure, the observer will also begin to exhibit emotional responses to the conditioned stimulus alone, even though he has not himself experienced the aversive stimulation directly.

Berger (1962) has recently conducted a series of studies in each of which one group of observers was informed that the performing model would receive a shock whenever a light dimmed, the dimming of the light being in each trial preceded by a buzzer. A second group of observers was instructed that the performer would make a voluntary arm movement whenever the light dimmed but that the performer was receiving no aversive stimulation. In two other conditions the model was supposedly shocked but refrained from making arm movements, or the model was neither shocked nor exhibited arm withdrawal responses. The measure of vicarious conditioning was the frequency of observers' galvanic skin responses to the buzzer, which served as the conditioned stimulus. Observers who were informed that the model was receiving aversive stimulation and who witnessed the model make avoidance responses displayed a greater degree of vicarious conditioning than observers in the other three groups. Had the models exhibited additional nonverbal and vocal pain cues characteristically associated with actual aversive stimulation, the vicarious conditioning effects would probably have been even more marked.

Although the phenomenon of vicarious conditioning has been clearly demonstrated, wide interindividual variability has been noted in the acquisition rate and stability of vicariously acquired conditioned responses. Since this process requires the observer to experience vicariously another person's pain responses, thereby producing emotional arousal in the observer, variables that influence an observer's general level of emotional arousal are likely to enhance or retard vicarious learning.

There are numerous investigations of *direct* aversive classical conditioning as a function of subjects' arousal level in which arousal is either manipulated by varying the intensity of unconditioned and stressor stimuli, or assessed in terms of personality measures of emotional proneness. These studies have shown that conditioned responses are developed more rapidly and, once acquired, extinguish less readily under conditions of high, as compared to low, arousal (Doerfler and Kramer, 1959; Spence, 1958, 1964). From these findings it might be expected that *vicarious* conditioning would likewise be positively related to degree of psychologically induced arousal.

A considerable body of recent experimentation exploring the interserver, variables that influence an observer's general level of emotional state (Schachter, 1964; Schachter and Singer, 1962; Schachter and Wheeler, 1962) indicates that administration of epinephrine, a sympathetic stimulant, may enhance observers' susceptibility to modeling influences. In particular, when given epinephrine without accurate information of its side-effects, subjects displayed much greater matching of models' aggressive, euphoric, and jocular behavior than subjects who were exposed to these models without prior psychological arousal, or who were given a sympathetic depressant.

Findings from studies concerning the effects of autonomic arousal on fearful and avoidant behavior, although not employing modeling procedures, nevertheless have implications for the vicarious instigation and acquisition of affective responses. Singer (1963), for example, found that rats injected with epinephrine displayed considerably more fear in response to aversive stimuli than placebo- or chlorpromazine-injected animals. However, available evidence (Latané and Schachter, 1962) indicates that acquisition of emotional responses through *direct* aversive conditioning is significantly influenced by the dose level of adrenalin employed: Small doses of adrenalin generally facilitate avoidance conditioning, whereas large doses have negligible effects on avoidance responses, suggesting a nonmonotonic relationship between autonomic arousal and conditioned emotional responses.

In order to determine the effects of varying degrees of arousal, manipulated both psychologically and physiologically, on vicarious conditioning processes, an experiment was conducted (Bandura and Rosenthal, 1965) that proceeded in the following manner. College students participated in a vicarious aversive conditioning paradigm in which a model emitted pain cues in conjunction with an auditory stimulus, and the observers' acquisition and extinction of galvanic skin responses to the conditioned stimulus were studied.

The following treatment conditions were included in the experiment: 1. *No injection nonthreat condition.* These observers were subjected to no direct experience of an emotion-provoking sort, and consequently provide an index of vicarious conditioning under relatively low arousal. 2. *Placebo injection.* Subjects in this condition received a placebo hypodermic without any knowledge of its contents which, for most subjects, constituted a moderately anxiety-arousing experience. 3. *Placebo injection plus threat of aversive stimulation.* This group of observers, which also received the placebo injection, was informed that following the conditioning of the model, they too would undergo the painful shock stimulation. The threat of impending shock was designed to induce an additional increment of emotional arousal. 4. *Epinephrine-induced arousal: small dose.* Observers assigned to this group received a dose of epinephrine sufficient to produce a noticeable physiological effect. 5. *Epinephrine-induced arousal: large dose.* The dosage level employed in this condition was capable of producing sizeable sympathetic arousal.

The two sets of experimental manipulations thus provided three degrees of psychologically induced emotional arousal (i.e., nonthreat, placebo injection, placebo injection plus shock threat) and three points on a physiological arousal continuum (epinephrine dosage of .2 cc and .5 cc, with the placebo injection condition serving as a 0 dosage group).

Immediately after the arousal manipulations the subjects observed the model, a confederate of the experimenter, perform on a pursuit rotor apparatus which served as the cover task for presenting the CS-UCS pairings to the model. At periodic intervals a buzzer, which served as the CS, was sounded, and shortly thereafter the model suddenly flexed his arm, dropped the stylus, and winced, creating the impression that painful shock had been delivered. Six CS-alone trials were interspersed among the ten vicarious acquisition trials as tests of the degree to which the CS was accruing conditioned aversive properties. During the test trials the buzzer was sounded, but the model exhibited no response whatsoever. At the completion of the acquisition-test series all subjects were given ten extinction trials in which the CS was presented alone.

Figure 6 shows the percentage of the total number of conditioning trials in which subjects from the various groups exhibited GSR responses.

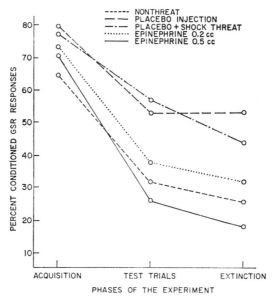

Fig. 6. Mean % conditioned GSR responses exhibited by subjects on each of three test periods for each of five treatment conditions representing differential levels of arousal. (Adapted from Bandura and Rosenthal, 1965.)

Subjects in all groups displayed a high frequency of GSR responsivity to the stimulus complex containing both the CS and the model's pain cues during the acquisition trials, and did not differ significantly in this respect. As can be seen from the test-trial scores in Fig. 6, however, the auditory stimulus itself had acquired differential aversive properties among groups of observers subjected to varying degrees of arousal. The differential vicarious conditioning revealed in the test trials is even more pronounced in the extinction phase of the experiment. Observers in both the placebo and the shock-threat groups continue to exhibit a significantly higher level of conditioned responses than either the low-aroused nonthreat group or the high-aroused epinephrine large-dose group.

The overall findings clearly reveal that observers' emotional arousal is a significant determinant of vicarious conditioning. This is demonstrated by the fact that the frequency of conditioned responses is a positive function of the degree of psychological stress. However, a monotonic decreasing function is obtained when, in addition to situational stress, subjects experience increasing physiologically induced arousal.

If it can be assumed that the five treatment conditions represent incremental levels of affective arousal on a single dimension, then the combined results suggest an inverted-U relationship between magnitude of arousal and vicarious conditioning. There are two sets of data that lend some support to this interpretation. First, subjects in the shock-threat group achieved the highest level of vicarious conditioning, but the placebo condition emerged superior in the extinction phase of the experiment. This reversal is probably due to the fact that the threat of impending shock stimulation produced a further heightening of emotional arousal in shock-threat observers as they entered the extinction series of trials. Second, within-treatments correlational analyses between a measure of emotional proneness and the vicarious conditioning and extinction scores furnished results that are indicative of a nonmonotonic relationship (Bandura and Rosenthal, 1965).

The failure of low-aroused subjects to exhibit much vicarious conditioning is readily explainable in terms of an activation hypothesis, but the equally poor conditioning in subjects administered the large dose of epinephrine may suggest alternative interpretations. One possible explanation is that epinephrine in the high dosage range has an inhibitory effect on the GSR response itself. This interpretation, however, cannot account for the differential conditioning rates, since no significant differences were obtained among groups in both the total number of trials to adaptation, and the frequency of GSR responsivity during acquisition, when the stimulus complex contained both the CS and the model's pain cues. Moreover, the fact that test trials were interspersed with acquisition trials, and the entire conditioning series was completed in a relatively brief period of time, rules out the possibility of any significant temporally related changes in drug action.

Although the data provide evidence of a relationship between arousal level and vicarious conditioning, the manner in which arousal produces facilitative or disruptive effects remains to be demonstrated. Subjects' replies to a post-experimental questionnaire suggested that disruptive effects may, in part, be mediated by self-generated competing responses designed to reduce the aversiveness of the vicarious instigation situation.

In some cases, this took the form of an intensive focus on irrelevant external stimuli, to the exclusion of the disturbing pain cues ("When I noticed how painful the shock was to him, I concentrated my vision on a spot which did not allow me to focus directly on either his face or hands.") Most observers attempted to decrease the aversive stimulation arising from the model's pain reactions by conjuring up competing cognitive responses. ("I tried to be cool. I thought about Latin verbs and about Latin composition.") A few subjects, however, marshalled considerably more potent contravening cognitive responses ("I finally just tried to think about the girl I slept with last night. It kept my mind off those damn shocks.")

To the extent that an observer who is confronted by a vicarious instigation situation succeeds either in attenuating unpleasant arousal by producing competing cognitive responses, or in curtailing attentional responses to the eliciting stimuli, the CS is likely to become endowed with relatively weak aversive properties. The deliberate use of avoidant and stimulus neutralization stratagems was reported most frequently by the most highly aroused subjects.

It should be noted that, unlike direct classical conditioning in which the subject is unable to modify the intensity of aversive stimulation administered to him, in vicarious conditioning situations the observer can readily engage in response-interference stratagems that serve to reduce vicariously instigated affective reactions. For this reason, investigations of direct and vicarious classical conditioning may not always yield equivalent relationships between variables. Similarly, findings based on vicarious classical conditioning may not be applicable to modeling processes involving instrumental classes of responses. Thus, as demonstrated in Schachter's experiments, a person experiencing high-intensity autonomic responses may welcome the opportunity to engage in matching social behavior, whereas in a classical conditioning situation permitting no motoric responses, high-aroused subjects can resort only to stimulus neutralization tactics as a means of reducing their discomfort.

The questionnaire data revealed additional complexities in the vicarious conditioning process that require systematic investigation. It was assumed that vicarious instigation of emotional responses is mediated by a process of stimulus generalization. That is, stimuli impinging upon a given person and the attendant reactions will arouse in the observer analogous emotional responses, the magnitude of the responses being a function of the degree of similarity between the participants. One would expect persons who possess similar characteristics to share many experiences in common. Results of experiments with infrahuman subjects discussed earlier (Church, 1959) reveal that the experience of repeated paired consequences is an important determinant of vicarious arousal. Moreover, Murphy *et al.* (1955) demonstrated that emotional responses in monkeys could be vicariously elicited not only by the sight of their experimental counterparts, but also through stimulus generalization by another monkey that was never involved in the original aversive contingencies.

The self-report data indicated that with a few notable exceptions subjects did, in fact, experience strong, empathetic reactions. Several of the observers, however, derived considerable satisfaction from witnessing pain being inflicted on the model (e.g., "My main reaction was sadistic. My main thoughts were, 'Oh, boy, is he getting it' " . . . "I was rather embarrassed to see that I was grinning when my partner got shocked and dropped the stylus with a suppressed groan.") On the assumption that such reactions are established through discordant, interindividual contingencies (Berger, 1962), a study is planned in which the level of vicarious conditioning will be measured as a function of antecedent paired aversive consequences, paired opposing consequences, and unassociated negative outcomes experienced by the model and observing subjects.

C. Higher-Order Vicarious Conditioning

In the experiments described above, observers' affective responses to the pain of the models undergoing direct aversive stimulation were conditioned to neutral stimuli. Social attitudes are frequently established on the basis of modeled higher-order pairings in which the names and discriminative attributes of target persons and objects are associated by the model with verbal stimuli likely to evoke in the observer intense, emotional responses on the basis of prior, first-order conditioning. The following quotation, taken from a report of a Ku Klux Klan rally (*San Francisco Chronicle*, 1963), provides a vivid illustration of how fear and hatred of Negroes can be conditioned in this manner and transmitted through modeling to the Klansmen's observant offspring.

> The speaker shouted, "In Washington and New York it weren't safe for a white woman to walk the streets by day." "Niggers," the crowd cried out.
> There was an attack on the Red Cross for not labelling blood "black and white." Another speaker was introduced as an expert on the subject. He told the people that there was a "round-shaped corpuscle in nigra blood" and that it was a "white child killer when it gets in our blood."
> From the platform came attacks on the "black communist conspiracy plot" . . . Shelton (Klan Grand Dragon) said "nigras" constituted 10 per cent of the Nation's population, but were responsible for 80 per cent of the crime, rape, illegitimate births, syphilis, and gonorrhea. . . . The grand commander of the Woman's Klan in Georgia was introduced. She said she was a mother and grandmother and then urged the people to "teach your children the difference between black and white. How do you know who

they'll marry? I'm fighting to keep mine pure and white." A woman sitting in front shook her head slowly. "Those damn niggers," she mumbled. "Damn niggers."

Many of the parents in the crowd had brought their young children to the meeting. On the fringe of the crowd three boys, not more than 10 years old, were playing the old American game of "king-of-the-mountain." They were on a mound of dirt pushing each other from the top. "Down, nigger, you get down there, you nigger," one of them said pushing his friend. "I ain't no nigger, you are," said another, as he scrambled to the top.

In view of the ample opportunities provided children to acquire prejudicial attitudes simply by observing the vehement, emotional responses displayed by bigoted models, it is not surprising that scapegoat theories of prejudice, based on a conflict-displacement paradigm (N. E. Miller, 1944, 1959) have yielded equivocal results (Berkowitz, 1958; Cowen *et al.*, 1959; Lindzey, 1950; Stagner and Condon, 1955; Weatherley, 1961). According to this theory, the objects and strength of displaced aggressive responses can be predicted by knowledge of three variables only—the strength of instigation to aggression by the original frustrating agents, the strength of inhibitory responses, and the degree of dissimilarity of the displaced objects to the original frustrators. This model thus makes no provision for the potentially powerful influence of social agents in transmitting and shaping highly discriminative patterns of prejudicial attitudes toward stimulus objects other than themselves (Bandura and Walters, 1963a). The predictive power of the conflict paradigm is likely to be particularly limited under conditions where the modeling cues and reinforcement contingencies displayed by the primary social agents have no consistent relationship to the similarity of the original frustrators to possible displaced objects.

IV. Vicarious Extinction

Autonomic and instrumental classes of responses can not only be acquired, but also extinguished on a vicarious basis. The latter outcome is achieved by exposing the observer to modeled stimulus events involving either the omission of reinforcement, or the presentation of opposing reinforcing stimuli to the performing subject. Some suggestive evidence for the occurrence of vicarious extinction of conditioned emotionality is provided by Masserman (1943) and Jones (1924) in exploratory studies of the relative therapeutic efficacy of modeling procedures.

Masserman produced strong feeding inhibitions in cats by pairing food approach responses to a conditioned stimulus with either air-blasts, grid-shocks, or both forms of noxious stimulation presented simultaneously. In the remedial phase of the experiment, the inhibited animals observed a cagemate which had never been negatively conditioned exhibit prompt approach and feeding responses. The observing subjects initially cowered at the presentation of the conditioned stimulus, but with continued exposure to their fearless companion, they advanced, at first hesitantly and then more boldly, to the goal box and consumed the food. Some of the animals, however, showed little reduction in avoidance behavior despite prolonged hunger and repeated modeling trials. Moreover, avoidance responses reappeared in a few of the animals after the normal cat was removed, indicating that in the latter cases the modeling stimuli served merely as temporary external inhibitors of avoidance responses. Jones (1924) similarly obtained variable results in extinguishing children's phobic responses by having them observe their peers behave in a non-anxious manner in the presence of the avoided objects.

In the cases cited above, the models responded to the most aversive stimulus situation at the onset, a modeling procedure that is likely to generate high levels of emotional arousal in observers. Under these conditions any avoidance responses performed by the observing subject that serve to attentuate or terminate the vicariously instigated aversive stimulation will in fact be reinforced rather than extinguished. Therefore, the efficacy of vicarious extinction procedures may depend to a large extent on the care with which the modeled performances are programmed.

Avoidance responses can be rapidly extinguished if subjects are exposed to a graduated series of aversive stimuli that progressively approximate the original intensity of the conditioned fear stimulus (Kimble and Kendall, 1953). In the application of this stimulus generalization principle to vicarious extinction, the subject might initially observe a model responding in a positive manner to relatively weak emotion-provoking cues. After these stimuli have lost their aversive properties for the observer, gradually increasing intensities of anxiety-arousing stimuli can be presented to the model until the most potent cues have been successfully neutralized.

If emotion-eliciting stimuli are repeatedly associated with positively reinforcing events, the former cues are likely to lose their aversive properties more rapidly than through mere repeated, nonreinforced presentation (Melvin and Brown, 1964; Wolpe, 1958). The induction of competing positive responses in observers during exposure to modeling trials may likewise expedite the vicarious extinction process. The latter principles and other factors known to facilitate extinction were systematically applied in an investigation of group vicarious extinction of dog phobias in young children (Bandura et al., 1965b).

The strength of avoidance responses toward dogs was measured by a standardized situational test in which children were instructed to engage in increasingly intimate interactions with a dog. Children who displayed avoidance responses were grouped into stratified levels of avoidance behavior and then assigned to one of four conditions.

One group of children participated in eight brief modeling sessions in which they observed a fearless peer model exhibit progressively longer, closer, and more active interactions with his canine companion. For these subjects, the modeled approach behavior was presented within the context of a highly positive, party atmosphere. A second group of children was exposed to the same graduated modeling stimuli, but in a neutral context.

In the latter two treatment conditions, the stimulus complex involved both modeling cues and repeated observation of the feared animal. Therefore, in order to control for the effects of exposure to the dog per se, a third group of children was presented the series of parties in the presence of the dog with the model absent. A fourth group participated in the positive activities but was never exposed to either the dog or the modeled displays.

Following the completion of the treatment series, the children were readministered, by a different experimenter, the situational test consisting of the graded sequence of interaction tasks with the test animal. They were asked, for example, to approach and to pet the dog, to release her from a play pen, to remove her leash, to feed her dog biscuits, and to spend a fixed period of time alone in the room with the animal while the experimenter departed to fetch an additional supply of canine cookies. The terminal test items required the children to climb into the play pen with the dog, to pet, and to remain alone with the animal under the exceedingly confining and potentially fear-provoking conditions.

In order to determine the generality of vicarious extinction effects, half the children in each of the four groups were tested initially with the experimental animal and then with an unfamiliar dog; the remaining children were presented the two dogs in the reversed order. In addition, the assessment procedures were repeated approximately one month later so as to assess the stability of the modeling-induced changes.

The modeling procedure produced highly stable and generalized vicarious extinction of avoidance responses. This is shown in the fact that the two groups of children, who had observed the peer model interact nonanxiously with the dog, displayed significantly greater approach behavior toward both the experimental and the unfamiliar animals than children in the exposure and control conditions, which did not differ from each other. The positive context, however, did not contribute any significant variance to the obtained outcomes. As might be expected, the positive context and repeated assessments also produced some decrease in avoidance behavior.

If symbolic modeling procedures, utilizing pictorial stimuli, should also prove efficacious in extinguishing conditioned emotional responses, then carefully programmed therapeutic films could be developed for preventive programs designed to eliminate common fears and anxieties before they become well established and widely generalized.

V. Concluding Remarks

Both the early and more recent conceptualizations of vicarious or observational learning have been developed and tested largely on the basis of a limited paradigm requiring observing subjects to perform matching responses as a precondition for their acquisition. A considerably more prevalent and significant vicarious phenomenon is evident in the occurrence of delayed reproduction of modeling behavior originally learned by observers under a nonresponse acquisition procedure.

The present paper is mainly concerned with the theoretical analysis of the process of no-trial learning. Unlike most previous accounts of modeling effects, which tend to highlight the reinforcing stimulus control of matching responses, the theory propounded by the author emphasizes the function of representational processes in observational learning. According to this formulation, matching responses are acquired on the basis of stimulus contiguity and are mediated by cue-producing symbolic responses which exercise discriminative stimulus control over corresponding overt performances. Thus, in this mode of response acquisition, imaginal and verbal representations of modeling stimuli constitute the enduring learning products of observational experiences. While the perceptual and cognitive aspects of vicarious learning are given emphasis, it is recognized that motivational and reinforcement variables may influence indirectly the level of *response acquisition* by augmenting or reducing the occurrence of requisite observing responses and facilitative covert rehearsal. There is considerable research evidence, however, that the *performance* of previously learned matching responses is primarily governed by reinforcement-related variables.

The theory advanced in this paper suggests that vicarious learning may be analyzed in the same manner as other associative learning processes. In the formation of novel responses, new associative connections between existing behavioral elements are established through observation. Since the observer does not engage in overt performances during the acquisition stage, the new integrations involve representational responses elicited by the modeling stimuli. In addition, the observer learns the sequential connections between modeling responses as they are exhibited in a continuous chain.

The fact that vicarious learning experiments employ social cues rather than nonsense syllables does not result in an acquisition process that is fundamentally different from traditional associative learning. There is no reason to believe, for example, that the principles governing the integration of elements in the mechanically displayed syllables ZXK, the modeled verbalization *supercalifragilisticexpialidocious,* or a modeled aggressive response consisting of several distinct components are essentially different simply because the former stimuli are presented to the observer in a nonsocial memory drum, whereas the latter stimuli are displayed socially. Nor are basically different learning processes involved in the acquisition of the clearly unique verbal response *supercalifragilisticex-pialidocious* when presented in the aperture of a memory drum or by a verbalizing model. Consequently, there is no need to search for enigmatic, psychological mechanisms and elusive, dynamic variables in accounting for learning by observation, imitation, or identification.

The study of the social transmission of response patterns is necessitated by the fact that the behavioral repertoires which constitute an enduring part of a culture are to a large extent transmitted on the basis of repeated observation of behavior displayed by social models rather than by memory drums. While the learning process is essentially the same, the characteristics of the social transmitters and other interpersonal variables can greatly affect the rate, level, and types of responses that will be acquired observationally. Moreover, the efficacy of parameters established on the basis of learning in one-person situations may differ in dyadic and group situations (Bandura *et al.*, 1963b). A comprehensive theory of behavior must therefore be based on experimentation involving both social and learning variables.

In addition to response learning, witnessing the reinforcement contingencies of a model is often highly influential in modifying the extent to which similar existing patterns of social behavior will later by exhibited by observers. The strength of inhibitory responses may likewise be significantly altered, and emotional responses may be vicariously conditioned and extinguished as a function of observing the reinforcing consequences to a model and his attendant affective reactions. The research findings reviewed in this chapter identify some of the social-learning variables determining the diverse behavioral effects on observers of exposure to socially modeled stimulus events.

REFERENCES

Allport, F. H. (1924). *Social psychology.* Cambridge, Mass.: Riverside Press.
Armstrong, E. A. (1942). *Bird display and behaviour.* London and New York: Cambridge Univer. Press.
Baer, D. M., and Sherman, J. A. (1964). Reinforcement control of generalized imitation in young children. *J. exp. Child Psychol.* **1**, 37–49.
Bandura, A. (1960). Relationship of family patterns to child behavior disorders. Stanford Univer. Progress Rep., Project No. M-1734, U.S. Public Health Service.

Bandura, A. (1962). Social learning through imitation. In M. R. Jones (Ed.), *Nebraska symposium on motivation: 1962.* Univer. of Nebraska Press, Lincoln, Nebr.: pp. 211–269.

Bandura, A. (1963). The role of imitation in personality development. *J. nursery Educ.* **18,** 207–215.

Bandura, A. (1965a). Behavioral modifications through modeling procedures. In L. Krasner and L. P. Ullmann (Eds.), *Research in behavior modification.* New York: Holt. pp. 310–340.

Bandura, A. (1965b). Influence of models' reinforcement contingencies on the acquisition of imitative responses. *J. Pers. soc. Psychol.* **1,** 589–595.

Bandura, A., and Huston, Aletha C. (1961). Identification as a process of incidental learning. *J. abnorm. soc. Psychol.* **63,** 311–318.

Bandura, A., and Kupers, Carol, J. (1964). Transmission of patterns of self reinforcement through modeling. *J. abnorm. soc. Psychol.* **69,** 1–9.

Bandura, A., and McDonald, F. J. (1963). The influence of social reinforcement and the behavior of models in shaping children's moral judgments. *J. abnorm. soc. Psychol.* **67,** 272–281.

Bandura, A., and Mischel, W. (1965). Modification of self-imposed delay of reward through exposure to live and symbolic models. *J. Pers. soc. Psychol.* **1,** (in press).

Bandura, A., and Rosenthal, T. L. (1965). Vicarious classical conditioning as a function of arousal level. *J. Pers. soc. Psychol.* **1,** (in press).

Bandura, A., and Walters, R. H. (1959). *Adolescent aggression.* New York: Ronald Press.

Bandura, A., and Walters, R. H. (1963a). *Social learning and personality development.* New York: Holt.

Bandura, A., and Walters, R. H. (1963b). Aggression. In H. W. Stevenson (ed.), *Child psychology: the sixty-second yearbook of the National Society for the Study of Education.* Chicago, Ill.: Nat. Soc. Study Educ., Part I, pp. 364–415.

Bandura, A., and Whalen, Carol K. (1965). The influence of antecedent reinforcement and divergent modeling cues on patterns of self-reward. *J. Pers. soc. Psychol.* **1,** (in press).

Bandura, A., Ross, Dorothea, and Ross, Sheila A. (1961). Transmission of aggression through imitation of aggressive models. *J. abnorm. soc. Psychol.* **63,** 575–582.

Bandura, A., Ross, Dorothea, and Ross, Sheila A. (1963a). Imitation of film-mediated aggressive models. *J. abnorm. soc. Psychol.* **66,** 3–11.

Bandura, A., Ross, Dorothea, and Ross, Sheila A. (1963b). A comparative test of the status envy, social power, and secondary reinforcement theories of identificatory learning. *J. abnorm. soc. Psychol.* **67,** 527–534.

Bandura, A., Ross, Dorothea, and Ross, Sheila A. (1963c). Vicarious reinforcement and imitative learning. *J. abnorm. soc. Psychol.* **67,** 601–607.

Bandura, A., Grusec, Joan E., and Menlove, Frances L. (1965a). The influence of symbolization and incentive set on observational learning. Unpublished manuscript, Stanford Univer.

Bandura, A., Grusec, Joan E., and Menlove, Frances L. (1965b). Vicarious extinction of avoidance responses. Unpublished manuscript, Stanford Univer.

Barnett, P. E., and Benedetti, D. T. (1960). A study in "vicarious conditioning." Paper read at Rocky Mt. Psychol. Ass., Glenwood Spring, Colorado.

Bayroff, A. G., and Lard, K. E. (1944). Experimental social behavior of animals: III. Imitational learning of white rats. *J. comp. Psychol.* **37**, 165–171.

Berger, S. M. (1961). Incidental learning through vicarious reinforcement. *Psychol. Rept.* **9**, 477–491.

Berger, S. M. (1962). Conditioning through vicarious instigation. *Psychol. Rev.* **69**, 450–466.

Berkowitz, L. (1958). The expression and reduction of hostility. *Psychol. Bull.* **55**, 257–283.

Berkowitz, L. (1962). *Aggression: a social psychological analysis.* New York: McGraw-Hill.

Berkowitz, L. (1964). Aggressive cues in aggressive behavior and hostility catharsis. *Psychol. Rev.* **71**, 104–122.

Berkowitz, L. (1965). Some aspects of observed aggression. *J. pers. soc. Psychol.* (in press).

Berkowitz, L., and Geen, R. G. (1965). Film violence and the cue properties of available targets. Unpublished manuscript, Univer. of Wisconsin.

Berkowitz, L., and Rawlings, Edna (1963). Effects of film violence on inhibitions against subsequent aggression. *J. abnorm. soc. Psychol.* **66**, 405–412.

Bierman, Mary M. (1965). The use of modeling, reinforcement, and problem-solving set in altering children's syntactic style. Unpublished manuscript, Stanford Univer.

Black, A. H. (1958). The extinction of avoidance responses under curare. *J. comp. physiol. Psychol.* **51**, 519–524.

Black, A. H., Carlson, N. J., and Solomon, R. L. (1962). Exploratory studies of the conditioning of autonomic responses in curarized dogs. *Psychol. Monogr.* **76**, No. 29 (Whole No. 548).

Blake, R. R. (1958). The other person in the situation. In R. Tagiuri and L. Petrullo (Eds.), *Person perception and interpersonal behavior.* Stanford Calif.: Stanford Univer. Press, pp. 229–242.

Blake, R. R., Rosenbaum, M. E., and Duryea, R. (1955). Gift-giving as a function of group standards. *Hum. Relat.* **8**, 61–73.

Blake, R. R., Mouton, Jane S., and Hain, J. D. (1956). Social forces in petition signing. *Sthwest. soc. Sci. Quart.* **36**, 385–390.

Bruning, J. L. (1965). Direct and vicarious effects of a shift in magnitude of reward on performance. *J. Pers. soc. Psychol.* **2**, 278–282.

Buchwald, A. M. (1959a). Extinction after acquisition under different verbal reinforcement combinations. *J. exp. Psychol.* **57**, 43–48.

Buchwald, A. M. (1959b). Experimental alterations in the effectiveness of verbal reinforcement combinations. *J. exp. Psychol.* **57**, 351–361.

Buchwald, A. M. (1960). Supplementary report: alteration of the reinforcement value of a positive reinforcer. *J. exp. Psychol.* **60**, 416–418.

Buss, A. H. (1961). *The psychology of aggression.* New York: Wiley.

Church, R. M. (1957). Transmission of learned behavior between rats. *J. abnorm. soc. Psychol.* **54**, 163–165.

Church, R. M. (1959). Emotional reactions of rats to the pain of others. *J. comp. physiol. Psychol.* **52**, 132–134.

Conant, M. B. (1964). Conditioned visual hallucinations. Unpublished manuscript, Stanford Univer.

Cowen, E. L., Landes, J., and Schaet, D. E. (1959). The effect of mild frustration on the expression of prejudiced attitudes. *J. abnorm. soc. Psychol.* **58**, 33–38.

Crandall, Virginia C. (1963). The reinforcement effects of adult reactions and non-reactions on children's achievement expectations. *Child Develpm.* **34,** 335–354.

Crandall, Virginia, C., Good, Suzanne, and Crandall, V. J. (1964). The reinforcement effects of adult reactions and non-reactions on children's achievement expectations: a replication study. *Child Develpm.* **35,** 435–497.

Crawford, M. P., and Spence, K. W. (1939). Observational learning of discrimination problems by chimpanzees. *J. comp. Psychol.* **27,** 133–147.

Darby, C. L., and Riopelle, A. J. (1959). Observational learning in the Rhesus monkey. *J. comp. physiol. Psychol.* **52,** 94–98.

Doerfler, L. G., and Kramer, Joan C. (1959). Unconditioned stimulus strength and the galvanic skin response. *J. Speech Hearing Res.* **2,** 184–192.

Dollard, J., and Miller, N. E. (1950). *Personality and psychotherapy.* New York: McGraw-Hill.

Duncker, K. (1938). Experimental modification of children's food preferences through social suggestion. *J. abnorm. soc. Psychol.* **33,** 489–507.

Dysinger, W. S., and Ruckmick, C. A. (1933). *The emotional responses of children to the motion picture situation.* New York: Macmillan.

Feshbach, S. (1961). The stimulating versus cathartic effects of a vicarious aggressive activity. *J. abnorm. soc. Psychol.* **63,** 381–385.

Feshbach, S. (1964). The function of aggression and the regulation of aggressive drive. *Psychol. Rev.* **71,** 257–272.

Freed, A., Chandler, P. J., Blake, R. R., and Mouton, Jane S. (1955). Stimulus and background factors in sign violation. *J. Pers.* **23,** 499.

Geen, R. G., and Berkowitz, L. (1965). Name-mediated aggressive cue properties. Unpublished manuscript, Univer. of Wisconsin.

Gelfand, Donna M. (1962). The influence of self-esteem on rate of verbal conditioning and social matching behavior. *J. abnorm. soc. Psychol.* **65,** 259–265.

Grosser, D., Polansky, N., and Lippitt, R. (1951). A laboratory study of behavioral contagion. *Hum. Relat.* **4,** 115–142.

Grusec, Joan E. (1965). Model characteristics, techniques of punishment, and reinforcement contigency as antecedents of self-criticism. Unpublished doctoral dissertation, Stanford Univer.

Grusec, Joan E. and Mischel, W. (1965). The model's characteristics as determinants of social learning. Unpublished manuscript, Stanford Univer.

Hall, K. R. (1963). Observational learning in monkeys and apes. *Brit. J. Psychol.* **54,** 201–226.

Hanlon, Camille. (1964). The effects of social isolation and characteristics of the model on accent imitation in fourth-grade children. Unpublished doctoral dissertation, Stanford Univer.

Hartmann, D. P. (1965). The influence of symbolically modeled instrumental aggression and pain cues on the disinhibition of aggressive behavior. Unpublished doctoral dissertation, Stanford Univer.

Hayes, K. J., and Hayes, Catherine (1952a). Imitation in a home-raised chimpanzee. *J. comp. physiol. Psychol.* **45,** 450–459.

Hayes, K. J., and Hayes, Catherine (1952b). Imitation in a home-raised chimpanzee. 16mm. silent film. State College, Pa., Psychol. Cinema Register.

Helson, H., Blake, R. R., Mouton, Jane S., and Olmstead, J. A. (1956). Attitudes as adjustments to stimulus, background, and residual factors. *J. abnorm. soc. Psychol.* **52,** 314–322.

Henker, Barbara A. (1964). The effect of adult model relationships on children's play and task imitation. Unpublished doctoral dissertation, Ohio State Univer.

Herbert, J. J., and Harsh, C. M. (1944). Observational learning by cats. *J. comp. Psychol.* **37**, 81–95.

Hicks, D. J. (1965). Imitation and retention of film-mediated aggressive peer and adult models. *J. Pers. soc. Psychol.* **2**, 97–100.

Hinde, R. A. (1953). The term "mimesis." *Brit. J. Anim. Behav.* **1**, 7–11.

Holt, E. B. (1931). *Animal drive and the learning process.* New York: Holt, Vol. 1.

Humphrey, G. (1921). Imitation and the conditioned reflex. *Pedag. Sem.* **28**, 1–21.

Imanishi, K. (1957). Social behavior in Japanese monkeys. *Macaca fuscata. Psychologia* **1**, 47–54.

Jones, Mary C. (1924). The elimination of children's fears. *J. exp. Psychol.* **7**, 383–390.

Kanareff, Vera T., and Lanzetta, J. T. (1960a). Effects of task definition and probability of reinforcement upon the acquisition and extinction of imitative responses. *J. exp. Psychol.* **60**, 340–348.

Kanareff, Vera T., and Lanzetta, J. T. (1960b). Effects of success-failure experiences and probability of reinforcement upon the acquisition and extinction of an imitative response. *Psychol. Rept.* **7**, 151–166.

Kanfer, F. H. (1965). Vicarious human reinforcement: a glimpse into the black box. In L. Krasner and L. P. Ullmann (Eds.), *Research in behavior modification.* New York: Holt. pp. 244–267.

Kanfer, F. H., and Marston, A. R. (1963). Human reinforcement: vicarious and direct. *J. exp. Psychol.* **65**, 292–296.

Katz, D., and Révész, G. (1921). Experimentelle Studien zur vergleichenden Psychologie (Versuche mit Hühnern. *Z. angew. Psychol.* **18**, 307–320.

Kawamura, S. (1963). The process of sub-culture propagation among Japanese Macaques. In C. H. Southwick (Ed.), *Primate social behavior.* Princeton, N.J.: Van Nostrand, pp. 82–90.

Kellogg, W. N., and Kellogg, L. A. (1933). *The ape and the child: a study of environmental influence upon early behavior.* New York: McGraw-Hill.

Kimble, G. A., and Kendall, J. W., Jr. (1953). A comparison of two methods of producing experimental extinction. *J. exp. Psychol.* **45**, 87–90.

Kimbrell, D., and Blake, R. R. (1958). Motivational factors in the violation of a prohibition. *J. abnorm. soc. Psychol.* **56**, 132–133.

Kriazhev, V. I. (1934). The objective investigation of the higher nervous activity in a collective experiment. *Psychol. Abstr.* **8**, 2532.

Lanzetta, J. T., and Kanareff, Vera T. (1959). The effects of a monetary reward on the acquisition of an imitative response. *J. abnorm. soc. Psychol.* **59**, 120–127.

Larder, Diane L. (1962). Effect of aggressive story content on nonverbal play behavior. *Psychol. Rep.* **11**, 14–15.

Latané, B., and Schachter, S. (1962). Adrenalin and avoidance learning. *J. comp. physiol. Psychol.* **55**, 368–372.

Lazarus, R. S., Speisman, J. C., Mordkoff, A. M., and Davison, L. A. (1962). A laboratory study of psychological stress produced by a motion picture film. *Psychol. Monogr.* **76**, No. 34 (Whole No. 553).

Lazowick, L. (1955). On the nature of identification. *J. abnorm. soc. Psychol.* **51**, 175–183.

Leaf, R. C. (1964). Avoidance response evocation as a function of prior discriminative fear conditioning under curare. *J. comp. physiol. Psychol.* **58,** 446–449.

Lefkowitz, M. M., Blake, R. R., and Mouton, Jane S. (1955). Status factors in pedestrian violation of traffic signals. *J. abnorm. soc. Psychol.* **51,** 704–706.

Leuba, C. (1940). Images as conditioned sensations. *J. exp. Psychol.* **26,** 345–351.

Lindzey, G. (1950). An experimental investigation of the scapegoat theory of prejudice. *J. abnorm. soc. Psychol.* **45,** 296–309.

Lövaas, O. I. (1961). Effect of exposure to symbolic aggression on aggressive behavior. *Child Develpm.* **32,** 37–44.

McDavid, J. W. (1962). Effects of ambiguity of environmental cues upon learning to imitate. *J. abnorm. soc. Psychol.* **65,** 381–386.

McDougall, W. (1908). *An introduction to social psychology.* London: Methuen.

McGuire, W. J. (1961). Interpolated motivational statements within a programmed series of instructions as a distribution of practice factor. In A. A. Lumsdaine (Ed.), *Student response in programmed instruction: a symposium.* Washington, D.C.: Natl. Acad. Sci.—Natl. Res. Council, pp. 411–415.

Marston, A. R., and Kanfer, F. H. (1963). Group size and number of vicarious reinforcements in verbal learning. *J. exp. Psychol.* **65,** 593–596.

Masserman, J. H. (1943). *Behavior and neurosis.* Chicago, Ill.: Univer. of Chicago Press.

Melvin, K. B., and Brown, J. S. (1964). Neutralization of an aversive light stimulus as a function of number of paired presentations with food. *J. comp. physiol. Psychol.* **58,** 350–353.

Metz, J. R. (1964). Teaching autistic children generalized imitation. Paper read at Amer. Psychol. Ass., Los Angeles.

Miller, N. E. (1944). Experimental studies of conflict. In J. McV. Hunt (Ed.), *Personality and the behavior disorders.* New York: Ronald Press, Vol. I, pp. 431–465.

Miller, N. E. (1959). Liberalization of basic S-R concepts: extension to conflict behavior, motivation, and social learning. In S. Koch (Ed.), *Psychology: a study of science,* New York: McGraw-Hill, Vol. 2, pp. 196–292.

Miller, N. E. (1964). Some implications of modern behavior theory for personality change and psychotherapy. In P. Worchel and D. Byrne (Eds.), *Personality change.* New York: Wiley, pp. 149–175.

Miller, N. E., and Dollard, J. (1940). *Social learning and imitation.* New Haven, Conn.: Yale Univer. Press.

Miller, R. E., Murphy, J. V., and Mirsky, I. A. (1959). Nonverbal communication of affect. *J. clin. Psychol.* **15,** 155–158.

Miller, R. E., Banks, J. H., and Ogawa, N. (1962). Communication of affect in "cooperative conditioning" of rhesus monkeys. *J. abnorm. soc. Psychol* **64,** 343–348.

Miller, R. E., Banks, J. H., and Ogawa, N. (1963). Role of facial expression in "cooperative-avoidance conditioning" in monkeys. *J. abnorm. soc. Psychol.* **67,** 24–30.

Mischel, W., and Grusec, Joan E. (1965). Determinants of the rehearsal and transmission of neutral and aversive behaviors. *J. pers. soc. Psychol.* (in press).

Morgan, C. L. (1896). *Habit and instinct.* London: Arnold.

Mowrer, O. H. (1950). Identification: a link between learning theory and psychotherapy. In *Learning theory and personality dynamics.* New York: Ronald Press, pp. 69–94.

Mowrer, O. H. (1960). *Learning theory and the symbolic processes.* New York: Wiley.

Murphy, J. V., Miller, R. E., and Mirsky, I. A. (1955). Interanimal conditioning in the monkey. *J. comp. physiol. Psychol.* **48**, 211–214.

Mussen, P. H., and Parker, Ann L. (1965). Mother-nurturance and girls' incidental imitative learning. *J. Pers. soc. Psychol.* **2**, 94–97.

Mussen, P. H., and Rutherford, E. (1961). Effects of aggressive cartoons on children's aggressive play. *J. abnorm. soc. Psychol.* **62**, 461–464.

Naruse, G., and Abonai, T. (1953). Decomposition and fusion of mental images in the drowsy and posthypnotic hallucinatory state. *J. clin. exp. Hyp.* **1**, 23–41.

Osgood, C. E., Suci, G. J., and Tannenbaum, P. H. (1957). *The measurement of meaning.* Urbana, Ill.: Univer. of Illinois Press.

Parsons, T., and Shils, E. A. Eds. (1951). *Toward a general theory of action.* Cambridge, Mass.: Harvard Univer. Press.

Piaget, J. (1951). *Play, dreams and imitation in childhood.* New York: Norton.

Riopelle, A. J. (1960). Complex processes. In R. H. Waters *et al.* (Eds.), *Principles of comparative psychology.* New York: McGraw-Hill, pp. 208–249.

Rosenbaum, M. E. (1956). The effect of stimulus and background factors on the volunteering response. *J. abnorm. soc. Psychol.* **53**, 118–121.

Rosenbaum, M. E., and Blake, R. R. (1955). Volunteering as a function of field structure. *J. abnorm. soc. Psychol.* **50**, 193–196.

Rosenbaum, M. E., and Bruning, J. L. (1961). Direct and vicarious effects of variations in percentage of reinforcement on performance. Unpublished manuscript, State Univer. of Iowa.

Rosenbaum, M. E., and deCharms, R. (1960). Direct and vicarious reduction of hostility. *J. abnorm. soc. Psychol.* **60**, 105–111.

Ross, Dorothea (1962). The relationship between dependency, intentional learning, and incidental learning in preschool children. Unpublished doctoral dissertation, Stanford Univer.

Ross, Sheila A. (1962). The effect of deviant and nondeviant models on the behavior of preschool children in a temptation situation. Unpublished doctoral dissertation, Stanford Univer.

San Francisco Chronicle, May 13, 1963. Klan rally—hate and fears, p. 17.

Schachter, S. (1964). The interaction of cognition and physiological determinants of emotional state. *Adv. exp. soc. Psychol.* **1**, 49–80.

Schachter, S., and Hall, R. (1952). Group-derived restraints and audience persuasion. *Hum. Relat.* **5**, 397–406.

Schachter S., and Singer, J. E. (1962). Cognitive, social and physiological determinants of emotional state. *Psychol. Rev.* **69**, 379–399.

Schachter, S., and Wheeler, L. (1962). Epinephrine, chlorpromazine, and amusement. *J. abnorm. soc. Psychol.* **65**, 121–128.

Schein, E. H. (1954). The effect of reward on adult imitative behavor. *J. abnorm. soc. Psychol.* **49**, 389–395.

Sears, R. R., Maccoby, Eleanor E., and Levin, H. (1957), *Patterns of child rearing.* New York: Harper.

Sheffield, F. D. (1961). Theoretical considerations in the learning of complex sequential tasks from demonstration and practice. In A. A. Lumsdaine (Ed.), *Student response in programmed instruction: a symposium.* Washington, D.C.: Natl. Acad. Sci.—Natl. Res. Council, pp. 13–32.

Sheffield, F. D., and Maccoby, N. (1961). Summary and interpretation on research on organizational principles in constructing filmed demonstrations. In A. A. Lumsdaine (Ed.), *Student response in programmed instruction: a symposium.* Washington, D.C.: Natl. Acad. Sci.—Natl. Res. Council, pp. 117–131.

Siegel, Alberta E. (1956). Film-mediated fantasy aggression and strength of aggressive drive. *Child Develpm.* **27,** 365–378.

Singer, J. E. (1963). Sympathetic activation, drugs, and fear. *J. comp. physiol. Psychol.* **56,** 612–615.

Skinner, B. F. (1953). *Science and human behavior.* New York: Macmillan.

Skinner, B. F. (1957). *Verbal behavior.* New York: Appleton.

Solomon, R. L., and Coles, M. R. (1954). A case of failure of generalization of imitation across drives and across situations. *J. abnorm. soc. Psychol.* **49,** 7–13.

Solomon, R. L., and Turner, L. H. (1962). Discriminative classical conditioning in dogs paralyzed by curare can later control discriminative avoidance responses in the normal state. *Psychol. Rev.* **69,** 202–219.

Speisman, J. C., Lazarus, R. S., Mordkoff, A., and Davison, L. (1964). Experimental reduction of stress based on ego-defense theory. *J. abnorm. soc. Psychol.* **68,** 367–380.

Spence, K. W. (1958). A theory of emotionally based drive (D) and its relation to performance in simple learning situations. *Amer. Psychologist* **13,** 131–141.

Spence, K. W. (1964). Anxiety (drive) level and performance in eyelid conditioning. *Psychol. Bull.* **61,** 129–139.

Staats, A. W., and Staats, Carolyn K. (1963). *Complex human behavior.* New York: Holt.

Stagner, R., and Congdon, C. S. (1955). Another failure to demonstrate displacement of aggression. *J. abnorm. soc. Psychol.* **51,** 695–696.

Tarde, G. (1903). *The laws of imitation.* New York: Holt.

Thorndike, E. L. (1898). Animal intelligence: an experimental study of the associative processes in animals. *Psychol. Rev. Monogr.* Suppl. 2, No. 4 (Whole No. 8).

Thorpe, W. H. (1956). *Learning and instinct in animals.* London: Methuen.

Tinbergen, N. (1951). *The study of instinct.* London and New York: Oxford Univer. Press (Clarendon).

Walters, R. H., and Llewellyn Thomas, E. (1963). Enhancement of punitive behavior by visual and audiovisual displays. *Canad. J. Psychol.* **17,** 244–255.

Walters, R. H., and Parke, R. D. (1964). Influence of response consequences to a social model on resistance to deviation. *J. exp. Child Psychol.* **1,** 269–280.

Walters, R. H., Leat, Marion, and Mezei, L. (1963). Inhibition and disinhibition of response through empathetic learning. *Canad. J. Psychol.* **17,** 235–243.

Warden, C. J., and Jackson, T. A. (1935). Imitative behavior in the Rhesus monkey. *J. genet. Psychol.* **46,** 103–125.

Warden, C. J., Fjeld, H. A., and Koch, A. M. (1940). Imitative behavior in Cebus and Rhesus monkeys. *J. genet. Psychol.* **56,** 311–322.

Watson, J. B. (1908). Imitation in monkeys. *Psychol. Bull.* **5,** 169–178.

Weatherley, D. (1961). Anti-semitism and the expression of fantasy aggression. *J. abnorm. soc. Psychol.* **62,** 454–457.

Wolpe, J. (1958). *Psychotherapy by reciprocal inhibition.* Stanford, Calif.: Stanford Univer. Press.

SELECTIVE EXPOSURE[1]

Jonathan L. Freedman and David O. Sears

STANFORD UNIVERSITY
STANFORD, CALIFORNIA
UNIVERSITY OF CALIFORNIA
LOS ANGELES, CALIFORNIA

". . . individuals engage in selective exposure . . . . Those least predisposed to change are least likely to allow themselves to be exposed to a persuasive communication . . . . If a new piece of information would weaken the existing structure of their ideas and emotions, it will be shunned; . . . if it reinforces the structure, it will be sought out . . . ."[2]

Behavioral Sciences Subpanel (1962), President's Science Advisory Committee.

[1] The preparation of this paper was supported in part by NSF grants to the authors.

[2] Deleted sections refer to selective perception and other processes which are also supposed to operate under the same conditions as selective exposure.

I. Introduction

Behavioral scientists, political leaders, advertisers, and many others have long been concerned with how best to change opinions. Vast amounts of time and money have been expended to produce opinion changes. These efforts have led to at least one important conclusion: It is extremely difficult to alter the beliefs of people holding clear opinions. A large number of voters appear to make final vote decisions before election campaigning even begins; brand loyalties toward cigarettes, toothpastes, and automobiles are strikingly enduring; few persons ever leave the religious groups in which they were raised; anti-prejudice campaigns are notoriously unsuccessful. Of course, under some circumstances opinions do change enormously. Herbert Hoover routed and was routed by successive Democratic presidential candidates in a period of four years; Crest toothpaste revolutionized the toothpaste market in a matter of months; and Bennington students demonstrated that broad scale changes in basic political and economic attitudes can occur, given appropriate circumstances.

Nevertheless, as Hovland (1959), Klapper (1960), and others have repeatedly noted, it is difficult to change people's opinions outside of an artificial laboratory situation. Why is this so? Two general types of explanations have been offered. One account makes use of a wide variety of mechanisms by which an individual resists accepting a discrepant persuasive message with which he has been confronted. Its persuasive impact may be diluted by previous learning of counterarguments (McGuire and Papageorgis, 1961) or by forewarnings about its content (Freedman and Sears, 1965). The individual may be so committed to his belief that he subverts its impact by derogating the communicator (Hovland *et al.*, 1957), by misperceiving the position taken in the message (Cooper and

Jahoda, 1947; Manis, 1961), by dissociating the communicator from any responsibility for the message (Harvey *et al.,* 1957), or by a variety of other subtle and unsubtle cognitive machinations (Abelson, 1959; Festinger and Aronson, 1960; Kelley, 1957). In a great many different ways, an individual can resist being influenced by a discrepant message with which he has been confronted.

A person can, however, spare himself much trouble if he simply avoids contact with any discrepant information. Thus a second type of explanation for the ineffectiveness of many propaganda campaigns concerns voluntary exposure to information. One of the most widely accepted principles of mass communications and social psychology is that voluntary exposure to information is highly selective: People seek out information that supports or reinforces their previous beliefs, and avoid information that challenges their opinions. To Festinger (1957), selective exposure is a central proposition in his theory of cognitive dissonance; to Klapper (1960), it is a factor of prime importance in determining the effectiveness of mass communications; to McGuire and Papageorgis (1961), it is a factor suggesting the need for immunizing techniques to produce resistance to persuasion; to Berelson and Steiner (1964), it is a basic principle of human behavior; and it is a fundamental assumption in the thinking of many other researchers about persuasion through mass communication.

Despite the importance of the principle of selective exposure, relatively little research has been done to test it directly, and there has been no recent thorough evaluation of the research literature.[3] The purpose of this paper is to reopen the question of whether or not a general psychological preference exists for information which is compatible with pre-existing beliefs, to assess the relevant evidence, and to present an analysis of factors which appear to affect voluntary exposure to information.

II. *De Facto* Selectivity in Exposure

The central issue is whether people seek supportive information and avoid nonsupportive information. This issue might be placed in clearer perspective, however, by first considering the question of whether or not exposure is in fact selective. That is, does any given individual typically get exposed to disproportionately more supportive than nonsupportive information? Put another way, is any given persuasive message more likely to reach those who will agree with it than those who will disagree with it?

[3] Steiner (1962) wrote a brief note which dealt with some of the issues in this area, but covered only a small part of the available research.

Some of the evidence on this point comes from extended propaganda campaigns. In the Erie County study, about two thirds of those whose voting intentions were constant throughout the election campaign of 1940 were exposed mainly to the publicity of their own party, while only about 20% were exposed mainly to the publicity of the opposite party (Lazarsfeld et al., 1948, p. 90). Similarly, Star and Hughes (1950) reported that exposure to a mass information campaign on the United Nations was greatest among persons who were favorable to the United Nations prior to the campaign. For example, of those exposed to the campaign through three or more media, 81% felt before the campaign that the "United States should take an active part in world affairs," and only 19% thought the United Nations would fail. Of those not exposed to the campaign at all, only 46% had endorsed the first of these principles, and 27% had thought the United Nations would fail (p. 398).

Similar findings have been reported for brief campaigns or one-shot mass communications. For example, according to Cartwright (1949) a week-long showing of a film designed to induce adults to take a more active part in the war effort in Bridgeport, Connecticut, attracted a disproportionate number of persons who had already donated blood. Of those attending the movie, about 40% had already given blood. By contrast, in a random sample of the city, only 20% of those not attending the movie had already given blood. Schramm and Carter (1959) found that 22% of the Republican respondents in a telephone survey had watched some portion of a twenty-nine-hour telethon given the previous weekend by the Republican gubernatorial candidate, Senator William Knowland. On the other hand, only 10% of the Democratic respondents had watched any part of it. In addition, the average Republican viewer had watched almost twice as much of the telethon as had the average Democratic viewer, and more people watched it in the average "Republican viewing home" than in the average "Democratic viewing home."

A final example is representative of evidence that might be gathered at almost any mass meeting arranged for an expressly ideological purpose. Wolfinger et al. (1964) sampled the audience of a Christian Anti-Communist Crusade "School" held for a week in Oakland, California, in 1962. The Crusade is largely organized and run by white Protestants of a conservative political persuasion. Wolfinger reports that more than 75% of those attending the school were Prostestants, that during the week of meetings his interviewers noticed only a "handful" of non-whites, and that the sample was 66% Republican and only 8% Democratic. In each of these respects, the school was grossly unrepresentative of either the city of Oakland or the San Francisco Bay Area as a whole.

Similar data could undoubtedly be collected at many gatherings of people, from the readership lists of newspapers, magazines, and journals, or from the audiences of mass communications in the mass media. Republican rallies are mainly attended by Republicans, Baptist services are attended mainly by Baptists, the readers of the *New Republic* are mostly liberals, and those of the *National Review* mostly conservatives. AMA journals are read primarily by doctors, and APA journals primarily by psychologists. The audiences for most mass communications are disproportionately made up of those with initial sympathy for the viewpoints expressed; and it is likely that most individuals are, throughout their lives, exposed more to mass communications with which they agree than those with which they disagree.

None of this, however, indicates a general psychological tendency to prefer supportive information. A great many social, economic, utilitarian, and psychological factors affect the type of information to which a person is exposed. Mississippi whites must have many reasons for not attending an NAACP rally; Republican political meetings may provide a businessman or lawyer with useful friendships and information; doctors read AMA journals to keep abreast of their field; and stockbrokers read the *Wall Street Journal* for its extensive coverage of financial and business news.

In all of these cases, the people involved may be exposed more to information with which they agree than to information with which they disagree, but this selectivity could be an incidental effect of other factors. It might be entirely independent of any preference for supportive information. This point is extremely important because the manifest ubiquity of *de facto* selective exposure has tempted many to conclude that psychological preferences for supportive information underly it. Clearly, such preferences need not be the only cause of *de facto* selectivity, nor must they even be *one* of the causes. It is often assumed that they are a major cause, however, and we now turn to the evidence for and against this assumption.

III. Seeking Supportive Information and Avoiding Nonsupportive Information

As indicated above, there are many reasons why a person might be exposed more to supportive than to nonsupportive information. The question here is whether or not a general psychological preference for supportive material is one of these. Stated more precisely, if a person is given a completely free choice between information which is likely to reinforce his initial opinions, and information which is likely to challenge his opinions, will he tend to choose the former more than the latter?

The research relevant to this question has generally followed a simple paradigm. The subject's opinion is measured, and he is given a choice of exposing himself to supportive or nonsupportive information. In some studies the dependent variable is his choice between the two (i.e., which one he picks first); in others, it is the sum of his ratings or rankings of several supportive and several nonsupportive materials. In a few studies the information is actually available to the subject, and the dependent variable is the amount of exposure to each type of information. All of the studies in this area have been classified according to whether they show a preference for supportive information, no preference, or a preference for nonsupportive information. They are discussed below in that order.

A. STUDIES INDICATING A PREFERENCE FOR SUPPORTIVE INFORMATION

In the study conducted by Ehrlich et al. (1957), two groups of respondents were interviewed. In one, each person had bought a new automobile four to six weeks earlier. In the other, each owned a car at least three years old. Among other things, each respondent was shown eight large envelopes bearing the names of the eight popular makes of automobiles, and containing advertising material about the make named. Each respondent was asked to choose two envelopes in order to read and comment on the enclosed material. As shown in Table I, 80.7%

TABLE I

PERCENTAGE OF SUBJECTS PREFERRING SUPPORTIVE
TO NONSUPPORTIVE INFORMATION

Authors	Issue	N	% Preferring supportive[a]	% supportive Chance	% supportive Less chance
Ehrlich et al. (1957)	Automobiles	119	80.7	25	+55.7
Adams (1961)	Child training	54	75.4	50	+25.4
Freedman and Sears (1963)	1962 election	77[b]	58.4	50	+ 8.4
Sears (1966)	Jury	96	50.0	50	0
Sears and Freedman (1963)	Jury	119	45.4	50	− 4.6
Sears and Freedman (1965)	Jury	102[b]	43.1	50	− 6.9
Sears (1965)	Jury	81	30.2	50	−19.8
Brodbeck (1956)	Wire tapping	153	20.2	42.9	−22.7
Freedman (1965a)	Interview	18	5.6	50	−44.4

[a] Entries are percentage of subjects who chose or ranked a source of supportive information ahead of any non-supportive source.

[b] Excluding subjects who indicated a neutral article as their first choice.

of the respondents selected an envelope bearing the name of their own autos as one of the two they wished to read, although by chance alone only 25% of the respondents would have done so. Ehrlich *et al.* also collected data on the automobile advertisements their respondents had read in recent issues of magazines and newspapers. They present the percentages of ads the respondents had noticed which were actually read. Of the ads they had noticed, both new and old car owners read more about their own cars than about other makes. Insofar as advertising material concerning one's own car may be considered as reinforcing one's decision to buy that car, these data indicate a highly significant preference for supportive information.

Adams (1961) asked mothers of young children whether they believed in hereditary or environmental theories of child development, and then offered them the opportunity to hear one of two speeches upholding these alternatives. In this sample, 75.4% selected the speech supporting their own opinions. While this too represents a highly significant preference for supportive information, one important feature of the setting confuses the picture. All but six of the one hundred subjects tested believed a child's behavior to be "mostly learned" rather than "mostly inborn." Hence the apparent preference for supportive information actually represents a preference for the "environmental" talk, which may have been more useful to mothers who have little control over the hereditary endowment of their children. Or it may have been more interesting for a variety of other reasons. In the absence of data indicating preferences for the hereditary talk by mothers who gave more weight to hereditary factors, an interpretation in terms of selectivity is somewhat equivocal.

Freedman and Sears (1963) asked California citizens to indicate their preferences among five pamphlets on the 1962 gubernatorial campaign between Governor Edmund G. Brown and former Vice-President Richard M. Nixon. Of those respondents who expressed candidate preferences and who picked one of the four partisan pamphlets as their first choice, 58.4% selected a pamphlet endorsing the election of the candidate they favored (56.8% for Nixon supporters, and 60.7% for Brown supporters).

Finally, two studies using college classroom situations have obtained preferences for consonant information, although in each case the data are somewhat ambiguous. Mills *et al.* (1959) told students in introductory psychology sections that each person would be allowed to choose whether he would take an essay or a multiple-choice exam for an upcoming test. After each subject made his (presumably irrevocable) decision, he was given a list of six articles about exams and asked to rank them in order of how much he would like to read them. Each subject received a list of article titles including three favorable to essay exams and three favorable to multiple choice exams. For some subjects, all six articles were positively oriented and supported the merits of these types of exams; while for the remaining subjects, all six articles were negative and critical. The dependent measure was the sum of the ranks assigned to the three articles favorable to the chosen type of exam. Mills *et al.* found that the three positive articles favorable to the chosen type of exam were significantly preferred over the three positive articles favorable to the unchosen type of exam (regardless of which exam the subject had selected). In direct contrast with this, however, the three negative articles favorable to the rejected type of exam were slightly (nonsignificantly) preferred to the three negative articles favorable to the chosen type of exam.[4] Half of the data, therefore, provide evidence for a preference for supportive information, while the other half indicate either no preference or a preference for nonsupportive information.

This study provides a good example of a recurrent problem in this area, that is, the definition of supportive and nonsupportive information. In the classroom situation, the subject is presumably primarily concerned with doing well on the test relative to the rest of the class. Dissonance-increasing information should be information that implies he will do poorly relative to the rest of the class on the test he has chosen when he knows that he wants to do well on the test. It is doubtful that any of the articles were really dissonance-producing according to this criterion. The articles concerned the difficulty of the tests, how much anxiety they would arouse, etc. They said nothing about performance relative to others in the class. It may be unpleasant to read that your test is harder or anxiety arousing, but it may not be dissonant if you have chosen one kind of exam because you think you will do better on it. Thus, it may be that the results of this study have little to do with preferences among supportive and nonsupportive information, since none of the articles was relevant to the major dimension on which support would be judged.

This problem was attacked directly in a study by Rosen (1961) in an attempt to replicate the Mills *et al.* experiment. Rosen gave each subject four of the positive article titles used by Mills *et al.* but included two new titles suggesting that the subject had made an incorrect choice,

---

[4] The greater preference for supportive information obtained here on positive articles parallels a result from the Freedman and Sears (1963) election study. Considering only the two positive pamphlets, 68.8% of subjects preferred the one advocating election of the preferred candidate, while preferences were exactly evenly divided between the two negative pamphlets.

e.g., "These authors present some evidence that students who prefer essay exams generally do a lot better on objective tests." Hence in terms of the principal criterion on which the subject made his decision (how well he might do on either kind of test), only these latter two article titles are clearly supportive or nonsupportive of the subject's decision.

Rosen's results were quite striking. Considering all six article titles (the four borrowed from Mills *et al.*, plus the two new ones), the subjects significantly preferred information favorable to the chosen type of test. However, on the two titles that were clearly consonant or dissonant (i.e., those that told them they would have performed better had they chosen the other type of test), 67% of the subjects preferred the dissonant article, a difference which was significant beyond the .001 level.

Although Rosen seems to take this result in his stride and still maintains that the study supports the selective exposure hypothesis, it would seem rather difficult to make any definite statements on the basis of these two studies. The positive articles elicited preferences for supportive material; the negative titles yielded essentially no preference; and the two titles that were most clearly relevant to the central issue in the decision drew strong preferences for nonsupportive information.

B. STUDIES INDICATING NO PREFERENCE

Several studies have indicated no preference for either supportive or nonsupportive information, or slight and nonsignificant preferences for nonsupportive material. Feather (1963) had subjects rank a list of 13 article titles, among which was one title suggesting that smoking causes cancer and another title suggesting that smoking does not cause cancer. He compared the ranks assigned to these two titles by smokers and nonsmokers in his subject population and found no appreciable difference.

Mills and Ross (1964) had college men state their position on whether or not college courses should be taught by television, and then asked them to indicate their degree of interest in reading articles for and against their position. Four articles were offered on each side of the issue, and the dependent measure was the sum of ranks for titles supporting the position the subject had taken. The overall mean was 17.8, which did not depart significantly from the chance value of 18. In none of the several experimental conditions was there a significant preference one way or the other.[5]

The present authors conducted a number of studies on voluntary exposure to information, several of which used a mock jury situation.

---

[5] Personal communication from Mills.

Typically the subjects were tested in separate cubicles. They first read what was described as a condensed version of the record from a real trial. Each subject reached a decision on a verdict without communicating with the other "jurors," and then indicated his preferences for further information on the case by rating or ranking a series of articles. The article titles were supportive, nonsupportive, and neutral.

Each of the studies was designed to test the effects of certain variables on information preferences, but for the purposes of this discussion, the data across all experimental conditions will be presented. In three of the studies, subjects were offered two supportive and two nonsupportive titles, and in each case no overall preference for supportive or nonsupportive information was obtained. Sears (1966) found exactly 50% ($n = 96$) preferred supportive articles, Sears and Freedman (1963) found 45.4% ($n = 119$) preferred supportive material, and Sears and Freedman (1965) found that 43.1% ($n = 102$) selected one of two possible supportive articles. All told, in these three studies 46.1% preferred one of the supportive articles, given the choice among four articles. This slight preference for nonsupportive information is not significant, nor are the preferences in any single study.

Two of these studies (Sears and Freedman, 1963, 1965) also provided data on actual exposure. Each subject was given a communication to read, and the length of time he spent reading it was recorded. Some subjects were given a supportive and some a nonsupportive communication. In the first study, exposure to the nonsupportive communication was greater than to the supportive; but in the second study, there was no difference between the two.

Although the data from these jury studies generally indicate no preference between supportive and nonsupportive information, it might be noted that presenting the overall results as we have done conceals a very real preference for nonsupportive information by those subjects voting for conviction. Whereas 51.2% of all pro-acquittal voters preferred supportive information, only 26.2% of the pro-conviction voters did. This difference is consistent with the point made above that information preferences in the Adams (1961) study might have depended on the specific positions held by the subjects. In order to evaluate selectivity on any issue, it is essential to test subjects on both sides of the issue.

Finally, Jecker (1964) set up two-man teams to play a competitive game, and then measured the time each subject spent exposing himself to supportive or nonsupportive information about his teammate. He reports no difference in exposure time between supportive and nonsupportive information, regardless of whether or not the subject had already selected his teammate.

C. STUDIES INDICATING A PREFERENCE FOR NONSUPPORTIVE INFORMATION

Several studies cited in the previous section produced some data that indicate a preference for nonsupportive information. The ratings of the two negative articles in Rosen's study (1961), the reading time data from one of the jury studies (Sears and Freedman, 1963), and the ratings by the pro-conviction voters in each of the jury experiments are all examples of such preferences. There are, in addition, several studies which provide clear evidence of a general preference for nonsupportive material. We shall now consider these.

Feather (1962) divided subjects into two groups, one of which was composed of persons believing there was no convincing evidence of a relationship between smoking and lung cancer, and the other composed of persons believing there was convincing evidence of such a relationship. Smokers in each group preferred an article *contradicting* their beliefs, while nonsmokers showed no particular exposure preferences, regardless of their position. Hence this represents evidence of a preference for nonsupportive information among subjects who were presumably highly ego-involved in an important issue.

Brodbeck (1956) tested college students in groups of eight. Each subject stated her opinion on wire tapping, and was led to believe the group was evenly divided on the issue. She then indicated which one of the other group members she would most like to hear discussing the issue. Although this study is often quoted as demonstrating that subjects tend to avoid people with whom they disagree, the actual results indicate no such preference. Only 20.2% of the subjects chose to listen to someone who shared their opinion on wire tapping, although by chance alone 42.9% of the subjects would have chosen to listen to someone of like belief. This represents a strong preference for hearing nonsupportive information.

A similar result was found by Sears (1965). He manipulated subjects' votes in a jury situation by giving case reports which were heavily weighted in either the pro-conviction or pro-acquittal direction. Of the subjects receiving the pro-conviction case, 26.7% ($n = 90$) selected supportive information, as did 34.1% ($n = 91$) of the subjects receiving the pro-acquittal case. If only those subjects who voted "correctly" are considered, a strong preference for nonsupportive information is manifested in both cases (only 27% of 74 subjects preferred supportive material in each case).

Finally, and perhaps most impressive, Freedman (1965a) told subjects that they were taking part in an investigation of social perceptiveness and stressed the importance of this ability. Each subject then heard one of two interviews between, allegedly, a candidate for an overseas conference and the person in charge of the conference. In one interview, the candidate sounded quite promising; in the other, quite unpromising. The subject evaluated the candidate and was then asked to choose between two evaluations of the candidate by people who knew the candidate well; one evaluation was described as quite favorable, and the other as quite unfavorable. The results were striking. Of 18 subjects tested, 17 chose the evaluation that disagreed with the evaluation they had made of the candidate after hearing the interview. This, of course, represents an extremely strong preference for nonsupportive information.

D. Summary and Conclusions

What does all this research show? One way of evaluating the evidence is simply to count how many results support the selective exposure hypothesis and how many do not. This is done in Table II, which divides

TABLE II

Tabulation of Studies Showing Preference for Supportive, Preference for Nonsupportive, and No Preference

Supportive preferred

Ehrlich et al. (1957)
Adams (1961)
Mills et al. (1959) positive articles only
Rosen (1961) positive articles only
Freedman and Sears (1963)

No preference

Feather (1963)
Mills et al. (1959) negative articles only
Mills and Ross (1964)
Jecker (1964)
Sears and Freedman (1963)
Sears and Freedman (1965)
Sears (1966)

Nonsupportive preferred

Brodbeck (1956)
Freedman (1965a)
Sears (1965)
Rosen (1961) negative articles only
Feather (1962)

the studies into those that showed a preference for supportive information, those that showed a preference for nonsupportive, and those that showed no preference. Studies such as those of Mills et al. (1959), and Rosen (1961), in which there were marked differences between experimental groups or different types of information, are put into more than one category. In all cases the results are taken at face value even though the data are often rather ambiguous.

This way of summarizing the data portrays a striking pattern of inconsistency. Five studies indicate a preference for supportive information, five show an opposite preference, and seven yield no particular preference at all.

That this inconsistency was not produced by a myriad of different dependent variables is shown in Table I, which presents the results of a large number of studies in terms of the same measure. All of these studies provided data on the percentage of subjects who chose a source of supportive information ahead of a nonsupportive source. The pattern of inconsistency is repeated. The percentages range from 80.7 all the way down to 5.6. Two studies (Adams, 1961; Ehrlich *et al.*, 1957) indicate a strong preference for supportive information; two others (Freedman, 1965a, Brodbeck, 1956) show a strong preference for nonsupportive information; and, of course, many show less clearly defined preferences.

These two tables make it rather easy to summarize the current status of the selective exposure hypothesis. Clearly, experimental evidence does not demonstrate that there is a general psychological tendency to avoid nonsupportive and to seek out supportive information. Equally clearly, the research does indicate that individuals' preferences must depend upon the particular circumstances. Under some conditions, there is a strong preference one way; under others, the preference is reversed. What is needed is a specification of the factors which affect these preferences. Festinger's theory of cognitive dissonance (Festinger, 1957) is a major source of hypotheses as to what some of these factors might be.

IV. Selectivity and the Magnitude of Dissonance

One of the core propositions of the theory of cognitive dissonance is that when dissonance is present, people will avoid dissonance-increasing information. A direct deduction from the theory is that the greater the dissonance, the stronger will be the resulting preference for information consistent with the person's beliefs. Efforts to test this hypothesis have relied upon two principal methods of manipulating the magnitude of dissonance: varying the salience or importance of a decision, and exposing subjects involuntarily to consonant or dissonant information.

A. Post-Decisional Dissonance

Perhaps the most straightforward deduction from dissonance theory is that following a decision, dissonance will be aroused by all cognitions which suggest that the decision was incorrect (i.e., by all positive aspects of the unchosen alternatives and by all negative aspects of the chosen alternative). A further implication of the theory is that the more salient, important, and/or final the decision is, the greater the dissonance aroused by any information inconsistent with the choice the subject has made. Several studies dealing with selective exposure have based manipulations of the magnitude of dissonance on this assumption.

Ehrlich *et al.* (1957) asked survey respondents which automobile ads they had read in a number of recent magazines. Some had bought a new car within the previous two months, while the others had purchased their car at least a year earlier and owned cars at least three years old. Two assumptions were made about the magnitude of dissonance. First, since the decision to buy a particular make of car was presumably more salient for the new car owners than for the old car owners, information inconsistent with the decision should produce more dissonance for new car owners than for old car owners. Second, positive aspects of makes that had been considered and rejected should be more dissonance-increasing than positive aspects of makes that had never been considered. Two predictions were thus made about selective exposure to automobile ads. First, that new car owners would seek out ads about the current models of their makes in preference to ads about the current models of other makes to a greater extent than would old car owners; and second, that new car owners would avoid ads about makes they had considered and rejected more than they would avoid ads about makes they had not considered.

Two kinds of data were obtained: Preference for automobile ads that they had never seen and the percentage of automobile ads subjects had actually noticed and read in recent magazines and newspapers. The advertisement preference data supported neither of the predictions. New and old car owners did not differ in these preferences. On the other hand, the data on percentage of ads noticed and ads that had been read did yield some support for the first hypothesis. Both new and old car owners read own car ads more than ads about other makes of cars; and as predicted, this difference between the two types of ads was greater for those owning the new cars. It must be noted, however, that in making this comparison the authors included some ads which had started running prior to the new car owners' purchases, i.e., ads which the subject might well have read *prior* to his decision. If such ads are excluded from the analysis, the difference between new and old car owners fails to attain the .05 level of significance. The second hypothesis was not supported at all. In direct contradiction to the prediction, moreover, ads about cars that had been considered and not bought were read somewhat more than ads about cars that had never been considered.

Several ambiguities in this study, by and large not representing problems in the studies discussed in the remainder of this section, should be mentioned. The comparison for the first prediction is between new car owners and persons owning old cars. It seems very likely that persons buying new cars would be, on balance, generally more interested in cars, and certainly more interested in their own car than someone who is content to drive around in a three-year-old car. People who buy new cars may resemble people who attend political meetings in certain respects. Each is more interested in one facet of human life than are many other people in the society. Not surprisingly, each keeps up with the mass media information on their interests to a greater extent than do people without such compelling interests. Secondly, in any given three-year period, especially during the early 1950's, radical changes in automobile styling and performance are likely to occur. It is hard to be certain that the owner of a rather down-at-the-heels, low-horsepower, 1950 Plymouth would find ads about new, flashy, high horsepower, tail-finned, 1955 Plymouths particularly supportive of his decision to buy a Plymouth. In fact, he may find that the ad makes his decision to buy an old second-hand model look rather bad. For these reasons, and because Ehrlich *et al.* (1957) only found marginally significant support for one of their predictions, and no support at all for the second prediction, it is hard to take this study as strong support for the dissonance hypotheses.

Mills *et al.* (1959) experimentally manipulated the magnitude of dissonance presumably felt by their subjects, utilizing the assumption that post-decision dissonance increases as a function of the importance of the decision. For some students, the exams they were to choose between counted 70% of their course grades (high dissonance), while for others the exams counted only 5% (low dissonance). Although a check on this manipulation indicated that it was successful, the high and low dissonance groups did not differ appreciably with respect to relative preferences for articles supporting or opposing their decision. Rosen (1961) attempted to replicate this experiment, and succeeded to the extent that a successful manipulation of decision importance again produced no differences in exposure preference.

Sears and Freedman (1963) experimentally varied strength of commitment to a verdict in the mock jury situation. Some subjects were told that their first decision was public, final, and completely irrevocable, while others were led to believe that their choice was confidential and only a current preference rather than a real decision. Presumably, the former group should show more selectivity of exposure, since information inconsistent with their decision should arouse more dissonance than it would in the less strongly committed subjects. There were, however, no

72   JONATHAN L. FREEDMAN AND DAVID O. SEARS

significant differences between the two commitment groups in preferences for supportive and nonsupportive information, nor did the groups differ in duration of exposure to subsequent supporting and opposing persuasive communications.

Mills and Ross (1964) manipulated commitment to a position by telling some subjects their opinions would be publicized (high commitment) and others that their opinions would be kept completely private (low commitment). Once again the groups did not differ in preference between supportive and nonsupportive articles.

In a final study, Jecker (1964) tested some subjects before they had chosen a teammate for a competitive game and other subjects after they had chosen their teammates. Each subject was exposed to favorable and unfavorable material about his prospective or selected teammate, and the duration of his exposure was timed. In both conditions, exposure to favorable material was slightly longer; but the two conditions did not differ significantly in the magnitude of this difference.

In each of these six studies, high and low dissonance groups were distinguished by differences in the salience, importance, or finality of a relevant decision. In only one of the studies, however, did the high and low dissonance groups differ significantly in selectivity of exposure. Even in that one study (Ehrlich et al., 1957), the data supported one dissonance prediction and were actually counter to a second, though not significantly so. In any event, this one source of support for the dissonance hypothesis is the weakest of the six studies, since it alone failed to utilize an experimental manipulation of dissonance.

B. EFFECTS OF INVOLUNTARY EXPOSURE TO DISSONANT INFORMATION

The second method of arousing dissonance has been to expose some subjects to information that was discrepant from their opinions, while exposing others to information consistent with their opinions. Presumably, exposure to discrepant information should arouse dissonance, which can be reduced by seeking information consistent with the original opinions and avoiding information inconsistent with them.

Brodbeck (1956) exposed all subjects to a talk favoring one side of the wire-tapping issue. The subjects then were told of the opinions held by the other subjects tested concurrently, and were asked which other subjects they would most like to listen to or speak with on the issue.

One way of deriving experimental conditions is in terms of whether or not they had been exposed to a discrepant communication. The subjects whose initial opinions disagreed with the talk can be considered high dissonance subjects, with the remainder being low dissonance subjects (although Brodbeck includes in this latter group five subjects who initially disagreed with the position taken in the talk, but changed their opinions to the position taken by the speaker). Considered in this way, the two groups did not differ appreciably, although the high dissonance subjects tended more to choose someone who shared their position.

Brodbeck distinguished, however, between two kinds of subjects in the high dissonance group. Those who initially disagreed and became less confident as a result of the talk were treated as the high dissonance group, leaving those who initially disagreed and became no less confident as a medium dissonance group. A comparison of this high dissonance group with the original low dissonance group showed greater selectivity among the former, although the difference is only marginally significant ($p < .06$). It is unfortunate that the original low dissonance group included some who initially disagreed but were converted, since by Brodbeck's argument these might well be considered as very high dissonance subjects. In any event, the difference is rather slight and depends upon an internal analysis, the assumptions of which are open to debate.

Maccoby et al. (1961) used a similar approach in a field experiment with young mothers on attitudes toward age of toilet training. Subjects were given pamphlets advocating relatively late toilet training, and several months later were asked about the opinions of others with whom they had discussed the issue in the interim. Again, separation of subjects into experimental conditions offers two options. As in the Brodbeck study, the simplest analysis would contrast those who initially disagreed with the pamphlet (high dissonance) with those who initially agreed with it (low dissonance). Considered in this way, the groups did not differ; regardless of whether they had originally agreed or disagreed with the position taken in the pamphlet, approximately 80% of the subjects subsequently discussed the issue with persons who shared their initial opinions.

Maccoby et al. (1961) argued, with Brodbeck, that only those exposed to a discrepant communication and who changed their opinions were really in a state of dissonance; and the more they changed, the greater the dissonance they felt. This is a plausible derivation from dissonance theory; dissonance should exist only to the extent that the subject holds cognitions which are inconsistent with his initial opinion, and the greater the proportion of inconsistent cognitions, the greater the dissonance.

However, Maccoby et al. arrived at a different prediction from that advanced by Brodbeck. Brodbeck suggested that the tendency toward selective exposure would increasingly favor information consistent with the subject's *initial* position, the greater the dissonance. Maccoby et al. predicted that with greater dissonance, selectivity would increasingly favor information consistent with the subject's *new, changed* position (that is, the position advocated in the discrepant communication). The data obtained by the Maccoby group supported their expectation. Those who changed considerably reported they talked more with people agreeing with the communication than did those who changed only moderately or did not change at all. Thus these last two studies actually obtained somewhat contradictory findings. Brodbeck's subjects who changed after hearing a discrepant communication chose informants who disagreed with the communication (presumably to help bolster the subject's initial opinion), while in the later investigation, those who changed apparently chose informants who agreed with the discrepant communication (supposedly to help the subject bolster her revised position). It should be noted, however, that the indicators of change in the two studies were not the same. Brodbeck measured change by decreased confidence in the initial opinion, while Maccoby *et al.* used the amount of actual opinion change. It is not clear what difference, if any, this might make in the outcome.

Adams (1961) also tested the hypothesis, but utilized a true experimental paradigm. In the two previous studies, subjects were separated into groups on the basis of initial opinion and reaction to a communication. In Adams' study, some subjects were randomly selected to be exposed to a communication opposing their beliefs, while others were given a supportive communication. Then, all subjects were asked whether they would like to hear a talk that agreed with their position or one that disagreed with it. The subjects who heard a nonsupportive communication (high dissonance) preferred the speech agreeing with their initial position slightly less than did the subjects who heard a consistent communication (low dissonance). This difference was in the opposite direction from that predicted, but it was not significant.

C. Summary and Conclusions

The original hypothesis being considered was that under high dissonance, subjects would show a greater preference for supportive over nonsupportive information than they would under low dissonance. The results of the studies dealing with this proposition are summarized in Table III, which indicates the difference in selectivity shown by high and low dissonance groups in each study.

The data are clearly quite discouraging. Only one study produced a significant difference between high and low dissonance groups, and that study (Ehrlich *et al.*, 1957) is of questionable value. Internal analyses produced more promising results in the Brodbeck and Maccoby *et al.* studies, but as noted above, these analyses showed contradictory trends. Nor is there any consistency in the direction of the differences found. Five showed greater preference for supportive than nonsupportive information by high dissonance subjects; four indicated greater preference by low dissonance groups.

It might be mentioned that most of these studies were done by experimenters who were attempting to prove the hypothesis and failed; they were not conducted by opponents of the theory. The experimental designs were quite varied, several different measures of preferences were used, and the issues were all different. Despite this, the results cited are dramatic in the consistency with which they failed to provide significant support for the hypothesis that greater dissonance leads to greater selective exposure. Although it is extremely difficult for negative findings to demon-

TABLE III
DIFFERENCES IN SELECTIVITY SHOWN BY HIGH AND LOW DISSONANCE GROUPS

Study	Measure of selectivity	Group showing greater selectivity[a]	p
Brodbeck (1956)	% choosing supportive first	High diss.	ns
Adams (1961)	% choosing supportive	Low diss.	ns
Maccoby et al. (1961)	% talking to supportive	Low diss.	ns
Ehrlich et al. (1957)	% own vs. % other ads read	High diss.	< .05
Mills et al. (1959)	Sum of ranks	Low diss.	ns
Rosen (1961)	Sum of ranks	High diss.	ns
Mills and Ross (1964)	Sum of ranks	High diss.	ns
Sears and Freedman (1963)	Mean rating	Low diss.	ns
Jecker (1964)	Viewing time	High diss.	ns

[a] The entry indicates only the direction of the difference between main experimental groups. Internal analyses are not considered.

strate that a particular hypothesis is untrue, these results probably come as close to this goal as is ordinarily possible.

Thus, the evidence reviewed in these last two sections supports neither the hypothesis that there is a general preference for supportive as opposed to nonsupportive information, nor the more specific hypothesis that whatever preference there is for supportive information will be greater under high than under low dissonance. It might further be pointed out that this paper has dealt largely with published research. Since both authors and editors are somewhat reluctant to publish negative results, it is quite possible that many other attempts to produce a selectivity effect have failed and passed quietly into oblivion.

As was mentioned at the beginning of this paper, there appears to be a widespread belief in the validity of both of these hypotheses. In addition, many of the studies described above are unaccountably cited as positive evidence for one or the other hypothesis, despite the fact that in most cases the actual data do not warrant this. Tabulations such as those presented in Tables I through III should be convincing demonstrations of the lack of positive evidence; and it would seem that acceptance of the selective exposure hypotheses should at least be suspended.

V. Selectivity and Confidence in Opinions

The research discussed in Sections III and IV indicates that, at the present time, there is no reason to believe that people prefer to be exposed to supportive information nor that any such preference is greater under high than under low dissonance. Despite this lack of any consistent evidence, however, the selective exposure hypothesis could still be entertained should an explanation be found for the negative results. A large number of such explanations are possible, but let us consider one that has been presented in detail.

Freedman and Sears (1963) and Festinger (1964) have suggested that the failure to find a selective exposure effect may be due to a misinterpretation of the experimental situations. They argue that in most of the experiments cited in Section IV, the subject may be trying to reduce dissonance rather than attempting to avoid its arousal. According to this line of reasoning, dissonance is aroused whenever the subject is presented with a choice of exposing himself to supportive or nonsupportive information. When he is given such a choice, he is in effect being told that some authorities disagree with his position. Knowing that such opposing information exists should in itself arouse dissonance. Since dissonance is aroused before the subject even sees the articles, he cannot avoid dissonance-arousal by avoiding exposure to the information. Hence his decision is not whether or not to permit dissonance to be aroused, but how best to reduce it.

Two distinctive modes of dissonance reduction are open to him at this point: He can expose himself to the information and hope to refute it, or he can avoid it and reduce dissonance by convincing himself that the information was unimportant, irrelevant, biased, or by disparaging it in some other way.

Two rather complex studies concerning voluntary exposure suggest that information seeking is affected by the specific expectations subjects have about the information, and in particular about whether the eventual effect of the information will be to support or to undermine their position (Festinger, 1957; Cohen et al., 1959). Recently, Festinger has hypothesized that the subject's choice between avoiding or seeking out opposing information is dependent upon how confident he is that his opinion is correct. If the subject is highly confident that he is right, he may seek out the nonsupportive information and try to refute it. If he has little confidence, on the other hand, perhaps he will avoid this information and seek additional supportive material to boost his confidence. According to this hypothesis, then, the lower the subject's confidence in his own opinion, the greater should be his preference for supportive information.

Canon (1964) conducted a study specifically designed to test this hypothesis and Freedman (1965b) attempted to replicate his findings. In both studies subjects read four cases presumably drawn from business school courses, and gave their decisions on each. On each of the first three cases, the subject was told whether or not he was correct and how many others in the group had given the same answer he did. Some subjects (high confidence) were told that their three decisions were all correct and that most other subjects had gotten them wrong; others (low confidence) were told that they had gotten the first case right but had missed the second and third, whereas most subjects had been correct on all. They then read the fourth case and gave their decision. They were not told whether or not this was correct, but instead were told that they would have to write an essay on this case. To help them write the essay, some articles were available for them to read, and they were asked to express their preferences among these five articles in the usual manner. Two of the articles supported their decision, two opposed it, and one was neutral.

Unfortunately, the two studies produced quite different results. Canon found that high confidence subjects preferred nonsupportive information, and low confidence subjects preferred supportive information, as predicted. Freedman, on the other hand, found no appreciable difference in selectivity resulting from variations in confidence. The only other difference between the two studies concerned checks on the power of the confidence manipulation. Freedman's check showed a significant difference between high and low confidence subjects, while Canon's check did not. Thus, if anything, the experimental manipulation seems to have been stronger in Freedman's attempted replication. In addition (see Section VI, C below), Freedman did replicate the other major finding in Canon's study. Since the procedures used were the same in both studies and one finding was repeated, the discrepancy in the results on confidence is somewhat puzzling. Whatever the reason for the difference, however, Freedman's study casts some doubt on the generality of Canon's results.

One piece of additional negative evidence comes from an experiment by Mills and Ross (1964). They attempted to manipulate certainty and then offered the subjects a choice of exposure to supportive or nonsupportive articles. They found no differences in preferences between the high and low certainty experimental groups. It should be noted, however, that a check on the confidence manipulation suggested that it had been unsuccessful so that this negative finding should be interpreted cautiously.

Additional evidence comes from several studies in which confidence was not manipulated experimentally but in which measures of actual confidence in opinions were obtained. In Brodbeck's experiment (Brodbeck, 1956), one group of subjects indicated decreased confidence in their opinions following exposure to a discrepant communication while a second group did not. Insofar as these two groups can be considered low and high confidence subjects respectively, we can get a further indication of the effect of confidence on exposure preferences. Of the decreased confidence subjects, 33% chose to listen to someone agreeing with them, while only 22% of those not changing in confidence chose agreers. This difference does not approach significance, but it is in the direction predicted by Festinger's analysis.

A series of studies by the present authors produced rather mixed correlations between confidence in initial opinions and selectivity of exposure. In the study on the 1962 California gubernatorial election (Freedman and Sears, 1963), high confidence subjects were significantly more selective than low confidence subjects. On the other hand, two of the mock jury experiments produced contradictory results. In one (Sears and Freedman, 1965), high confidence subjects manifested greater selectivity than did low confidence subjects; while in the other (Sears, 1965), this difference was reversed. Neither of these results approached significance, and they are offered only as evidence suggesting the lack of consistency in the relationship between confidence and selectivity.

A final suggestion is that the relationship is even more complicated than Festinger has proposed. Mills and Ross (1964) hypothesized that with high commitment to an initial position, less certain subjects will be more selective than their more certain counterparts. With low commitment, however, the highly certain subjects will supposedly be more selective. Their data failed to support this hypothesis with experimentally manipulated groups, but some correlational data were consistent with it.

At the present time, therefore, neither the experimental data nor the correlational data provide consistent support for the hypothesized relationship between confidence and selectivity of exposure to information. This hypothesis has been considered in some detail, however, both because it is an important notion, and because it illustrates the kind of contingencies that might determine whether or not information selectivity will arise. It is to be hoped that once the lack of evidence for selective exposure is widely accepted, more attention will be paid to the rather special circumstances under which selectivity may occur. Perhaps selectivity does generally occur under the combined conditions of low confidence, high dissonance, and high commitment, or perhaps it does not. In any case, this kind of hypothesis should produce more adequate tests for selective exposure, and also perhaps contribute to fuller understanding of the mechanisms underlying exposure preferences in general.

VI. Voluntary Exposure to Information

It is possible to take an entirely different approach to the lack of support for the selective exposure hypotheses. Rather than attempting to explain, or explain away the negative results, it might be fruitful to accept them at face value, at least for the time being. We can then turn instead to the more general problem of the factors that do affect voluntary exposure to information. In this way, it might be possible to understand more about exposure in general, and to answer such questions as why *de facto* selectivity occurs, and under what conditions, if any, people do prefer supportive information.

A. BASE RATES OF EXPOSURE

To put this discussion into perspective, we will return to the evidence for *de facto* selectivity. There are, as cited in Section II, considerable data indicating that people are exposed disproportionately to supportive information. These data suggest, however, that exposure is determined by the particular conditions under which it is measured. For example, the classic study by Lazarsfeld *et al.* (1948) found that about two thirds of those with consistent voting preferences were exposed primarily to propaganda favoring their candidate. A breakdown into parties, however, reveals the startling fact that this held only for persons with Republican predispositions. Far from being selectively exposed, those with Democratic predispositions were almost evenly divided: 50.4% being exposed primarily to Democratic publicity, and 49.6% primarily to Republican propaganda (p. 96). Thus, selectivity was very different for Republicans and Democrats.

However, if one considers the relative availability of pro-Republican and pro-Democratic propaganda, the finding becomes even more paradoxical. Lazarsfeld *et al.* report that 68.8% of all available partisan propaganda in the overall campaign was pro-Republican (*ibid.,* p. 111). It is thus hardly surprising that 69.7% of those with Republican predispositions were exposed primarily to pro-Republican information, and 30.3% primarily to pro-Democratic publicity (*ibid.,* p. 96). The exposure of those with Republican predispositions almost exactly matched the partisan division of available information. In fact, looked at from this point of view, it was the Democrats who were selectively exposed, since they were exposed to considerably less Republican propaganda than might have been expected, even though they were actually exposed to equal amounts of supportive and nonsupportive information.

The point here should be obvious and is mentioned only because it appears sometimes to be overlooked. *Selectivity of exposure must be defined in terms of deviations from a baseline determined by information availability.* We are all exposed more to information supporting the belief that the world is round than to information attacking this belief. This is hardly selective exposure in any meaningful sense of the term since there is very little nonsupportive information available. However, it might fall into the category of *de facto* selectivity as it is usually defined. Simple availability of information, of course, serves as a limiting factor on exposure. Let us now consider some of the other factors which affect exposure, and see if they are in some way related to selectivity.

B. INDIVIDUAL DIFFERENCES: EDUCATION AND SOCIAL CLASS

At one extreme are factors which may be classified as individual differences or predispositions theoretically independent of partisan preferences. As an example, let us consider briefly what is clearly the most powerful known predictor of voluntary exposure to informational and public affairs presentations in the mass media—education and social class. Star and Hughes (1950) reported that 68% of their college-educated respondents were exposed to the U.N. campaign in at least three media, while only 17% of the grammar-school-educated respondents were. Key (1961, p. 349) presented SRC data indicating that college-educated persons comprised 40% of those exposed to the 1956 presidential campaign in at least four media, while grammar-school-educated respondents only made up 9% of this group. Conversely, of those who were not exposed to the campaign in the mass media, 3% were college-educated and 58% had only grade school educations. G. A. Steiner (1963, pp. 168–170) found somewhat weaker but still sizable differences due to education in the composition of audiences for television news, information, and public affairs programs. Lazarsfeld *et al.* (1948) also obtained substantial differences in exposure to campaign propaganda relating to socioeconomic status and education.

These differences resulting from education and social status appear to hold even when selective exposure would demand greater exposure from the less educated, working-class respondents. Key (1961, p. 354) cited the example of speeches by New Deal leaders in which high SES respondents were almost twice as likely to listen to the speeches as low SES respondents, despite the considerably greater support for the leaders among the latter group.

Since these correlations with education and class are so well-known, one would think that these factors would be controlled in investigations of selective exposure. Yet, this has frequently not been done. Star and Hughes (1950) reported that internationalists were most likely to be exposed to a campaign for the United Nations; but highly educated people were also most likely to be internationalist (Key, 1961) as well as being most likely to be exposed to mass media information on any topic. Blood donors were more likely than non-donors to attend meetings designed to enhance civilian participation in the war effort (Cartwright, 1949) but persons of superior education and social status were more likely to attend such meetings and also, probably, give blood than were other citizens. Similarly, where Schramm and Carter (1959) found a greater rate of exposure to the Knowland telethon among Republicans than Democrats, we must remember that Republicans are generally better-educated than Democrats, and thus more likely to be in *any* public affairs audience. In none of these studies was there evidence of selectivity *within* educational or class levels.

It is, therefore, quite possible that many reports of *de facto* selective exposure represent little more than cases in which highly educated persons, who normally are overrepresented in any audience for public affairs presentations, also share a common set of political, social, and/or economic attitudes. Star and Hughes (1950, p. 397) are clearly on solid ground in recommending that information campaigns be directed especially at "women, the relatively uneducated, the elderly, and the poor," since they are normally least likely to be reached. However, low rates of exposure of such population groups must be distinguished from alleged avoidance of information due to discrepant political opinions.

C. UTILITY OF INFORMATION

Another factor which may affect exposure preferences is the perceived utility of the information. Although this has often been ignored in previous research, it is obvious that information varies greatly in the extent to which it will serve a useful, practical purpose. It seems likely that the greater the perceived utility of the information the greater will be the subject's desire to be exposed to it. A student might want information that will help him do well on a test he is going to take (as in Mills *et al.,* 1959; and Rosen, 1961); or a mother, information that will help her do a good job raising her children (Adams, 1961; Maccoby *et al.,* 1962); or a discussant information providing material with which to prepare a talk or rebut counterarguments (Canon, 1964; Freedman, 1965b; Sears and Freedman, 1963). In all of these cases, it might be expected that information will be preferred to the extent that it is useful.

The evidence supports this supposition. In the Adams study, women were offered a choice between a talk on environmental factors and hereditary factors in child behavior. The former was potentially of greater practical importance and was preferred by a three to one margin. Similarly, Maccoby et al. offered housewives a pamphlet on toilet training and recorded how many requested the pamphlet; and they sent the pamphlet to a different group of women and recorded how many actually read it. The subjects were divided into those who had an only child between the ages of three and twelve months (critical group), those who had an older child (post-group) and those who had no children (pre-group). Presumably the pamphlet was most useful for the critical group. This group expressed more interest in getting the pamphlet (71% versus 36% and 38% for the other groups); and a greater percentage of them read it when it was sent to them (88% vs. 48% and 47%).

Mills et al. (1959) and Rosen (1961) told students that they would have to take an examination, and gave them a choice of the type of exam they would take. They then offered them a choice among various pamphlets concerning the two types of exams. They found that subjects preferred pamphlets dealing with their own exam, regardless of whether the article was favorable or unfavorable to the exam, although the effect was stronger with favorable information.

Finally, Canon (1964) and Freedman (1965b) explicitly varied utility. The subjects made a decision on what was supposedly a case study in business, and were then offered a choice of articles supportive or nonsupportive of their choice. Before rating the articles, they were told either that they would have to present their reasons for deciding on the case as they did, or that they would engage in a written debate in which they would have to rebut arguments from the opposing side. It was assumed that in the former case supportive information would be more useful, since it would provide necessary reasons for their decision. In the latter case, nonsupportive information would presumably be more useful, since the subjects could not prepare rebuttals without knowing what the opposition believed. In both studies, the more useful information was significantly preferred to the less useful, regardless of which was consistent with the subject's decision.

Thus, the evidence strongly supports the contention that information which is expected to serve a practical purpose is preferred to less useful information. This finding has interesting implications for selective exposure, because it is apparent that differential utility can produce greater exposure to supportive or nonsupportive information, or no difference between the two, depending on the particular conditions.

As an illustration, in Adams' study the pro-environmental talk was both more useful and more supportive, and consequently, strongly preferred to the pro-heredity talk. In the Mills *et al.* and Rosen studies, positive information about the chosen type of exam was both supportive and useful, whereas negative information about the chosen exam was nonsupportive but useful. Indeed, the experimenters found that with both positive and negative articles the subjects preferred information about the exam they would have to take, thereby manifesting preferences for supportive information in one case and nonsupportive in the other, but preferring the more useful information in both cases.

One implication of this is that it is essential to hold utility constant in order to provide a rigorous, unambiguous test of the selective exposure hypothesis. Sears and Freedman (1963) and Freedman (1965b) attempted to do this by making all information as useless as possible; while Jecker attempted to equate utility directly. Although it is difficult to be certain how successfully information utility was equated in these studies, it should be noted that all of them failed to show a selective exposure effect.

D. PAST HISTORY OF EXPOSURE ON THE ISSUE

Information can be relevant to an opinion without being clearly supportive or nonsupportive. It can provide substance, organization, background, structure; it can put an opinion in truer perspective; it can make an issue more real; etc. Even information that is clearly supportive or nonsupportive may be important for these other reasons. People seem to spend a considerable time seeking out information, and it is unlikely that their only or even primary concern is to defend existing beliefs.

Opinions are frequently formed on the basis of rather limited information. Children form political party preferences in grade school; adults often make final vote decisions prior to the nomination of candidates, and the recommendations of significant reference groups or reference persons are often adopted without much in the way of supporting logic (see Lane and Sears, 1964, pp. 17–71). Yet, having committed themselves (however prematurely) to definite positions, people do not cease exposing themselves to relevant information. A person's position may not change with further exposure to information, but the panoply of opinions about a particular issue may be broadened substantially as the person becomes better informed. He may become more able to make distinctions, to introduce appropriate qualifications, to account for inconsistencies in his thinking, and to perform a variety of cognitive operations as he becomes more aware of the complexities of the issue. Let us then examine information preferences as they manifest themselves in the process of opinion development, subsequent to the expression of an initial opinion, with the hope that they will clarify the utilities of various dimensions of information.

1. One-Sided vs. Two-Sided Presentations

Perhaps the simplest psychological hypothesis one might entertain is that a person early in the process of developing an opinion has a greater need to review the available alternatives than does a person who has been exposed to more information. The easiest way for a person to review the alternatives is for him to expose himself to a presentation which contains all of them, rather than exposing himself to a presentation containing only one.

The classic example of the two-sided presentation is the formal debate. Existing data do not permit refined comparisons of the drawing power of debates as opposed to one-sided presentations. However, it seems highly likely that each of the televised debates in the 1960 presidential campaign attracted an audience considerably larger than either candidate could have gotten by himself. The most reliable estimates place the size of the audience for the first debate at between 60% and 65% of the total adult population (Katz and Feldman, 1962). This audience compares very favorably with available estimates for one-sided presentations, such as the 11.5% found to be watching some part of a 29-hour-telethon given by former Senator Knowland (Schramm and Carter, 1959). Even if the audience for the 1960 debate was atypically large, the very magnitude of the difference is impressive.

Data collected in the mock jury situation suggest that two-sided presentations are preferred insofar as the individual has not been exposed to the arguments of either side. Sears (1966) gave each subject a brief case report of a trial, then gave some subjects the prosecution summation, some the defense summation, others both summations, and a fourth group of subjects no summations at all. Each subject was then asked for his preferences among five articles, one of which was "Johnny Burdick: An Overview of the Case," allegedly authored by the professor who had collected the several articles for a casebook. This "overview" was the first choice of 65% of the subjects who had been exposed to no summations, 43.6% of those who had read one summation, and 39.5% of those who had read two summations. The mean rank assigned to the "overview" was significantly higher in the no-summation condition than in the two-summation condition ($t = 2.13$, 56 df, $p < .05$). While the data are not truly comparable, it is interesting to note that in another study in which the same five articles were offered, but in which all subjects were initially exposed to both attorneys' summations and the judge's charge to the jury, in addition to the case report, first choices of the overview were lower still. Only 22.7% of the 119 subjects tested preferred the overview to each of the four one-sided articles offered (Sears and Freedman, 1963).

These data suggest that a two-sided presentation (made by one individual in the jury studies, but often in field situations by two disputants) is preferred most by individuals who have not been previously exposed to the partisan arguments on either side. This has interesting implications for selective exposure. Presumably, the relatively naive person is the one who is most susceptible to persuasive pressure, but he is evidently also the one who most prefers two-sided presentations. Thus, the man whom everyone wants to reach is the one who is least likely to expose himself to either side alone.

2. Preferences among One-Sided Presentations

A more general hypothesis derived from the previous discussion is that any information which will help the naive individual become familiar with both sides of the issue will be favored, regardless of whether or not it supports his initial preference. We have seen that this process gives rise to a preference for two-sided presentations. It should also be an important determinant of preferences among one-sided presentations.

A person who has an initial preference based upon relatively little information in general but disproportionate exposure to information favoring one side should, according to the hypothesis proposed above, have a particular need to hear "the other side of the story." Data relevant to this point were collected by Sears (1966) in the experiment cited above. The subjects in the single-summation conditions who voted in line with the summation given them, subsequently preferred the opposing one-sided articles, while those who voted counter to the summation they had read subsequently preferred supportive articles ($F = 9.23$, 1/38 df, $p < .01$ for the difference between the two sets of subjects). That is, both sets of subjects, each of whom had been exposed to the arguments of only one attorney, evidenced a preference for seeing arguments favorable to the other attorney's position, despite the fact that "the other side" in this case was supportive for some subjects, and nonsupportive for others.[6] Neither the no-summation nor the two-summation subjects showed any significant preference for supportive or nonsupportive articles.

[6] These data provide a possible explanation of Brodbeck's (1956) finding that subjects who had been exposed to dissonant information considered supportive information somewhat more attractive than did subjects who had been exposed to a consonant communication. This marginally significant difference might have been produced by a desire of all subjects to hear the side other than the one they had just heard. Those who had been exposed to a dissonant communication would thus want to hear the other side, which was consonant information; while those who had heard a consonant communication would also tend to prefer the other side, which was dissonant information.

Additional evidence is provided by a second study (Sears, 1965) in which the subject's expectations about his familiarity with further information were varied. Each subject received highly condensed case reports of criminal trials that were heavily biased toward one verdict or the other. The subjects were then asked to indicate whether they would prefer to read, verbatim, the defense summation or the prosecution summation from the trial. Some subjects were told that the arguments contained in these summations had already largely been covered in the case report (old information), while the others were told that the summations included arguments that were not covered in the brief case reports (new information).

This situation is, therefore, one in which the subject indicates his information preferences after being exposed only to information heavily weighted toward one side or the other. As the hypothesis would predict, the subjects strongly preferred the summation advocating a verdict opposite to that strongly suggested by the biased case report ($F = 28.52$, $1/360$ df, $p < .001$).

More relevant to our present concern, however, are the differences between experimental conditions. The "old information" subjects showed a greater preference for nonsupportive information than did the "new information" subjects ($F = 3.99$, $1/360$ df, $p < .05$). That is, preference for seeing or hearing "the other side" among persons who have already been exposed to one side is greatest if they feel they are completely familiar with the supportive arguments, and less marked (though still significant: $F = 5.58$, $p < .05$) if the subject feels he may learn still more about the side he favors.

In short, preferences among one-sided presentations are related to the individual's past history of exposure to information on the issue. If in some controversy he has been exposed to one side's arguments but not the other's, he seems to prefer the side with which he is unfamiliar, even if it means being exposed to nonsupportive information. This preference is less clear, however, if a subject is offered the opportunity of seeing unfamiliar arguments; he then is more willing to expose himself to supportive material.

This last finding could be interpreted in terms of selective exposure. When old information is expected, the nonsupportive information offers little threat. The subjects may, therefore, be quite confident that they will be able to refute it, and seek it out in order to do this. With the new information, the nonsupportive material is an unknown quantity and may be very dangerous. Under these circumstances, the subject is less confident of being able to refute it and, therefore, shows relatively little desire to seek it out.

According to this analysis, specific expectations about the information may determine the subject's preferences; the familiarity of the information is one of the factors which shape these expectations and thus affect preferences. It should be noted, of course, that with both new and old information there was a strong preference for nonsupportive information; so that, even if the above reasoning is correct, the effect of supportiveness is obviously extremely weak compared to other factors in the situation.

3. Positive vs. Negative Arguments

Finally, if the view is taken that the individual's task, when he is trying to develop a viable opinion, is to review the available alternatives, it is necessary to turn to a factor which has been stressed in both conflict theory (Miller, 1944) and dissonance theory (Brehm and Cohen, 1962): differences between positive and negative attributes of the alternatives. In most situations, a propagandist can stress the positive advantages of his position, or he can stress the negative and iniquitous character of the opposition.

It appears that positive arguments are generally preferred to negative arguments. Data collected during the 1962 election campaign (Freedman and Sears, 1963) indicated that 57.4% of those choosing a partisan article first preferred positive articles, while 42.6% preferred negative articles. Similarly, considering the several mock jury studies, 61.9% of 318 subjects made a positive article their first choice among two positive and two negative alternatives.

Several studies suggest that positive attributes of the alternatives in American public affairs may be more important than negative attributes. Almond and Verba (1963, p. 131) observed that Americans generally speak of even their political opponents in positive terms (unlike Italians, Mexicans, or the British), and Campbell et al. (1954, pp. 53–54) reported that negative comments about the nonpreferred presidential candidate exceed positive comments by only slight margins. Similarly, Lazarsfeld et al. (1948, p. 31) stated that *none* of their respondents explained their own vote intentions by alluding to something the preferred candidate opposed.

Whatever the baselines for the relative utility of positive or negative information, or the relative importance of positive and negative considerations in opinion formation among Americans, our concern here is with the differential utility of positive and negative information at different points in the opinion formation process.

Hovland (1952) has suggested that positive instances are more useful in the early stages of concept formation than are negative instances. However, later on, when the subject has developed firmer hypotheses about the correct answer, negative instances seem to be more useful.

Perhaps when people are forming opinions, the same generalization holds. Until an individual is familiar with the positive arguments used by each side, negative information will avail him little (criticism is of little use until one knows what is being criticized). When he knows what each side stands for, perhaps then it will be useful to find out where each side feels the other has erred.

This expectation is borne out by the mock jury study discussed above (Sears, 1966). Of those given no summations, 80% selected a positive article (as opposed to a negative article) as their first choice. In the one-summation conditions 69.2% chose a positive article, while in the two-summation condition only 47.4% selected a positive article as their first choice. The no-summation subjects rated the positive articles higher, and negative articles lower, than did the two-summation subjects ($F = 4.01$, $p < .05$). These data suggest that preferences switch from positive to negative information as the individual becomes more familiar with the arguments on either side.

Additional data suggesting that prior experience with the issue produces greater preferences for negative information are provided by the 1962 election study (Freedman and Sears, 1963). Four groups of subjects were tested: a night-school class and a Methodists' men's club, three graduate classes in educational psychology, an introductory psychology class, and a group of Young Democrats and Young Republicans from UCLA. Considering only those subjects who expressed preferences for positive or negative articles in their ratings, 84.0% of the night-school-Methodists group preferred positive pamphlets, 65.8% of the graduate students in education did so, 52.4% of the introductory psychology students did so, while only 36.1% of the Young Democrats and Republicans preferred positive information. An analysis of variance for the linear trend across these four groups, done in this order, yields $F = 12.76$, $1/235$ df, $p < .001$, while if the education and psychology groups are reversed, the linear trend is still highly significant ($F = 9.22$, $1/235$ df, $p < .01$). These data suggest that interest in negative information increases as the subject becomes more familiar with the issue, and perhaps also as he becomes more partisan.

Finally, there are some supporting data about the content of propaganda campaigns as they progress, and therefore presumably as the recipients of propaganda become more familiar with the campaign. Lazarsfeld *et al.* (1948, p. 111) found that positive statements about the candidates (Roosevelt and Wilkie) exceeded negative statements by 10% in early August, while by mid-October, shortly before the election, negative statements predominated by 15%. The data from these two studies of election campaigns are of course ambiguous and subject to several interpretations, but they are at least consistent with the notion that positive information is preferred insofar as the individual is unfamiliar with the arguments advanced by both sides.

E. SUMMARY

The data discussed in this section indicate that substantial preferences among information alternatives do exist on matters which involve opinions. We have dealt with a number of factors that determine such preferences. Individual differences such as education level and socio-economic class, the utility of the information itself, and the past history of exposure of the individual all have very powerful effects on exposure preferences.

In some instances variations in preference caused by the factors discussed in this section produce greater exposure to supportive than to nonsupportive information; in some instances they do not. This *de facto* selectivity is, of course, no evidence of a preference for supportive information. It is merely an incidental result of the effect of these other variables.

The great relative strength of these factors has two important implications for this discussion. In the first place, investigation of selectivity must take these factors into account. If they are not carefully controlled and held constant, any selective exposure effects may be swamped by effects due to these more powerful variables. In addition, the possibility must be considered that people prefer supportive information only under certain limited conditions defined by variations in these factors.

The second implication concerns research strategy. Perhaps more attention should be paid to these factors which are manifestly so powerful. A more thorough investigation of the operation of certain of these factors may reveal a great deal about the determinants of exposure preferences, and may even enable us to specify the conditions under which people prefer supportive to nonsupportive information.

VII. Concluding Remarks

A. THE PARADOX OF *De Facto* SELECTIVITY WITHOUT PREFERENCES FOR SUPPORTIVE INFORMATION

This paper has been concerned primarily with evaluating the evidence for the existence of selectivity in voluntary exposure to information. There seems to be ample evidence, both systematic and anecdotal, for the existence of *de facto* selectivity. Most audiences for mass communications apparently tend to overrepresent persons already sympathetic to the views

being propounded, and most persons seem to be exposed disproportionately to communications which support their opinions.

On the other hand, a considerable amount of experimental research
has uncovered no general psychological preference for supportive information. Under some circumstances, people seem to prefer information which
supports their opinions; under other circumstances, people seem to prefer
information which contradicts their opinions. In no way can the available
evidence be said to support the contention that people generally seek
out supportive information and avoid nonsupportive information.

These two conclusions are paradoxical. How can it be that people
are in fact selective, yet display no trace of a general preference for
supportive information? The simplest answer, and yet one easily overlooked, is that most of the examples of *de facto* selectivity come from
mass communication settings in which exposure is determined by a great
many complex factors which are incidental to the supportiveness of the
information.

An unequivocal expression of an information preference occurs
when a randomly selected respondent is asked to choose between two
pieces of information. Survey data on, for example, exposure to a televised
political speech involve several other variables. The viewer must have
a television set, he must be watching it rather than tippling in a bar
or playing pool, and the set must be tuned to the correct channel. Even
then, we cannot be sure that the viewer is expressing a genuine preference
for supportive information. If he prefers watching Senator Knowland
to Jackie Gleason, he is expressing a preference, to be sure, but the
dimension of preference is unclear. Selectivity in newspaper and magazine
reading also consists of highly complex sequences of behavior. May a
financier be said to indulge in selective exposure along partisan political
lines simply because he opens the *Wall Street Journal* rather than the
New York Post when he arrives at his office?

In many cases, then, people are disproportionately exposed to supportive information, but for reasons other than its supportiveness. In
fact, these reasons often have nothing at all to do with *information* preferences. A Southern housewife may leave her radio turned to a hillbilly
music station all day, a station which also happens to carry a politically
conservative fundamentalist preacher. Or a person may go to a political
rally simply in order to see a potential president in the flesh, or perhaps
more often in order to see the stable of movie stars with whom the
candidate goes to the country.

On other occasions, people have perfectly genuine information preferences which produce *de facto* selectivity quite by accident. One general
class of variables affecting information preferences concerns simple prac-

tical utility. For example, financiers read the *Wall Street Journal* and farmers listen to farm reports on the radio, both for reasons having to do with the practical utility of the information for their livelihoods. Yet in each case, the individual may be indulging, quite incidentally, in *de facto* selectivity, since the *Wall Street Journal* shares a common set of political opinions with many financiers, and many farm reporters agree politically with farmers. Hence, exposure often occurs as a result of some need that the information may serve; and the information turns out to support the individual's pre-existing political or social opinions as well.

Individual differences in absolute rate of exposure may also incidentally produce *de facto* selectivity. *De facto* selectivity may occur whenever those with high rates of exposure share certain opinions not held by persons with low rates of exposure. For example, large differences in opinion are associated with educational level on a number of issues, such as internationalism, tolerance for ethnic minorities, and support for civil liberties. In each case, those holding the more "liberal" opinions are also more likely to be exposed to any public affairs material in the mass media, by virtue of their greater education. Hence, "liberal" propaganda on these issues is indeed most likely to reach "liberal" citizens; but the reason has little or nothing to do with preferences for supportive information.

The presence of *de facto* selectivity in the absence of general preferences for supportive information is thus not as unlikely as it might seem at first glance. Most instances of *de facto* selectivity involve complex and multiply determined acts, produced by numerous variables more powerful than whatever slight preference for supportive information might be present. Our purpose has been to indicate that at the current time there is no evidence for a psychological preference for supportive information, and to demonstrate that cases of *de facto* selectivity are nevertheless quite explicable.

B. PERHAPS MAN IS VERY SELECTIVE ONLY SOMETIMES

Nonetheless, the selective exposure hypothesis seems too plausible to be completely incorrect. We seem to derive pleasure from having our opinions supported, and pain from having them attacked; and it seems only reasonable that most of us would try to arrange things so that we can maximize pleasure and minimize pain. Even if the "fit" of communicator and respondent opinions is usually a trivial factor in determining information preferences, it must be important on occasion. Indeed, the data given in Tables I and II clearly indicate substantial variations between issues, subjects, and situations in the degree of preference for supportive information. Some of this variance may be attributable to genuine differences in preferences. The problem, perhaps, is simply to distinguish between conditions which elicit preferences for supportive information, and those which elicit no preference, or preference for non-supportive information.

The major effort to define such conditions has been made within the context of cognitive dissonance theory. The basic hypothesis is that selectivity increases with greater magnitudes of dissonance, everything else being equal. A related hypothesis is that selectivity decreases with greater confidence in one's opinion. Both of these hypotheses are plausible, but the data relevant to them are contradictory. It has not been possible to demonstrate any systematic relationships between selectivity and the magnitude of dissonance or level of confidence. Unfortunately, dissonance theory has, in a sense, pre-empted the field; there are no alternative theories at the moment. Hence, it may be true that "Man is very selective only sometimes," but at the present time we cannot say when he is, and when he is not.

C. Perhaps Man is a Little Selective All the Time

Conversely, the notion might be entertained that people are clearly selective only when observed over a rather long period of time. At any given moment, the supportiveness or non-supportiveness of a communication may be inconsequential relative to other reasons for seeking or avoiding or ignoring it; but over the long term, non-supportive information could cause too much trouble and thus might tend to be avoided. One could easily imagine that people are ably equipped to rebut and disparage given pieces of discrepant information. This may be a tiring and aggravating job, however—something to be undertaken only at widely separated moments of particular intellectual fortitude. Hence, dramatic preferences may not appear at any given moment in time; but over a long period, people may organize their surroundings such that they are exposed largely to supportive information. Berelson et al. (1954) and Newcomb (1961, 1963) have most clearly enunciated this argument. Their evidence has been ingeniously collected and analyzed; but since it deals largely with the acquisition of friends and marital partners, rather than with information preferences, it lies somewhat beyond the scope of this paper.

D. Selective Exposure and Coping with Discrepant Information

As indicated at the beginning of this paper, considerable amounts of evidence have been accumulating in recent years suggesting that people cope with discrepant information in a variety of predictable ways. Some of these involve mechanisms by which a person confronted with discrepant information is able to minimize or resist its impact on his opinions. Others, to greater or lesser degree, involve mechanisms by which a person avoids being confronted with veridical representations of discrepant arguments. In this latter category fall such mechanisms as selective perception and selective retention, and perhaps most clearly, selective exposure. In other words, it has been generally assumed that selective exposure represents one way in which people actively avoid being confronted with arguments counter to their own opinions. Selective exposure has, therefore, been used frequently as a reason for the apparent ineffectiveness of propaganda and information campaigns (cf. Klapper, 1960).

The evidence reviewed above leads to the conclusion that selectivity of exposure is not as ubiquitous a way of dealing with discrepant propaganda as has been commonly supposed. Much of the *de facto* selectivity is in all probability primarily a function of factors such as information availability or chronic reading habits. The principal means by which people deal with discrepant propaganda, therefore, appear to be those elicited upon confrontation with the material. The problem faced by those who conduct information campaigns is, thus, not so much how to reach people who are actively avoiding being reached, but rather how to reach people who are apathetic, who habitually expose themselves to other media, who have little interest in public affairs, etc., and then how to produce acceptance of discrepant messages.

E. IMPLICATIONS

A substantial research effort has been made in the last decade to determine the variables which affect selectivity of exposure. As is evident from this review, the cumulative effect of this research has been to eliminate some of the more obvious possibilities. One strategy would be to attempt to continue the search for variables which affect selectivity. Given the paucity of theoretical notions, and the rather discouraging record of previous research, perhaps it would be wiser to seek alternatives.

Two major alternatives have been proposed in this review. The first, an accelerated attack on mechanisms by which people resist persuasive messages with which they have been confronted, lies somewhat beyond the scope of this paper. Yet it is clear that such mechanisms serve the same functions that selectivity has been thought to serve, and it is clear that very little is actually known about how people resist influence.

The second major alternative is to direct greater research effort to the general problem of information preferences. It seems clear from the research on selectivity that behavioral scientists are, in general, quite unclear about the reasons why people seek different kinds of information. If indeed, as we have argued, *de facto* selectivity is often an artifact of other, more potent, information preferences, it is highly appropriate to turn research efforts to the consideration of these more basic factors affecting information preferences.

Such research on general information preferences can take two directions. First, it can be addressed toward determining the respondent and situational variables which affect voluntary exposure to information. We have dealt with three of these in particular in Section VI above: education, information utility, and the individual's past history of exposure to information on the issue. They are probably among the major determinants of the extent to which a person desires to be exposed to a particular piece of information. Greater attention to these variables should thus lead to a fuller understanding of exposure preferences, and may eventually enable us to specify the conditions under which people prefer supportive information and those under which they do not.

A second approach might be to broaden the dimensions of information which are investigated. The dimension with which previous research has been almost solely preoccupied is the extent to which information supports an individual's pre-existing opinions. Yet there are a number of other dimensions of propagandistic information, some of which probably are of considerably greater significance. We have dealt with several of these in Section VI: one-sided vs. two-sided presentations, biased vs. unbiased sources, familiar vs. unfamiliar arguments, positive vs. negative arguments, arguments concerning the individual's position vs. arguments concerning an alternative position, and so forth.

F. FINAL CONCLUSIONS

The final conclusions of this paper may be summarized as follows:

1. People are, in fact, exposed to disproportionate amounts of supportive information, although this is not an overwhelming nor completely ubiquitous phenomenon.

2. Laboratory evidence does not support the hypothesis that people prefer to be exposed to supportive as opposed to non-supportive information.

3. The evidence does not support the hypothesis that the greater the magnitude of cognitive dissonance the greater will be the relative preference for exposure to supportive as opposed to nonsupportive information.

4. Although a variety of other factors such as confidence and familiarity may limit the conditions under which selective exposure occurs, at the present time there is not sufficient evidence to support any hypothesis concerning the effect of these factors on selectivity.

5. It is suggested that research in this area turn away from questions dealing primarily with the selective exposure hypotheses, and focus more

on the questions of what factors chiefly determine voluntary exposure to information and how people resist persuasive messages with which they have been confronted.

REFERENCES

Abelson, R. P. (1959). Modes of resolution of belief dilemmas. *J. confl. res.* 3, 343–352.

Adams, J. S. (1961). Reduction of cognitive dissonance by seeking consonant information. *J. abnorm. soc. Psychol.* 62, 74–78.

Almond, G. A., and Verba, S. (1963). *The civic culture.* Princeton, N.J.: Princeton Univer. Press.

Behavioral Sciences Subpanel (1962). President's Science Advisory Committee. Report to the President. *Behav. Sci.* 7, 277.

Berelson, B. R., and Steiner, G. A. (1964). *Human behavior.* New York: Harcourt Brace.

Berelson, B. R., Lazarsfeld, P. F., and McPhee, W. N. (1954). *Voting: a study of opinion formation in a presidential election.* Chicago, Ill.: Univer. of Chicago Press.

Brehm, J. W., and Cohen, A. R. (1962). *Explorations in cognitive dissonance.* New York: Wiley.

Brodbeck, May (1956). The role of small groups in mediating the effects of propaganda. *J. abnorm. soc. Psychol.* 52, 166–170.

Campbell, A., Gurin, G., and Miller, N. E. (1954). *The voter decides.* Evanston, Ill.: Row, Peterson.

Canon, L. K. (1964). Self-confidence and selective exposure to information. In Festinger, L. (Ed.), *Conflict, decision and dissonance.* Stanford, Calif.: Stanford Univer. Press, pp. 83–95.

Cartwright, D. (1949). Some principles of mass persuasion: selected findings of research on the sale of United States war bonds. *Hum. Rel.* 2, 253–267.

Cohen, A. R., Brehm, J. W., and Latané, B. (1959). Choice of strategy and voluntary exposure to information under public and private conditions. *J. Pers.* 27, 63–73.

Cooper, Eunice, and Jahoda, Marie (1947). The evasion of propaganda: How prejudiced people respond to anti-prejudice propaganda. *J. Psychol.* 23, 15–25.

Ehrlich, Danuta, Guttmann, I., Schonbach, P., and Mills, J. (1957). Post-decision exposure to relevant information. *J. abnorm. soc. Psychol.* 54, 98–102.

Feather, N. T. (1962). Cigarette smoking and lung cancer: a study of cognitive dissonance. *Austral. J. of Psychol.* 14, 55–64.

Feather, N. T. (1963). Cognitive dissonance, sensitivity, and evaluation. *J. abnorm. soc. Psychol.* 66, 157–163.

Festinger, L. (1957). *A theory of cognitive dissonance.* Stanford, Calif.: Stanford Univer. Press.

Festinger, L. (1964). *Conflict, decision and dissonance.* Stanford, Calif.: Stanford Univer. Press.

Festinger, L., and Aronson, E. (1960). The arousal and reduction of dissonance in social contexts. In Cartwright, D., and Zander, A. (Eds.), *Group dynamics* (2nd ed.). Evanston, Ill.: Row, Peterson, pp. 214–231.

Freedman, J. L. (1965a). Preference for dissonant information. *J. Pers. soc. Psychol.* 2, 287–289.

Freedman, J. L. (1965b). Confidence, utility and selective exposure to information: a partial replication. *J. Pers. soc. Psychol.* (in press).

Freedman, J. L., and Sears, D. O. (1963). Voters' preferences among types of information. *Amer. Psychol.* **18**, 375.

Freedman, J. L., and Sears, D. O. (1965). Warning, distraction, and resistance to influence. *J. Pers. soc. Psychol.* **1**, 262–266.

Harvey, O. J., Kelley, H. H., and Shapiro, M. M. (1957). Reactions to unfavorable evaluations of the self made by other persons. *J. Pers.* **25**, 393–411.

Hovland, C. I. (1952). A "communication analysis" of concept learning. *Psychol. Rev.* **59**, 461–472.

Hovland, C. I. (1959). Reconciling conflicting results derived from experimental and survey studies of attitude change. *Amer. Psychol.* **14**, 8–17.

Hovland, C. I., Harvey, O. J., and Sherif, M. (1957). Assimilation and contrast effects in reactions to communication and attitude change. *J. abnorm. soc. Psychol.* **55**, 244–252.

Jecker, J. D. (1964). Selective exposure to new information. In Festinger, L. (Ed.), *Conflict, decision and dissonance.* Stanford, Calif.: Stanford Univer. Press, pp. 65–81.

Katz, E., and Feldman, J. J. (1962). The debates in the light of research: a survey of surveys. In Kraus, S. (Ed.), *The great debates.* Bloomington, Ind.: Indiana Univer. Press.

Kelley, H. H. (1957). Resistance to change and the effects of persuasive communications. In Sherif, M., and Wilson, M. O. (Eds.), *Emerging problems in social psychology.* Norman, Okla.

Key, V. O., Jr. (1961). *Public opinion and American democracy.* New York: Knopf.

Klapper, J. T. (1960). *The effects of mass communications.* Chicago, Ill.: Free Press of Glencoe.

Lane, R. E., and Sears, D. O. (1964). *Public opinion.* Englewood Cliffs, N.J.: Prentice-Hall.

Lazarsfeld, P. F., Berelson, B., and Gaudet, Hazel (1948). *The people's choice* (2nd ed.). New York: Columbia Univer. Press.

Maccoby, Eleanor E., Maccoby, N., Romney, A. K., and Adams, J. S. (1961). Social reinforcement in attitude change. *J. abnorm. soc. Psychol.* **63**, 109–115.

Maccoby, N., Romney, A. K., Adams, J. S., and Maccoby, Eleanor E. (1962). "Critical periods" in seeking and accepting information. In *Paris-Stanford studies in communication.* Stanford, Calif.: Inst. for Communications Res., pp. 47–57.

McGuire, W. J., and Papageorgis, D. (1961). The relative efficacy of various types of prior belief-defense in producing immunity against persuasion. *J. abnorm. soc. Psychol.* **62**, 327–337.

Manis, M. (1961). Interpretation of opinion statements as a function of recipient attitude and source prestige. *J. abnorm. soc. Psychol.* **63**, 82–86.

Miller, N. E. (1944). Experimental studies of conflict. In Hunt, J. McV. (Ed.), *Personality and the behavior disorders.* New York: Ronald Press.

Mills, J., Aronson, E., and Robinson, J. (1959). Selectivity in exposure to information. *J. abnorm. soc. Psychol.* **59**, 250–253.

Mills, J., and Ross, A. (1964). Effects of commitment and certainty upon interest in supporting information. *J. abnorm. soc. Psychol.* **68**, 552–555.

Newcomb, T. M. (1961). *The acquaintance process.* New York: Holt.

Newcomb, T. M. (1963). Persistance and regression of changed attitudes: long-range studies. *J. soc. Issues* **19**, 3–14.

Rosen, S. (1961). Post-decision affinity for incompatible information. *J. abnorm. soc. Psychol.* **63**, 188–190.

Schramm, W., and Carter, R. F.(1959). Effectiveness of a political telethon. *Publ. Opin. Quart.* **23**, 121–126.

Sears, D. O. (1966). Opinion formation and information preferences in an adversary situation. *J. exp. soc. Psychol.* (in press).

Sears, D. O. (1965). Biased indoctrination and selectivity of exposure to new information. *Sociometry* (in press).

Sears, D. O., and Freedman, J. L. (1963). Commitment, information utility, and selective exposure. *USN tech. Rep. (ONR)* Nonr-233(54) NR 171–350, No. 12, August.

Sears, D. O., and Freedman, J. L. (1965). The effects of expected familiarity with arguments upon opinion change and selective exposure. *J. Pers. soc. Psychol.* **2**, 420–426.

Star, Shirley A., and Hughes, Helen M. (1950). Report on an educational campaign: the Cincinnati plan for the United Nations. *Amer. J. Sociol.* **55**, 389–400.

Steiner, G. A. (1963). *The people look at television.* New York: Knopf.

Steiner, I. D. (1962). Receptivity to supportive versus nonsupportive communications. *J. abnorm. soc. Psychol.* **65**, 266–267.

Wolfinger, R. E., Wolfinger, Barbara K., Prewitt, K., and Rosenhack, Sheliah (1964). America's Radical Right: Politics and Ideology. In Apter, D. (Ed.), *Ideology and discontent.* New York: The Free Press of Glencoe, pp. 263–289.

GROUP PROBLEM SOLVING[1]

L. Richard Hoffman

GRADUATE SCHOOL OF BUSINESS
UNIVERSITY OF CHICAGO
CHICAGO, ILLINOIS

I. Introduction

The basic question to be answered in the study of group problem solving is: How best can a group use the resources of its members in solving a given problem? This phrasing of the question assumes that the necessary resources do lie in the group. Furthermore, most experimenters have used problems whose difficulty is presumably commensurate with the level of ability of the group members.

[1] This chapter was prepared in conjunction with United States Public Health Service Grant MH-2704, N.R.F. Maier, principal investigator. The author was then with the Department of Psychology, University of Michigan.

From a broad point of view, however, this assumption avoids several interesting questions which could easily arise in naturalistic settings. How does a group know when its members have the resources which are needed to solve a problem? How long will the group persist in attempting to solve the problem if it does not possess the necessary resources? What actions does a group take when it decides it is unable to solve the problem? To my knowledge, there have been no experimental attempts to answer these questions. In fact, Feather's (1961) analysis of the motivational and expectational bases for persistence in individual problem solving is almost unique in its concern with these questions.

Even if the group members have the capability of solving the problems assigned to them, other questions remain. What factors tend to prevent the effective utilization of the group's resources, and what conditions promote problem-solving efficiency? This separation of inhibiting and facilitating factors suggests that the removal of the impediments to problem solution is often insufficient to produce effective group problem solving; facilitating factors must be brought to bear before the group's resources are mobilized effectively.

This chapter will review the experimental evidence which bears on these questions. The discussion will focus primarily on group problem solving and will bring in the classical group-versus-individual controversy only where it seems relevant. We assume here that it is helpful to conceive of groups as groups without necessarily falling into the trap of reifying the group and its processes independently of the members (Allport, 1924). Furthermore, since the management of large organizations often requires that various committees rather than single individuals must do the work, the question of how groups can solve their problems most effectively is of considerable practical importance.[2]

II. Factors Inhibiting Effective Problem Solving

The major barriers to effective problem solving are those conditions which prevent the free expression of ideas in a group. Restraints can decrease the likelihood that the correct solution or the elements of such a solution will be made available to the group. Factors both obvious and subtle can work against the group's use of its resources.

[2] The organizational requirement for group problem solving rests primarily on two assumptions: (1) the information needed for most management decisions must come from a variety of sources whose functional interdependence requires its simultaneous consideration and evaluation by all concerned; and (2) the acceptance of such decisions by the persons affected is often more important than the objective quality of the decision, and acceptance is promoted by participation in decision making.

A. PRESSURES TOWARD UNIFORMITY

1. The Value of Unanimity

The continued existence of the group is itself a subtle barrier against the free expression of ideas. In laboratory groups there is a strong tendency for the members to agree on a single solution to a problem, even when instructed to ignore the prior discussion in reporting their own conclusions. It is as if the members did not want the group to be divided at the end of the session. We have often had subjects who violently opposed the majority's solution announce their capitulation with, "I thought we were all supposed to agree!"

The experimental evidence is quite clear on this point. Groups tend to produce unanimous decisions, and discussions tend to increase the uniformity of their members' individual judgments. Thomas and Fink (1961) gave Maier's Horse Trading Problem to groups varying in size from two to five people. Each member was asked for his individual answer after the discussion. Sixty-four percent of the groups regardless of size gave unanimous answers. Despite the instructions to the members to disregard the group's discussion if they wished this degree of uniformity was obtained on a relatively simple, if tricky, arithmetic reasoning problem. Almost half of these groups, moreover, were unanimously incorrect. Interestingly enough, the members of unanimous groups were more satisfied with their decisions than were members of split groups, whether they were correct or incorrect. We shall return to this phenomenon later.

Pennington et al. (1958), in a design similar to Edith Bennett's (1955), showed that groups which were required either just to discuss the problems assigned to them or to reach decisions on these problems (or to do both) agreed more following the group sessions than before. On the other hand, members of groups which merely reconsidered their judgments showed practically no change. However, Bass (1963) demonstrated recently that coalescence (increased agreement) has only a modest correlation with the effectiveness of the decisions ($r = .29$). Even on these objective problems there is no guarantee that unanimity produces truth; in fact, there often is very little relationship between the two. The more complex the problems, then, the more detrimental will this tendency be for the group members to promote consensus at the possible expense of arriving at a more effective solution.

2. Majority Rule

The majority's ability to coerce the people holding the minority view was recognized early by Thorndike (1938) and Timmons (1942). They showed that the majority generally produced only a slightly better solution than the average group member. When it is wrong, moreover, the majority frequently suppresses the expression of the correct solution. This was demonstrated by Maier and Solem (1952). Where the majority was initially correct, 60% of the persons who were initially incorrect adopted the correct answer following discussion. If a minority of the members was initially correct, however, and there was no appointed leader in the group, only 46% of the incorrect subjects adopted the correct answer. When a leader was appointed, however, 72% of the incorrect subjects changed to correct answers. The effect of the leader's presence was most apparent in those groups where only one of the five or six members was initially correct, thus supporting the investigators' argument that the leader served to protect the minority opinion from majority suppression.

Pressures toward uniformity may be merely the result of the typical experimental situation. The experimental conditions may have made the subjects think that proper performance as subjects required them to arrive at a single solution to the problem (Orne, 1962). In real life, on the other hand, there is often very little motivation to arrive at a unanimous decision, but just how often is hard to tell and worthy of study. No matter how frequently the phenomenon arises in naturalistic settings, pressures toward opinion uniformity may be detrimental to the group's effectiveness if it prevents search for and discussion of alternative possibilities.

B. Sources of Pressure Toward Uniformity

1. Personal Characteristics

Whatever the source of the uniformity pressures, these conditions cause many subjects to refrain from solving the assigned problem themselves and to depend on particular members of the group for the correct answer. The cited effects of majority influence—right or, especially, wrong—exemplify this abdication of individual problem solving (Maier and Solem, 1952; Thomas and Fink, 1961). As one might expect, then, Hochbaum (1954) found that subjects who were induced to lack confidence in their ability to do the problem given them were more inclined to conform to a fictitious group norm than were subjects who were made to be high in self confidence. Furthermore, the subjects' confidence in their own judgment was increased by conformity to the group norm. Thus, a person who feels uncertain of his own abilities can feel secure and successful by adhering to others suggestions.

Many people also exhibit a tendency to agree with the other group members if they believe that by agreeing with them, they might improve their popularity or standing with these others. Jackson and Saltzstein (1958) found that subjects who were highly attracted to the group they were in were likely to conform to the group norm. But in addition, subjects who previously had not been accepted by their groups conformed to the group judgment as much on an individual task as on a problem for which the group as a whole was to be evaluated. Thus, the insecurity generated by possible rejection by the group provides a strong incentive to prove oneself worthy by agreeing with the other members.[3] If the subject holds an opinion which deviates from that of the majority, he is presented with a difficult dilemma. Since deviation can lead to ultimate rejection by the group, he should conform in order to preserve his standing in the group (Schachter, 1951). On the other hand, if he fails to contribute the correct answer to the group, he has done the group a disservice. Experimental evidence suggests that he chooses the first alternative over the second to the extent that he values his membership in the group and feels threatened by rejection.

2. Group Members' Perceived Ability

The tendency to depend on other group members can also be rational, i.e., rational to the degree that the subject regards the other members as being able to solve the assigned problem. Mausner (1954) paired his subjects with a confederate who was either successful or unsuccessful on a previous task similar to the test task. Subjects paired with successful confederates tended to conform to the confederate's erroneous judgments in the test situation more than did subjects paired with unsuccessful confederates. In a somewhat similar investigation, Berkowitz (1957) showed that persons who where induced to like their ficticious partners rated them as more proficient and conformed more to their purported judgments than did subjects who were made to like their partners less. Thus, not only will subjects conform to the opinions of people they like, but they will judge these people to be more proficient. Believing the liked person to be proficient, of course, also heightens adherence to his views.

3. Prior Experience

An essentially similar phenomenon has been observed at the group level in the subjects' tendency to rely on the total group's ability to solve their problems. Kidd and Campbell (1955) gave three-person groups differential success experiences on an anagram task. They then had the

---

[3] The extensive literature on conformity pressures is clearly relevant here (e.g., Asch, 1956; Crutchfield, 1959; Tuddenham, 1959) but, since it has been reviewed elsewhere, I have limited this discussion to conformity in group problem solving.

group members make individual judgments about the number of flickers of a light, gave the subjects a purported group average, and then permitted them to change their judgments. There was an increase in the subjects' degree of conformity to the group average on the light judgments which corresponded to the degree of prior group success on the anagram task.

This generalization of group influence from one type of task to another can clearly be a detriment to an effective attack on some problems. Problems vary considerably in their solution requirements. Prior success may promote adoption of a readily available but poor solution (Hoffman *et al.*, 1963). Berkowitz and Levy (1956) suggested that success generates both pride in the work group and more positive motivation to work on group problems. While these may be salutary effects, the omniscient and omnipotent powers thus given to the group remind one of those questionable personnel selection decisions which assume that success in one situation predicts success in another: great generals make great executives; the best graduate students make the best professors.

It may well be that the more successes a group has had on one type of problem, the more inflexible it will be in attacking other types of problems. Thus, there must be careful feedback. A group must have information providing for continued motivation, but, at the same time, the members must never lose the ability to search for varied alternatives in attempting to solve new and different problems. The question of how to separate these two functions of feedback is important for research.

C. PARTICIPATION BIASES

1. Feedback

Unfortunately, it is often difficult to control the type and amount of feedback given to group members. People have a natural tendency to participate more actively in group discussion the more favorably their contributions are evaluated. Oakes and his colleagues (Oakes *et al.*, 1960) increased the participation of certain arbitrarily chosen members by indicating to them that their contributions were "insightful" and decreased the participation of other members by indicating that their contributions were "not insightful." Furthermore, this difference was maintained, even though not significantly, during a subsequent period in which feedback was not provided and the authors expected participation to "extinguish." Thus, the person whose ideas are initially accepted by the group is likely to increase his participation, while one whose suggestions are rejected will withdraw from the discussion (Pepinsky *et al.*, 1958).

Oakes (1962) later showed that the effectiveness of the feedback he provided in enhancing participation varied with the relevance of the purported source (professional psychologists versus peers of the subjects versus laymen) for the problem at hand. Nevertheless, since the feedback that one usually receives is typically relevant to the problem, the recipient of this information is likely to be influenced by it.

2. Influence on Solution Adoption

Riecken's study (1958) of the impact of the talkative member on the group's decision-making process identified a major barrier to successful problem solving. In groups which had solved two previous problems he determined who were the most talkative and least talkative members. He then gave a "hint" [the elegant solution to Maier's Parasol Assembly Problem (Maier, 1952)] to one member of each group: to the most talkative member in half the groups and to the least talkative member in the other half. Groups with the most talkative hint-holders generally adopted the elegant solution, while those with the least talkative hint-holders rejected it for the most part.

Riecken attributed this difference to the supporting remarks made by the highly talkative hint-holders. More recently, our own research has indicated that the solution which receives the highest number of favorable comments becomes the group's solution, but that most of the comments often come from a single member (Hoffman and Maier, 1964; cf. also Thomas and Fink, 1961). Thus, he who talks the most is likely to promote his solution to the group successfully.

There is a complementary aspect to this relationship. The person who talks the most is also most likely to be selected as a leader by the other group members. Slater (1955), Kirscht et al. (1959), and Blake and Mouton (1961) all found that leaders selected by their groups were generally the most talkative members. Even in the Shaw and Gilchrist study (1956), where subjects "interacted" only through notes placed in mailboxes at various times, the leaders elected in almost all of the groups had sent the most number of items, especially items relating to the means of organizing the group and to information about the problem.

More definitively, Mann (1961) factor analyzed members' behaviors as rated by peers and by observers and as coded by observers (Bales' system) on two different problems. He found a Task Prominence factor in both analyses. This factor included peer ratings of leadership and talkativeness, observer ratings of leadership, and observer coding of talkativeness and making suggestions, thus supporting the relationship between talkativeness and rated leadership.

This relationship would not interfere with group performance if all or most of the talk contributed to effective solutions to the problems. In Mann's study, however, as in most investigations, the relationship holds regardless of the quality of the solutions obtained from the group. As was noted earlier, Riecken (1958) demonstrated experimentally that the elegant solution was rarely adopted when its proponent was the least talkative member of the group, but was almost always adopted when he was the most talkative member.

3. Personal Characteristics

Undue personal influence is considered a barrier to effective problem solving. The reason becomes clear when we examine the personality characteristics of the more talkative members. Mann (1959) reported significant correlations on two problems of .25 and .36 between the Task Prominence behavioral factor referred to above and a Social Extroversion personality factor, marked most clearly by the General Activity, Ascendance, and Sociability scales of the Guilford-Zimmerman Temperament Survey. These scales also were positively correlated with leadership nominations in groups studied by Kaess et al. (1961). Reference to this phenomenon as the "GAS" syndrome—referring to the initial letters of the three traits—is probably apt in view of the amount of hot air which emerges. Unfortunately, these three variables have generally been found to be unrelated to any measures of cognitive ability (Joan S. Guilford, 1952; Mann, 1959).

Shaw's Individual Prominence scale (1959) shows the same relationship to talkativeness and influence and gives us some clue to the type of person identified by the GAS syndrome. He is the outgoing, domineering, yet friendly person who invests tremendous energy in all his activities. He takes the initiative in social situations, enjoys being with other people, and is able to mobilize others to gain ends that he sets.

Another kind of emergent leader is the one highly motivated to find a good solution. The member with a high stake in achieving a successful outcome is likely to enter the discussion early and to attempt to organize and discuss the problem his way (Hemphill et al. 1957). The persons selected to discuss their groups' solutions with representatives of other groups in the Blake and Mouton (1961) and the Kirscht et al. (1959) studies were identified as dominating the group and engaging in more directive and influencing acts than other members. Crockett's (1955) observations of management conferences revealed that, even in formal groups, leaders emerged who had higher stakes in the issues than the other members and who were generally higher in organizational rank, rated expertise, and rated expression of self-oriented needs. Unfortunately, the expression of self-oriented needs was judged to be related to ineffective group performance in these management conferences (Fouriezos et al., 1950).

The ability of these extroverted and highly motivated people to influence the other group members suggests that, when faced with complex problems, people are willing to rely on those who sound as if they know the answer. Thus, the self-confident manner in which the socially aggressive person presents his opinion may enhance its merit to others. Such a mechanism would account for the surprising findings by Shaw (1963) and Shaw and Penrod (1962). These investigators obtained a negative relationship between the amount of additional information about the problem they gave to certain members and the amount of influence those members had over the group's decision. Shaw's suggested explanation, consistent with the present hypothesis, was that the subjects with the least amount of additional information were able to promote a single solution, whereas those with even more information had several equally good alternatives. Thus, the first group could self-confidently influence the other members to adopt their proposed solutions, while the latter subjects were less confident in supporting several possibilities. A corollary hypothesis, of course, is that the more self-confident members prevent a group from utilizing all of the relevant information available to it.

D. GROUP STRUCTURE

1. Group Size

The disproportionate influence of the self-confident member on the group's decision would seem to grow with increases in group size. As groups grow the distribution of participation among the members becomes severely skewed, with one or two people doing most of the talking (Bales and Borgatta, 1955; Stephan and Mishler, 1952). The larger the group the more inhibited the introverted people are, unless they have a strong stake in the outcome. In such cases those who are willing to speak will railroad their ideas through the meeting. Potential dissenters are often reluctant to voice their opinion for fear of being thought deviant.

2. Formal Structure

These personality characteristics which often lead to an undue influence upon group members typically have their greatest effect in formally leaderless groups. These traits become somewhat less important in groups with some type of formal structure. Shaw (1959), for example, found a positive relationship between scores on his Individual Prominence scale and a person's influence over the decision in groups in which no decision power structure existed. No relationship was found, however, where some members were given more decision-making authority. Similarly, Crockett (1955) found that leaders emerged in management conferences more frequently when the formal leaders were less active in setting goals and proposing problems or their solutions and, thus, when the group structure was relatively ambiguous. A clear-cut status structure in the group seems to inhibit the tendency of the GAS personalities to dominate the discussion.

3. Power Structures

Power structures in groups, while possibly mitigating the negative effects of personality factors, may also create new barriers to effective problem solving. Torrance's series of studies (1955) of problem solving in Air Force crews demonstrated that the lowest-ranked member was least likely to influence the group's decision, even when he was correct. There are probably several reasons for this finding. For one, high-status members expect to exercise influence and require little support from the other group members in order to have their ideas adopted. (This explanation seems consistent with the self-confidence hypothesis stated above. Expecting to influence, the high-status person may assert his ideas more forcefully than the other group members.) Then, too, Torrance suggested that a low-status member may go along with the person in authority even when he knows his personal opinion is better. This notion is supported by the findings of Maier and Hoffman (1961) that people who are strongly identified with their organizations are especially likely to accept the suggestions of the authority person.

The presence of authority relations in a group seems to change the character of the discussion. There is a greater concentration on the ideas of the high-status person, and the group has to spend considerable time either supporting or rejecting his views rather than searching for alternatives (Maier and Hoffman, 1960b). Bass (1963) provided evidence supporting this characterization. He noted that in unstructured groups increases in group participation enhanced the quality of group judgments, whereas in highly structured groups, extent of participation was negatively correlated with the profitability of the discussions and the increases in agreement among the group members. Thus, leaders in formal authority positions should either refrain from suggesting solutions to a group or should be very certain that they are right if they want to avoid introducing error into the problem-solving process.

The inhibiting effect of an authority figure in the group may also be due to the threat he implies to other group members. We are all familiar with the insecure person who is afraid to contradict the boss. The study of bargaining in two-man groups by Deutsch and Krauss (1960) suggests that even implied threats can produce reactions which are harmful to the threatener. Only when neither member of the dyad could threaten the other were they able to develop a cooperative solution to the bargaining problem so that both could make a profit. Neither member was able to make a profit when either or both were able to threaten the other.

Communication between the people involved in the bargaining situation may help overcome some of the negative consequences of implied threat. Loomis (1959) demonstrated that permitting communication in varying degrees between the partners increased the members' perception of the others' trustworthiness and also increased trustworthy behavior on the same problem. Thus, some of the adverse effects produced by the presence of high status group members may be traced to restraints upon communication. Authority figures may be seen as potential threats and inhibit the free expression of ideas, as Mellinger (1956) and Read (1962) demonstrated. But whatever the reason for the negative consequences, the implied threat created by the presence of authority may lessen the members' motivation to arrive at the best possible decision (Hoffman, 1961) in favor of what is apparently acceptable to the boss.

Status differences affect the behavior of those who are high in authority as well as those with little power. Placing a person in a leadership position generally influences his actions in the group. Even in laboratory groups where one person is told he is the "leader" of a group, but is without any real power, he tends to participate more actively and to direct and organize the group's effort, more than the other group members. Berkowitz (1956) showed that persons occupying central positions in a communication net, whether they were strongly ascendant or weakly submissive personalities, tended to dominate the problem-solving process of the group. In a recent unpublished study of our own, we found that subjects who were randomly selected to be leaders were almost invariably the most active members of the group, often engaging in as many problem-directed acts as the other three members combined. Furthermore these acts were critical in determining which of a variety of solutions being discussed by the group was finally selected. The appelation "leader" seems to legitimize the high volume of attempted direction giving and also serves to focus the control of the group's operation in his hands. This control may or may not enhance the effectiveness of the group, depending on the leader's ability to solve the problem (Fiedler and Meuwese, 1963). When power to reward and punish is added to the title, the focus seems to become even sharper. An apparent dilemma is thereby created. The more power a leader has the more effectively he can control the group's procedure, but the more likely he is to become a barrier to the free exchange of ideas.

It is important to repeat here that the barriers to problem solving that I have just discussed have their negative impact on the creative aspects of group problem solving. In terms of other criteria of group effectiveness, however, these conditions may be beneficial. For example, the pressures toward uniformity may be useful when time is an important factor or where solution alternatives are of approximately equal quality. Where, however, an exchange of ideas is needed or only one member has the necessary information, these barriers seem to prevent effective group problem solving.

E. FAILURE TO SEARCH FOR PROBLEMS

Another contributor to ineffective problem solving is the failure of most groups to organize or plan their attack on the problem. Shure *et al.* (1962) showed that groups tend not to use the opportunity to organize for effective problem solving. The pressure to reach a solution (cf. Maier and Solem, 1962) probably inhibits discussion of the problem or of how to attack it, thus preventing the group from systematically reviewing the problem requirements or their approach to it.

This lack of planning is most clearly seen in the Cohen and Bennis study (1962) of changes in communication networks. Groups which remained in circle networks persisted in a circuit problem-solving system, in which each member received all information and solved the problem himself, rather than developing the more efficient hierarchical system. Groups which shifted from wheel to circle networks, on the other hand, almost invariably developed a hierarchical communication flow. Apparently the necessity for concentrating on the problem activities in the all-circle groups prevented their consideration of problem-solving organization. But the wheel-to-circle groups were able to benefit from their previous experience and explore the possibilities of organizing within the circle network. Even in the original study by Bales and Strodtbeck (1951) on phases in group problem solving, only 6 of the 22 groups actually conformed to the orientation-evaluation-control sequence postulated by the researchers. Whether their definition of orientation is equivalent to "defining the problem" or not, it is clear that comparatively few groups spend much time on that activity.

III. Factors Promoting Effective Problem Solving

A. GROUP COMPOSITION

1. Ability

Several theories have been offered to relate the abilities of the group members to the outcome of the group's problem-solving efforts (e.g., Ekman, 1955; Lorge and Solomon, 1955; Thomas and Fink, 1961).

These have generally applied to so-called "insight" problems in which there is a single key to obtaining the correct answer to the problem. The Lorge and Solomon and the Ekman accounts assume that the group product reflects the ability of the most able member. Thus, they claim, if one member of a group can solve the problem, the group as a whole will solve it. They explain the typical superiority of groups over individuals on these problems as the greater probability of having at least one able person in a group. By extension, groups should be even more superior than individuals on more complex problems, since the probability of having one person who can solve one part of the problem and another who can solve another part, etc., is much greater than having individuals who can solve all parts.

Thomas and Fink (1961) showed, however, that such a model was grossly inadequate for the Horse Trading Problem which requires only a single insight. On the basis of solutions collected from individual members following group discussion, they found a much smaller proportion of unanimously correct groups and a much larger proportion of unanimously incorrect groups than expected on the basis of the "rational" probabilistic model. Thomas and Fink proposed a "consensus model" which predicts that group members will tend to converge on a single answer. This solution is likely to be correct or incorrect according to the difficulty and "verifiability" of the problem.

These theoretical formulations dealing with ability in group problem solving face the difficult task of measuring the relevant abilities. While mathematical reasoning scores on general intelligence tests are usually positively correlated with individual success on deductive reasoning problems, they are completely uncorrelated with success on the Horse Trading Problem and other similar insight problems. Thus, for any particular problem it is difficult to determine the ability level of the group or its most able member other than by having subjects solve the problem itself. Such a procedure obviously introduces new complexities (e.g., practice effects) into the research.

Furthermore, having examined the barriers of personality and social structure to effective group problem solving in previous sections, we can understand why the few studies which varied the general level and distribution of abilities of the group members produced inconsistent findings. In some instances the group product reflected the most able member's ability (Palmer, 1962; Comrey and Staats, 1955; Wiest et al., 1961). In other cases, however, group performance was either uncorrelated with the ability of the most able member (Roby and Lanzetta, 1961), or the member with the right answer was actually suppressed (Maier and Solem, 1952).

Tuckman and Lorge (1962) tested the hypothesis that the group product reflects the best member's ability. Using the relatively complex Mined Road Problem, they had groups of five solve the problem first individually and then as groups. Although they concluded that the group product was no better than the best individual's, their data show that in some groups the group product was considerably better than the best individual's, in others considerably worse, and in a few exactly the same. There is also some suggestion in the group problem-solving literature that the less straightforward the problem, the less the group product reflects the single, most able individual. The evidence presented in succeeding sections suggests that the group product is rarely a simple extension of the combinational model which Lorge and Solomon (1955) offered to account for insight problems. Rather, the group answer typically represents a utilization of abilities in identifying deficiencies, recommending solutions, and applying the appropriate evaluative criteria to select the correct one. Occasionally it means skillfully combining several alternatives into a single elegant package.

2. Other Factors

Characteristics other than the intellectual ability of the group members have been shown to affect a group's problem-solving performance. Two factors appear to stand out as promoting creative problem solving: (1) the members' motivation to work cooperatively on the probem, and (2) the diversity of the points of view and information relevant to the problem within the group.

a. Motivation. In general, all-female groups tend to do less well than male groups. While this may reflect ability differences between the sexes, the equivalence and occasional superiority of mixed-sex groups to all-male groups suggests a motivational explanation (Hoffman & Maier, 1961a, 1961b; Hoffman et al., 1962). Women in all-female groups probably reinforce each other's rejection of the problem-solving task, as when they solve problems individually (Carey, 1958). Thus, such groups presumably fail to put as much effort into the task as is needed. When the problem is more involving, as when they are role-playing with men or dealing with a problem of feelings, all-female groups seem able to function effectively. Men are generally relatively highly motivated to solve problems, although it is not clear how they would act if faced with problems more clearly feminine in content (Milton, 1958). In an unpublished study, we have found that the same male groups which were substantially superior to female groups on the Horse Trading Problem were slightly inferior to them on a human relations problem. Whether these results are a product of the men's reduced motivation on the human relations problem or of the women's increased motivation is not known at this time.

The work of Stock and Thelen (1958) also suggests that personality factors in the group members may promote or inhibit effective group interaction. Working from Bion's framework (1959), they define people's orientations to groups in terms of tendencies toward fight, flight, dependency, and counter-dependency. People with flight or dependency tendencies avoid conflict by denying it or surrendering. They supposedly are less likely than the other two types to engage in the expression and adjustment of different points of view necessary for creative problem solving. J. C. Glidewell's study (reported in Stock and Thelen, 1958) compared the problem-solving effectiveness of groups which he characterized as having one of these four orientations. The fight groups which were able to focus their conflicts on the task produced the most effective solutions. The use of the Reactions to Group Situations Test, an incomplete-sentence, projective device developed by Stock and Thelen, should permit the identification of group members with productive or inhibiting personalities and provide further insight into the emotional factors in group problem solving.

b. Diversity of viewpoints. The superiority of mixed-sex groups even to all-male groups in certain instances may be attributable, in part, to the divergent approaches and orientations of men and women to the assigned problem (Hoffman and Maier, 1961a; Hoffman et al., 1962). The seemingly greater sensitivity of women to feelings and interpersonal relations combined with men's ability to find the facts provides a potent combination for many complex human relations problems.

Other evidence of the value of diverse approaches to problems was supplied by Hoffman (1959), and Hoffman and Maier (1961a) with heterogeneous personalities, Ghiselli and Lodahl (1958) with heterogeneous decision-making approaches, Ziller and Exline (1958) with heterogeneous age groupings, and Triandis et al. (1962) with heterogeneous religious and political attitudes. In all of these studies the more heterogeneous groups were more effective and/or more creative. The usual explanation for these successes is that in heterogeneous groups there are more different kinds of ideas or different possible directions available for approaching the problem (Hoffman, 1961).

It is not clear, however, how one determines whether a group will be sufficiently heterogeneous or not heterogeneous enough to be effective. On what dimensions should group members be heterogeneous? Shaw (1960) showed that group problem-solving performance was either uncorrelated or negatively correlated with the variance (heterogeneity) of member characteristics on such scales, taken singly, as Acceptance of

Authority and Individual Prominence. Heterogeneity clearly has to be relevant to the problem requirements, yet we rarely know what these requirements are. The successes of the heterogeneous groups cited earlier probably stem from the wide variety of characteristics on which the members differed.

The two exceptions to the positive relationship between heterogeneity and effectiveness occur in the all-female groups of the Ziller and Exline study (1958) and in the comparison of homogeneous and heterogeneous religious groups in Holland done by Fiedler et al. (1961). Both results are probably due to the lack of appropriate motivation in the group. The poor performance of the all-female groups is consistent with the explanation, given above, that women tend to lack interest in problem-solving tasks. As for the other study, the religious groups (Calvinist and Catholic) have a long history of antagonism in Holland which Fielder et al. implied, restricted communication among the group members. It would seem that a diversity of viewpoints must be accompanied by a tolerance for differences of opinion if a group is to exploit its potential creativity.

B. GROUP PROCESS

1. Idea Generation

It is apparent, however, that even when diversity exists in a group, the varied viewpoints are not always heard. The many barriers listed above can operate successfully to restrict the benefits of diversity. As Osborn (1953) pointed out, and as Hoffman and Maier (1964) have confirmed quantitatively, one of the most effective barriers is the tendency for group members to evaluate suggested solutions as they appear, instead of waiting until all suggestions are in and then making their choice. This tendency to evaluate suggestions one at a time may promote a mediocre solution or it may kill off a good one early. Frequently groups will evaluate the pros and cons of one solution for a considerable length of time before discarding it. During this period the suggestions made prior to the discarded solution have been forgotten and may never be recovered (Hoffman and Maier, 1964).

As a cure for these difficulties Osborn (1953) offered the brain-storming technique, in which an evaluation-free period of idea production permits the exploration of even the most harebrained solutions. By delaying the evaluation and by systematically recording all solutions offered, brainstorming prevents the amassing of support for a single solution, as well as the slaughter and forgetting of solutions which occurs in ordinary discussion (Hoffman and Maier, 1964).

Experimental evaluations of the usefulness of brainstorming have produced generally favorable results when individuals with training in the technique are compared to those without training (Parnes and Meadow, 1959). But despite the introduction of brainstorming as a group problem-solving technique (Osborn, 1953), we have not located any experimental tests of its superiority to free discussion. The technique is, in any case, difficult to evaluate. The difficulty can be illustrated in a study by Weisskopf-Joelson and Eliseo (1961) in which brainstorming groups were compared with groups instructed to be "critical" in developing possible brand names for three different products: a cigar, a deodorant, and an automobile. (Note that this was an advertising-like task for which Mr. Osborn originally developed the brainstorming technique.) The brainstorming groups produced significantly more possible names than did the critical groups, as expected. Next, 150 students at the same university rated each of the 902 different brand names suggested on a five-point scale of attractiveness, with a high degree of agreement. The superior production of the brainstorming groups apparently resulted primarily from a higher number of poor quality suggestions. The same number of high quality suggestions was produced by groups with both types of instructions. We cannot question the validity of the student ratings for judging the effectiveness of these groups since the groups' task was to produce brand names which would "attract the Purdue male." The results do not, however, refute the creative advantages of the brainstorming technique. As the authors indicate, "such conventional names as 'Sportsmen,' 'Esquire,' or 'Century' were among the three most highly rated names [which] suggests that the imaginative ideas of the brainstormers were wasted on the conservative taste of the judges."

A period of idea-production free from evaluation can lead to a solution of high quality—if the members can refrain from being self-critical and can avoid staying in particular directions. The studies by Taylor et al. (1958) and by Dunnette et al. (1963) suggest that brainstorming groups tend to follow a particular train of thought and fail to use all the members' ideas.

2. Solution Evaluation and Selection

Brainstorming is not, however, a panacea. While the brainstorming technique may produce a large number of possible solutions to a problem, the increase in number does not guarantee that the group will adopt the best or most creative solution. The process of evaluating and selecting from the enlarged pool of ideas creates new opportunities for the old biases and individual personality and motivational factors to operate again.

In a recent study in our own laboratory, Springborn (1963) found a significant *negative* correlation between the number of alternative solutions suggested by a group and the quality of its final solution. The great number of proposed solutions may increase the ambiguity of the group situation and thus heighten the extent to which sources of error can operate. Little attention has been given and much invention is needed to develop effective techniques for evaluating solution suggestions.

Maier's Screening Principles (1960) appear to offer a highly sophisticated means for forcing a group to attend more carefully to the facts given in a problem. The four principles he describes are designed to eliminate solution possibilities which cannot be supported by the facts in the case, or whose support cannot be agreed upon by the group members. Solutions selected in accord with the Maier principles are those which have the largest number of facts from different sources of information. While it is analytically meaningful, however, this technique has not been subjected to experimental test. The difficulties in validating this procedure are similar to the problems of evaluating the brainstorming technique. In any case, if ideas are to be produced in a way which avoids the motivational and social problems common to group problem solving, the evaluation and selection of final solutions must be governed by the realities of the problem situation.

3. Identifying the Problem

Both of these phases (idea-generation and solution-evaluation) will be assisted immeasurably if the group first identifies the problem requirements. More often than not, a group will begin to offer solutions to the immediately perceived problem rather than exploring the facts to define the real problem. As Maier pointed out early with respect to individual problem solving, the direction which the person initially takes in solving the problem may prevent him from finding the correct answer (Maier, 1930). In the same way a group may fall into a rut and produce an inferior solution by agreeing early on an inadequate definition of the problem requirements.

Maier and Solem (1962) have shown that when a group first explores the circumstances surrounding a problem before attempting to solve it, they are more likely to produce a creative solution to the problem. They used a three-step procedure. After the problem was presented by the foreman, there was: (1) a brief airing of everyone's view; (2) a listing of the important factors in the problem by the group; and (3) a use of the list as the basis for the final solution. The groups which followed this procedure produced significantly more creative solutions than groups which used the usual free discussion, presumably because the former groups were more likely to consider all facets of the problem before they offered possible solutions.

4. Exploiting Conflict

Hoffman (1961) suggested that ideational conflicts can be conducive to creative problem solving. Faced with differing alternatives, none of which is acceptable to the entire group, the members may be encouraged either to search for new solutions or to integrate the alternative suggestions into a more complete and more effective single possibility. Experimental support for this idea was provided (Hoffman *et al.*, 1962) by encouraging low-status members, via the wording of their role instructions, to oppose the suggestion of a high-status member to change their work method. The resulting conflict produced more creative solutions than did the comparable, less conflictful situations.

One has to be sure, however, that the conflict is based principally on different facts or on different ways of interpreting the facts, rather than on the likes and dislikes the group members have for each other. Guetzkow and Gyr (1954) made this distinction in their comparisons of effective and ineffective management conferences. Successful conferences were marked by substantive conflict, while unsuccessful ones suffered from emotional difficulties.

It is extremely difficult, too, to dissociate your feelings about another persons from your feelings about his ideas (Hoffman, 1961). When someone disagrees with you, you dislike him, yet from disagreement can come creativity.

Furthermore, when differences are resolved creatively, positive feelings are generated. Maier and Hoffman (1964) found that group members were more satisfied with their group's solutions to a role-playing problem where creative solutions emerged than where their initially preferred, but objectively less adequate, solution was adopted. The successful resolution of conflict appears to be a satisfying experience.

C. LEADERSHIP IN GROUP PROBLEM SOLVING

1. The Function of a Leader

Is a leader necessary for the effective functioning of a problem-solving group? In a now classical article, Benne and Sheats (1948) suggested that the important consideration was whether the functions they listed—energizing, recording, harmonizing, etc.—were performed, not who performed them. This proposition has never been tested empirically, so the question remains unanswered.

As pointed out earlier, those who are usually called the group leaders, i.e., those who emerge to direct the operations of the group, do not necessarily help the group reach effective solutions. Furthermore, formally appointed leaders (managers, deans, etc.) tend to dominate and limit the range of discussion. Maier and Solem (1952) showed, however, that a formally appointed leader can enhance a group's effectiveness by ensuring the hearing of a minority, but correct, viewpoint. Without the leader the incorrect viewpoint favored by the majority usually prevailed. Thus, when the leader acts to ensure the free expression of ideas, he enhances the group's effectiveness. If, on the other hand, he tends to dominate the discussion (Section II, C, 2), he hinders the group's operation. He is especially likely to dominate if he holds a position of authority in the group, as was pointed out earlier (Torrance, 1955).

2. Skills and Techniques

Struck by the effectiveness of the "democratic" leader in the studies of children's groups (Lewin et al., 1939; Lippitt, 1940), and seeing the relevance of the non-directive method developed by Rogers (1942, 1951), Maier trained foremen in permissive conference leadership (Maier, 1952, Chapter 2). He evaluated the training by having the trainees and an untrained control group lead role-playing problem-solving conferences. While the control groups produced no creative solutions to the problem, almost 40% of the trained leaders' groups did so (Maier, 1953). Since then Maier has had a continuing interest in developing more refined leadership skills based on empirical research for formal leaders, usually in hierarchial settings (Maier, 1963). While the principles and techniques enunciated thus far require considerable refinement and further development, they seem promising as ways of overcoming some of the barriers to effective problem solving noted earlier and stimulating group members to more creative thought.

These principles and techniques provided a loose framework for a series of experiments concerned with the quality of problem solving by groups. For example, the principle that groups should be *problem-minded* rather than *solution-minded* (Maier, 1958) was tested by Maier and Solem (1962) by having experimental groups review the facts of the problem under the leader's direction, before they tried to solve the problem. In contrast to control groups, these experimental groups produced more than three and a half times as many inventive solutions.

Maier also demonstrated that the quality of a group's decision could be improved when the leader asked stimulating questions causing the group to question its current approach or to consider other aspects of the problem (Maier, 1950). Asking stimulating questions must still be done within the context of a permissive atmosphere which encourages free expression of divergent viewpoints. But this procedure faces difficulties. What the leader considers to be a "stimulating question" may be rejected by the group as irrelevant. When his questions point to facts which merely support his position, they may serve as a barrier to effectiveness. Nevertheless, to the extent that his questions call the group's attention to previously neglected facts, their potential for improving quality is great.

The "developmental discussion" technique (Maier, 1952, p. 53 ff.) was introduced both to separate the influence of feelings and facts on decisions and to ensure the systematic attention of the group to the several facets of the problem. The technique in its most advanced form consists first of analyzing the total problem into sub-parts, then discussing and solving these sub-problems in turn before reaching a final total decision. In this way the group members can avoid the difficulties in communication which arise when two people disagree with each other because they are talking about different facets of a complex problem, not because they truly disagree.

The usefulness of the developmental discussion technique in promoting good solutions to a complex problem has been demonstrated experimentally (Maier and Maier, 1957), especially when the leaders have been trained in its use (Maier and Hoffman, 1960a). Maier succeeded in reducing the proportion of poor quality decisions (in comparison to that produced by permissively led groups) merely by asking group leaders to follow written descriptions of the developmental technique. The majority of decisions were still, however, of poor quality. Maier and Hoffman then trained leaders in the use of the technique and succeeded in producing good decisions in more than 60% of their groups.

The screening principles, noted earlier (Maier, 1960), are the most recent contribution to the discussion leader's skill repertoire. These techniques were designed to depersonalize the evaluation process and focus the group more closely on the facts of a complex, ambiguous, and uncertain problem situation.

Besides these techniques for improving the use of information by a group, leaders in positions of authority have been advised to have their groups come up with two different solutions to a problem from which a choice might be made. An experimental test of this technique on groups of students and nursing administrators showed the second solution to be an inventive one three and a half to five times as often as their first solutions (Maier and Hoffman, 1960b). This process of resolving a problem is thought to have two advantages: (1) it restores the group to a state of *problem-mindedness* (cf. Maier and Solem, 1962) and starts them thinking again about the problem requirements and the character of the information available; and (2) it permits the leader, the authority figure, to pay more attention to the members' views, since his need to arrive at a solution was met by the first solution.

3. Attitudes

The leader's attitude toward the group and toward his proper function as leader also has come under investigation. It is clear that his group's problem solving effectiveness is greater: (1) the more the leader sees his role as stimulating the most creative thoughts in the group and encouraging the members to air their ideas and make their own decisions, and (2) the less he feels it necessary to be the final arbiter of the decision. In one role-playing problem, Solem (1958) instructed half the foremen to decide on the best solution to the problem before they started the meeting. The other half were told merely to present the problem to the group members and to accept their solution. The groups whose foremen had not thought of a solution before the meeting were the more creative. Solem suggests that the group leaders who came into the meeting with a formed opinion were even less open to other ideas than were the "bosses" in the control groups and, therefore, less effective in utilizing the creative potential in the group.

The leader is often not completely free to accept whatever the group's decision is. He is often limited, or believes himself to be limited, by the desires and orders of people above him in the organization to which he and the other group members belong. Epstein (1955) reported an ingenious attempt to introduce the leader's organizational superiors into the group problem-solving discussion by means of instructions. As part of the leader's role instructions, he was told that his boss had asked him to solve his problem and would either (1) support whatever he came up with, or (2) support actions only within a limited realm. The clarity of each of these admonitions was also varied. The major differences in quality of solutions favored the clearly free leaders over the clearly restricted leaders, with the leaders given vague instructions of both types producing solutions of intermediate quality. The clearly restricted foremen tended to be more concerned with management's goals and less with the workers', to restrict discussion, and generally to reject the various ideas brought forth by the group members. Thus, the process of effective group problem solving may be hampered by the leader's attitude, which is created by his perception of higher management's expectations.

D. ACCEPTANCE

These leadership principles and techniques have been developed to improve the quality of problem solving in groups. They have grown, however, within the context of a free and permissive discussion atmosphere, which reflects Lewin's concern (cf. K. Lewin, 1947) about the members' identification with the group's decision. In keeping with this concern, Maier early distinguished between two dimensions of a solution to a problem—*quality* and *acceptance* (Maier, 1952). Quality "refers to the objective features of a decision" while acceptance "refers to the degree to which the group that must execute the decision accepts it" (Maier, 1963, p. 253). The theoretical usefulness of this distinction lies in the fact that the quality of a decision reflects the group's ability to produce and utilize information effectively, while acceptance reflects the members' feelings about the solution and about the way it was reached. This is a helpful distinction since effective real-life decisions require both high quality and high acceptance, else they fail from lack of attention to the facts or from the members' unwillingness to carry out the decision. Yet the two concepts merge, as Hoffman (1961) demonstrated. Our ideas at times are so affect-laden that we feel proud when they are accepted by the group. If they are rejected, on the other hand, we may feel rejected also and may lower our regard for the group.

A number of experiments have investigated the relationship between acceptance and quality. Acceptance has been measured most often by the subjects' responses to a five- or six-point, Likert-type question, "How satisfied are you with the group's solution?" While such an item can have but limited reliability, it has been employed successfully and certainly has face validity as a measure of acceptance.

In the studies noted earlier, which compared the problem-solving effectiveness of groups composed of heterogeneous and homogeneous personalities (Hoffman, 1959; Hoffman and Maier, 1961a), the heterogeneous groups produced higher quality solutions than did the homogeneous groups, but the general level of members' satisfaction with the solutions hardly differed. Correlations between the quality score and members' satisfaction ratings further confirmed the lack of relationship between the quality and acceptance of solutions in these groups. Furthermore, members' ratings of satisfaction with the solutions were highly correlated with the subjects' own ratings of satisfaction with their influence over the decision, although they were uncorrelated with the other members' ratings of each member's influence over the decision. Thus, acceptance seems to be related to the freedom of the problem solving process, rather than to the objective quality of the decision itself. A group member will feel satisfied to the extent that he feels he has influenced the group decision appropriately.

The importance of the leader in promoting this feeling of shared influence and, thereby, encouraging member acceptance is illustrated in studies by Maier and Hoffman (1960b; 1962). When members were asked whether their leader used group decision making or whether he made the final decision himself, members of groups characterized by unilateral decisions were least satisfied with the decision, while members of group-decision groups were most satisfied. The proportion of satisfied members in a group had no relationship to the character of the solution produced.

More recent research, using a newly developed method for quantifying the problem-solving interaction in a group, provides additional evidence. These findings suggest that the most important factor in determining the members' acceptance of a solution to a complex problem is the amount of influence they actually exerted over the final decision (Hoffman et al., 1963). The rated satisfaction with the solution was correlated .59 with the amount of verbal support given by the member for the solution finally adopted by the group. Considering the modest reliability of the satisfaction measure, this value probably accounts for a considerable portion of the common variance. Acceptance, again, was completely unrelated to the quality of the solution.

If this relationship is confirmed in future studies, it suggests that acceptance can be increased if everybody is encouraged to express his feelings about the solution to be adopted. If the feelings are favorable, their expression will presumably promote the member's commitment to the decision. If unfavorable feelings are exhibited, however, they may be emotionally based and their mere expression may relieve the resistance to the proposed solution. Voicing negative feelings which are based upon information can promote a search for new and perhaps superior alternatives. High acceptance and high quality, while not necessarily positively correlated, may be associated when the problem-solving process considers both aspects of the solution. The leader's attitudes and skills will be of paramount importance in determining their joint consideration.

IV. The Present State of Group Problem-Solving Research

Although the history of the experimental study of group problem solving is a long one, it is replete with discontinuities. A survey of the literature reveals numerous difficulties which have been relatively ignored over the years, but which have retarded the advance of knowledge in this area. An enumeration of these difficulties may help in defining problems for needed research and analysis.

A. THE NATURE OF PROBLEM-SOLVING TASKS

1. Problem Content

One of the foremost difficulties concerns the term "problem solving" itself. Problem solving has been used with reference to tasks as varied as judging the number of dots briefly displayed on a large card, to providing answers to arithmetic reasoning problems, to solving the complex problems faced by the managements of large business organizations. On a priori grounds one might expect that the factors producing effective performance should vary greatly in these different types of problems, just as qualitatively different abilities are required for individuals to solve simple addition problems as against problems in topology, even though both are "mathematics" problems. This rather obvious point has generally been neglected. It calls for the systematic development of a taxonomy of problems.[4]

The few experiments in which the same groups solved more than one problem have almost invariably produced discrepant or ambiguous conclusions. For example, in our study of the effects on group problem solving of homogeneous personality composition (Hoffman and Maier, 1961a) the same groups were compared on four different problems. The quality of the solutions produced varied considerably from problem to problem, as did the magnitudes of the differences between the two types of groups. At our present state of knowledge it is impossible to identify the causes of these variations in results. In some general sense all of the problems are somewhat similar; they are all complex and deal with relations among people in quasi-real situations. There were many specific differences, however, in the character of the problems and in the circumstances surrounding their administration and scoring which could account, singly or in combination, for the differences obtained. As one question we might ask, what different requirements are placed on groups when all the members share all the information, as compared to problems where only part of the information is generally known?

The data obtained from this study show clearly that the assigned problems elicited substantially different amounts of problem-related activity among the group members. In addition, we found consistent differences among groups as well as significant and varied interactions between groups and problems (Hoffman and Smith, 1960). In other words, each problem produced a particular reaction from the group members, which was modified somewhat by the idiosyncratic nature of the groups to which they belonged. Our inability to identify these behavioral differences in relation to the quality of the group products limits our ability to theorize about the determinants of effective problem solving.

2. Grading the Quality of Solutions

Related to these difficulties is the lack of suitable methods for assessing the quality of solutions to complex problems. How can we compare,

---

[4] This need for a taxonomy of problems, as I have indicated elsewhere (Hoffman, 1961), is also pressing in the study of individual problem solving, but Guilford's work (J. P. Guilford, 1956) in this area has provided at least one approach to its satisfaction.

using an appropriate metric, the adequacy of the solutions to altogether different problems? Thus, on one problem used in the previously cited study of homogeneous and heterogeneous groups the range of possible scores went from 0 to 100, while on another problem there were only three qualitatively different categories of solutions. If we try to answer the question, "Did the homogeneous groups do relatively worse on the one problem than the other?" we are stymied by a lack of comparable scales for measuring solution quality. If, as was done, we compare the percentage of groups of each type whose solutions were above the median score on each problem, we ignore possible differences in the difficulty level of the two problems. To the extent that the problems are either very easy or very difficult, the effects of the experimental variation may be obscured. I believe we will not develop adequate, comparative scoring systems until a method for identifying task requirements is obtained. Without a good theoretical reason for making particular distinctions among solutions to problems, scores assigned to represent differences in quality must remain arbitrary and limit the generality of most experimental results (Coombs, 1963).

3. Analysis of the Process

Roby and Lanzetta (1958) made the most systematic attempt to provide an adequate framework for a taxonomy of group problems. Although their paradigm was designed for use with all group tasks and populations of groups, they illustrated its application to the "common symbol" task, which is used so frequently in studies of communication nets. They first recommend that the properties of the problem and the distribution of these properties among the group members be described in elemental terms. There then can be an analysis of the ways in which these properties are transformed during the group interaction into some output (the group's solution). Recognizing that we are unable to describe the elements of the task and the group members so specifically at present, Roby and Lanzetta suggested a more macroscopic analysis of the task and the group process in terms of the "critical demands" required to produce an effective solution.

Unfortunately, little effort has been directed toward applying this paradigm to group problem solving. Most systems for observing group interaction (e.g., Bales, 1950; Heyns and Lippitt, 1954) ignore the relevance of what is being said for the solutions to the problem. These systems, while useful for determining the general socioemotional versus task atmosphere of the group interaction, yield little information about the quality of such interaction for effective group problem solving. The assumption, frequently made, "that the process would surely be self-defeating and self-limiting if there were more . . . negative reactions than positive" (Bales, 1953) must be open to question in view of our findings of the creative possibilities in exploiting conflict among group members (Hoffman *et al.*, 1962).

A few attempts have been made to relate the activities of the group to the solutions produced. Oakes *et al.* (1960), in reinforcing suggestions for particular solutions, recorded the number of suggestions made for each of three solutions. They found an increase in the number of favorable comments made for the arbitrarily reinforced solution, which led to its selection by the group in most cases. Hoffman and Maier (1964) developed a more elaborate system, based on some ideas proposed by Hoffman (1961), for recording the types of comments made about the suggested solutions offered in a group. They distinguish among several different types of remarks, e.g., descriptions of the solution, justifications for it, criticisms of it, both favorable and unfavorable. With this technique they were able to follow the course of a potential solution through the group discussion and found consistent relationships with the group's selection of a final solution and with the members' satisfaction with the decision.

Such recording systems, however, represent only a beginning in the analysis of the cognitive aspects of group problem solving. There also should be a systematic examination of the way the information available to the group is offered and used. As Roby and Lanzetta (1958) implied, giving more attention to the cognitive requirements of group problem-solving tasks may greatly increase our understanding of the group problem-solving process.

B. POPULATION CHARACTERISTICS

1. Group Composition

A collateral difficulty arises from the fact that the particular characteristics of the groups studied may severely restrict the generality of the results obtained. While most experiments have been conducted on that favorite subject, the college freshman or sophomore, the intellectual quality of students at different universities varies considerably and may often be the principal source of discrepant conclusions in similar experiments (e.g., Shaw, 1961). Calvin *et al.* (1957) compared groups of "low" I.Q. and "high" I.Q. students in "authoritarian" and "permissive" experimental atmospheres on Twenty Questions problems at Michigan State and Hollins Colleges. In two sessions run in Michigan, the permissive, bright subjects used fewer questions per problem and solved a higher percentage of problems, while at Hollins the results showed a slightly reversed trend.

Similarly, the oft-noted description of subjects as "members of a class in introductory psychology" neglects the sex composition of the group (a group characteristic whose importance has already been discussed; in Section III, A, 2, a), as well as other factors such as age, personality, socio-economic status, etc. The unknown characteristics of groups formed from other populations, of course, also should limit statements regarding the generality of the experimental results, but rarely do. The approaches taken by Cattell and Wispe (1948) and by Hemphill and Westie (1950) in identifying the dimensions of groups on a variety of tasks could be followed profitably in more specific studies of group problem solving. If such an effort sampled groups from many diverse populations, it would provide a framework of norms into which specific experiments could be classified. Until the characteristics of different populations relevant to problem solving have been systematically studied and identified, the comparative interpretation of different experimental results will remain obscure.

2. Real and Ad Hoc Groups

In the same vein, the criticism by Lorge et al. (1958) that the groups studied in comparison with individuals are almost invariably ad hoc, temporary groups without history, tradition or norms, holds almost equally true for studies of group problem solving per se. Unfortunately, these authors provided no directions or clues as to the differences one might expect to find between these two types of groups. Their criticism, while potentially valid, thus serves principally as a reminder that generalizations from experiments on ad hoc groups may have only questionable validity for "traditioned" groups.[5]

Probably the major difficulties which experimenters avoid by remaining with the study of laboratory groups are: (1) the lack of comparability of problems, and (2) the members' involvement in the problems, which one meets in studying the problem solving of real groups. As mentioned earlier, even in comparing groups of men and women on laboratory problems, we find that the females' reduced motivation often results in poor performance. To try to find a problem which might be of considerable interest to a sample of executives from different companies is clearly an almost insuperable obstacle.

The Michigan Conference Research Project (Guetzkow and Gyr, 1954) encountered a major difficulty in trying to study the problem solving of executive groups in business and government. Their decision to use

[5] Before I am accused of taking a "holier-than-thou" position about these difficulties, I should like to admit my own contributions to these problems and recognize the considerable difficulty in overcoming them.

the number of agenda items completed as an index of the effectiveness of the meetings observed seems a far cry from even the arbitrary systems discussed earlier. In a number of cases an agenda item was "completed" by tabling it for the future, presumably when the conflict it generated in the group could not be resolved. An ability to classify different tasks would probably have helped immeasurably.

Another difficulty in studying real groups stems from the experimenter's usual lack of knowledge of the past history of the group. In a typical existing group the members have developed a shorthand language through their shared experiences which permits them to refer to complex issues in terms foreign to the outside observer. To study a group solving its real problems, the experimenter must familiarize himself with the group's history and environment. This often requires more time than we care to invest. Unless we are willing to spend the time required to study groups outside University and college settings, we must settle for a very restricted theory of group problem solving.

These difficulties—the absence of taxonomies for types of problems and for populations of groups and of systems for describing the cognitive aspects of the problem-solving process—have provided major barriers to any attempt to integrate the literature on group problem solving. With rare exceptions there has been a notable lack of a continued, consistent, and additive effort in this area. The typical experimenter does one or two studies on a single facet of the topic, with a problem (described in too general and vague terms) which nobody else has ever used. He produces suggestive, but inconclusive results, and is never heard from again. This practice has left the literature on group problem solving a large conglomeration of unrelated experiments, with only the faintest suggestion of commonality. Also, most of the experiments to date have concentrated on identifying the barriers to effective problem solving, rather than on discovering means to stimulate group creativity. Admittedly, the barriers discovered so far occur so ubiquitously that, unless they are overcome, the chance of promoting creative problem solving is rather small. Nevertheless, effort directed to inventing and testing new ways of encouraging creative group problem solving should advance our understanding of the problem-solving process and, when successful, would have practical value for society as well.

REFERENCES

Allport, F. H. (1924). *Social psychology*. Boston, Mass.: Houghton Mifflin.
Asch, S. E. (1956). Studies of independence and conformity. A minority of one against a unanimous majority. *Psychol. Monogr.* **70**, No. 9 (Whole No. 416).
Bales, R. F. (1950). *Interaction process analysis: a method for the study of small groups*. Reading, Mass.: Addison-Wesley.

Bales, R. F. (1953). The equilibrium problem in small groups. In T. Parsons, R. F. Bales, and E. A. Shils (Eds.), *Working papers in the theory of action.* New York: Free Press, 111–161.

Bales, R. F., and Borgatta, E. F. (1955). Size of group as a factor in the interaction profile. In A. P. Hare, E. F. Borgatta, and R. F. Bales (Eds.), *Small groups: studies in social interaction.* New York: Knopf, pp. 396–413.

Bales, R. F., and Strodtbeck, F. L. (1951). Phases in group problem solving. *J. abnorm. soc. Psychol.* 46, 485–495.

Bass, B. M. (1963). Amount of participation, coalescence and profitability of decision-making discussions. *J. abnorm. soc. Psychol.* 67, 92–94.

Benne, K. D., and Sheats, P. (1948). Functional roles of group members. *J. soc. Issues* 4, 41–49.

Bennett, Edith (1955). Discussion, decision, commitment and consensus in "group decision." *Hum. Relat.* 8, 251–274.

Berkowitz, L. (1956). Personality and group position. *Sociometry* 19, 210–222.

Berkowitz, L. (1957). Liking for the group and the perceived merit of the group's behavior. *J. abnorm. soc. Psychol.* 54, 353–357.

Berkowitz, L., and Levy, B. I. (1956). Pride in group performance and group task motivation. *J. abnorm. soc. Psychol.* 53, 300–306.

Bion, W. R. (1959). *Experiences in Groups.* New York: Basic Books.

Blake, R. R., and Mouton, Jane S. (1961). *Group dynamics—key to decision making.* Houston, Texas: Gulf Publ. Co.

Calvin, A. D., Hoffmann, F. K., and Harden, E. L. (1957). The effect of intelligence and social atmosphere on group problem solving behavior. *J. soc. Psychol.* 45, 61–74.

Carey, Gloria J. (1958). Sex differences in problem-solving performance as a function of attitude differences. *J. abnorm. soc. Psychol.* 56, 256–260.

Cattell, R. B., and Wispe, L. G. (1948). The dimensions of syntality in small groups. *J. soc. Psychol.* 28, 57–78.

Cohen, A. M., and Bennis, W. G. (1962). Predicting organization in changed communication networks. *J. Psychol.* 54, 391–416.

Comrey, A. L., and Staats, Carolyn K. (1955). Group performance in a cognitive task. *J. appl. Psychol.* 39, 354–356.

Coombs, C. H. (1963). *A theory of data.* New York: Wiley.

Crockett, W. H. (1955). Emergent leadership in small, decision-making groups. *J. abnorm. soc. Psychol.* 51, 378–383.

Crutchfield, R. S. (1959). Personal and situational factors in conformity to group pressure. *Acta Psychol.* 15, 386–388.

Deutsch, M. and Krauss, R. M. (1960). The effect of threat upon interpersonal bargaining. *J. abnorm. soc. Psychol.* 61, 181–189.

Dunnette, M. D., Campbell, J., and Jaastad, Kay (1963). The effect of group participation on brainstorming effectiveness for two industrial samples. *J. appl. Psychol.* 47, 30–37.

Ekman, G. (1955). The four effects of cooperation. *J. soc. Psychol.* 41, 149–162.

Epstein, S. (1955). An experimental study of some of the effect of variations in the clarity and extent of a supervisor's area of freedom upon his supervisory behavior. Unpublished Ph.D. thesis, Univer. of Michigan.

Feather, N. T. (1961). The relationship of persistence at a task to expectation of success and achievement related motives. *J. abnorm. soc. Psychol.* 63, 552–561.

Fiedler, F. E., and Meuwese, W. A. T. (1963). Leader's contribution to task performance in cohesive and uncohesive groups. *J. abnorm. soc. Psychol.* **67**, 83–87.

Fiedler, F. E., Meuwese, W., and Oonk, Sophie (1961). An exploratory study of group creativity in laboratory tasks. *Acta Psychol.* **18**, 100–119.

Fouriezos, N. T., Hutt, M. L., and Guetzkow, H. (1950). Measurement of self-oriented needs in discussion groups. *J. abnorm. soc. Psychol.* **45**, 682–690.

Ghiselli, E. E., and Lodahl, T. M. (1958). Patterns of managerial traits and group effectiveness. *J. abnorm. soc. Psychol.* **57**, 61–66.

Guetzkow, H., and Gyr, J. (1954). An analysis of conflict in decision-making groups. *Hum. Relat.* **7**, 367–382.

Guilford, Joan S. (1952). Temperament traits of executives and supervisors measured by the Guilford personality inventories. *J. appl. Psychol.* **36**, 228–233.

Guilford, J. P. (1956). The structure of intellect. *Psychol. Bull.* **53**, 267–293.

Hemphill, J. K., and Westie, C. M. (1950). The measurement of group dimensions. *J. Psychol.* **29**, 325–342.

Hemphill, J. K., Pepinsky, Pauline N., Kaufman, A. E., and Lipetz, M. E. (1957). Effects of task motivation and expectancy of accomplishment upon attempts to lead. *Psychol. Monogr.* **71**, No. 22 (Whole no. 451).

Heyns, R. W., and Lippitt, R. (1954). Systematic observational techniques. In G. Lindzey (Ed.), *Handbook of social psychology.* Reading, Mass.: Addison-Wesley, pp. 370–404.

Hochbaum, G. M. (1954). The relation between group members' selfconfidence and their reactions to group pressures to uniformity. *Amer. sociol. Rev.* **79**, 678–687.

Hoffman, L. R. (1959). Homogeneity of member personality and its effect on group problem-solving *J. abnorm. soc. Psychol.* **58**, 27–32.

Hoffman, L. R. (1961). Conditions for creative problem solving. *J. Psychol.* **52**, 429–444.

Hoffman, L. R., and Maier, N. R. F. (1961a). Quality and acceptance of problem solutions by members of homogeneous and heterogeneous groups. *J. abnorm. soc. Psychol.* **62**, 401–407.

Hoffman, L. R., and Maier, N. R. F. (1961b). Sex differences, sex composition, and group problem solving. *J. abnorm. soc. Psychol.* **63**, 453–456.

Hoffman, L. R., and Maier, N. R. F. (1964). Valence in the adoption of solutions by problem-solving groups: concept, method and results. *J. abnorm. soc. Psychol.* **69**, 264–271.

Hoffman, L. R., and Smith, C. G. (1960). Some factors affecting the behaviors of members of problem-solving groups. *Sociometry* **23**, 273–291.

Hoffman, L. R., Harburg, E., and Maier, N. R. F. (1962). Differences and disagreement as factors in creative group problem solving. *J. abnorm. soc. Psychol.* **64**, 206–214.

Hoffman, L. R., Burke, R. J., and Maier, N. R. F. (1963). Does training with differential reinforcement on similar problems help in solving a new problem? *Psychol. Rep.* **13**, 147–154.

Jackson, J. M., and Saltzstein, H. D. (1958). The effect of person-group relationships on conformity processes. *J. abnorm. soc. Psychol.* **57**, 17–24.

Kaess, W. A., Witryol, S. L., and Nolan, R. E. (1961). Reliability, sex differences, and validity in the leaderless group discussion technique. *J. appl. Psychol.* **45**, 345–350.

Kidd, J. S., and Campbell, D. T. (1955). Conformity to groups as a function of group success. *J. abnorm. soc. Psychol.* **51**, 390–393.

Kirscht, J. P., Lodahl, T. M., and Haire, M. (1959). Some factors in the selection of leaders by members of small groups. *J. abnorm. soc. Psychol.* **58**, 406–408.

Lewin, K. (1947). Group decision and social change. In T. M. Newcomb and E. L. Hartley (Eds.) *Readings in Social Psychology.* New York: Holt, pp. 330–344.

Lewin, K., Lippitt, R., and White, R. K. (1939). Patterns of aggressive behavior in experimentally created "social climates." *J. soc. Psychol.* **10**, 271–299.

Lippitt, R. (1940). An experimental study of the effect of democratic and authoritarian group atmosphere. *Univer. Iowa Stud. Child Welf.* No. 16.

Loomis, J. L. (1959). Communication, the development of trust, and cooperative behavior. *Hum. Relat.* **12**, 305–315.

Lorge, I., and Solomon, H. (1955). Two models of group behavior in the solution of Eureka-type problems. *Psychometrika* **20**, 139–148.

Lorge, I., Fox, D., Davitz, J., and Brenner, M. (1958). A survey of studies contrasting the quality of group performance and individual performance, 1920–1957. *Psychol. Bull.* **55**, 337–372.

Maier, N. R. F. (1930). Reasoning in humans. I. On direction. *J. comp. Psychol.* **10**, 115–143.

Maier, N. R. F. (1950). The quality of group decisions as influenced by the discussion leader. *Hum. Relat.* **3**, 155–174.

Maier, N. R. F. (1952). *Principles of Human Relations.* New York: Wiley.

Maier, N. R. F. (1953). An experimental test of the effect of training on discussion leadership. *Hum. Relat.* **6**, 161–173.

Maier, N. R. F. (1958). The appraisal interview: objectives, methods and skills. New York: Wiley.

Maier, N. R. F. (1960). Screening solutions to upgrade quality: A new approach to problem solving under conditions of uncertainty. *J. Psychol.* **49**, 217–231.

Maier, N. R. F. (1963). *Problem-solving discussions and conferences: leadership methods and skills.* New York: McGraw-Hill.

Maier, N. R. F., and Hoffman, L. R. (1960a). Using trained "developmental" discussion leaders to improve further the quality of group decisions. *J. appl. Psychol.* **44**, 247–251.

Maier, N. R. F., and Hoffman, L. R. (1960b). Quality of first and second solutions in group problem solving. *J. appl. Psychol.* **44**, 278–283.

Maier, N. R. F., and Hoffman, L. R. (1961). Organization and creative problem solving. *J. appl. Psychol.* **45**, 277–280.

Maier, N. R. F., and Hoffman, L. R. (1962). Group decision in England and the United States. *Personnel Psychol.* **15**, 75–87.

Maier, N. R. F., and Hoffman, L. R. (1964). Financial incentives and group decision in motivating change. *J. soc. Psychol.* **64**, 369–378.

Maier, N. R. F., and Maier, R. A. (1957). An experimental test of the effects of "developmental" vs. "free" discussions on the quality of group decisions. *J. appl. Psychol.* **41**, 320–323.

Maier, N. R. F., and Solem, A. R. (1952). The contribution of a discussion leader to the quality of group thinking: the effective use of minority opinions. *Hum. Relat.* **5**, 277–288.

Maier, N. R. F., and Solem, A. R. (1962). Improving solutions by turning choice situations into problems. *Personn. Psychol.* **15**, 151–157.

Mann, R. D. (1959). The relation between personality characteristics and individual performance in small groups. Unpublished Ph.D. thesis, Univer. of Michigan.

Mann, R. D. (1961). Dimensions of individual performance in small groups under task and social-emotional conditions. *J. abnorm. soc. Psychol.* **62**, 674–682.

Mausner, B. (1954). The effect of one partner's success in a relevant task on the interaction of observer pairs. *J. abnorm. soc. Psychol.* **49**, 557–560.

Mellinger, G. D. (1956). Interpersonal trust as a factor in communication. *J. abnorm. soc. Psychol.* **52**, 304–309.

Milton, G. A. (1958). Five studies of the relation between sex-role identification and achievement in problem solving. Tech. Rep. No. 3, Departments of Industrial Administration and Psychology, Yale University [Contract Nonr609 (20)].

Oakes, W. F. (1962). Effectiveness of signal light reinforcers given various meanings on participation in group discussion. *Psychol. Rep.* **11**, 469–470.

Oakes, W. F., Droge, A. E., and August, Barbara (1960). Reinforcement effects on participation in group discussion. *Psychol. Rep.* **7**, 503–514.

Orne, M. T. (1962). On the social psychology of the psychological experiment: with particular reference to demand characteristics and their implications. *Amer. Psychologist* **17**, 776–783.

Osborn, A. F. (1953). *Applied Imagination.* New York: Scribner's.

Palmer, G. J. Jr. (1962). Task ability and effective leadership. *Psychol. Rep.* **10**, 863–866.

Parnes, S. F., and Meadow, A. (1959). Effects of "brainstorming" instructions on creative problem solving by trained and untrained subjects. *J. educ. Psychol.* **50**, 171–176.

Pennington, D. F., Jr., Haravey, F., and Bass, B. M. (1958). Some effects of decision and discussion on coalescence, change, and effectiveness. *J. appl. Psychol.* **42**, 404–408.

Pepinsky, Pauline, Hemphill, J. K., and Shevitz, R. N. (1958). Attempts to lead, group productivity, and morale under conditions of acceptance and rejection. *J. abnorm. soc. Psychol.* **57**, 47–54.

Read, W. H. (1962). Upward communication in industrial hierarchies. *Hum. Relat.* **15**, 3–15.

Riecken, H. W. (1958). The effect of talkativeness on ability to influence group solutions of problems. *Sociometry* **21**, 309–321.

Roby, T. B., and Lanzetta, J. T. (1958). Considerations in the analysis of group tasks. *Psychol. Bull.* **55**, 88–101.

Roby, T. B., and Lanzetta, J. T. (1961). A study of an "assembly effect" in small group task performance. *J. soc. Psychol.* **53**, 53–68.

Rogers, C. R., (1942). *Counseling and psychotherapy.* Boston, Mass.: Houghton-Mifflin.

Rogers, C. R. (1951). *Client-centered therapy.* Boston, Mass.: Houghton-Mifflin.

Schachter, S. (1951). Deviation, rejection, and communication. *J. abnorm. soc. Psychol.* **46**, 190–207.

Shaw, M. E. (1959). Some effects of individually prominent behavior upon group effectiveness and member satisfaction. *J. abnorm. soc. Psychol.* **59**, 382–386.

Shaw, M. E. (1960). A note concerning homogeneity of membership and group problem solving. *J. abnorm. soc. Psychol.* **60**, 448–450.

Shaw, M. E. (1961). Some factors influencing the use of information in small groups. *Psychol. Rep.* **8**, 187–198.

Shaw, M. E. (1963). Some effects of varying amounts of information exclusively possessed by a group member upon his behavior in the group. *J. gen. Psychol.* **68,** 71–79.

Shaw, M. E., and Gilchrist, J. C. (1956). Intra-group communication and leader choice. *J. soc. Psychol.* **43,** 133–138.

Shaw, M. E., and Penrod, W. T., Jr. (1962). Does more information available to a group always improve group performance? *Sociometry* **25,** 377–390.

Shure, G. H., Rogers, M. S., Larsen, Ida M., and Tassone, J. (1962). Group planning and task effectiveness. *Sociometry* **25,** 263–282.

Slater, P. E. (1955). Role differentiation in small groups. *Amer. sociol. Rev.* **20,** 300–310.

Solem, A. R. (1958). An evaluation of two attitudinal approaches to delegation. *J. appl. Psychol.* **42,** 36–39.

Springborn, B. A. (1963). Some determinants and consequences of the locus of evaluation in small group problem solving. Unpublished Ph.D. thesis, Univer. of Michigan.

Stephan, F. F., and Mishler, E. G. (1952). The distribution of participation in small groups: an exponential approximation. *Amer. sociol. Rev.* **17,** 598–608.

Stock, Dorothy, and Thelen, H. A. (1958). *Emotional dynamics and group culture.* Washington, D.C.: National Training Laboratory.

Taylor, D. W., Berry, P. C., and Block, C. H. (1958). Does group participation when using brainstorming facilitate or inhibit creative thinking? *Admin. sci. Quart.* **3,** 23–47.

Thomas, E. J., and Fink, C. F. (1961). Models of group problem solving. *J. abnorm. soc. Psychol.* **68,** 53–63.

Thorndike, R. L. (1938). The effect of discussion upon the correctness of group decisions, when the factor of majority influence is allowed for. *J. soc. Psychol.* **9,** 343–362.

Timmons, W. M. (1942). Can the product superiority of discussors be attributed to averaging or majority influences? *J. soc. Psychol.* **15,** 23–32.

Torrance, E. P. (1955). Some consequences of power differences on decision making in permanent and temporary three-man groups. In A. P. Hare, E. F. Borgatta, and R. F. Bales (Eds.), *Small groups: studies in social interaction.* New York: Knopf, pp. 482–492.

Triandis, H. C., Mikesell, Eleanor H., and Ewen, R. B. (1962). Task set and attitudinal heterogeneity as determinants of dyadic creativity. Tech. Rep. No. 8, Univer. Illinois.

Tuckman, J., and Lorge, I. (1962). Individual ability as a determinant of group superiority. *Hum. Relat.* **15,** 45–51.

Tuddenham, R. D. (1959). Correlates of yielding to a distorted group norm. *J. Pers.* **27,** 272–284.

Weisskopf-Joelson, Edith, and Eliseo, T. (1961). An experimental study of the effectiveness of brainstorming. *J. appl. Psychol.* **45,** 45–49.

Wiest, W., Porter, L. W., and Ghiselli, E. E. (1961). Relationships between individual proficiency and team performance and efficiency. *J. appl. Psychol.* **45,** 435–440.

Ziller, R. C., and Exline, R. V. (1958). Some consequences of age heterogeneity in decision-making groups. *Sociometry,* **21,** 198–211.

SITUATIONAL FACTORS IN CONFORMITY[1]

Vernon L. Allen
DEPARTMENT OF PSYCHOLOGY
UNIVERSITY OF WISCONSIN
MADISON, WISCONSIN

I. Introduction

A. CONTEXT OF CONTEMPORARY RESEARCH

One of the most active research areas in social psychology in recent years has been the study of the conformity of the individual to the group.

[1] Helpful comments on this paper were made by J. C. Gilchrist and I. D. Steiner.

Interest in this problem is not at all a new development. Terman's (1904) investigations, for example, are not dissimilar to contemporary research on conformity, both in terms of substance and methodology. That groups exert influence upon their members is not a startling disclosure to social psychologists. Two series of studies have, nevertheless, dramatized the fact in clear and convincing fashion. Much of the impetus to the recent research on group influence is due to the classic studies of Sherif (1935) and Asch (1951). Sherif's experiment served as a paradigm for the formation and change of social norms, while Asch's study demonstrated that influence of the group extended even to matters of undisputed fact.

The term conformity has acquired a variety of meanings, some of which were intended to be explanatory and the others only descriptive. Sometimes the term is used to "explain" an instance of agreement of a person with a group. This type of explanation has been common practice in the past. By contrast, the term "conformity" is frequently used in contemporary research, and will be used in this paper, to *describe* behavior which is influenced by a group, the result being to create increased congruence between the individual and the group. According to this usage, then, the term "social influence" is broader than conformity; conformity is only one instance of social influence, and is here said to result from other group members' opposition to the individual's views. Care must be taken to distinguish between this particular definition of conformity and other cases of uniformity of behavior. Conformity should not be equated with behavioral uniformity which is the result of persons responding independently to the same stimuli in the absence of group pressure (i.e., opposition from other group members).

Conformity has often been contrasted with nonconformity or independence, terms implying the failure of attempted group influence. To regard conformity as the opposite of nonconformity as Walker and Heyns (1962) do, or of independence as Asch (1952) and Crutchfield (1955) do, assumes a continuum with conformity at one end and its opposite (nonconformity or independence) at the other. Such unidimensional formulations are inadequate, according to some writers (Krech et al., 1962; Willis and Hollander, 1964) who argue that nonconformity consists of two conceptually distinct types of behavior. Nonconformity may reflect independence, or it may actually be anticonformity (or as Crutchfield calls it, counterformity). These three types of behavior—conformity, independence, and anticonformity—are related to each other as the apexes of a triangle. Therefore, it is necessary to posit at least two dimensions: conformity—anticonformity, and independence—dependence (Willis, 1963).

The two-dimensional conception emphasizes that both conformers and anticonformers are similar in the sense that both take cognizance of the group norm to an unusual degree; the conformer in order to agree with the norm, the anticonformer in order to disagree. The independent differs from both the conformer and the anticonformer in evaluating the stimulus independently of the group norm, i.e., the norm is not given any weight in his judgment. It is not suggested that a person engages exclusively in one of these types of responses. The formulation is not a typology of persons but a differentiation of responses. A person may exhibit all three types of responses within an experimental session.

When the term conformity is used, it is understood that we mean conformity to something. In studying the influence of a group, social psychologists usually deal with the effect of social pressure in producing conformity to a group norm or standard. Most current research is conducted with a small group, or as Goffman (1961) so aptly puts it, a "little group" of four or five persons. Only a few studies have used natural groups. Sometimes an attempt is made to enhance the interdependence among group members. But by and large, no effort is made to create a psychological relationship among an aggregation of individuals. To claim that most current research deals only with temporary collections of people who interact little if at all is not necessarily a cogent criticism. For purposes of generalization, the type of groups typically employed is probably representative of the kind of relationships we often have with other persons.

A norm usually refers to a set of expectations held by members of a group concerning how one ought to behave (Rommetveit, 1955). Strictly and operationally speaking, however, most research on conformity deals with the (usually manipulated) majority or consensus among group members, and has little to do with these "ought" or morally obligatory qualities. Nevertheless, pressure is generally placed on the individual member to adhere to the group consensus. The concept of social pressure used in conjunction with conformity research has a variety of operational meanings. In its most general sense, the term means that group members oppose a person, either actively or passively. In some experiments, the individual is the object of active social pressure communicated by face-to-face oral or written discussion in which others may urge him to change his position. In other experiments social pressure is passive, consisting only of the naive subject's awareness that other group members disagree with him.

It is worth noting in passing that conformity has captured the interest of social psychologists and laymen alike and has been thoroughly censured by both. We can readily understand why conformity has acquired a negative connotation. For many people the term implies a slavish submission to others or a cowardly yielding of one's own beliefs. Consistent with such an interpretation, most psychological experiments in this area have been designed in such a manner that conformity was by necessity maladaptive: factually incorrect, detrimental to the group and the individual, or simply dishonest. Such a view of conformity is often oversimplified, however. Conformity frequently improves the functioning of a group. Further, a person may go along with beliefs expressed by most of the other people around him because he realizes that opinions shared by many are often more likely to be correct than the opinions held by a single individual, and that to be too honest may be embarrassing and inappropriate. That conformity can serve a very positive function is illustrated dramatically by Milgram's (1965) study. In some situations conformity is constructive and appropriate; in other situations it is not.

B. SCOPE OF THE PRESENT PAPER

The present paper will be restricted to experimental studies of the influence of small face-to-face groups on the behavior of the individual. Excluded are other types of social influence such as persuasive communication, studies of two-person interaction, and imitation. Such investigations will be referred to when directly relevant, but our focus will be on the effect of the group on the individual. It can be argued that all studies of social influence, in the broadest sense of the term, are pertinent to the group pressure situation. This is probably true in general, although evidence exists that different kinds of social influence situations are not correlated (Stukat, 1958; Moore, 1964). At any rate, within a group certain phenomena may occur which are not possible in a two-person influence or persuasive communication situation (e.g., coalitions, a deviant against a majority). The scope of the paper will also be limited to situational factors, that is, conditions which are manipulated experimentally. The role of stable, individual properties and dispositions will be excluded. Thus, this chapter will not deal with correlates of conformity such as personality and physiological variables.

II. Public Compliance and Private Change

A. TAXONOMY OF GROUP INFLUENCE

One of the most important advances in the area of group influence has been the realization that conformity and nonconformity cannot be satisfactorily conceptualized by restricting analysis to the phenotypic level. Two responses which are phenotypically identical may differ in terms of their meaning for the individual, tne psychological processes which produced them, and in consequences for future behavior.

In attempting to differentiate meaningfully among the various categories of a gross concept such as conformity, two salient dimensions which must be considered are the nature of the public and the private response given in the face of opposition by the group. Festinger (1953), Jahoda (1959), and Kelman (1958) have stressed the importance of making such a distinction.

Assume that a person is exposed to unanimous disagreement from a group. When confronted with such group pressure, the person may publicly conform or not conform to the group. Regardless of his public response, the individual can privately agree or disagree with the group. Hence, the following different categories are possible: (a) public conformity and private agreement, (b) public conformity and private disagreement, (c) public nonconformity and private disagreement, (d) public nonconformity and private agreement. Two of the categories indicate correspondence between public and private responses [(a) and (c)], and two indicate a lack of correspondence [(b) and (d)]. Two ostensibly identical responses of public conformity may thus really reflect two quite different psychological states (conformity with or without private agreement with the group). Similarly, nonconformity may represent two very different psychological conditions (nonconformity with or without private disagreement with the group).

Subsequent behavior can vary as a function of the psychological process involved in conformity or nonconformity. For example, a person who conforms publicly to the group may have truly changed his own position, or his private opinion may have remained intact. Adopting the group's position publicly but not accepting it privately is public compliance, and is not a case of actual change of one's own belief. Behavior which is only public compliance and not a true change would not be expected to be the same in the absence of the group. In contrast, if conformity to the group represented an actual change in one's private position, then the behavior should not change when the group is no longer present. Clearly, two responses which seem on the surface to be identical are extremely different psychologically.

B. THEORY

Ability to predict when group pressure produces only public compliance and when it produces public conformity accompanied by private change would greatly enhance our understanding of group influence phenomena. An identification of the crucial variables which control the different psychological processes is needed.

Deutsch and Gerard (1955) identified two different influence processes: normative and informational influence. They did not discuss the role of these different influence types relative to the problem of public compliance and private change, but we can assume that informational influence would be more likely to lead to public conformity with private change than would normative influence.

Festinger (1953) discussed group influence from the point of view of the conditions hypothesized to produce only public agreement with the group, as opposed to public agreement with private acceptance. He stated that public conformity will be accompanied by private acceptance if the person wants to remain a member of the group which is attempting to influence him. When the person no longer cares to be a member of the group, then private acceptance will be less likely to occur.

Public agreement with the group without private acceptance presumably will occur if the person is restrained from leaving the group, and if reward and punishment can be administered to induce compliance. Punishment or threat of punishment to obtain agreement with the group will be effective in producing compliance, but will not produce a true change at any time. Festinger suggested the important point that reward may operate in a somewhat different manner from punishment. Both reward for agreeing with the group or punishment for not agreeing will effectively produce public compliance. If continued, however, the use of reward to induce agreement may increase the attractiveness of the group. The person would then have a greater desire to maintain membership in the group, which could ultimately result in private acceptance as well as public compliance.

Kelman (1958, 1961) presented a theoretical formulation in which he posits three types of social influence. According to Kelman's theoretical analysis, social influence phenomena may be understood in terms of three different psychological processes: compliance, identification, and internalization. Compliance is produced when the influence source has means control over the individual, e.g., when the individual may be rewarded or punished. Identification occurs when adoption of the influence agent's position is based on attractiveness or satisfyingness of the relationship between the influence agent and the individual. Internalization is based on the credibility of the influence agent and congruence of the issues with the person's value system.

The three processes discussed by Kelman are conceptually distinct, but in most social influence situations they are probably not easily untangled. Most cases of social influence are most likely the result of the contribution of all three processes. Kelman (1958) has reported an experiment in which influence was produced by controlling the variables hypothesized to create the three processes. Results confirmed the prediction that conditions necessary for the subsequent private performance of behavior produced by social influence differs for compliance, identification, and internalization.

Obvious similarities can be found between Kelman's and Festinger's ideas. One difference is that Kelman does not differentiate between conformity produced by reward and conformity produced by punishment, as Festinger did. Kelman considered reward and punishment as part of the compliance process. As pointed out by Festinger, however, public compliance produced by reward may have different implications for subsequent behavior than public compliance produced by punishment. It might be profitable to attempt an integration of Festinger's and Kelman's formulations with the two types of influence discussed by Deutsch and Gerard (1955), informational and normative influence.

The need to determine empirically when group influence produces only public compliance and when it also produces concommitant private change introduces an important methodological problem. Several criteria which could be used will be discussed. Some of the criteria below were first discussed by Festinger (1953).

First, both a person's public and private response could be assessed as nearly simultaneously as possible while under social pressure. For example, a person could give a public response orally, and at the same time give a written response which would be concealed from the group. Whether public compliance was accompanied by private acceptance could be determined by correspondence or lack of correspondence between public behavior and private response. Difficulties inherent in this technique make its implementation troublesome, however. In practice it is virtually impossible to obtain a private and a public response at exactly the same point in time; one response must be made prior to the other. A commitment could be made to the response given first, which would then affect the following response. Often a private response is obtained shortly after the public response, but while the person remains in the group. It obviously is not easy to devise a procedure for measuring public and private response simultaneously and which will still sound reasonable to the subject. Another problem with this method is that we may not obtain the person's private response. Since the response will be seen by the experimenter, the subject may regard the situation as considerably less than private, and his response will be affected accordingly.

A second method of investigating the relation between public and private opinions utilizes withdrawal of social pressure. Public behavior can be observed while the person is exposed to social pressure, and his response on the same topic observed again when the group is not present. It is assumed that true change has occurred if the response given in the absence of social pressure coincides with the response given previously under social pressure. However, this assumption often may not be tenable. A correspondence between a person's behavior and his prior public behavior upon removal of group pressure does not justify the inference that correspondence between public and private behavior existed when social pressure was present. The private response might have changed toward congruence with the public response as a result of other influences during the intervening time. It is also possible that the group caused only public compliance initially and that private change occurred later through other psychological processes. Suppose that according to this criterion private change did not occur. It is possible that real change did occur in the presence of the group, but that the effect dissipated when the person left the group.

A third possibility for investigating the relation between public compliance and private acceptance is to employ retrospective verbal reports. Interviews might be conducted to determine whether private acceptance was present when a person publicly agreed with the group. Limitations of this method are the same as limitations of any retrospective account of experience: The report could easily be purposely biased; the subject might rationalize his previous behavior, with or without conscious intent; the report may be inaccurate due to memory distortions; and relevant information might be inaccessible to verbal report.

A fourth technique involves the transfer paradigm. Assuming private change is produced when a person publicly agrees with a group, we can test for transfer of the behavior to closely related areas. True acceptance of a particular position implies that transfer to other related areas should occur. If private acceptance occurred, a person's responses on other issues could be predicted. One problem with this technique is that when transfer fails to occur it cannot be determined whether the failure should be attributed to lack of private acceptance or to other unknown reasons.

C. LITERATURE REVIEW

In this section we will attempt to determine whether public compliance or true change is produced in three types of experimental situations which have served as paradigms for much of the research on group influence. Many investigations of group influence were not designed to provide evidence concerning the relation between public compliance and private acceptance. A few studies have explicitly investigated the problem, however, and in other studies relevant data can be located. Unfortunately, sufficient data are not available to permit pursuing this type of analysis in depth in each section of this paper.

Consider first the social influence procedure introduced by Sherif (1935) in which judgments are made of the extent of perceived movement of a stable pinpoint of light (the autokinetic effect). Characteristics of this procedure are: the task is extremely ambiguous since objectively correct answers are not available; many successive judgments are given; there is no social interaction among subjects; and social pressure is passive, consisting only of a person listening to other judgments.

In his original experiment, Sherif (1935) was interested in whether the obtained social influence was temporary or permanent. Observing subjects' judgments 24 hours after the social influence session, Sherif discovered that the effect of the social influence still persisted when subjects judged alone.

Two other studies have investigated social influence in the autokinetic situation over even longer periods of time. In Bovard's (1948) study, persons made judgments alone 28 days after having been influenced by a confederate of the experimenter. Almost all the subjects' judgments were still close to the judgments they gave in the presence of the confederate. Stability of social influence in the autokinetic situation was studied after a period of one year by Rohrer et al. (1954). A high relation was found between amount of movement when judging in the social influence session and when judging alone one year later.

Further evidence that true change occurs in the autokinetic situation is available in an investigation by Hood and Sherif (1962). A confederate gave judgments, and a naive subject listened but did not make judgments while presumably being dark-adapted. It was found that judgments given alone by the subject converged toward the norm of the responses previously "overheard" from the confederate.

The results of these studies indicate that social influence occurring in the autokinetic situation is true change and not just public compliance. It is also often found that subjects in the autokinetic situation are unaware of the extent of their agreement with the confederate, and do not realize they have been influenced (Hood and Sherif, 1962; Rohrer et al., 1954). In a situation where the stimulus is so ambiguous as to permit many equally appropriate or correct alternatives, and when the person is unaware of being influenced, it is very unlikely that only public compliance would occur. A person would have to be aware that others were trying to influence him, and experience conflict between his and the group's position, for public compliance without private acceptance to take place.

In the autokinetic situation the question of correspondence between one's visual experience and verbal report still remains. After shifting one's estimate toward another person, does the amount of movement *look* different? Linton (1954) questioned subjects whose judgments had been influenced, and tried to determine the nature of the change toward closer agreement with the confederate. All but one of 14 subjects said that the confederate's responses had caused a change in the scale they used to estimate amount of movement. According to the retrospective reports of experience by Linton's subjects, it seems that social influence in the autokinetic situation affects the judgmental process rather than visual experience per se.

A second type of experimental procedure has been used by Festinger and his associates (Festinger, 1957; Festinger and Thibaut, 1951; Gerard, 1954). In their research we find: the task has no objectively correct answer, although it is not completely ambiguous (an opinion); some interaction among subjects takes place; active influence attempts may be made by the group; repeated measures are taken on one opinion topic.

A few studies have tried to ascertain whether social influence produced by this type of procedure is true private change or only public compliance. Two studies conducted by H. Burdick and D. McBride, reported by Festinger (1957), investigated the effect of group pressure on public agreement and private acceptance. High school students indicated their opinion regarding a curfew regulation. After a discussion conducted with notes (controlled by the experimenter), public opinion was reassessed, then anonymous opinions were taken. Promise of reward or threat of punishment was employed via faked notes to induce agreement with the group. Both reward and threat were successful in producing agreement with the group: 37 percent of the students in the reward condition and 28 percent of those in the threat condition changed to agree with the group consensus. Further analysis of these data revealed that 16 percent of the reward group and 10 percent of the threat group showed private change from the beginning. In the reward group 21 percent of the students showed public compliance, as compared with 18 percent in the threat conditions.

Hardy (1957) investigated public behavior and private response on the topic of divorce. In one condition the subject had a partner who agreed with his private opinion; in the other condition the subject was unanimously opposed by six confederates. After giving public responses subjects went into separate rooms and filled out another questionnaire to indicate their private response. Almost half the subjects showed public compliance by shifting substantially toward the group, as compared with earlier private responses. Private acceptance also occurred, as indicated by the fact that about 45 percent of the subjects privately changed toward the group on at least half the twelve statements. Furthermore, a significantly greater amount of private attitude change occurred under unanimous group opposition than when a partner was present, although public agreement with the group did not differ significantly in the two conditions.

Two other studies investigating the effect of group pressure on opinion have found private acceptance to accompany public agreement with the group (Gerard, 1954; Raven, 1959).

A third type of procedure for studying group influence was employed by Asch (1951). Characteristics of this procedure are: there is a difference between the group's response and a person's sensory input; the task is simple and unambiguous, having a correct answer; the group unanimously opposes the naive subject; there is no interaction among the subjects; active influence is not attempted.

Is conformity in the Asch situation an instance of only public compliance, or is the overt agreement with the group also accompanied by private acceptance? Judging from Asch's (1956) monograph, it would seem that private acceptance is very unusual. His interview data suggest that actual change in perception of the stimulus is extremely rare, being reported by only a few persons. In contrast, many persons said they had agreed with the group but were certain at the time that the group was wrong. Even those few people who reported a perceptual change may have been rationalizing their agreement with the group. Nevertheless, it is possible that a true perceptual change sometimes might have occurred. Bovard (1953a) noted that a few persons who conformed to a group majority stated that the size of a rectangle looked different on a second estimate.

Luchins and Luchins (1955b) used an Asch-type situation with three confederates. After the group session the entire set of stimuli (lines) was readministered to the naive subject in the absence of the confederates. This time, when judging alone, no objectively incorrect choices were made, although many persons had agreed with the group shortly before by selecting the incorrect alternative. In another experiment by Luchins and Luchins (1961), immediately after the social pressure subjects gave private responses to the same item in the presence of the confederates. The effect of the group still persisted when subjects answered privately (i.e., they gave incorrect answers). Interestingly, when these subjects rejudged the same items alone one day after the experiment, no errors were made. When queried as to why their answers differed from answers given the previous day, many persons insisted that the stimuli were different.

An attempt was made by Israel (1963) to determine whether the Asch procedure could successfully be used to change private opinion. In one condition a simulated group gave extreme attitudes enhancing the self; in the other condition the group's attitudes devalued the self. After presenting two-thirds of the pressure items, the experimenter pretended the apparatus had broken and asked the subjects to answer the same items privately on paper. About 31 percent of the subjects conformed publicly to the group. Of this number, around 20 percent also indicated private acceptance. No one expressed private acceptance who had not also previously agreed openly with the false group consensus. Interestingly, there was a larger percentage of private acceptance with attitudes which underrated the self than with those which overevaluated the self.

Israel (1963) also asked whether the privately accepted attitudes would transfer to a different situation. At the end of the experimental session, subjects rated themselves on intelligence, appearance, orderliness, and leadership. Transfer did occur. For example, when group pressure was in the direction of overevaluating the self, subjects who had actually changed their opinion of themselves also overevaluated themselves on the later ratings.

In summary, when objective stimuli are used in the Asch situation, available evidence appears to indicate that public compliance occurs, but not private acceptance. It is possible, however, that if more difficult objective stimuli were used or if more response alternatives were available, some degree of private change might be produced. Private change arises in the Asch-type situation when opinions are used as stimuli.

It can be seen from studies discussed in this section that overt agreement with a group is accompanied by private acceptance in many situations. In other instances, however, agreement with the group may represent only public compliance and not private change. Studies of forced compliance conducted by Festinger and colleagues are relevant at this point. Research indicates that an attitude discrepant from one's voluntarily undertaken overt behavior tends to change toward closer agreement with the behavior. If a person publicly complies with the group but disagrees privately, his private opinion may ultimately change so that it becomes more consistent with the behavior. Evidence exists that such a process does occur in group pressure situations. In the previously cited Burdick and McBride studies (see Festinger, 1957), of the subjects who publicly complied under the promise of reward or threat of punishment, one-third ultimately showed private change in agreement with their public behavior. Dissonance between behavior and cognition was reduced by changing the cognition in line with the behavior.

Raven's study (1959) is also pertinent. Persons distorted their private opinions when writing notes to each other in order to appear more closely in agreement with the group. Yet during and after writing the distortions, private opinion tended to change. Pressure of the group was effective in producing the distorted communication, after which opinion change reduced the discrepancy between public behavior and private opinion.

III. Conditions of Responding

A. Public and Private

In the previous section the relation between public response and private acceptance was discussed. The frequent existence of a discrepancy between public and private behavior suggests that the condition under which the response is given is important. This section will focus on the context of the response—whether it is given publicly or privately—as an independent variable. Thus, in studies discussed in this section, a person's behavior is observed in either a public or a private condition, while the studies reviewed earlier sought to determine the relation between public response and private acceptance by observing both public and private behavior of one person.

Classification of a response as public or private is, of course, a matter of degree. At the public end of the continuum is a response given aloud when the person is in a face-to-face group. Asch (1956) used this situation. The term "private," on the other hand, generally refers to a response given anonymously when individuals cannot see each other.

Deutsch and Gerard (1955) made a comparison of degree of agreement with the group in two situations differing in amount of privacy. In one condition subjects in face-to-face groups announced their judgments aloud; in another condition subjects could not see each other because of partitions, and they responded by pressing a button. As we would expect, more conformity was found in the face-to-face condition than in the more anonymous, private condition. In one of Asch's (1956) procedures the person recorded his response privately on a sheet of paper instead of publicly (aloud). Frequency of errors was much less in this private condition; yielding occurred only about one-third as much as when responses were made publicly. Moreover, the errors that were made were moderate ones.

Levy (1960) studied conformity in a face-to-face situation and in a simulated group (using the Crutchfield apparatus to simulate others' responses). Since individuals could see each other when reacting by the Crutchfield apparatus, this situation is somewhat less private than the Deutsch and Gerard (1955) private condition. Levy found more conformity in the face-to-face groups than in the simulated groups (36 to 19 percent).

It should be recognized that the use of an apparatus such as that described by Crutchfield does not afford complete anonymity and privacy. As a case in point, many of the Deutsch and Gerard (1955) subjects thought that others would be able to identify them from their position in the sequence. And of course, responses made through a Crutchfield-type apparatus are public to a certain extent because the answers are seen by others, even though the source cannot be identified. The fact that responses will be seen by the experimenter also contributes to making the situation less than completely private. Asch's (1956) subjects reported that they had assumed the experimenter would see their responses and compare them with responses made by others. A more completely private condition can be devised, as attested by Argyle's (1957) procedure. In Argyle's private condition, the person's final opinion was put in a sealed envelope. The subject was told that results would be treated statistically by an assistant, and that data could not be connected with him personally.

Olmstead and Blake (1955) compared conformity in a face-to-face condition and in a simulated group. Clicks were heard through earphones; the voices of other persons (actually a tape-recording) incorrectly reported the number of clicks. The subjects heard the opinions of other people, therefore, but never saw these others. In terms of anonymity and privacy, this situation would seem to be slightly different from that employed by Deutsch and Gerard (1955). The difference between the conditions is that in the Olmstead and Blake study subjects answered aloud, while in Deutsch and Gerard's study subjects pressed a button. Answering aloud is more public, since identification of one's voice is possible. Therefore, Olmstead and Blake's public and private conditions probably did not differ greatly on the public-private continuum. Amount of conformity was slightly greater in face-to-face groups (51 to 43%), but the difference was not statistically significant. Anonymity in responding was studied by Mouton *et al.* (1956) in a click-counting task. In one condition subjects gave their names before each trial, while in another condition they remained anonymous. Although subjects could not see other group members, identification by name provides a more public situation. Identification before each response produced a larger number of highly yielding subjects than did anonymity.

Because more conformity occurs when responding publicly than privately, can we infer that persons comply only when the response is given publicly; that they merely avoid public disagreement with the group yet keep their own attitudinal position intact? At first thought such a conclusion would appear warranted, but further examination suggests additional possibilities. The greater effect of the face-to-face group may not be the result only of mere public compliance. Instead, in the more public situation the group may be regarded as more convincing, so that actual private change as well as public compliance could be greater in the public than in private conditions.

B. COMMITMENT

An interesting variable in studies of group pressure has to do with the person's commitment to some belief or attitude. When an individual expresses an opinion in the face of group pressures, we may say, (a) he has made a decision—i.e., to yield to the group or not to do so—and (b) he may feel committed to this decision. According to cognitive dissonance theory, after a decision is made, the attractiveness of the chosen alternative (such as to yield to the group) increases and attractiveness of the unchosen possibility decreases. Brehm and Cohen (1962) maintain that commitment is a necessary condition for producing cognitive dissonance. All in all, this reasoning implies that the group member who has committed himself to a given position early in the session may maintain this position for some time. In the Asch-type experiment there is rather high consistency over trials in a person's responses (Asch, 1956); and the consistency remains high even if items differ in content (Crutchfield, 1955). Persons who yield to the group early in the experiment continue to do so, while those who are nonconformers early in the session tend to be nonconformers throughout. In fact, from knowledge of an individual's behavior on the first few pressure trials, his response on subsequent trials can be readily predicted. The person apparently commits himself to a general course of behavior.

Of course, consistency of response in the Asch situation might not be completely due to commitment. An equally plausible explanation is that subjects who undertake a certain action on the first trials, i.e., who yield or do not do so, have personality characteristics that dispose them to continue this behavior on all trials. Experimental evidence is needed to support the hypothesis that commitment is responsible for the consistent behavior. Let us look at evidence for commitment to nonconformity or independence. Deutsch and Gerard (1955) explored the effect on conformity of three degrees of commitment to one's private judgment prior to learning the group's responses. Lengths of lines were judged in an Asch procedure, and public responses were given after confederates had answered. One commitment condition used a "magic pad," on which the subject wrote his judgment before seeing others' responses. After each trial the subject erased his response; only the subject himself could be aware of his original judgment. In a second commitment variation, the subject wrote his initial judgment on a sheet of paper before seeing responses of other people. The sheets were not signed by name, and subjects were told the sheets would not be collected. For the third variation, public commitment was used. In this condition the subject wrote his initial judgment on a sheet of paper before seeing the judgments of the others. But after every trial the subject signed his name on the paper and gave it to the experimenter. These three types of commitment range from very private to very public.

Results of the conditions, ordered in terms of increasing error (conformity to the erroneous group opinion) were: public, unsigned, and magic pad. A condition with little or no public commitment had higher conformity than any of the other commitment conditions. Unexpectedly, the unsigned commitment condition was as effective in reducing conformity as the public condition. The authors suggested that subjects regarded the unsigned condition as a public commitment. Although the subjects threw the unsigned paper in a waste basket, if they were socialized in the mores of psychology experiments they probably believed that the experimenter could later identify their answers. Consequently, there was a tendency to maintain initial (independent) judgments. The tendency to maintain the first response in the face of contradictory evidence is also clearly evident in the Kelley and Shapiro (1954) study.

Gerard (1964) recently reanalyzed some data collected in the Deutsch and Gerard (1955) study. In the face-to-face situation he confirmed Asch's (1956) finding that people who yield early tend to continue to yield, and subjects who initially are independent remain so. As trials progressed, however, a larger number of independent subjects yielded in the semi-anonymous condition (Crutchfield apparatus) than in the face-to-face situation. Commitment, whether to conformity or to nonconformity, is stronger, of course, in a public condition than in an anonymous condition. Repeated confrontation with disagreement from others presumably decreased the subjects' confidence in the correctness of their initial views, thereby causing more yielding in the anonymous condition as trials progressed. In spite of this decreased confidence, however, public commitment to their initial position prevented many subjects from changing their behavior.

When a person commits himself publicly, at least two factors contribute to maintenance of the behavior in the future. One factor might be called "face saving." Appearance of inconsistency and vacillation will probably be negatively evaluated by other members, as well as by the person himself. A second factor is that a continuation of the type of response made initially helps reduce post-decision dissonance. For both these reasons, there would be a tendency to be consistent with prior public behavior over a series of trials.

Once a person commits himself to nonconformity, is it possible for the group to change his behavior in the direction of conformity? Fisher et al. (1956) have findings relevant to this question. In a commitment condition the subject gave a public response first; the accomplice gave an incorrect response, then the subject gave a second response. The subjects in this study did not change their responses toward the partner after having made a public commitment. The effect of the partner was, however, reflected on subsequent trials. The partner gave incorrect answers consistently in one direction. In this situation the subjects could anticipate the direction of their partner's response and influence could occur at the first public estimate, before knowing the partner's estimate.

IV. The Person-Group Relationship

A. ATTRACTIVENESS OF THE GROUP

In considering the person-group relationship, one of the most important factors is the degree of attraction the group holds for the person. A number of plausible reasons can be advanced to support the expectation of more conformity in more attractive groups. Nevertheless, is there an empirical relation between group attractiveness and conformity? The Festinger et al. (1950) field study demonstrated that number of friendship choices in a group was positively correlated with conformity to group standards. Attractiveness of the group was manipulated experimentally by Festinger et al. (1952). High attraction to the group was created by telling subjects that the group had been composed so that they would like each other and get along well; low attraction was established by telling subjects that the composition of the group was such that they might not like each other. Results showed that more persons whose opinions differed from the alleged group consensus changed toward the majority position in the high than in the low attraction-to-group condition. The difference was, however, only marginally significant. Gerard (1954) also found more opinion change toward the group in high than in low attraction groups. And evidence from Schachter's (1951) study suggests there is more pressure toward conformity in high than in low attraction groups.

Gerard's (1954) experiment showed, further, that when the subject's opinion was challenged a week later by a confederate, fewer persons changed toward the confederate in the high attraction condition than in the low. There apparently had been a stronger acceptance of the views held by the attractive group, so that these opinions were then relatively impervious to opposing arguments. Berkowitz's (1954) study also found that the effect of group influence in a high attraction condition continued to exist when direct pressure was removed. Thus it seems that the greater change produced by high attraction groups is private change and not just public compliance.

In Bovard's (1951) study, sections of an introductory course were conducted by either a leader-centered or a group-centered technique. The techniques differed most importantly in the greater amount of verbal interaction that occurred among members of group-centered classes. This factor was probably responsible for the finding that persons in group-centered classes liked their group more than persons in leader-centered classes. Data collected at the end of the semester showed that after announcement of the group's average judgment of the length of a rectangle, there was a greater convergence toward the class's mean estimate in group-centered than in leader-centered classes. That is to say, effect of the group was greater in groups that were better liked by their members.

Several studies have used natural groups instead of laboratory groups. One advantage of using natural groups is that, as a consequence of long acquaintance, group attraction is likely to be much stronger than attraction produced by instructions given in the laboratory. Another advantage is that members will continue to associate with each other in the future. Future contact provides opportunity for subsequent positive or negative sanctions from group members. (One study casts doubt on the importance of limited future contact, per se. Gerard and Rotter (1961) hypothesized that expectation of longer association with a group in the future—one versus four experimental sessions—would produce more conformity. The hypothesis was not confirmed.)

Lott and Lott (1961) studied the relation of conformity and group attraction in fifteen natural friendship groups. Ratings of mutual liking among members of the groups and attractiveness of the group as a whole constituted the operational definition of group attraction. Change of opinion toward the reported group position was significantly correlated (.54) with group attraction for these groups of college students. Greater conformity has been found in groups of acquaintances than in groups of strangers (Lambert and Lowy, 1957; Thibaut and Strickland, 1956). But amount of group influence in stable groups as compared with temporary groups has yielded conflicting findings (Bovard, 1953a,b).

The role of attraction of the group in the autokinetic situation has been investigated by Downing (1958). Attraction was varied by telling people they had been matched on personality questionnaires so that they would like each other, or would not. Amount of influence did not differ significantly in the high and low attraction conditions. In fact, there was evidence that subjects were influenced slightly more in the low attraction condition. Results of this study clearly contradict results of studies which have used opinions as the object of social influence. Downing suggested that the discrepant findings in the two types of procedures are due to a person's feeling morally obligated to adhere to group consensus on matters of opinion. In contrast, the person may feel no obligation to agree with an attractive group on matters of visual judgment. But

Sherif and Sherif (1956) report a study by D. Zeaman in which the subject was positively influenced by a strongly liked partner and seemed to be negatively influenced by a disliked partner. A confirmation of this finding appeared recently (Sampson and Insko, 1964).

The relation of group attraction and conformity has also been studied in the Asch situation (Harper, 1961). Results showed no significant differences in amount of conformity on visual perceptual items among three types of friendship groups (close, distant, mixed). Another study using extreme norms found no difference between liked and disliked groups in conformity on a click-counting task (Wilson, 1960). On attitude judgment there was more yielding in the liked than the disliked groups for persons with particular personality traits, but not for all subjects.

Attraction to a group may derive from many different sources (Festinger, 1950; Cartwright and Zander, 1960). Back (1951) employed three different bases of attraction: personal attraction, effective performance, and prestige. He found different patterns of communication and influence as a function of basis of attraction, but in all cases there was more influence in the more attractive groups. Whether different bases of attraction produce different types of influence (e.g., private change versus public compliance) has not been determined.

As the foregoing review indicates, studies of group attraction and conformity are not without contradictory results. One source of conflicting findings may be the manipulation of attraction. The conditions being compared in some studies may be too similar in level of attraction to affect conformity differentially. Further, post-experimental measures may not validly reflect group attraction, but instead may assess only the subject's acceptance of the experimenter's instructions that they will or will not like each other. Another factor to consider is whether the subject believes that conforming behavior is conducive to gaining rewards from the group—if he cares whether he is accepted or liked more by an attractive group than by an unattractive group and regards conformity as a way of achieving this acceptance.

A study reported by Walker and Heyns (1962) may help explain the negative results obtained in some studies. Attractiveness was manipulated by telling some groups that they were selected for their competence in the task. No difference in amount of conformity was found between attractive and unattractive groups. In fact there was some tendency for subjects who liked the group more actually to conform less. Walker and Heyns argued that conformity must be instrumental to being liked by others before high attraction will lead to high conformity. In another study (Walker and Heyns, 1962), subjects were explicitly informed by the experimenter that people tend to like one another better when they agree about problems. To emphasize this information, subjects were required to rate their liking of the group after each influence attempt. Results of this experiment did show more conformity in the high attraction condition than in the low.

Yet another important factor is the complex relations among attraction to the group, acceptance as a member, and nature of the task. Jackson and Saltzstein (1958) found that when a group score was given on a task, more conformity occurred in the high than in the low attraction condition when subjects believed they were accepted by the group. No difference in conformity in the high and low attraction conditions was found when subjects were not accepted as group members. Furthermore, no difference in conformity between high and low attraction groups was found when individual scores instead of group scores were given. This finding underscores the importance of the interrelation of group attraction, normative expectations, group interdependence, and conformity.

B. STATUS IN THE GROUP

One aspect of group structure which could reasonably be expected to be an important determinant of conformity is status in the group. Status is a general term denoting one's relative rank in the group on some dimension. Power, popularity, and leadership are among the important status dimensions that have been studied. It is often assumed that a person is aware of his position or status in the group, although in many cases this may not be true.

Let us look first at leadership. Does the leader conform to group norms more or less than other group members? Reasonable arguments can be advanced in support of either prediction. A number of considerations suggest that the leader would conform more than other group members. As a representative of the group, the leader is expected to reflect accurately its norms when dealing with other groups. The leader would also be expected to serve as an example to other members by upholding the group norms. In sum, the leader may find it necessary to conform to the group's norms in order to maintain his position of leadership in the group (Merei, 1949).

A case can be made also for expecting the leader to conform less than other group members. A successful leader must at times deviate from group norms. During crises, for example, rigid adherence to group traditions could prove fatal to the leader's position and to the group as well (Hamblin, 1958). In addition, by virtue of his high status, the leader may be granted more freedom to violate the norms of the group with impunity (Hollander, 1958).

Reasonable arguments can likewise be advanced for expecting high conformity for both the second ranking person and the lowest ranking person in the group on the leadership dimension. The second ranking person, being close to the top position, might try to improve his standing by closely adhering to the group norms. The lowest ranking person might try to avoid being rejected from the group by conforming.

Relevant experimental findings from natural groups are available concerning the relation between leadership and conformity. A study by Harvey and Consalvi (1960) compared conformity of leaders with other members of the group who differed in rank. On the basis of sociometric data from cliques of delinquent boys, subjects were selected for study whose position on the leadership dimension was either leader, second ranking member, or lowest ranking member. With two other members of their clique, the boys judged the distance between simultaneous flashes of light in a dark room. It was found that greatest conformity occurred with the second ranking person. Least conformity occurred with the leaders, but they did not differ significantly from the lowest ranking people.

The dimensions of leadership and popularity are conceptually independent, but in reality they are probably frequently correlated. Harvey and Rutherford (1960) found a high positive correlation (.78) between popularity and leadership in grade school children. Wilson (1960) found the relation between popularity (liking) and yielding in high school boys to be curvilinear. There was less yielding by liked and disliked boys than by boys of middle rank. This relation was found on both attitude items and click-counting, but was stronger for attitudes. A problem of interpretation exists when popularity or leadership is not created experimentally. Difference in conformity between persons of high and low popularity or leadership might be due to their personality characteristics. That is, personality characteristics of persons which determine their status may determine their conformity as well.

Another aspect of status is the extent to which the group accepts and values a person as a member. Kelley and Shapiro (1954) assumed that when a person believed he was accepted and highly valued by others, he would feel freer to disagree with the group than when he felt less accepted. Through fictitious ratings, subjects were led to think they were either highly acceptable or much less acceptable as a co-worker. Contrary to expectation, highly accepted persons showed greater conformity on a judgmental task than persons with low acceptance, but the difference was not statistically significant. A problem in manipulating acceptance is that attraction to the group covaries with acceptance (Kiesler, 1963; Kelley and Shapiro, 1954). In a later study, Dittes and Kelley (1956) attempted to hold attraction to the group constant. This time change toward the group was greater for persons who had average acceptance with a possibility of changing for the better, than for subjects who had high or low acceptance ratings. In public discussion, persons in the very low acceptance condition adhered more closely to the group's decision than people at other acceptance levels, indicating that the men at other acceptance levels were .freer to deviate from the norm. Low acceptance persons did not highly value the group, and we may assume that their high public conformity was motivated by an attempt to avoid complete rejection and its attendant embarrassment.

There is evidence that the effect of acceptance on conformity varies as a function of the interdependence of the group members. One study found that under high acceptance conditions there was more conformity when group scores were given (interdependent group) than when only individual scores were given (Jackson and Saltzstein, 1958).

A study by Berkowitz and Macaulay (1961) helps elucidate the basis of the relation between status and conformity. Persons with high status (leadership) whose status was subject to change were more highly attracted to the group and had greater preference for high status than high status persons whose position was secure. Unfortunately, conformity was not significantly related to status level or status stability in this experiment. Berkowitz and Macaulay interpreted the finding between status and attraction in terms of McClelland's motivation theory (McClelland et al., 1953). According to this analysis a high status person whose position is unclear, or a second ranking person, experiences a small discrepancy from the desired state or goal: secure high status. Such a small discrepancy should heighten the desirability of this goal, and the group is seen as being attractive. A person low in rank, whether his status is stable or unstable, will experience negative affect and not be attracted to the group because of the large discrepancy between his position and the desired high status.

Homans (1950) and Hollander (1958) have advanced opposing hypotheses regarding the relation between status and conformity. Hollander's (1958) thesis is that a high status person will have freedom to deviate from group norms because of positive impressions or "credits" previously received from the group. Berkowitz and Macaulay (1961) pointed out that even if the hypothesis is sufficient to explain the nonconformity of high status persons (Hollander, 1960, 1961), it still cannot explain the even greater nonconformity sometimes found among persons of medium or second ranking status. Homans (1950) hypothesized that the person with highest social rank will more closely follow the group norms; furthermore, the relation is asserted to be linear. Homans also stated that the more certain a person is about his rank, the less he will conform to the norms of the group. Both Homans' and Hollander's hypotheses receive some support; both also run counter to much available empirical data. Much of the apparent contradiction among studies in this area may partially be due to the failure to give sufficient attention to the nature and relevance of the task. Kelley and Shapiro (1954) have suggested that popularity may be positively related to conformity when conformity is good for the group but negatively related when conformity is bad for the group, as was the case in their experiment. Harvey and Consalvi (1960) cited an unpublished dissertation by E. Sundby which is highly suggestive. Sundby found that status was positively related to conformity when the task was relevant to the group.

C. INTERDEPENDENCE

Two functions of social norms, comparative and normative, have been distinguished by Kelley (1952). Group norms provide information for purposes of self-comparison; they also specify how a person ought to behave. Deutsch and Gerard (1955) discussed two functions of group norms in terms of different types of social influence. Conforming to the group because of positive expectations of the group (and of oneself) is normative influence. Conforming to the group because its behavior is taken as evidence about reality is informational influence. Deutsch and Gerard argued that most studies of conformity deal primarily with informational rather than normative influence. The argument is probably valid, since in most studies subjects merely respond in the presence of others; there is usually neither a common goal nor an explicit set of expected behaviors. The motivation of a person in such a situation is to achieve his goal without regard to the goals of others in the group. In an interdependent relationship, group members are dependent on each other for the achievement of a common goal. Consider the consequences of the promise of a group prize. Since each member must contribute toward attaining the group's objective (the prize) before any member can benefit, the people in the group can affect each other's chances of reaching this goal. Interdependence may exist relative to a variety of goals; the goal may be to achieve a unanimous decision, or to be a "good" and congenial group.

In a two-person situation, Berkowitz (1957) found that group task motivation was higher when the persons were interdependent than when they were independent. That is, when subjects were told both could receive a valued reward, they worked more rapidly at the task than when they thought only one could attain the goal. Berkowitz considered conformity to group norms a special case of the relation between interdependence and motivation to conform to relevant expectations.

The Deutsch and Gerard (1955) experiment is one of the few studies of group conformity that has manipulated the interdependence of group members. Interdependent groups were created by telling some persons that a reward would be given to the five best groups—the five groups that made the fewest errors. (The reward was a pair of tickets for a Broadway show to each member of the group.) It was made clear that each error made by a member would be counted against the group. In this interdependent condition, subjects conformed about twice as much as in the noninterdependent condition. That is, the subjects agreed more often with the (fictitious) obviously erroneous responses of others even when told the most accurate group would win a prize. A very similar procedure, using the same type of prize, was employed in an investigation by Jones et al. (1958). When the experimenter gave feedback that agreed with the false group consensus, there was more conformity in interdependent groups than in noninterdependent groups.

In R. S. Crutchfield's study (cited in Krech et al., 1962) a money reward was used. Crutchfield presented several different kinds of items to subjects, who responded by using an apparatus. To create interdependence some groups were told that a ten-dollar prize would be given to the best (most accurate) group tested during the semester. Other groups were told that a ten-dollar prize would be given to the best individual in the group. More conformity was found in the interdependent groups. In a similar study, Julian and Steiner (1961) failed to obtain a statistically significant difference between interdependent and independent groups, although results were in the predicted direction.

An example of a goal other than money or a prize is provided by the Thibaut and Strickland (1956) experiment. In one condition subjects were told that their group was competing against other groups. No prize was offered, but subjects were informed that effectiveness of their cooperation would determine how good a group they were. In another condition there was no attempt by the experimenter to urge consensus or cooperation in the group; in fact, the opposite was made clearly acceptable. More conformity was found in the former condition (interdependent) than in the latter (independent). In addition, when group pressure was greater, conformity increased in the interdependent groups, but decreased slightly in independent groups.

How can we account for the generally consistent results of more conformity in interdependent than in independent groups? One explanation can be offered in terms of the social responsibility norm (Berkowitz and Daniels, 1963). Proper social behavior at times demands conformity to the expectations of dependent others. Another factor may be due not to normative influence—conforming to expectations of others—but to informational influence. When a group prize is offered, a person may become motivated to try harder for accuracy. Contrary to such an explanation, results cited earlier show that in such a situation persons may actually make more errors in conforming to the group consensus. How can we account for this apparent paradox of a person trying harder but doing worse? We must not overlook the fact that the person is aware that others in the group are also trying harder. Simply in terms of probability of the group's being correct, others are more likely to be considered correct when trying harder. Hence, the tendency to accept the responses of others as evidence about reality—informational influence—may be stronger in interdependent groups.

Both normative and informational influence are no doubt present in varying degrees in all group pressure situations. When groups are interdependent, presumably most of the influence is normative. An interesting condition was used in Di Vesta's study (1959) which exemplifies minimum normative influence. On about half of a series of trials, signal lights on a Crutchfield apparatus displayed incorrect answers. The subjects were told that the experimenter controlled the lights, which were used only to let the subjects know when to respond. It was made clear that the lights were selected randomly and had nothing to do with others' responses. In this condition there should be no normative influence. Nevertheless, there were more errors than in control groups. Although subjects were informed that the lights did not represent others' responses, their judgments were still influenced. One explanation is that since the lights did reflect veridical answers on about half the trials (nonpressure trials), the subjects may have concluded that accurate information was conveyed somehow on all trials in spite of the experimenter's disclaimer (Di Vesta, 1959). In this condition, informational influence was no doubt present in a much "purer" form than found in most studies.

V. Characteristics of the Group

A. COMPOSITION

The composition of the group is an important factor to consider in relation to conformity. Other persons in a group create the social pressure; their characteristics have relevance for predicting one's conformity to that group. The individual regards certain groups as important and appropriate groups with which to compare himself on a given issue. If members of a group differ from a person in some important respect, the group may be less acceptable as a comparison group (Festinger, 1954).

Long ago, Cooley (1902) proposed that one type of nonconformity (as opposed to rebellious behavior) was the result of the influence of other, remote standards which were acting upon the individual at the time. Hence, no definite line can be said to exist between conformity and nonconformity; rather, people may respond to different influence sources. Thus, if a person disagrees with a laboratory group on a given issue, he may perhaps be conforming to his conception of the norms held by other more important or more appropriate groups which are his reference groups on this particular matter.

Although importance of the reference group concept is tacitly acknowledged, reference groups are rarely treated as a variable in studying conforming behavior. Nevertheless, a few relevant studies can be found. White's (1957) experiment, for one, indicates that the group of which a person is nominally a member is not the only relevant source of social pressure. Persons who believed that important reference groups strongly opposed a (reported) class consensus conformed less than persons who perceived that the important reference groups held a position similar to the classroom group. In another study (Walker and Heyns, 1962) the source of the purported norms was either from other girls on the campus, from other sorority girls in general, or from the person's own sorority group. Greatest effect of the reported group opinion occurred when the subject's own sorority was the source of the norm.

Investigations by Gordon (1952) and McKeachie (1954) demonstrate the effect of the individual's conception of the group norm. In Gordon's experiment, persons stating their opinions publicly tended to conform to, or more partially toward, their conception of the group norm. Likewise, McKeachie found a correlation between change in attitude and change in subjects' perception of the group norm in classroom groups.

Interesting comments were made by some of Israel's (1963) subjects in post-experimental interviews which support the reference group analysis. The subjects reported that before answering they frequently tried to imagine how their friends or family would feel about the question at hand. Surely this is an instance of referring an opinion to a group more salient than the one in which the subject happens to be physically present.

The crux of the preceding discussion may be summarized by saying that it is important to know to what a person is conforming. The experimenter may be inclined to assume that the subject will conform to the norms of the group of which he is physically a member during the experiment. But the situation may be interpreted less simply by the subject. Numerous social influences must be impinging on the person simultaneously. Some influence emanates from the face-to-face group, other influence derives from reference groups which are not physically present.

It can be predicted that greater the similarity of the group to the person, the greater the likelihood that the group will be an acceptable reference group. Therefore, greater conformity can be expected when there is considerable similarity between the person and the group on certain important dimensions. Several pertinent studies can be mentioned.

Groups of similar (homogeneous) persons have been composed by telling subjects that everyone in the group had equal skill, knowledge, and ability to perform a task, while dissimilar or heterogeneous groups have been established by informing individuals they differed widely in ability and qualifications for a task. Using such groups, Gerard (1953) found no change toward the announced group opinion in heterogeneous groups. In homogeneous-high pressure groups, individuals with minority opinions did change in the direction of the majority. In a similar experiment (Festinger and Thibaut, 1951) there was no difference between heterogeneous and homogeneous groups with a case study task; with a football strategy task, on the other hand, there was greater change toward the group in the homogeneous condition than in the heterogeneous.

One study investigated an interesting aspect of similarity of the person to the group (Linde and Patterson, 1964). A face-to-face group was composed either of paraplegic persons (confined to wheelchairs) or of normals. Results disclosed higher conformity in the Asch situation when the groups were homogeneous (all disabled or all able) than when the naive subject differed from the rest of the group (able-bodied person with disabled group, or disabled person with able-bodied group).

A highly visible and readily detectable aspect of group composition is sex of the members. Difference in amount of conformity for males and females has been repeatedly demonstrated, with females generally conforming more than males (Crutchfield, 1955; Tuddenham, 1958). The finding holds, it should be noted, for groups composed of like-sex members, but must be qualified when sex composition is varied. Tuddenham et al. (1958) formed three types of groups: five men; three men and two women; and two men and three women. The same three types of groups were formed also with females. It was hypothesized that yielding by men would vary directly with the number of men in the group, while yielding by women would vary inversely with the number of women in the group. Results were generally consistent with these predictions. Tuddenham et al. (1958) interpreted the data in terms of the cultural sex stereotype which assumes that men are superior to women in cognitive processes such as perceptual judgments. In terms of similarity of the person to the group, the more homogeneous groups produced more conformity for males, but less for females. Results of this study emphasize that the effect of homogeneity of the group depends on the relevance to conformity of the dimension on which the homogeneity is based.

The composition of the group does seem to affect the extent of conformity displayed by its members. While the effect of similarity between the person and group may be interpreted in terms of the reference group concept, other interpretations can also be suggested. In homogeneous groups the person might perceive that similar others also hold similar attitudes, and this attitudinal similarity could lead to increased attraction (Newcomb, 1961); as we have seen, group attractiveness often produces a high level of conformity. In heterogeneous groups, furthermore, there may be more tolerance for disagreement among the members than in homogeneous groups; thus, more pressure toward conformity would be felt in homogeneous groups.

B. Size and Unanimity

Only slight attention has been given to the effect on conformity of the size of the group opposing a person. Asch (1956) studied groups of 1, 2, 3, 4, 6, 7, and 15 opponents. Conformity increased markedly from 1 to 3 opponents, and then evidently reached a plateau at this size, although the relation was slightly curvilinear. Rosenberg's (1961) study provides evidence that the apparent curvilinearity found by Asch was not just a leveling-off effect. Greatest conformity occurred with three partners present, and the decrease from three to four partners was statistically significant.

Two studies have failed to find a significant relation between group size and conformity. Kidd (1958) used one, three, or five opponents. There was a slight but insignificant increase in yielding as size of the group increased. One, two, or three opponents were employed by Goldberg (1954). Larger groups resulted in somewhat more conformity, but the difference was statistically insignificant. In both these studies which obtained negative results for group size, group pressure was presented by the experimenter's report of the group's judgments. If the subjects were conforming to the experimenter, as Goldberg (1954) suggested, it is reasonable that increase in group size made little difference.

One of the distinctive characteristics of the Asch procedure is that a single individual is opposed by a unanimous majority. In Asch's (1951, 1952, 1955) studies, experiments were conducted to determine the effect on conformity of a nonunanimous group. When a confederate gave the correct answer throughout, thereby serving as a partner for the subject, conformity decreased drastically (from about 35 to about 5 percent). In another variation a unanimous majority gave correct answers in the early trials. The interesting finding was that the naive subject was independent as long as anyone agreed with him; once he was alone, however, conformity to the majority increased abruptly. Thus, the person who regards himself as being alone in his opinion is evidently relatively susceptible to influence from the others around him.

There are at least two reasons why social support tends to decrease conformity. One, the partner's opinion could provide information about reality, thereby reinforcing the person's confidence in the veridicality of his own perception. Alternatively, the effect could be due to the partner's dissent from the views expressed by the other group members; it may be much easier to disagree if someone else takes the initiative in this opposition. Asch (1955) arranged two conditions which furnish data relevant to these hypotheses. In one condition the partner chose an incorrect alternative intermediate between the group's extreme error and the correct response. Conformity decreased by about one-third, and most of the errors were moderate ones which, incidentally, were the kind made by the partner. In another condition the dissenter chose the extreme alternative, in disagreement with the group's moderate error. In this case, errors dropped to only nine percent. It appears from these results that the effect of a partner is not primarily informational, but perhaps creates the perception of greater tolerance for dissent which frees the naive subject from the influence of the group majority to a remarkable degree.

In another interesting experiment a confederate answered correctly on six trials, then always agreed with the majority (Asch, 1955). Later when the partner "left" the subject and no longer sided with him, there was a sudden increase in conformity. Asch concluded that this was due to the person's feeling that the partner had "deserted" him, and not just to the lack of a partner. To test this idea, the instructed partner merely left the room after six trials. Although conformity increased when the partner left the room, conformity was less than when the partner "deserted."

Malof and Lott (1962) reported an interesting experiment that is relevant to this matter of social support. They composed groups of six males who judged length of lines. In each group one confederate disagreed with the unanimous group, and gave the correct judgment. In half the groups the confederate was Caucasian and in half he was Negro. Both high and low ethnocentric subjects accepted social support from the Negro as well as from the Caucasian partner and did not conform to the group.

The effect of social support on conformity has been investigated using attitudes instead of objective stimuli (Hardy, 1957). More public conformity occurred when the group unanimously opposed the person than when social support was present, but the difference was not statistically significant at the usual level ($P = .11$). Yet, the effect of social support on private acceptance was much more striking. Amount of attitude change (toward the group) was significantly greater when the group unanimously opposed the person than when social support was present.

Clearly, social isolation is a major determinant of the extent to which the group can influence an individual member. Another finding by Asch (1952) further illustrates the importance of this factor. When one confederate made incorrect judgments in disagreement with a group of sixteen naive individuals, the naive subjects reacted with laughter, sympathy, or indifference. But when two confederates disagreed with the group, the two were taken much more seriously and the laughter ceased.

C. EXTREMENESS OF THE NORM

The α position of the group norm in relation to the individual's position is a variable that is often uncontrolled, but which affects amount of conformity. There may well be a direct relation between conformity and extremeness of the norm because extreme norms produce greater conflict and greater social pressure upon the individual holding the deviant opinion. But other factors must be taken into account as the discrepancy between the group and the person increases. Some writers have hypothesized that rejection of the group is likely to occur in the presence of extreme norms (Festinger, 1957; Hovland and Pritzker, 1957), and one study has confirmed this hypothesis (Johnson, 1964). Furthermore, suspiciousness of the group's veracity and of the experimental procedure will increase with extreme norms, particularly when objective stimuli are used.

Tuddenham (1961) varied the discrepancy between the person and the group norm, by locating the false group consensus at either the fiftieth, seventy-fifth or ninety-ninth percentile of responses given by a control group. For both males and females, yielding was greater with the extremely distorted norm than with the moderately distorted one. Interestingly, variability in the extreme norm condition was much greater than in the moderate norm condition. The moderate norm seemed to affect persons fairly uniformly, causing some movement toward the group for all. In contrast, when the norm was extreme some persons were influenced very little and others considerably more. Placing the norm at the control group mode (fiftieth percentile) resulted in even less variance than in control conditions.

Helson et al. (1958) examined degree of shift toward the group on opinion items as a function of the extremeness of the norm. The percent of subjects who gave responses different from the control's modal response increased at each of three discrepancies. But the effect of discrepancy between the person and the group was not linear; the curve seemed to reach a plateau at the larger discrepancies. A curvilinear relation between influence and discrepancy of the confederate's response has also been found in the autokinetic situation (Whittaker, 1964). Very large or very small discrepancies produced less change than moderate discrepancies.

The relation between conformity and extremeness of the norm is somewhat ambiguous for objective stimuli. Using a task in which subjects were to count the number of clicks, Olmstead and Blake (195) varied the simulated group norm by either one, two, or three clicks from the correct answer. In general, there was most conformity at the small discrepancy (one click). Least conformity was found at the middle discrepancy (two clicks from the veridical). This finding was not confirmed by Schroder and Hunt (1958), however, who used the same task. Asch (1956) varied the discrepancy between a standard and a comparison line by one-quarter, one-half, and three-fourths of an inch. Frequency of errors (conformity) was an inverse function of the size of the discrepancy. As extremeness of the norm increases, incredulity probably becomes a more important factor with objective stimuli than with subjective or ambiguous stimuli, such as judging intelligence from photographs (Goldberg, 1954).

Results of studies of extremeness of the norm may depend partially on the stimulus context. Sometimes stimuli are presented in conjunction with several other degrees of extremeness of the norm in a single series of trials (Olmstead and Blake, 1955); sometimes only one degree of extremeness of the norm is presented to a person in a series of trials (Tuddenham, 1958).

When the group is in opposition to an individual, the latter's expressed judgment often shifts somewhat toward the position held by the group, but the change typically is short of complete agreement with the group. Goldberg's (1954) study showed that the farther the distance of the group from the person's judgment the greater the conformity. Amount of conformity for each person was converted to a percentage of amount "demanded" by the group (extremeness of the norm). The subjects appeared to reduce the difference between themselves and the group by about 30% of the initial disagreement. Tuddenham's (1958) data also indicate that persons' responses shift somewhat toward the group. This effect can be detected if several response categories are provided. Evidence that compromise responses occur when they are possible is also found in Asch's (1956) study. When the majority made an extreme error, some of the subjects' errors were moderate ones.

It has been suggested that conformity to moderate and to extreme norms may involve different psychological processes (Olmstead and Blake,

1955; Schroder and Hunt, 1958). One process seems to be due to informational influence (at reasonable norms), and the other due to normative influence (at extreme norms). Schroder and Hunt (1958) have found personality differences between persons who conform at moderate and at extreme norms. Similarly, McDavid (1959) found there were personality differences between persons who yielded to informational and to normative influence. These data appear to support the hypothesis that different psychological processes are involved in conformity to norms of different discrepancies from the veridical or control response.

VI. Nature of the Task

A. Competence on the Task

In group pressure studies some task must be employed. Persons in a group may differ in their ability relevant to the task. If one person is aware of his superior ability in comparison with others in the group, he should be less subject to the others' influence. Superior ability may be intrinsic to the person because of his possession of characteristics relevant to the task, or an experimental procedure may be arranged to convince him that he has such relevant characteristics.

Perceived competence could be enhanced by having a person succeed on a relevant task or by having others fail; relative difference between the person and the group would be the same. But this does not exclude the possibility that self esteem is differentially affected by one's succeeding, as compared to others' failing. Such a general effect on self esteem could influence conformity to the group. Furthermore, success or failure of a group may alter the attractiveness of the group, which in turn could affect conformity. Groups that have experienced success have been found to be more attractive than groups that have undergone failure (Gilchrist, 1952).

Let us first discuss studies in which the person's competence on a task has been manipulated prior to the application of group pressure. Samelson (1957) presented a nonsense syllable tachistoscopically and asked subjects to identify it from four alternatives. Prior to the main part of the experiment, in one condition practice trials led the naive subject to believe that he had better vision than others in the group. Significantly less conformity occurred when an individual thought his eyesight was better than that of the others in the group. Hochbaum (1954) gave subjects clear evidence of ability relative to other group members on the same type of task that was later used with group pressure (making predictions on case histories). Results showed that those people who held deviant opinions and had failed on the practice tasks changed their opinion toward the group more than persons who had succeeded.

Other experiments in which success or failure was manipulated have yielded results consistent with these studies cited, using opinion items (Di Vesta, 1959) as well as objective stimuli (Rosenberg, 1963), and in two-person situations employing objective stimuli (Mausner, 1954a) and the autokinetic effect (Kelman, 1950). In one experiment, Mausner (1954b) varied the success or failure of the subject's partner on a task somewhat different but relevant to the one used in measuring influence. The subject's responses converged toward the previously successful partner, but did not shift toward the unsuccessful partner. This study is interesting because the task used to manipulate the partner's supposed competence was different from the experimental task. The two tasks were probably perceived as being somewhat similar, however, since they required the same type of skill. For success or failure experience to affect conformity, at least some perceived similarity must exist between the prior task on which one has demonstrated competence and the subsequent task used during group pressure (Croner and Willis, 1961).

Fagen (1963) studied the effect on conformity of real task-relevant ability and reports by the experimenter of the person's ability. It was found that both real and reported ability affected conformity. That is, when a person actually had high ability on the task as well as when the experimenter reported that he had high ability, there was less conformity than when ability was low or reported to be low.

Crutchfield (1955) gave feedback to persons concerning the correctness of their judgments (on items having correct answers) during the group pressure session itself. The feedback indicated that the false group consensus was correct. Under this condition there was a substantial increase in amount of conformity on items similar to those on which the group had supposedly been correct. Data from an experiment by Jones et al. (1958) suggest that feedback from the experimenter which repudiates the false group consensus decreases conformity more than feedback that supports the group's false judgments increases conformity. In one investigation feedback successfully influenced subjects' conformity apparently without their awareness of the influence (Walker and Heyns, 1962). Experimentally increased conformity on objective items has been found to generalize to other items (both objective and subjective) that did not receive feedback (Allen and Crutchfield, 1963).

The number of group pressure trials in the first half of a series of 86 items was varied by Di Vesta (1959). Accuracy was greater (i.e., there was less conformity) in the second half of the series of trials when there had been a larger number of critical trials in the first half of the series. In this condition the subject probably perceived that the group made more errors, which increased his feeling of competence relative to the group. Related to this finding is the fact that amount of conformity was greater in the first half of the series than in the second half. One explanation is that as the absolute number of pressure trials increases, the subject concludes that the group is less competent. It should be noted that Asch (1956) observed a nonsignificant but clear trend for less conformity as the percentage of neutral trials in a series increased. The studies differ in that Di Vesta measured conformity in a subsequent series of items as a function of the absolute number of pressure trials in a prior series.

A problem exists when a person's alleged success or failure is conveyed by the report of the experimenter. The subject may not believe the information given him. A more convincing technique than merely reporting the subject's performance to him was devised in one experiment (Wolf and Zolman, 1959). The subject was allowed to examine the objective evidence of his performance by actually counting the number of paratroopers that he had estimated on a card. A bogus card was substituted, of course, and the subject was convinced that he really had been accurate or inaccurate in his estimates.

B. CONFIDENCE

The subjective counterpart of objective competence is feelings of confidence. We can assume that the possession of objective competence is accompained by confidence concerning the relevant task; the converse will not necessarily be true. A person might have high confidence without objective justification.

Several investigators have obtained an interesting correlation between certainty of judgment and yielding (Crutchfield in Krech et al., 1962; Hochbaum, 1954). After persons changed their opinion to agreement with the group, they also expressed high confidence in the correctness of the new response. This was found even on items for which a person had previously indicated that his original position was probably correct. The confidence in the correctness of the altered belief is probably the result of dissonance reduction.

Certainty of judgment was studied experimentally by Kelley and Lamb (1957). Subjects rated the taste of a substance (phenylthiourea) that is bitter to some people and tasteless to others. Groups were composed of two tasters and one nontaster, or two nontasters and one taster. The taster majority affected the nontaster, but the nontaster majority did not influence the taster. Certainty of the subjects' ratings of unpleasantness can account for the results; ratings of tasters indicated more certainty than ratings of nontasters.

Certainty or confidence in one's opinion is no doubt correlated with stimulus ambiguity, although a distinction can be made conceptually. Ambiguity can be defined as the probability of interpreting a stimulus in a certain way (Wiener *et al.,* 1957). In a two-choice situation, for example, if most persons give the same interpretation to a stimulus, it is less ambiguous than when about half the persons interpret the stimulus one way and the other people the other way.

Crutchfield (1955) studied ambiguity by presenting items for which none of the alternative answers was correct. As an example, the subject was instructed to choose the larger of two circles when they were actually objectively equal; or to report whether two words were synonyms or antonyms when they were really neither. More conformity occurred with such ambiguous items than with items which had objectively correct answers. Other studies have found social influence more effective when ambiguous stimuli were used (Luchins, 1945; Luchins and Luchins, 1955a; Walker and Heyns, 1962; Wiener, 1958). The existence of a general relation between conformity and stimulus ambiguity was challenged by Luchins and Luchins (1963), who pointed out that there are situations in which the relation would not be found.

C. DIFFICULTY AND IMPORTANCE

Difficulty of the task has been investigated in a number of studies. Presumably, difficulty as well as ambiguity affect confidence in a person's judgment and thereby his yielding to the group.

Difficulty of a number of items was determined in one experiment by the percent of control subjects who gave incorrect answers on questions concerned with current events, geography, government, literature, language, and science (Coleman *et al.,* 1958). For twelve pressure items the rank correlation between difficulty and conformity to the group was .58 for men and .89 for women. Range of difficulty in this study was not large; the most difficult item was one on which 54 percent of the control group gave an incorrect answer.

Other studies report more yielding on difficult items than on easier ones (Crutchfield, 1955; Blake *et al.,* 1957; London and Lim, 1964). One investigation did not find any significant difference in conformity for counting two different speeds of clicks (Moulton *et al.,* 1956). (The researchers assumed that when the rate of clicks was faster the task was more difficult.) It should be more difficult to make judgments when stimuli are not physically present but must be judged from memory.

Deutsch and Gerard (1955) found more conformity on line judgments when responses were made several seconds after the removal of the stimuli.

The more information a person has about a stimulus the less difficult the judgment should be. In H. Burdick's study (see Walker and Heyns, 1962) the group's influence was greatest on stimuli with which the persons had little acquaintance and familiarity. Information about a topic was controlled experimentally by Snyder *et al.* (1960). Persons having little information about art were given a taped lecture on art history. Persons who had heard the lecture were more resistant to the group than a control group who had listened to a lecture on music. The result is somewhat puzzling in view of the fact that the group pressure came from persons who had also heard the lecture and hence had the same information as the subject.

The more important a topic is to a person the less we might expect his behavior to be affected by other people's responses. Instructions given by Di Vesta (1959) can be interpreted as increasing the importance of the task. When told that responses to items correlated highly with intelligence, persons were less influenced by the group. Two studies have used the Allport-Vernon-Lindzey scale of values to determine importance of a value area to an individual (Snyder *et al.*, 1960; Vaughan and Mangan, 1963). In both studies less conformity to the group was found when the task involved more important value areas.

An increase in importance of the task may not, however, always produce less conformity. If one is aware that a task is very important both for himself and also for other members of the group, there may be more conformity (Krech *et al.*, 1962; Crowne and Liverant, 1963).

VII. Conclusions

This review began by pointing out that conformity to the group is a complex phenomenon which should be differentiated into several distinct psychological processes. Relevant data were not available from most studies to enable one to discern which psychological process is represented by the gross response of agreement or disagreement with the group. It makes a great deal of difference whether agreement with the group is public compliance or true private change, or whether nonconformity represents independence or anticonformity. Were such information available, the literature could be integrated more meaningfully; many contradictory results might be seen to be due to forced inclusion of psychologically different phenomena in the same category.

Nevertheless, in spite of this paucity of adequate data, there is a remarkable degree of agreement among studies in the area of conformity.

Ambiguities and contradictions that do exist may very likely be due to numerous and unknown differences in procedure, method, and population. But it is readily apparent that two important factors are rarely controlled or systematically studied, and that these factors clearly affect the results of studies of conformity: the nature of the task and the extremeness of the norm. Selection of stimuli or task and placement of the norm often seem to be done in a most casual manner. In many studies the position of the norm is unspecified. And too often the task is trivial or its relevance and importance for the person is unknown. Systematic examination of the interaction of the nature of the task with other variables is lacking.

Another important feature of laboratory studies of conformity that has received practically no attention is the role of the experimenter, who probably affects results more than we realize. The role of "demand characteristics" (Orne, 1959, 1962) in group pressure studies is an important problem that has not been investigated. It may be that behavior under group pressure is partially a response to perceived pressure from the experimenter; the subjects may be responding in the way they think the experimenter wants them to. Furthermore, instructions often imply or even explicitly state that subjects should agree with one another.

A number of other important problems in conformity need investigation. Although there have been a few studies of generalization of conformity (Allen and Crutchfield, 1963; Walker and Heyns, 1962), little is known of the generality of conformity. Investigations have not been conducted on the generality of conformity across situations outside the laboratory. The use of some type of representative design (Brunswik, 1956) might be very profitable in this area. Another important problem is suggested by the fact that the majority of people conform little if at all under group pressure. Research should be directed toward understanding the variables that affect nonconformity, as well as conformity. Nonconformity may not be just the mirror image of conformity. Neither should we fail to realize that other modes of response to group pressure are available to a person in addition to conformity and nonconformity (Steiner and Rogers, 1963).

Theories of conformity which have been advanced in recent years include psychoanalytic (Hoffman, 1953), cognitive (Asch, 1956), reinforcement (Mausner, 1955), and even mathematical models (Cohen, 1963). These formulations have not been very useful in suggesting new research. Even if one limits the scope of a theory to the explanation of public behavior under group pressure, the psychological situation is still a complex one involving the interaction of numerous variables. A subject in a conformity situation has information and beliefs about several important features of the situation: the task, other members of the group, and the experimenter. Moreover, he thinks about how the group and the experimenter are reacting to him and to the task. Superimposed on these aspects of the situation are certain goals of the subject which are created by the relative salience of cues in the experimental situation. We can assume that the subject engages in some type of cognitive weighing of these factors, which determines the resultant response. The outcome of this weighing is presumably the response that•maximizes the possibility of achieving the momentarily most relevant and salient goal.

REFERENCES

Allen, V. L., and Crutchfield, R. S. (1963). Generalization of experimentally reinforced conformity. *J. abnorm. soc. Psychol.* **67**, 326–333.

Argyle, M. (1957). Social pressure in public and private situations. *J. abnorm. .soc. Psychol.* **54**, 172–175.

Asch, S. E. (1951). Effects of group pressure upon the modification and distortion of judgment. In H. Guetzkow (Ed.), *Groups, leadership and men.* Pittsburgh, Penn.: Carnegie Press, pp. 177–190.

Asch, S. E. (1952). *Social psychology.* Englewood Cliffs, N.J.: Prentice-Hall.

Asch, S. E. (1955). Opinions and social pressure. *Sci. American* **193**, 31–35.

Asch, S. E. (1956). Studies of independence and submission to group pressure: I. A minority of one against a unanimous majority. *Psychol. Monogr.* **70**, No. 9 (Whole No. 417).

Back, K. (1951). The exertion of influence through social communication. *J. abnorm. soc. Psychol.* **46**, 9–24.

Berkowitz, L. (1954). Group standard, cohesiveness, and productivity. *Hum. Relat.* **7**, 509–519.

Berkowitz, L. (1957). Effects of perceived dependency relationships upon conformity to group expectations. *J. abnorm. soc. Psychol.* **55**, 350–354.

Berkowitz, L., and Daniels, L. (1963). Responsibility and dependency. *J. abnorm. soc. Psychol.* **66**, 427–436.

Berkowitz, L., and Macaulay, J. R. (1961). Some effects of differences in status level and status stability. *Hum. Relat.* **14**, 135–147.

Blake, R. R., Helson, H., and Mouton, J. S. (1957). The generality of conformity behavior as a function of factual anchorage, difficulty of task, and amount of social pressure. *J. Pers.* **25**, 294–305.

Bovard, E. W., Jr. (1948). Social norms and the individual. *J. abnorm. soc. Psychol.* **43**, 62–69.

Bovard, E. W., Jr. (1951). Group structure and perception. *J. abnorm. soc. Psychol.* **46**, 398–405.

Bovard, E. W., Jr. (1953a). Conformity to social norms in stable and temporary groups. *Science* **117**, 361–363.

Bovard, E. W., Jr. (1953b). Conformity to social norms and attraction to the group. *Science* **118**, 598–599.

Brehm, J. W., and Cohen, A. R. (1962). *Explorations in cognitive dissonance.* New York: Wiley.

Brunswik, E. (1956). *Perception and the representative design of psychological experiments.* Berkeley and Los Angeles, Calif.: Univer. of Calif. Press.
Cartwright, D., and Zander, A. (1960). *Group dynamics* (2nd ed.) New York: Harper.
Cohen, B. P. (1963). *Conflict and conformity.* Cambridge, Mass.: M.I.T. Press.
Coleman, J. F., Blake, R. R., and Mouton, J. S. (1958). Task difficulty and conformity pressures. *J. abnorm. soc. Psychol.* **57**, 120–122.
Cooley, C. H. (1902). *Human nature and the social order.* New York: Scribner.
Croner, M. D., and Willis, R. H. (1961). Perceived differences in task competence and asymmetry of dyadic influence. *J. abnorm. soc. Psychol.* **62**, 705–708.
Crowne, D. P., and Liverant, S. (1963). Conformity under varying conditions of personal commitment. *J. abnorm. soc. Psychol.* **66**, 547–555.
Crutchfield, R. S. (1955). Conformity and character. *Amer. Psychologist* **10**, 191–198.
Deutsch, M., and Gerard, H. B. (1955). A study of normative and informational social influences upon individual judgment. *J. abnorm. soc. Psychol.* **51**, 629–636.
Dittes, J. E., and Kelley, H. H. (1956). Effect of different conditions of acceptance upon conformity to group norms. *J. abnorm. soc. Psychol.* **53**, 100–107.
Di Vesta, F. J. (1959). Effects of confidence and motivation on susceptibility to informational social influence. *J. abnorm. soc. Psychol.* **59**, 204–209.
Downing, J. (1958). Cohesiveness, perception, and values. *Hum. Relat.* **11**, 157–166.
Fagen, S. A. (1963). The effects of real and experimentally reported ability on confidence and conformity. *Amer. Psychologist* **18**, 357–358 (Abst.).
Festinger, L. (1950). A theory of social comparison processes. *Hum. Relat.* **7**, 117–140.
Festinger, L. (1953). An analysis of compliant behavior. In M. Sherif and M. O. Wilson (Eds.), *Group relations at the crossroads* New York: Harper, pp. 232–256.
Festinger, L. (1954). A theory of social comparison processes. *Hum. Relat.* **7**, 117–140.
Festinger, L. (1957). *A theory of cognitive dissonance.* Evanston, Ill.: Row, Peterson.
Festinger, L., and Thibaut, J. (1951). Interpersonal communications in small groups. *J. abnorm. soc. Psychol.* **46**, 92–100.
Festinger, L., Schachter, S., and Back, K. (1950). *Social pressures in informal groups.* New York: Harper.
Festinger, L., Gerard, H. B., Hymovitch, B., Kelley, H. B., and Raven, B. (1952). The influence process in the presence of extreme deviants. *Hum. Relat.* **5**, 327–346.
Fisher, S., Rubinstein, I., and Freeman, R. W. (1956). Intertrial effects of immediate self-committal in a continuous social influence situation. *J. abnorm. soc. Psychol.* **52**, 200–207.
Gerard, H. B. (1953). The effect of different dimensions of disagreement on the communication process in small groups. *Hum. Relat.* **6**, 249–272.
Gerard, H. B. (1954). The anchorage of opinions in face-to-face groups. *Hum. Relat.* **7**, 313–326.
Gerard, H. B. (1964). Conformity and commitment to the group. *J. abnorm. soc. Psychol.* **68**, 209–210,

Gerard, H. B., and Rotter, G. S. (1961). Time perspective, consistency of attitude and social influence. *J. abnorm. soc. Psychol.* **62**, 565–572.

Gilchrist, J. C. (1952). The formation of social groups under conditions of success and failure. *J. abnorm. soc. Psychol.* **47**, 174–187.

Goffman, E. (1961). *Encounters.* Indianapolis, Ind.: Bobbs-Merrill.

Goldberg, S. C. (1954). Three situational determinants of conformity to social norms. *J. abnorm. soc. Psychol.* **49**, 325–329.

Gordon, R. L. (1952). Interaction between attitude and the definition of the situation in the expression of opinion. *Amer. sociol. Rev.* **17**, 50–58.

Hamblin, R. L. (1958). Leadership and crisis. *Sociometry* **21**, 322–325.

Hardy, K. R. (1957). Determinants of conformity and attitude change. *J. abnorm. soc. Psychol.* **54**, 289–294.

Harper, F. B. W. (1961). The sociometric composition of the group as a determinant of yielding to a distorted norm. Unpublished Ph.D. dissertation, Univer. of California (Berkeley).

Harvey, O. J., and Consalvi, C. (1960). Status and conformity to pressures in informal groups. *J. abnorm. soc. Psychol.* **60**, 182–187.

Harvey, O. J., and Rutherford, J. (1960). Status in the informal group: influence and influencibility at differing age levels. *Child Develpm.* **31**, 377–385.

Helson, H., Blake, R. R., and Mouton, J. S. (1958). An experimental investigation of the effectiveness of the "big lie" in shifting attitudes. *J. soc. Psychol.* **48**, 51–60.

Hochbaum, G. M. (1954). The relation between group members' self-confidence and their reactions to group pressure to conformity. *Amer. sociol. Rev.* **19**, 678–687.

Hoffman, M. L. (1953). Some psychodynamic factors in compulsive conformity. *J. abnorm. soc. Psychol.* **48**, 383–393.

Hollander, E. P. (1958). Conformity, status, and idiosyncrasy credit. *Psychol. Rev.* **65**, 117–127.

Hollander, E. P. (1960). Competence and conformity in the acceptance of influence. *J. abnorm. soc. Psychol.* **61**, 365–369.

Hollander, E. P. (1961). Some effects of perceived status on responses to innovative behavior. *J. abnorm. soc. Psychol.* **63**, 247–250.

Homans, G. C. (1950). *The human group.* New York: Harcourt, Brace.

Hood, W. R., and Sherif, M. (1962). Verbal report and judgment of an unstructured stimulus. *J. Psychol.* **54**, 121–130.

Hovland, C. I., and Pritzker, H. A. (1957). Extent of opinion change as a function of amount of changed advocated. *J. abnorm. soc. Psychol.* **54**, 257–261.

Israel, J. (1963). Experimental change of attitude using the Asch-effect. *Acta Sociol.* **7**, 95–104.

Jackson, J. M., and Saltzstein, H. D. (1958). The effect of person-group relationships on conformity pressures. *J. abnorm. soc. Psychol.* **57**, 17–24.

Jahoda, M. (1959). Conformity and independence. *Hum. Relat.* 12, 99–120.

Johnson, H. H. (1964). Some effects of discrepancy level on responses to adverse information about one's self. Unpublished Ph.D. dissertation, Univer. of Illinois.

Jones, E. E., Wells, H. H., and Torrey, R. (1958). Some effects of feedback from the experimenter on conformity behavior. *J. abnorm. soc. Psychol.* **57**, 207–213.

Julian, J. W., and Steiner, I. D. (1961). Perceived acceptance as a determinant of conformity behavior. *J. soc. Psychol.* **55**, 191–198.

Kelley, H. H. (1952). Two functions of reference groups. In G. E. Swanson et al. (Eds.), *Readings in social psychology* (rev. ed.). New York: Holt, pp. 410–414.

Kelley, H. H., and Lamb, T. W. (1957). Certainty of judgment and resistance to social influence. *J. abnorm. soc. Psychol.* **55**, 137–139.

Kelley, H. H., and Shapiro, M. M. (1954). An experiment on conformity to group norms where conformity is detrimental to group achievement. *Amer. sociol. Rev.* **19**, 667–677.

Kelman, H. C. (1950). Effects of success and failure on "suggestibility" in the autokinetic situation. *J. abnorm. soc. Psychol.* **45**, 267–285.

Kelman, H. C. (1958). Compliance, identification, and internalization: three processes of attitude change. *J. Conflict Resol.* **2**, 51–60.

Kelman, H. C. (1961). Processes of opinion change. *Public Opin. Quart.* **25**, 57–78.

Kidd, J. S. (1958). Social influence phenomena in a task-oriented group situation. *J. abnorm. soc. Psychol.* **56**, 13–17.

Kiesler, C. A. (1963). Attraction to the group and conformity to group norms. *J. Pers.* **31**, 559–569.

Krech, D., Crutchfield, R. S., and Ballachey, E. L. (1962). *Individual in society.* New York: McGraw-Hill.

Lambert, W. E., and Lowy, F. H. (1957). Effects of the presence and discussion of others on expressed attitudes. *Canad. J. Psychol.* **11**, 151–156.

Levy, L. (1960). Studies in conformity behavior: a methodological note. *J. Psychol.* **50**, 39–41.

Linde, T. F., and Patterson, C. H. (1964). Influence of orthopedic disability on conforming behavior. *J. abnorm. soc. Psychol.* **68**, 115–118.

Linton, H. B. (1954). Autokinetic judgment as a measure of influence. *J. abnorm. soc. Psychol.* **49**, 464–466.

London, P., and Lim, H. (1964). Yielding reason to social pressure: task complexity and expectation in conformity. *J. Pers.* **32**, 75–89.

Lott, A. J., and Lott, B. E. (1961). Group cohesiveness, communication level, and conformity. *J. abnorm. soc. Psychol.* **62**, 408–412.

Luchins, A. S. (1945). Social influences on perception of complex drawings. *J. soc. Psychol.* **21**, 257–273.

Luchins, A. S., and Luchins, E. H. (1955a). Previous experience with ambiguous and non-ambiguous perceptual stimuli under various social influences. *J. soc. Psychol.* **42**, 249–270.

Luchins, A. S., and Luchins, E. H. (1955b). On conformity with true and false communications. *J. soc. Psychol.* **42**, 283–303.

Luchins, A. S., and Luchins, E. H. (1961). On conformity with judgments of a majority or an authority. *J. soc. Psychol.* **53**, 303–316.

Luchins, A. S., and Luchins, E. H. (1963). The role of understanding in social influences on judgment. *J. soc. Psychol.* **61**, 133–150.

McClelland, D. C., Atkinson, J. W., Clark, R. A., and Lowell, E. L. (1953). *The achievement motive.* New York: Appleton.

McDavid, J., Jr. (1959). Personality and situational determinants of conformity. *J. abnorm. soc. Psychol.* **58**, 241–246.

McKeachie, W. J. (1954). Individual conformity to attitudes of classroom groups. *J. abnorm. soc. Psychol.* **49**, 282–289.

Malof, M., and Lott, A. J. (1962). Ethnocentrism and the acceptance of Negro support in a group pressure situation. *J. abnorm. soc. Psychol.* **65**, 254–258.

Mausner, B. (1954a). The effect of prior reinforcement on the interaction of observer pairs. *J. abnorm. soc. Psychol.* **49**, 65–68.

Mausner, B. (1954b). The effect of one partner's success in a relevant task on the interaction of observer pairs. *J. abnorm. soc. Psychol.* **49**, 557–560.

Mausner, B. (1955). Studies in social interaction: I. A conceptual scheme. *J. soc. Psychol.* **41**, 259–270.

Merei, F. (1949). Group leadership and institutionalization. *Hum. Relat.* **2**, 23–39.

Milgram, S. (1965). Liberating effects of group pressure. *J. per. soc. Psychol.* **1**, 127–134.

Moore, R. K. (1964). Susceptibility to hypnosis and susceptibility to social influence. *J. abnorm. soc. Psychol.* **68**, 282–294.

Mouton, J. S., Blake, R. R, and Olmstead, J. A. (1956). The relationship between frequency of yielding and the disclosure of personal identity. *J. Pers.* **24**, 339–347.

Newcomb, T. M. (1961). *The acquaintance process.* New York: Holt.

Olmstead, J. A., and Blake, R. R. (1955). The use of simulated groups to produce modifications in judgment. *J. Pers.* **23**, 335–345.

Orne, M. T. (1959). The nature of hypnosis: artifact and essence. *J. abnorm. soc. Psychol.* **58**, 277–299.

Orne, M. T. (1962). On the social psychology of the psychological experiment: With particular reference to demand characteristics and their implications. *Amer. Psychologist* **17**, 776–783.

Raven, B. H. (1959). Social influence on opinions and the communication of related content. *J. abnorm. soc. Psychol.* **58**, 119–128.

Rohrer, J. H., Baron, S. H., Hoffman, E. L., and Swander, D. V. (1954). The stability of autokinetic judgments. *J. abnorm soc. Psychol.* **49**, 595–597.

Rommetveit, R. (1955). *Social norms and roles.* Minneapolis, Minn.: Univer. of Minnesota Press.

Rosenberg, L. A. (1961). Group size, prior experience, and conformity. *J. abnorm. soc. Psychol.* **63**, 436–437.

Rosenberg, L. A. (1963). Conformity as a function of confidence in self and confidence in partner. *Hum. Relat.* **16**, 131–139.

Samelson, F. (1957). Conforming behavior under two conditions of conflict in the cognitive field. *J. abnorm. soc. Psychol.* **55**, 181–187.

Sampson, E. E., and Insko, C. A. (1964). Cognitive consistency and performance in the autokinetic situation. *J. abnorm. soc. Psychol.* **68**, 184–192.

Schachter, S. (1951). Deviation, rejection, and communication. *J. abnorm. soc. Psychol.* **46**, 190–207.

Schroder, H. M., and Hunt, D. E. (1958). Dispositional effects upon conformity at different levels of discrepancy. *J. Pers.* **26**, 243–258.

Sherif, M. (1935). A study of some social factors in perception. *Arch. Psychol.* **27**, No. 187.

Sherif, M., and Sherif, C. W. (1956). An outline of social psychology. New York: Harper.

Snyder, A., Mischel, W., and Lott, B. E. (1960). Value, information, and conformity behavior. *J. Pers.* **28**, 333–341.

Steiner, I. D., and Rogers, E. D. (1963). Alternative responses to dissonance. *J. abnorm. soc. Psychol.* **66**, 128–136.

Stukát, K. G. (1958). Suggestibility: a factorial and experimental analysis. *Acta Psychologica,* Gothoburgensia, II. Stockholm: Almqvist & Wiksell.

Terman, L. M. (1904). A preliminary study of the psychology and pedagogy of leadership. *Pedag. Sem.* **11**, 413–451.

Thibaut, J. W., and Strickland, L. H. (1956). Psychological set and social conformity. *J. Pers.* **25**, 115–129.

Tuddenham, R. D. (1958). The influence of a distorted group norm upon individual judgment. *J. Psychol.* **46**, 227–241.

Tuddenham, R. D. (1961). The influence upon judgment of the apparent discrepancy between self and others. *J. soc. Psychol.* **53**, 69–79.

Tuddenham, R. D., Macbride, P., and Zahn, V. (1958). The influence of sex composition of the group upon yielding to a distorted norm. *J. Psychol.* **46**, 243–251.

Vaughan, G. M., and Mangan, G. L. (1963). Conformity to group pressure in relation to the value of the task material. *J. abnorm. soc. Psychol.* **66**, 179–182.

Walker, E. L., and Heyns, R. W. (1962). *An anatomy for conformity.* Englewood Cliffs, N.J.: Prentice-Hall.

White, M. S. (1957). Attitude change as related to perceived majority opinion. Crew Res. Lab. Air Force Res. & Develpm. Comm. (Randolph A.F. Base, Texas) Res. Rep. No. AFPTRC-TN-S7-79.

Whittaker, J. O. (1964). Parameters of social influence in the autokinetic situation. *Sociometry*, **27**, 88–95.

Wiener, M. (1958). Certainty of judgment as a variable in conformity behavior. *J. soc. Psychol.* **48**, 257–263.

Wiener, M., Carpenter, J. T., and Carpenter, B. (1957). Some determinants of conformity behavior. *J. soc. Psychol.* **45**, 289–297.

Willis, R. H. (1963). Two dimensions of conformity-nonconformity. *Sociometry* **26**, 499–513.

Willis, R. H., and Hollander, E. P. (1964). An experimental study of three response modes in social influence situations. *J. abnorm. soc. Psychol.* **69**, 150–156.

Wilson, R. S. (1960). Personality patterns, source attractiveness, and conformity. *J. Pers.* **28**, 186–199.

Wolf, I. S., and Zolman, J. F. (1959). Social influence: self-confidence and prestige determinants. *Psychol. Rec.* **9**, 71–79.

SOCIAL POWER

John Schopler[1]

DEPARTMENT OF PSYCHOLOGY
UNIVERSITY OF NORTH CAROLINA
CHAPEL HILL, NORTH CAROLINA

I. Overview of Social Power

In his 1953 presidential address to the Society for the Psychological Study of Social Issues, Dorwin Cartwright chided social psychologists for neglecting the variable of power. It was his contention that any social psychological theory was incomplete without this construct and that "a concerted attack on the problem of power should produce a major advance in the field of social psychology" (Cartwright, 1959a, p. 13). While the research activities during the following decade did not constitute a concerted attack, they did evidence increasing interest in power. Of course, power explanations of interpersonal behavior have been used in all of the social sciences. Cartwright is not alone in his evaluation of their

[1] A preliminary version of this chapter was read by Professor Edward E. Jones. His thoughtful suggestions and comments are gratefully acknowledged.

degree of importance. For example, power was characterized as a fundamental concept in the social sciences by Russell (1938) and had been
elevated to a similar status in political science since the late 1920's,
according to Lane (1963).

The potential importance of a power concept is easy to document,
as are the difficulties of placing it in a coherent theory. One immediate
problem revealed by even a casual perusal of the power literature is
the variety of meanings associated with the term. In part this appears
to be the fate of any construct which has been entrenched in everyday
vocabulary, thereby acquiring a rich heritage of connotative and denotative
meanings. The dilemma created by such popularity for anyone wishing
to use the concept systematically is poignantly described by Dahl (1957)
who confesses to two contrary suspicions:

> First (following the axiom that where there is smoke there is fire), if so
> many people at so many different times have felt the need to attach the
> label power, or something like it, to some Thing they believe they have
> observed, one is tempted to suppose that the Thing must exist; and not
> only exist, but exist in a form capable of being studied more or less sys-
> tematically (p. 201).

Dahl's second suspicion, evidently following the axiom that where there
is smoke there may be smoke-machines, is that the Thing which generates
so much attention ". . . is probably not a Thing at all but many Things."
Dahl's dilemma applies to the social scientists wishing to use power systematically as well as to someone wishing to summarize their work. In
order to proceed with the main aim of the present chapter, to review
the theoretical and empirical developments involving power, primarily
from the standpoint of social psychology, it will be necessary to delineate
what aspects of the Thing are going to be covered.

In a general way the concept of social power has been used to
account for the changes which occur in the course of an interaction
sequence. Any relationship, whether it be two strangers meeting, a parent
with his child, or a president and congress, contains potentialities for
the exercise of influence and for the induction of change in one or both
of the participants. Power has been used as an explanatory construct
for coordinating the behavior changes in one participant to the prior
actions of his partner. At this level of generality it is evident that power
could subsume such traditional content areas as learning, attitude change,
leadership, conformity behavior, etc. The present review, however, is
limited to the theories and experiments explicitly dealing with power as
a characteristic of a social relationship, involving at least two persons,
where the amount of power is defined by the events occurring in the
relationship. Treatments of power based on viewing it as a personality

trait will not be included. The network of related variables with which power has been prominently linked will be mentioned only illustratively. Specific reviews relating power to certain other areas are available elsewhere. Power and organizations have been extensively reviewed by Cartwright (in press), power and leadership by Janda (1960), and the community power studies have been summarized by Herson (1961).

Within these restrictions, the recent power literature will be surveyed. One of its striking features is the relative independence of the empirical research from the theoretical formulations. The major theoretical analyses of power typically have little data uniquely related to them, nor have they generated anything like a distinctive and coherent set of testable issues. The empirical research, on the other hand, although often acknowledging a particular theoretical parentage, is ordinarily tied to that systematic position in a tenuous manner. It will therefore faithfully reflect the current status of the area to summarize the theoretical positions separately from the experimental work. At the conclusion of these summaries a general evaluation of the power literature will be made.

II. Systematic Positions

Three kinds of power formulations will be discussed. For convenience these frameworks are labeled "field theory," "decision-making," and "interaction." They differ primarily in the level of abstraction of their concepts, the segment of the interaction sequence on which they focus, and especially in the kind of information they require to establish the manifestation of power. Although each kind of formulation lends itself to somewhat different experimental operations or observations, there is little difficulty in stating one position in the terminology of another.

A. Field Theory Framework

The most prevalent definition of power appearing in the literature has its roots in Lewinian field theory and has been comprehensively articulated by Cartwright (1959b). The essence of this system consists of specifying relationships among various types of psychological forces. Power is defined as the maximum "resultant" force A can bring to bear on B with respect to a particular region of B's life space.[2] The resultant force is in turn composed of the strength of the force to "comply" minus

---

[2] Power formulations are almost always illustrated by a dyadic relationship in which one member has more power than his partner. Many conventions exist for designating the participants. For example, in Cartwright's dyads O always has power over P. However, because of their slight mnemonic advantage the letters A and B will be used in this chapter to designate the more powerful and less powerful person, respectively.

the strength of the force to "resist." In other words, A has power over B if A enacts a particular behavior x which both induces a compliance force on B to locomote in a particular direction yz and is greater than the accompanying resistance force. In Cartwright's formulation, A's power is not dependent on B's actual movement in the direction yz. The behavior of B is considered to depend on the sum of all of the forces, or the "combined" forces, acting on him at the time of A's act. For instance, a professor may assign an outside reading with sufficient vigor to convince a particular student that the benefits of doing the work outweigh the benefits of not doing it. According to Cartwright, the professor has demonstrated power over the student, even if the student decides to pursue an especially attractive date instead of working on the assignment. If the combined forces (the "attractive date" in the example) are sufficiently large, B may not move at all, or he may go in a different direction from that desired by A. In this instance, B would be showing opposition. Cartwright uses the term "control" to describe A's ability to overcome B's opposition and distinguishes control from power, which is conceptually related only to overcoming the resistance force. Most of the other authors who use a field theory framework do not make this distinction, but coordinate A's power with changes in B.

In order for A to be able to activate a compliance force, his act must have some significance for B; it must mesh in some way with B's motive base. The magnitude of the inducing force on B is a joint function of the strength of A's act and the motive base to which it is relevant. To illustrate the latter point, consider a father who wants to have his teen-age son cut the lawn on Saturday afternoon and promises the use of the family car that night for compliance. The father will have more power if the son has a date for Saturday night than if he has decided to remain home. It is this feature of power relationships which has given rise to definitions of power based on A's possession of valuable resources or on his control of B's need satisfaction or goal attainment (Pepitone, 1950; Berkowitz, 1957; Stotland, 1959; Cohen, 1959). An exception to this formulation can also be cited. Horwitz (1958) holds that the amount of social power an individual expects to have will rise as the strength of his own need increases. Stronger needs are thought to enhance the legitimacy of the position advocated. If both participants have equal weight in determining a joint decision, the one whose needs are greater will expect to have more power.

1. Bases of Power

In principle, any need or desire of B could serve as a source of A's power. Moreover, if a satisfactory classification of motives were available, it could be coordinated to various bases of power. Such an analysis has not yet been undertaken. However, French and Raven (1959) have devised a taxonomy of bases that is consistent with the field force framework. Their bases of power are distinguished by the meaning A's acts have to B and by the kind of relationship they imply. Five types of bases of power are specified; reward, coercive, legitimate, referent, and expert. These have become sufficiently important to warrant further discussion before proceeding with other aspects of Cartwright's framework (1959b).

a. Reward power. Reward power resides in B's belief that A has the ability to mediate rewards for him. The use of reward power rests on A's possession of some resource that B values and which B believes he can obtain by conforming to A's act. Similar to Rotter's (1954) basic formulation of social learning theory, French and Raven assume that the strength of reward power increases as the amount of reward increases and with B's estimate of the likelihood of attaining them if he conforms. Because B's conformity is based on the prospect of being rewarded, use of reward power depends on A's ability to observe B's behavior. Reward power is also likely to increase the attraction of B toward A and, over time, to shade into referent power. When influence is based solely on reward power, French and Raven suggest that B will maintain the changes only in those instances where A's power is salient.

b. Coercive power. Coercive power, B's belief that A can mediate punishments, is conceptually similar to reward power in several ways. Its strength depends on the magnitude of the negative valences controlled by A, and on B's estimate of the likelihood of avoiding them by conforming. Its use requires A to maintain surveillance over B, who will maintain changes only as A's power is salient. Certain consequences of coercive power are thought to be distinctly different from reward power. The use of coercive power over time will presumably tend to lower B's attraction for A and will tend to generalize negative valences to other regions of the life space. The use of this power base may also require A to set up restraints to keep B from withdrawing.

c. Legitimate power. The existence of legitimate power requires prior socialization of B. It stems from the values internalized by B which give him a feeling that A "should" or "has a right" to exert influence and that he (B) has an obligation to accept it. French and Raven suggest such sources of legitimate power as cultural values, the acceptance of the social structure and designation by a "legitimizing agent." Although the range of legitimate power may vary widely, it is ordinarily specific to the internal value which is its source. The changes achieved by use of this kind of power are thought to be dependent on the presence of

A, who will not have to monitor B's behavior. However, even in A's absence the changes may generalize to other situations if the internalized values instigated by A remain salient to B. In addition to being a source of power in its own right, legitimacy is often an important characteristic of reward and coercive power, and is capable of changing the meaning of these power bases. The previous discussion was premised on A's holding legitimate reward or coercive power. French and Raven note the illegitimacy of reward power implied by the word "bribe."

d. Referent power. Referent power is equated with the process of identification. A's referent power over B depends on B's desire for, or feeling of, "oneness" with A. Identification is thought to stem primarily from A's attractiveness to B and to be manifest in such positive feelings as liking. Referent power can occur independent of A's intention to influence B. It, of course, does not require surveillance, although A's presence may influence the stability of changes. The range of referent power may be limited if, for example, it is based on a specific attribute of A. A political group, for instance, may have considerable power over a member's political attitudes, but none over his religious attitudes. But of the five types, referent power is considered to be most likely to generalize to a wide range of topics. French and Raven hypothesize that the amount of attraction and the extent of the range are positively correlated.

e. Expert power. Expert power exists when B perceives A as possessing knowledge or skills in a particular area. B must also believe that A is being truthful and is acting in good faith. The exercise of expert power does not depend on maintaining surveillance and the range of power is thought to be limited to the areas of A's expertness, although some generalizations may occur to other areas. After all, the political opinions of prominent military leaders have been known to be influential.

Although the five bases of power are conceptually distinct, French and Raven recognize that they often occur in combination with each other. Some of these combinations, such as reward and referent power, are considered to occur more frequently than others, but no systematic analysis has been attempted of all possible combinations. These writers also leave open the question of whether an increase in the number of bases results in an increase in amount of power.

2. Resistance Forces

The French and Raven analysis of power bases amplifies the meaning of induction forces in Cartwright's system. Unfortunately, the meaning of resistance forces is not as clear. Resistance forces, it will be recalled, are those forces in B's life space specifically activated by A's act. Cartwright presents no referents by which they might be identified. It is possible to gain some understanding of them through French's (1956) discussion of his formal model, which is based on the application of the concepts of directed linear graphs to the force field definition of power. He holds that resistance forces might be composed of factors such as "certainty of own position" and of such personality characteristics as rigidity and authoritarianism.

3. Directionality of Power

Because power is defined by the ability to overcome resistance forces, A's amount of power can vary independently of B's power. Cartwright characterizes power relationships as nonsymmetric. The statement "A has power over B" has no necessary implications for the statement "B has power over A." (When amount of power is defined by the difference between A and B's power, i.e., as a relative power advantage, power relationships must be asymmetrical.) For Cartwright the consequences of having a relative power advantage are related to maintaining control of the partner and to overcoming the combined forces existing in his life space.

In Cartwright's system power is also linked to a particular act of an agent. An act can be referred to several attribute dimensions. The content of an act, e.g., a promise, a command, or a suggestion, relates to the "form" of power. The properties of the forces it activates, especially in B's life space, characterize the strength of the act. In addition, an act of A—for example, commands such as "mow the lawn," "produce more units," etc.—usually specifies a direction for B's movement. This direction can ordinarily be equated with revealing A's intentions; it specifies what it is he wishes B to do. In fact some definitions of power have focused on its intentional characteristic: Russell (1938) says, "Power may be defined as the production of intended effects" (p. 35), and Heider (1958) formulates power as a function of intentions and abilities. For Cartwright the manifestation of power involves changes coordinated with A's intentions. On the other hand, Lippitt et al. (1952) have coined the term "behavioral contagion" to represent power devoid of intention to influence. Behavioral contagion refers to the spontaneous imitation by B of A's behavior in a social context where A displays no intention of having B imitate him.

A related, although minor, issue is raised by the B who moves in a direction that is opposite to the one specified by A. The "negativism" of smaller children or the result of an influence attempt by a disliked person are illustrations of this point. Is it reasonable to speak of power when the consequences of A's act are contradictory to his intentions?

Cartwright interprets this seeming paradox as a result of the combined forces acting on B and therefore regards it as a problem of control. Other authors, in particular Dahl (1957), are willing to speak about "negative power." In so far as the movement in an opposite direction is highly predictable, A might still obtain a desired effect by merely disguising his intentions. Of course, B might anticipate such a reversal, and so on. It is sufficient to note that most authors avoid these problems by assuming A's act veridically reflects his own intentions, which are accurately perceived by B.

4. Degree of Power and Amount of Change

It follows from the definition of power that the distance B moves in the direction specified by A is an index of A's power, granting the absence of forces outside the A-B system. In order to predict how A and B will resolve some difference, such as an opinion difference, it is only necessary to know their initial positions and the extent of their power. In groups containing more than two members predictions about the results of mutual influence attempts are complicated by the existence of various types of communication structures. French's (1956) formal model of social power derives theorems about the consequences of the influence process on the attitude positions held by the group members. (Variables assuming an underlying continuum, such as attitudes, are particularly suited for the concepts of the force field framework because they are able to reflect degrees of change.) By combining the initial attitude position of each member with various group structures, defined by the degree of "connectedness" between pairs, French is able to predict the members' attitude positions at the end of each subsequent unit of influence. A generalization of this model has been proposed by Harary (1959). He provides a mathematical demonstration of how every power structure necessarily converges to a stable distribution of ultimate attitude positions. Harary's extension proceeds from recognizing an isomorphism between French's model and the successive transition probabilities in Markov chains.

5. Summary

In summary, the field theory framework, as represented by Cartwright's (1959b) position, details the functional relationships among the variables implied by the concept of forces. Power is defined as a potential for inducing a resultant force whose direction and magnitude depends on specific characteristics of the interaction.

Cartwright's aim was to place power in a network of variables that was grounded in a general theory of behavior and only incidentally to develop hypotheses about the determinants and consequences of power. Because of this orientation, the emphasis of his work falls ". . . more on the vocabulary of power than on its syntax" (Jones, 1960). It does not serve as a guideline for generating research questions, and his position has exerted power, but little control, over social psychologists.

B. DECISION-MAKING FRAMEWORK

Most of the authors whose writings are included under this heading have sought to clarify the problem of how to make power comparisons among individuals who are not necessarily in the same relationship. Despite a prevailing political-science orientation, for instance, how to compare the power of different senators, their formulations of power are relevant to a wider domain. These writers also have accepted the general characteristics of power outlined by Simon (1953), who likened an influence relation to a causal relation, and for whom the exercise of power consists in affecting the policies of others. Power and influence are therefore equated and a power relationship must be asymmetrical. Power is always manifested either by changes in the probability of eliciting a response from B or in the probability of affecting some state of nature.

1. The March Analysis

It is March's (1955) contention that a large segment of human behavior can be treated as exemplifications of a decision-making process. He explicitly places the concept of power, or influence, in a decision-making context. March comments, "Influence is to the study of decision-making what force is to the study of motion—a generic explanation of the basic observable phenomena" (p. 432). Influence is defined by March in terms of the inducement of change in an organism. In order to recognize influence it is necessary to observe an organism at one point in time and from that observation to be able to predict what he will do at a second point. If the organism deviates from the predicted path, granting the validity of the laws used to make the prediction, influence has occurred and has been the source of the change. March attempts to build a theory of influence based on a general conception of the decision-making process. He employs the formal terminology of set theory to develop a model of the organism whose state is defined in terms of elementary sets, trichotomous values ($+$, $-$, and 0) attached to the elements of those sets, and probability connections among the elements. The organism makes a decision whenever an evoked state contains an element whose chain of probability connections terminates in a $+$ and $-$ value.

In keeping with his model, March specifies four general influence processes. The most evident process by which an organism can be changed is by affecting the probability connections among elements in the evocable set. The threat of punishment or the promise of a reward are examples of activities aimed at changing probability connections. The promised use of the family car changes the son's perception of the likelihood that desirable outcomes will result from mowing the lawn. Influence can also be exerted by changing the values connected with the elements contained in the evocable set. Because such a change alters what an individual will desire or value, March illustrates this kind of influence process by referring to the cultural determinants of individual behavior, as represented by the process of internalization or socialization. Instances of the last two processes are less frequent, but follow logically from the model. They involve expanding the responses contained in a set that is connected to an evocable set, and, lastly, changing the connections between an evocable set and the environmental cues necessary to its arousal.

March (1957) has also discussed the problems associated with measuring amount of influence, particularly with respect to comparing degrees of power. In keeping with his earlier analysis, influence is defined by the kind of changes a particular intervention produces on some state of nature. His focus is on sets of behaviors enacted by individuals in different roles. March maintains it is crucial to separate the influence stemming from a role from that of a particular behavior. In order to make power comparisons it is necessary to observe the consequences of comparable behaviors for each role on a specific state of nature, such as the passage of a bill. Suppose the power of a husband and wife are to be compared with respect to whether they purchase a new house. As a matter of convenience their behaviors will be restricted to saying "yes" or "no," and the outcome of each combination will be represented as a probability value. A hypothetical array of such probabilities is presented in Table I. The specific probability of purchasing a house is a

TABLE I
AN ILLUSTRATION OF MARCH'S POWER COMPARISON

Wife \ Husband	"Yes"	"No"
"Yes"	.9	.3
"No"	.7	.1

joint function of the behaviors enacted: the highest value occurs when both husband and wife say "yes," the lowest when both say "no," etc. A role is considered to be more influential if it is ". . . more successful than the other at narrowing the range of possible outcomes" (p. 210), either for a given behavior or over a set of behaviors.

In the example, the husband has more influence over the purchase of a house with respect to saying "yes" because this constrains the outcome to .9 or .7, compared to the .9 or .3 associated with the wife's identical response. In the same way the husband is also more influential when he says "no." The diagonals need not sum to unity and it is not inevitable, in even the two-alternative situation, that greater influence for one behavior implies greater influence for the other. The influence of a particular behavior would be ascertained by determining its consequences regardless of the role-player enacting it.

2. Dahl's Formulation

The analysis begun by March has been extended by Dahl (1957). He accepts March's general definition of power but modifies its referents. A's power over B is defined as the net increase in the probability of B enacting a behavior after A has made an intervention, compared to the probability of B's enacting the behavior in the absence of A's intervention. The probability of B doing x given that A has done w is written as:

(1) $P_1 = P(B,x/A,w)$

The probability of B doing x without A having done w is written as:

(2) $P_2 = P(B,x/A,\overline{w})$

Amount of power (M) is then given by the statement:

(3) $M = P_1 - P_2$

Dahl points out several features of his formulation. When P_1 equals P_2 no power relation exists, and this is equivalent to the statistical meaning of independence. When M equals $+1$, power is at a maximum, an instance of B doing something he would never have done without A's intervention. When M equals -1, A also has maximum power, but it is "negative power" because his intervention results in B's not making a response he would otherwise always make. Dahl suggests negative power need not be linked to A's intentions. Basically, it depends only on the specification of a direction for B's movement.

Dahl's major aim is to specify the requisite conditions for making power comparisons among individuals not necessarily in the same relationship. To this end the value of M by itself is not sufficient. Power comparisons between two actors must also include: (1) the bases of their power, (2) the means by which their bases are invoked, (3) the scope of their power, i.e., the number of areas or types of responses over which they have power, and (4) the number of comparable respondents over whom power is exercised. Although the bases and means of power appear to be implied by A's act w, the other two variables are clearly separate. Dahl notes there is currently no way reasonably to combine each of these factors into a single power index and contends, as did March, that comparisons can only be made for one dimension when the other ones are held constant. However, some latitude in actual application is condoned by Dahl. Through judicious use of a number of assumptions, he demonstrates how his concepts can be applied to making power rankings in the U.S. Senate.

3. Other Analyses

Another addition to this framework has been made by Harsanyi (1962a) to include the expected consequences for both participants of conformity or nonconformity. According to Harsanyi, any power comparisons must include, aside from the variables noted by Dahl, the "opportunity costs" to both A and B. The opportunity costs involved in A's power over B are defined as the expected value (a weighted average) of the costs A would incur when B conforms, such as rewarding B, and those he would incur by B's failure to conform, such as punishing B. The opportunity costs to B, on the other hand, are defined as the net disadvantage to B of not conforming. The disutility of not conforming can also be seen as an index of the incentives A can bring to bear on B and are termed the "strength" of A's power. In other words, the parent who induces his child to brush his teeth by promising him a dime does not have as much power as another parent who obtains the same result by offering only a penny (assuming the utility of money is comparable for both parents). Harsanyi develops a measure of amount of power in the unilateral power situation which he modifies slightly for the bilateral power situation. In an accompanying paper he develops a measure for n-person reciprocal power situations (Harsanyi, 1962b).

A different kind of solution to the problem of power comparability has been suggested by Tannenbaum (1962). He too is not entirely satisfied with Dahl's formulation because it neglects the importance B attaches to the behavior desired by A. Tannenbaum argues that even small changes in important behaviors might represent more power than larger alterations in unimportant behaviors. A woman who changes the probability of her boyfriend's proposing marriage from .1 to .5 may well be considered to have more power than a woman who has changed her colleague's likelihood of paying for her morning coffee from .1 to .99. Tannenbaum also wishes to include what Harsanyi called B's opportunity costs. In Tannenbuam's formulation opportunity costs are stated as the price B has paid for conforming through not enacting the other possible responses available to him. He proposes to take account of both of these factors—the importance of the behavior and the opportunities foregone—by use of Floyd Allport's event-structure theory. In this way he is able to provide a "common denominator" for comparing power over different actors in different circumstances.

Event-structure theory is a formulation of individual need arousal and need reduction. An organism is thought to experience a "primary state of energic upset" at the beginning of a behavior cycle which terminates in closure. Primary energies may vary in number and intensity aroused and behaviors vary in the extent of closure they provide. The importance of a particular behavior is a function of the number of primary energies to which it is relevant and the anticipated degree of closure it will provide. Dahl's formula for amount of power (M) is weighted by Tannenbaum by the primary energies involved in the requested act (x), as well as those energies that are prevented from receiving closure because B has decided to do x. Power comparisons become possible by determining the amount of B's motivational energies at A's disposal.

Although the conceptual reduction of power to motivational energies implies a comparison basis that is less restrictive than all those previously discussed, the operational problems requiring solution to activate this formulation are equally formidable.

Taken together, the formulations reviewed in this section have focused on variables which any comprehensive theory of power must be able to take into account. They are in no instance contradictory to the field theory formulations, although they often demand a type of measurement that is different from that originating in the field force framework.

C. INTERACTION FRAMEWORK: THE THIBAUT AND KELLEY ANALYSIS

The formulations discussed so far, except for Cartwright's, have all coordinated power to changes in B. The attribute dimension of the response deemed to be important has differed—for example, overcoming resistance forces, increments in probability of enacting a response, reduction of motivational energies—as have the additional variables thought to be necessary to specify power. But A's amount of power has always been coordinated to the change occurring in B. By contrast, the systems grouped under the "interaction framework" heading lack such a focus. Although they have much in common with the decision-making formulations, they concentrate on the nature of the outcomes each participant can provide for the other, and are only secondarily concerned with change.

The interaction framework is best exemplified by the work of Thibaut and Kelley (1959). The power-relevant features of their formulation will be summarized below. Somewhat parallel treatments can be found in Homans (1958, 1961), and Blau (1964), in which interaction is viewed as an "exchange" process. An attempt to apply the interaction framework to balance concepts has been made by Emerson (1962). Karlsson (1962) has proposed a mathematical model based on a general concept of utility which is consistent with the interaction formulation.

The Thibaut and Kelley conception of power is based on their analysis of the way individuals interact. For these writers the major conceptual unit is the individual's repertoire of behavior sequences. It consists of all the responses a person is capable of enacting. Two people interact by performing some of the sequences from their repertoire. The successive pairing of behavior sequences produces a series of outcomes, each of which has a particular subjective value to the individual on a goodness-poorness scale. One way of summarizing a particular interaction is by the distribution of outcomes each participant has experienced. Power is defined by Thibaut and Kelley as the ability to affect the quality of the partner's outcomes. Specifically, the amount of power A has over B is determined by the range of outcomes through which he potentially could move B in the course of their interaction. The larger the range of outcomes that B could experience, the greater is A's power.

It is of some importance for Thibaut and Kelley to be able to specify the general limits that bound a particular outcome range. The upper limit of each participant's range is of course determined by the best available outcome, while the lower limit is set by the worst outcome the individual will endure without leaving the relationship. Thibaut and Kelley maintain that a person will leave a relationship, not necessarily because the outcomes are poor, but, because they are generally worse than the expected outcomes available in a different relationship which can be substituted for the current one. The substitute relationship, which in some instances may be the alternative of being alone, is termed "the comparison level for alternatives" (C. L.$_{alt.}$).

A person's amount of power does not directly reflect his ability to exert influence, according to this analysis. The amount of power which can effectively be utilized to influence the partner is termed "usable power" and is characterized by Thibaut and Kelley as the degree to which its use does not penalize its possessor. They describe several possible sources of penalties. One source derives from the amount of power possessed by the partner. As B's power increases, A's usable power—or relative power—is diminished because the extent to which he can profit by using that power, by giving B poor outcomes as well as good, is curtailed.

Another kind of restriction on A's use of power stems from the particular pattern of interdependence between A and B which determines the control one person has in assigning outcomes to his partner. Thibaut and Kelley distinguish *fate control* from *behavior control*. In a fate control situation A's response assigns an outcome to B regardless of the behavior B enacts. An example of fate control is presented in Table II. For

TABLE II
An Example of Fate Control

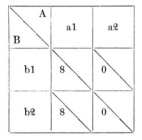

the sake of simplicity A and B are confined to making one of two responses and only B's outcomes are represented. The outcome array illustrates that A's response determines the outcome value experienced by B, who can not alter his fate. If A enacts a1, B will receive 8 outcome units whether B enacts b1 or b2. It should be noted that fate control is the limiting case of March's (1957) idea that power restricts the range of possible outcomes. In the example, either of A's responses have a probability of 1 of achieving a specific outcome. Power based on the ability to administer a wide range of outcomes is not contradictory to March's formulation in which the wide range reflects a lack of control over achieving a particular effect.

The ultimate advantage in possessing power resides in the ability to elicit desired responses from the partner. Behavior control refers to those situations where this is accomplished directly. Person A has behavior control if, by varying his behaviors, he can make it desirable for B to vary his behavior too. The amount of behavior control will increase as B stands to gain more by adjusting his behavior to the choices A has made. Behavior control occurs in any interaction where the outcome value of a particular behavior is in some measure determined by the nature of the partner's response with which it is paired. For example, the outcome value of saying "Hello" to a stranger will depend on whether he responds menacingly or cordially. Thibaut and Kelley discuss additional features of the outcome matrix which relate to the possibilities of exercising power, such as the amount of control A has over his own outcomes and the degree to which variation of A's outcomes correspond to the changes in B's outcomes. A game-theoretic extension to classifying types of interdependencies, consistent with their framework, has been suggested by Wilson and Bixenstine (1962).

Although fate control is defined by how one person's responses affect his partner's outcomes, it too can be converted to behavior control by the introduction of a rule or norm that governs both participant's responses. Consider the relationship depicted in Table II. If A wishes B to enact response b1 he would always reward its enactment (by doing a1) and discourage the occurrence of b2 (by doing a2). Fate control can be converted explicitly, by stating the rule, or implicitly, by enacting the appropriate matching behaviors. The implicit conversion of fate control in a situation where both A and B have mutual fate control has been demonstrated by Sidowski *et al.* (1956) and more recently by Kelley *et al.* (1963).

From their characterization of control Thibaut and Kelley are able to coordinate the psychology of norms to power. A norm, defined as a rule accepted by both participants, restricts the range of outcomes the low-power person is likely to receive. The norm will specify what combinations of behaviors will probably occur, as well as the unlikely combinations. Thibaut and Kelley point out that the development of norms is advantageous to both participants because it introduces regularity and control into the relationship. It removes the necessity for A's direct personal application of power, while B achieves a certain degree of dependability and stability in the outcomes he will expect to obtain.

Thibaut and Kelley also use their formulation to analyze various techniques for increasing power. These strategies have the common aim of changing the range of available outcomes from its existing size. Person A can increase his power by extending the range of outcomes he administers to B. For example, the upper (positive) end of the range can be extended through A originating such behaviors as flattery or praise, while the lower end can be extended by developing the ability to injure, harm, or molest. However, if B has an alternative relationship to which he would turn if his outcomes were to become worse, instituting the techniques for extending the negative end of the range might first require A to reduce the value of B's $C._{\mathrm{alt.}}$ by either eliminating the alternative relationship or convincing B he has over-valued its expected attractiveness. Person A can also increase his power by restricting the range of outcomes through which B can move him. To this end A would try to develop better alternative relationships or devalue the best available outcomes.

For Thibaut and Kelley, power is a potential for exercising influence which is activated under specifiable conditions of mutual control and is affected by the outcome matrix characterizing a relationship. The power one person has to induce behavior changes in his partner is mediated through learning mechanisms. Thibaut and Kelley's concepts appear to be extremely useful for organizing interaction events. But, similar to the other frameworks discussed, the operational specification of the major variables must be accomplished before the research potential of their system can fully be realized.

III. Empirical Studies

The survey of the empirical literature on power will begin with the studies contrasting various bases of power. The remaining studies are grouped according to whether they have focused on relationships of power inequality, relationships of power equality, or the perceptual concomitants of power.

A. Bases of Power

The research on bases of power is probably the most interesting set of studies in the power literature. These investigations also face the largest number of procedural problems. Any particular two power bases can not easily be arrayed on a unitary dimension. An investigator who wishes to contrast the amount of conformity obtained by two different bases, for instance, expert and referent power, has no guidelines or zero points by which to select appropriate operations. The results of such an experiment would depend on the strength of the operation selected to define each power base. Moreover, whenever reward or coercive power is included in a study, additional complications arise. These are the only two bases whose use requires Person A to make a contingent response to B's behavior, i.e., rewarding conformity and not rewarding deviation or punishing deviation and not punishing conformity. If the extent of B's conformity is a dependent variable measure, the actual use of reward or coercive power during the experiment will confound the power base manipulation with the dependent variable measure. For these reasons, the research in this section will be described in some detail.

1. The French and Raven Bases of Power

Coercive power, Person A's ability to mediate punishments for B, has most often been pitted against some other base. In general, the conceptual underpinning for these studies has been the French and Raven contention that coercive acts are most likely to induce the largest resistance force in B, and thereby reduce his conformity as well as his liking for A. The main procedural problem confronting these experiments is how to equate the strengths of inducing forces from two different bases in order to allow the resistance forces to vary. (If the "resultant" forces are equal for two bases the amount of conformity obtained through each must be equal, by definition.)

One way in which the induction forces—for instance, of reward and coercive bases—have been equated is by manipulating a specific, monetary amount. Reward power then becomes A's ability to add an amount for B's conformity, for instance, fifty cents, while coercive power is the ability to take away fifty cents for nonconformity. The objective symmetry of adding or subtracting fifty cents may not create subjective equality. In recognition of the problem of subjective differences, most studies have obtained ratings of the perceived strength of the induction force and have claimed comparability if no significant differences were found. In the absence of any independent validity for these ratings, however, it is impossible to distinguish between the results which would occur from a poor item, i.e., one that produces mostly error variance, and those that occur from true comparability of the induction forces.

In addition, the use of rewards or punishments during an experiment requires a response to the subject's behavior. As was mentioned above, the dependent variable measure may be confounded. This does not apply to experiments in which subjects are confronted only with the threat of punishment or the promise of a reward. However, several studies have attempted to solve this problem by programming a fixed schedule of rewards or punishments over a number of work units. The drawback to this solution is that the subject's actual conformity, in this instance determined by the amount of work he does, does not determine the amount of punishment or reward he will experience. The subjects in the coercive condition lose money, while those in the reward condition gain money, regardless of the extent of their conformity. Retrospective recall of the subject's feelings about the power figure, the typical way in which resistance forces are measured, may therefore reflect only the effects of the appropriateness of the particular schedule on which the subject happened to be placed. If all subjects attempt to conform, those in the reward condition should be pleased at having their increased efforts recognized, while the subjects in the coercive condition can be expected to feel irritated because their increased work has been met with punishment.

The hypothesis that reward power produces less resistance than coercive power was tested by Zipf (1960). Subjects were required to sort punched cards during a number of work units. At the end of each unit their performance was evaluated by a "supervisor." For half of the subjects the supervisor had reward power (he could add to the money subjects had earned) and for the other half he had coercive power (he could take away money subjects had earned). The resistance force was measured by the number of negative characteristics attributed to the supervisor on a post-experimental checklist, while the conformity forces were measured by a rating of how much the subject wanted to obtain the reward or how much he wanted to avoid the fine. Zipf showed that conformity, the increase in number of cards sorted after the supervisor's instruction to go faster, was positively correlated to the strength of the conformity force and tended to be negatively related to the resistance force. The resistance force was greater for coercive than reward power, but the amount of conformity obtained for both bases of power was comparable. She had also predicted that persons with a stronger need for independence would display more resistance, but obtained only a trend in this direction.

The results obtained by Kipnis (1958) indicate the amount of conformity obtained by reward or coercive bases depends on the leadership style employed by the powerful person. Grammar school children were exposed to propaganda about the desirability of a nonpreferred type of comic book by an adult who could either reward conformity by giving free movie passes or punish nonconformity by taking passes away. Each power condition was divided into a lecture and a group discussion condition. At the end of the experiment, subjects rated their comic book preferences. Although the amount of public compliance at the end of the experiment was similar in both power conditions, a check of the children's comic book preferences made one week later, in a context devoid of the former power implications, revealed a striking difference. Reward power was more effective in maintaining changes than coercive power for the children who had been in the group discussion, but reward power was less effective than coercive power for the children exposed to the lecture method. Kipnis suggested that the locus of change is shared in the discussion situation, thereby making the resistance forces induced by coercion more salient and reducing the amount of conformity which is retained over time. Kipnis also reported the expected greater liking for the reward figure than for the coercive figure.

Any conclusions about the relative efficacy of reward or coercive bases in obtaining conformity are further complicated by the data reported by Brigante (1958). Junior High School students were interrogated by a board composed of judges who could either reward, punish, or not affect the subject. In the first study reported, no differences were found for conformity to the opinions of the three types of judges when the measure was taken while the subjects were still in the power situation.

But ratings made one week later revealed a trend for the *neutral* judge
to be most influential. In a second study based on a similar format,
the neutral judge was found to have more overt and covert influence
than either the rewarding or punishing figures. Because the subjects tended
to rate themselves as being more like the neutral judge than the other
two judges, Brigante suggested his findings may be mediated by the subjects' closer identification with the neutral judge.

One of the by-products of power relationships discussed by French
and Raven is the necessity for A to maintain surveillance over B. They
hold that surveillance is especially critical for reward and coercive power.
Thibaut and Kelley (1959) make a similar analysis, although they contend
the use of rewards will permit A to decrease his surveillance efforts
because B, the trainee, will be motivated to demonstrate his conformity
in order to gain the reward. Coercion requires the trainer to arrange
surveillance opportunities in order to detect deviation. In any event, the
use of rewards or coercion by A requires him to know whether B has
conformed or deviated.

Kelley and Ring (1961) have pointed out that in most "training"
situations the trainer cannot monitor the trainee on all occasions. Their
study tested the hypothesis that a trainee would conceal his responses
less when placed on a "suspicious" training schedule (almost all responses
concealed from the trainer are punished) than when he is on a "trusting"
training schedule (almost all responses concealed from the trainer are
rewarded). Subjects were required to make successive judgments as to
which of two symptoms implied the greater personality pathology in a
situation where they could choose to conceal their response from the
"trainer." Their results, at least for a plausible training criterion, showed
that persons under a "suspicious" training schedule, in contrast to a "trusting" schedule, are more willing to bring their responses to the trainers
attention, learned his criterion to a greater degree, and expressed greater
feelings of control over the trainer's action toward them.

In an accompanying study Ring and Kelley (1963) investigated the
differences between the influence techniques of "augmentation" and
"reduction" of rewards. Subjects were either generously rewarded for
correct responses or excessively punished for incorrect responses. The
reward schedule produced greater incidence of showing responses as well
as learning the trainer's behavioral standard. They concluded on the basis
of both studies that the optimum training technique seems to be a combination of generously rewarding revealed correct responses, punishing
concealment, and mildly punishing the showing of incorrect responses.

French *et al.* (1960) studied coercive power. They separated coercive
power into the components of "punishment" forces and "resistance" forces.

Their major predictions were: (1) the greater the strength of the punishment force, the greater the amount of conformity, and (2) the greater the resistance force, the less the conformity and the less the liking for the power figure. Each of these hypotheses received supporting evidence in an experiment whose format was similar to the one Zipf used. In addition, they varied the legitimacy of the supervisor's coercive act, which either corresponded to or exceeded the maximum amount the subject had been told the supervisor could take away. They also showed that the strength of the resisting forces decreased with increasing legitimacy of a coercive influence attempt. Contrary to their prediction, the attraction toward the supervisor did not increase with increasing legitimacy of his power base.

The superiority of legitimate power in its ability to obtain conformity, even when contrasted to nonlegitimate power, has not been satisfactorily established. Raven and French (1958a) had each experimental group "elect" one of its members as a supervisor who was to monitor their work in cutting out cardboard forms. One of three stooges planted in the group was always proclaimed the winner. Prior to the start of the first work period, a second stooge started an argument with the elected supervisor. The legitimate power groups heard the announced winner retain his role, while the nonlegitimate power groups heard the second stooge taking over the supervisor's role. Only a weak trend was revealed for subjects in the legitimate power condition to conform more than subjects in the nonlegitimate condition. Although this effect was strengthened after subjects were eliminated whose pre- and post-supervisor preference ratings made it appear that the manipulation had failed, the effect was not replicated in a second study (Raven and French, 1958b), whose format was similar to the previous one. Obviously, more work is needed to establish under what conditions nonlegitimate access to a power position will penalize the occupant.

Other by-products of legitimate power were established in both of the Raven and French experiments. Chief among these was that perceptions of the extent of legitimacy were positively associated both with ratings of the justifiability of the supervisor exercising power and with the supervisor's degree of attractiveness.

Legitimacy has been defined in terms of legal accession to a particular position and in terms of enacting behaviors in keeping with an induced role prescription. In their theoretical analysis French and Raven also describe legitimacy in terms of the acceptance by B of A's right to prescribe behavior. It is in this sense of legitimacy that the conformity studies using distorted group norms can be coordinated to a power analysis. Campbell (1961) has noted that the false information attributed to other subjects in the experiment places the real subject in a situation where he must reconcile the conflict between his own perceptions and the information obtained from the other subjects. A subject in a typical conformity experiment may see twenty dots flashed on a screen. When he hears the other "subjects" announce they have seen fifty dots, his final judgment must somehow take into account this information. Campbell views the subject's final response as a weighted composite of the two sources of information. The stooges in these experiments have legitimate power because they represent a social source of information which, in many other situations, has been an accepted means of gaining valid information about the environment. The extent of acceptance of such information is enhanced by a task requiring no special abilities and by the subject's assumption the stooges are not motivated to deceive him. Any experimental manipulation which increases the legitimacy of the source of false information should increase the amount of conformity obtained.

Referent power is primarily mediated by B's identification with A. In an imaginative extension of power analysis to a level of aspiration situation, Zander and Curtis (1962) contrasted referent power with coercive power. They assumed referent power to be more likely than coercive power to lead to changes in a person's private cognitions. A standard of performance attributed to an A who has referent power should then have more influence on B's internal level of aspiration than a standard attributed to an A with coercive power. If that standard is very high, the referent power group should have a higher internal level of aspiration. For a situation in which persons fail to attain a standard of performance proposed for them by others, Zander and Curtis deduce that the referent group, in contrast to the coercive group, will perform better, be less satisfied with their performance, show greater acceptance of A's pressure, and more attraction to A. The greater discrepancy between actual performance and the internal aspiration level expected for the referent group led Zander and Curtis to predict more discrediting of the importance of the task by the referent group.

In their study, male high school seniors were led to believe that Rotter's level of aspiration board was a test of muscle control, and was to be the instrument of a state-wide competition. Prior to working on the "test," subjects were informed of unrealistically high standards of performance which a group of peers expected them to attain. Subjects in the coercive condition thought this peer group had the power to select the team which would represent the high school, while referent subjects thought they already had a place on the team which included the prestigeful peer group. With the exception of the predictions concerning the discrediting of the importance of the task, the major hypotheses were confirmed. Referent subjects actually attained better scores and expressed less satisfaction with their performance. This seeming contradiction lends considerable credence to their rationale. However, the experimental operations defining the two bases of power may have confounded the results. Some difficulty is created by the referent subjects' belief they have been assured team membership, while subjects in the coercive condition think their task performance is to be used in evaluating their acceptability as team members. Moreover, subjects in the referent condition were also told that the unusually high standard was the average score attained by the peer group on the task the subject was about to perform. The same high standard was represented to subjects in the coercive condition as a discussion consensus reached by the peer group who had not attempted the task. It seems likely that a standard attributed to a group discussion is less credible than one which represents the average of a group's actual performance, especially when that standard is beyond the subject's own performance. If, for this reason, subjects in the coercive group rejected the standard, their internal aspiration levels would have been correspondingly lowered. This could account for the Zander and Curtis results, aside from any difference created by the particular basis of power.

Although disagreements exist about the proper placement of the term "cohesiveness" in the web connecting reward power, referent power, "attraction," and "liking," it is an obvious power base. A number of studies have shown a group's increased ability to obtain conformity with increasing cohesiveness (Back, 1951; Schachter et al., 1951; Festinger et al., 1950). In analyses of dyadic interactions, extent of mutual liking has played a central role. In the cognitive balance models, [for instance in those of Heider (1958) and Newcomb (1953)], the nature of the affective bond between two persons is assumed to be a potent determinant of attitude change. Liking and attitude similarity are assumed to go together as are disliking and attitude dissimilarity.

In most laboratory experiments, extent of liking has been the independent variable and attitude change has been the dependent variable. There are some indications that in field situations liking is a consequence of attitude similarity. Newcomb (1963) reports that in a group of unacquainted people, initial attitude similarity is a better predictor of interpersonal attraction measured after 16 weeks of interaction than initial ratings of attraction. In a situation where each person is free to seek out others he likes, and where there is no pressure toward consensus, attraction seems to be based on attitude similarity rather than the other way around.

Referent power, as well as legitimate and expert power, permit B to gain rewards for conforming that are independent of any additional actions by A. The form of A's control is not direct, and B retains personal initiative for complying. This is one feature of referent power which minimizes resistance to its use. Although no study has directly tested the relation between amount of conformity and the degree to which the target person retains the initiative for conforming, Walster and Festinger (1962) conducted a study which bears closely on this point. In their study, subjects who thought they were "overhearing" a group discussion containing persuasive information, showed more attitude change than subjects who heard the identical discussion, but thought the participants were aware of their presence. Walster and Festinger conclude the effect, which holds up only for issues in which the person is involved, represents the enhancement of influence by a source that has no apparent motive to influence. From the respondent's point of view there are no "hidden charges" to being influenced, and, most likely, no feeling of constraint about his own freedom of action. The contexts in which referent power will be an effective influence strategy is still uncertain.

The old master on power matters, Machiavelli (reprinted 1940), whose discussion of power contains many of the hypotheses under current investigation, argues, in what is essentially a contrast between referent and coercive power, " . . . men love at their own free will, but fear at the will of the prince, and that a wise prince must rely on what is in his power and not on what is in the power of others . . ." (p. 63). On the other hand, after summarizing a number of studies showing a positive association between low status and poor mental health, French (1963) suggests an ingenious remedy: poor mental health might be alleviated by raising the power of low status roles, by increasing their referent power. He suggests the resistance of high power people will not be mobilized because an increase in the low's referent power will not alter the relative power positions. It is, however, difficult to see how a supervisor will not have less relative power if he likes his subordinates more.

The effectiveness of expertness as a base of power has been frequently demonstrated in studies using the closely allied concepts of "perceived competence," "credibility," or "skill." Croner and Willis (1961) showed that a stooge whose performance is presented as being good on one task will be able to exert more influence on a subsequent task. Their study takes on added significance because they show the relationship holds only when the second task is comparable to the first. They substantiate French and Raven's (1959) prediction that the scope of expertness is limited to the areas on which the expertness is based. On the other hand, the importance of both relevant and irrelevant aspects of credibility in determining successful influence has been demonstrated by Aronson and Golden (1962). A persuasive message about arithmetic which was attributed to an engineer produced more attitude change than when the same message was attributed to a dishwasher. In this respect their results are similar to those of many other studies. However, half of the subjects in each condition saw a Negro communicator and half saw a Caucasian. No differences were found for the amount of influence attributable to the race of·the communicator. But when the subjects' amount of prejudice was taken into account, a significant difference was found for the impact made by the Negro communicator. Prejudiced subjects were "under influenced" and unprejudiced subjects were "over-influenced." An attribute of the communicator which was irrelevant to his credibility affected the extent and direction of his influence.

Thibaut and Kelley (1959) interpret expertness as an ability to cut the partner's costs. They suggest that one of the problems associated with expert power is the possibility that its use will, over time, obviate the recipient's need. The extent to which a particular expert is vulnerable to communicating his expertness and thereby using up his base is a function of a number of variables, including the complexity of the knowledge and the degree to which the expert's decision-process is open to view. Their analysis suggests the expert's maintenance of power is dependent on his ability to keep the recipient in ignorance about the basis for making recommendations, as well as preventing him access to relevant information. The popularization of medical practices would, in these terms, produce more problems for the general practitioner than for the surgeon.

The question of the consequences of using up a power base could also be raised with respect to reward and coercive power. Harsanyi (1962a) has drawn attention to this feature of power relationships. His concept of opportunity costs refers to the costs A must incur to reward conformity or punish nonconformity. In most experiments A has an unlimited, or at least an impersonal, supply of money, electricity, "points," experimental credit, etc. Little is known about A's ability to change B under various conditions of opportunity costs to A.

Other problems involving power bases deserving more research attention can also be cited. The relative ability to produce conformity by one or another power base is still unclear. In addition, few studies have attempted to assess the long-range effects of a particular base, not only on the degree of conformity retained over a given time period, but also on the concomitant changes in B that are not necessarily intended. For instance, it seems intuitively correct to accept French and Raven's hypothesis about the long-range superiority of reward power over coercive power, but this does not seem to apply to the dimension of effectiveness. In addition to the research already discussed, such observations as Bettelheim's (1943) of the effective use of extreme coercive techniques, indicate the importance of studying interpersonal dimensions other than effectiveness of obtaining changes.

It is interesting to note that the role of punishment in traditional learning experiments is not completely settled. In his review of research on punishment, R. L. Solomon (1964) lists a number of conditions which affect the effectiveness of punishment as a controller of behavior, such as the intensity of the punishment, the nature of the response to which it is applied, the pre-training conditions for establishing the response, etc. Solomon also suggests the general acceptance of the efficacy of reward techniques testifies more to their appeal as acceptable, humanistic values than to the existence of experimental evidence demonstrating their superiority over punishment techniques. Many of the studies of reward and coercive power bases appear to suffer from a similar experimenter orientation.

2. Power Based on Accurate Predictions

Despite the lack of any direct, empirical research, it seems worthwhile to mention the ability to predict as a base of power. If A is able to predict what B is going to do, A is likely to enjoy certain advantages. Consider a typical game matrix where B must select one of the columns and A one of the rows. To the extent that A can predict which column B will select, A will be able to obtain the best outcome available within the limitations established by B's response. In this instance A is not necessarily interested in changing B's behavior, but he is able to capitalize on whatever B intends doing in order either to maximize his own outcomes, or to assign to B the outcome value he wishes. A successful poker player is likely to have the chief source of his power stemming from his ability to predict accurately the meaning of his opponent's behaviors.

The extent to which this power base is used will probably be inversely related to the amount of direct control an individual possesses over his partner or over his own outcomes. It is likely to appeal most to the person with less power. However, the high-power individual may also use predictions, especially in situations where he can control some environmental event whose effect on B is predictable. Cartwright (in press) speaks of "ecological control" and notes its use whenever B's ". . . behavior is predictably related to some manipulable feature of (B's) physical or social environment."

There are some conceptual difficulties attendant to classifying the ability to predict as a power base. This base is in logical contradiction to the frameworks defining power as A's ability to change B's behavior, because its use requires A to modify his own behavior in accordance with what he expects B to do. Any changes which occur happen in Person A, blurring the usual, causal order of events indicative of influence. Simon (1953) refers to this problem as "the rule of anticipatory reaction" and notes that its occurrence hinders observation of the influence process. In order to preserve the directionality of influence in power relationships, Simon suggests the necessity for assuming ignorance or fallible predictions on the part of the participants. While Simon's position may be unnecessarily severe (see March, 1955), it should be noted that when power is defined in terms of A's ability to affect the quality of B's outcomes or his ability to maximize his own outcomes, no contradiction exists with power based on making accurate predictions.

B. Relationships of Power Inequality

In any relationship the participants can be scaled on the dimension of how much power each possesses. If a sufficiently sensitive metric of power existed it would be rare to find a relationship, even a dyadic one, in which the participants had equal amounts of power with regard to a specific domain or interaction goal. One person will usually have a relative power advantage. However, the observable coordinates of power are fairly gross, and in practice a distinction can be made between relationships in which the participants have unequal power from those in which they have equal power. Studies of the former class of relationships have typically focused on the interpersonal consequences of exercising power; studies of the later type of relationships have been concerned with the kinds of accommodations made by participants who begin an interaction on an equal footing.

1. Obtaining Change

The possession of power is intimately linked with the ability to induce change in the partner. As already noted, power is often defined by the production of change. An experiment which demonstrated that increasing amounts of power produced increasing degrees of change would, therefore, do little more than validate a particular set of experimental procedures. It would hold little theoretical interest. This same relation has, of course, been demonstrated for variables closely associated with power, such as leadership and high status. For example, Strodtbeck (1951) showed that culturally approved patterns of sex-dominance are reflected in the pattern of dominance shown by husband-wife pairs from three different cultures on a decision-making task. In a like way, status in the wider society was shown to correlate positively with the amount of influence exerted on decisions made in a jury situation (Strodtbeck et al., 1958). Torrance (1955) demonstrated that the leader of a three-man military group exerts the most influence on a decision-making task. In the area of attitude change, the relationship is illustrated by the "prestige" suggestion experiment, in which a high-status source typically obtains more change than a neutral or low-status source.

In a field study guided by a general conception of power as the ability to influence, Lippitt et al. (1952) studied the relation between a person's amount of power and "behavioral contagion," the extent to which he is imitated by others in situations in which he does not intend to influence. According to their findings a group member is more likely to imitate the behavior of those group members to whom he has attributed high power. The acceptance of influence attempts is also higher when initiated by high-power members. The correlations on which these findings are based are vulnerable to several artifacts. One of these is the positive correlation between high power and total behavior output. However, the relations remain significant when total behavior output is controlled.

The conditions facilitating imitation have also been studied by Bandura et al. (1963). Their experiment is the only one found in the literature which contrasts predictions from a power framework with those of a different theory. Experimentally contrived three-person groups representing prototypes of the nuclear family were used to test three different predictions. From a power framework it was deduced that the person who controls valued resources will be the major source of identification and subsequent imitation. The consumer of resources was predicted to be the target of imitation from Whiting's status envy theory. It claims that when a child competes unsuccessfully for scarce resources he will envy the consumer of these resources and consequently identify with him.

Their final prediction came from applying the concept of secondary reinforcement to imitation. According to this view, if the behavioral attributes of a model are paired with positive reinforcement of the child, the attributes will acquire secondary reward value. Through stimulus generalization the child can elicit reinforcement by imitating the model. Appropriate experimental counterparts for each prediction were arranged. Imitation was greatest for the power condition, although its superiority over the secondary reinforcement condition was attributed to a theoretically irrelevant aspect of the procedure. Imitation was clearly greatest for the person who controlled the valued resources.

In unequal power relationships the consequences for the low-power person are usually clear—he will enact responses or make other changes which the high-power person desires. What can be said about changes which might occur in the high-power person? Ordinarily it is assumed that he remains stable, because the changes he has caused should have optimal value for him and there is no reason for him to change. (In addition, the high-power person in experiments is often an accomplice of the experimenter. Investigators have not been interested in how their accomplices are affected by the experiment.) It is possible to imagine a situation in which successful influence could generate pressures on the inducer to change. For instance, if a disliked person is induced to change his attitude to resemble that of the high-power person, the latter will experience some degree of cognitive imbalance and may subsequently change his attitude.

An analogous problem has been raised with respect to the power a group has over its leader's conformity to important group norms. It has been suggested that a leader displays the greatest amount of conformity to the group's norms (Homans, 1950). In so far as the leader has the most power over the group, it can also be argued, he will be able to deviate with impunity from the norms adhered to by the other members. Hollander (1958) has made one attempt at resolving this difference. He introduced the concept of "idiosyncrasy credits," defined as the ". . . accumulation of positively-disposed impressions residing in the perceptions of relevant others . . ." (p. 120). Idiosyncrasy credits are obtained by possessing qualities or enacting behaviors which are positively valued by members of the group. Increasing amounts of these credits relate to attaining higher status in the group and to the ability to deviate successfully from group norms. Hollander differentiates the process by which one becomes a leader—accruing credits through activities such as conforming—and the prerogatives of being a leader, which includes having enough credits to be able to deviate. He demonstrated (Hollander, 1961) that when someone who possesses a high degree of task competence deviates during a group's early phase he cannot exert as much influence as he might if he deviated during a later period.

Berkowitz and Macaulay (1961) contest the comprehensiveness of the idiosyncrasy credit explanation because it can not account for the experimental results showing that the greatest amount of conformity is displayed by group members who are only moderately accepted. In order to understand these results, Berkowitz and Macaulay contend status instability, which is viewed as a source of approach motivation to the group, must be considered. They predict the highly accepted members whose status is not secure, in contrast to highly accepted members whose status is stable, will show greater conformity, admit to a greater desire for high status, and be more attracted to the group. Although the conformity prediction was not confirmed, their other predictions were supported.

2. *Other Consequences for the Relationship*

Aside from being able to induce change, the high-power person enjoys certain other advantages over his low-power partner. The analysis of these factors advanced by Thibaut and Kelley (1959) will serve to guide this discussion. The high-power person is typically able to initiate behaviors, thereby gaining the advantage of having any shifts in activities occur when he wishes. The low-power person usually follows changes and is always in some danger of not completing a particular sequence or being unprepared for a shift. Inmates typically suffer this disadvantage when the staff enforces rigid schedules which are geared to the convenience of the institution rather than to the task activities of the inmates.

The high typically has greater freedom of action, in contrast to the low's caution and need carefully to monitor his own behavior. Riesman (1954) makes a similar point when he writes, ". . . if one has power one does not feel the need of insight. . . " (p. 169). Hurwitz *et al.* (1953) conducted a controlled conference composed of high- and low-status mental health workers. They found that low-status mental health workers approach high-status ones with deference and fear. Lippitt *et al.* (1952) document a similar point for adolescents in a summer camp, while Cohen (1958) has added experimental confirmation.

A person who has high power in many relationships, and is therefore typically able to obtain conformity to his own values and attitudes, has the additional advantage of remaining consistent when moving from one relationship to another. The low-power person is vulnerable to the tensions associated with cognitive imbalance or inconsistency. It is much easier for a university professor to maintain a consistent viewpoint favoring racial integration in the south than for an hourly worker in a grocery store.

The various advantages enjoyed by the high-power person often translate into other psychological consequences. For instance, the highs tend to show more satisfaction with any given interaction. Zander and Cohen (1955) used a role-playing technique in which members of a group reacted to one of their members as if he had high status and to one as if he had low status. The post-experimental ratings by the highs showed greater satisfaction and enjoyment of the interaction than did those of the lows. In artificially created communication networks, occupancy of the position of greatest power produces the largest amount of satisfaction (Bavelas, 1960). Mulder (1960) interprets these results as indicating that the exercise of power is in itself satisfying. When the communication structure of a group is left free, highs participate more than lows and are more often the targets of communicative acts. The tendency of the lows to communicate upwards was interpreted by Thibaut

(1950) as a form of substitute locomotion, while Hurwitz *et al.* (1953) see it as an ego defensive reaction. Finally, the possession of power seems to be one basis for developing trust. L. Solomon (1960) found that in a game situation, trusting responses were more likely when the person possessed high power.

3. Power Strategies

Whenever a person attempts to improve his power position he is engaging in a power strategy. Although persons having high or low power may use power strategies, the disadvantages attendant to having low power typically motivate the low-power person to improve his power position.

It is not clear under what conditions a person will desire to employ power strategies. The mere existence of power inequalities is neither a necessary nor sufficient condition for such attempts. The low-power person, even though he sees conflicts resolved in his partner's favor, may still be getting much better outcomes from the relationship than he could obtain from any other alternative. He will then be satisfied with the existing power distribution and have little reason to develop power strategies. Some authors have linked the lack of power with the creation of personal threat, either when the low-power person feels unable to reach his goal (Stotland, 1959) or when he feels inadequate to gain need satisfaction (Cohen, 1959). Cohen (1959) found that lack of structure in a situation significantly enhances the threat felt by a low-power person from a partner having what was essentially fate control. Stotland (1959) showed that peer-group support heightens persistence on a task controlled by a threatening power figure, as well as expressions of direct hostility and negative evaluations of the power holder.

Horwitz (1958) maintains a reduction of a person's expected amount of power will produce threat and lead that person to efforts to restore his power. He summarizes a series of experiments stemming from this theme. His main independent variable manipulation, reduction of power, involved a stooge successfully ignoring the experimental instructions of how much weight the subjects' opinions should be given in making a task decision. This manipulation is similar to the one used by French *et al.* (1960) in their study of legitimate power bases. Horwitz's results are comparable in that the reduction of power produced expressions of hostility and negative ratings of the power figure. In addition, the power figure was seen as acting on "inner" determinants for his behavior. These reactions were mollified in another study to the extent to which power was restored.

The Thibaut and Kelley (1959) framework lends itself to a somewhat different analysis of power strategies. Consistent with their range of outcomes definition, an individual's power strategies are aimed at either restricting the range of outcomes he can experience (giving up the best ones or eliminating the worst) or extending the range through which he can move his partner (giving him better or poorer outcomes than were previously possible). Within this general format various specific interpersonal strategies are possible. Power can be extended, for example, by such techniques as flattery, praise, short-run concessions, or by eliminating the partner's best alternative relationship. Although it is not typically conceived of in this way, the conforming act can itself be a power-increasing strategy in a relationship which will endure beyond the point of conformity. Because conforming is presumably the best response B can make from A's view point, it maximizes A's outcomes. Person B extends, or at least develops, a range of outcomes through which he can move A, if he has the possibility of not conforming in the future. Schopler and Bateson (1962) suggest this argument with respect to understanding the subjects' responses to an experimenter, especially when the experimenter has made them do something unpleasant. They interpret the Aronson and Mills (1959) finding of greater liking for a dull discussion made by subjects experiencing a severe initiation into the group, in contrast to ones having a mild initiation, in power terms. The severe initiation created a wider range of outcomes through which the experimenter moved these subjects. Their expression of greater liking was viewed as representing conformity to a powerful experimenter's attitude. In a similar manner Jones (1964) has interpreted ingratiation techniques in terms of their power significance. He distinguishes between the total behavior repertoire and that portion considered relevant to the relationship. The ingratiator attempts to extend the range of relevance beyond what is implicitly accepted by both participants. He is oriented, for example, toward exploiting behavior which is not task-centered.

Another kind of power strategy is available in situations where it is possible to form coalitions. Ordinarily potentials for coalition formation require, at a minimum, a three-person group and an arrangement whereby two of the people can act jointly to affect the outcomes of the third. The literature in this area is sufficiently extensive to warrant a separate chapter (Gamson, 1964) and will not be reviewed here.

In a broader sense, any human interaction contains coalition potentials with agents who are external to the relationship. Thibaut and Kelley (1959) interpret parents invoking such agents as God or Santa Claus to obtain conformity in their children as a parental strategy to increase power. Their analysis has received some empirical support from Nunn (1964), who demonstrated that families representing God as an agent who punishes "bad" behavior are characterized by lower socioeconomic indices of power than families who do not represent God in this way. A theoretical extension of the power potentials based on personal convictions of being in a coalition with a powerful agent of control has been made by Thibaut (1964).

Thibaut and Kelley (1959) also include the formation of coalitions with norms as a way of increasing power. They maintain that if a request for a certain behavior can be referred to a norm, it will obviate the necessity for the use of personal power. This strategy is illustrated by the parent who asks his child to eat spinach because spinach is good for his health. Its effectiveness will depend on the extent to which the norm has been accepted by the target person. Whatever cost he incurs from the conforming act will be compensated by the rewards obtained from conforming to a norm which he accepts. It is probably also true that the more important a norm is to a group, the more effective it will be as a "coalition partner." In addition to the likelihood that important norms will have a wider degree of acceptance, they are frequently maintained by powerful agents in the society. Deviation from these norms, even in a dyadic relationship, incurs the risk of invoking the power of these agents. A professor who wants his entire class to attend a final examination will have little difficulty in obtaining compliance if the university administration has defined attendance as an important norm.

The existence of norms also places certain constraints on the high-power person in his exercise of power. The strategy of non-violence when employed as an influence technique can be seen in this light. The low-power minority group is able to obtain changes despite its weakness by dramatizing both its weakness and the norm it wishes upheld. Again, the effectiveness of this strategy will depend on the degree of acceptance of the norm by the more powerful group. For instance, Berkowitz (1957) and Berkowitz and Daniels (1963) showed that a partner's dependence can serve as an effective source of motivation for giving him help. The essential point in both of these studies was that the subjects will work harder when they believe their partner stands to win money than when their partner is not affected by the amount they work. They interpret the partner's dependence to be a cue for arousing the norm of "social responsibility." In effect the dependent partner is able to exert influence by his ability to arouse the norm.

In subsequent studies (Daniels and Berkowitz, 1963; Berkowitz and Daniels, 1964), they show that the dependent partner's ability to influence is increased not only by conditions which arouse the norm, such as the subject being helped on a prior task, but also by factors which motivate the subject to conform to the norm, such as liking for the partner. In each of these studies high dependence was manipulated by telling the subject he was working for a supervisor who stood to gain a reward, while subjects in the small-dependence condition were told their supervisor's chance of winning a reward were in no way affected by the subjects' work. The lower work output of the subjects having a minimally dependent partner could be based on the lack of justification for doing any work. They have no control over the partner's outcomes whether they work hard or not at all.

In a study employing a range-of-outcomes definition of dependence, Schopler and Bateson (1965) showed that the degree of help given by a powerful person increases as the amount of his own reward he must sacrifice decreases. The Berkowitz finding of greater yielding to high dependence was repeated for females, but not males, where the direction was reversed, producing an interaction effect between degree of dependence and sex of subject on amount of yielding.

C. Relationships of Power Equality

In interactions where each participant has the same amount of power, his ability to cause change or to influence will also be equal. In situations requiring the exercise of power, i.e., when conflicts of interest arise, each member will be equally represented. It is possible that such groups would not be able to resolve the conflict. Of course, in practice, power differentation usually occurs with respect to a particular area. It is also possible that the final resolution represents the best compromise available for the group. Siegel and Fouraker (1960) devised a bargaining situation involving supply and demand schedules. They explicitly excluded the kinds of interpersonal variables which might create power structuring by having subjects communicate by notes with bargaining partners whose identity was not known. Bargaining pairs tended to reach the best common solution of maximizing joint payoffs, in repeated bargaining sessions. In situations where a compromise is not possible for a particular conflict, the group would be expected to work out some kind of trading norm that insures each person a fair turn at optimizing his own outcomes.

In groups where each participant begins with a similar amount of power, power differences may quickly develop through interaction. One member may convey greater expertness about the task, make himself more attractive, etc., thereby establishing some degree of power differentiation. Several experiments have investigated the kinds of accommodations which are reached and their effect on the influence process. Atthowe (1961), for example, had pairs of subjects make joint decisions on a gambling-type task. Maximal decision-making inefficiency was associated with increasing verbal interaction, moderate initial individual differences, and a weak leader-follower relationship.

Eskola (1961) has conducted the most extensive work on equal power relationships. He reports two studies conceptually based on Cartwright's analysis, but primarily focused on methodological problems and empirical associations among the measures. He required pairs of subjects to work on a variety of decision-making tasks until they arrived at a common solution. The subjects had given answers to each task prior to the experimental interaction. One of his major analyses was based on categorizing the decisions into one of three categories of dominance, compromise, or intermediate solution types. Although he notes many of his relationships to be affected by the nature of the task, he has some general findings. For example, intermediate solutions are much more likely if the initial opinion discrepancy in the dyad is large. Initial accuracy and power were positively associated, but the correlations varied widely from task to task.

It is perhaps a testimony to the difficulty of generating deductive hypotheses from power frameworks that a large portion of Eskola's careful work centers on methodological problems inherent in his situation. For example, on a task requiring the recall of items contained in a picture, he discovered the person recalling more items, regardless of his objective accuracy, was usually more influential than his partner on the joint decision. Eskola's inventive interpretation involves postulating greater resistance to lowering the number of items recalled because it is ". . . easier for people to admit that they did not see everything, than to admit they saw something which did not exist" (p. 66).

When power is equal it is possible to distinguish groups in which everyone holds high power from those in which each person holds low power. In Back's (1951) study, dyads composed of members who were highly attracted to each other not only made more influence attempts, but also influenced each other more. On the other hand, Deutsch and Krauss (1960) showed that high-power dyads who were engaged in a competitive game gained fewer rewards compared to low-power dyads. The addition of power (the ability to block the other's goal attainment) prevented mutually optimum solutions from being reached. The extent to which their results can be generalized beyond the specific features of their game has been questioned by Borah (1963).

D. PERCEPTUAL CONCOMITANTS OF POWER

When group members are asked to rate each other with respect to how much power they perceive others to possess, a reasonable amount of agreement is usually found. Furthermore, each member seems to be aware of the amount of power he possesses in the group. According to Lippitt *et al.* (1952) individuals are accurate in rating their own power position in their group. The power self-ratings of campers who have been rated high on power by their peers are significantly higher than the self-ratings of campers who have been rated low on power. The accuracy of discerning ones own position is evidently affected by the individual's degree of adjustment. Rosen (1959) reports that adjusted campers are more accurate than maladjusted campers in perceiving their own amount of power.

The accuracy of perceiving power ought to be affected by the general conditions which lower or enhance perceptual accuracy. For example, Pepitone (1950) predicted the occurrence of distortions in line with personal goal attainment in the amount of power attributed to others. His study is an example of an early "balance" formulation and used the perception of amount of power merely as a vehicle to test the general formulation. In the section of his study relevant to power subjects faced a three-man board, each of whom had objectively equal power in deciding whether the subjects would be granted a valued athletic ticket. The subjects found one man to be friendly, one hostile, and one neutral. Subjects were divided according to whether they were highly motivated or not to win the ticket. In post-experimental ratings of the judges' degree of power, the friendly judge was seen to have more power by the motivated group than by the less motivated.

This difference was consistent with the prediction, but its meaning was obscured by the tendency of the highly motivated subjects to attribute more power to all of the judges than the less motivated subjects. Although this was not directly at issue in the Pepitone study, it is also likely that perceived friendliness and amount of power of another person are positively correlated. In a study using peer ratings by college subjects, Tagiuri and Kogan (1960) found ratings of liking of others and extent of being influenced by others to be positively correlated for most subjects. On the other hand, the conference data on high- and low-power participants, collected by Hurwitz et al. (1953), is consistent with Pepitone's hypothesis. They report their low-power subjects as showing a greater need to see high-power members as liking them.

The question of what characteristics are associated with being seen as having power has also been investigated. In the camp situation, Lippitt et al. (1952) found amount of attributed power not to be associated with either age or intelligence when all of their groups were combined, but intelligence was shown to be positively correlated with power in their group of adjusted campers. Gold (1958) interviewed children in order to identify characteristics which they viewed as valuable and important. Although the importance of these characteristics varied with age and sex of the child, the individual who possessed many important characteristics was seen by his peers as better able to influence them than an individual who possessed only a few. Rosen *et al.* (1961) found about the same amount of agreement between a group of campers and a sample of teachers on rankings of how important six characteristics were for the possession of power. The perceived importance of a characteristic was thought to be a function of the number of situations eliciting it and the frequency of occurrence of those situations. Much as the search for characteristics associated with leadership has seemed to depend on such factors as the goals of the group and the context of their interaction, the characteristics linked with power are likely to depend on the same situational factors.

A person's perception of his own amount of power is undoubtedly affected by his recognition of whether he possesses the appropriate traits. In addition, Levinger (1959) demonstrated that an individual's perception of his own power is affected by the favorableness of initial information concerning his relative resource potential in the group and the way in which other group members respond to him. Finally, Rosen *et al.* (1960) report, for a group of campers, the more power attributed to a member the less he will want to change himself and the less he will want to see changes in others.

IV. Conclusion

The increased research efforts in the area of power over the past decade were noted at the beginning of this chapter. The theoretical formulations and the empirical research, taken together, form an impressive beginning to understanding the phenomena of power and justify a certain degree of optimism about the future of research on power. On the other hand, signs of disenchantment with the concept are also evident. March (1963), in a critical analysis of six general power models, considers their predictive ability meager and their measurement prerequisites difficult to meet, especially in natural settings. Although March expresses some hope for its productive use in laboratory studies, he judges power to be a "disappointing variable."

The brunt of evidence to date appears to favor March's judgment, but the ultimate usefulness of a power concept will depend on several possible lines of development. One of these is advances in theoretical formulations which place power in a well-defined construct network capable of generating meaningful research issues. Despite some notable beginnings, this goal has not yet been attained. No other single advance would do as much for replacing the taxonomic advantages with truly substantive ones. It would also tend to coordinate various research efforts. The variety of meanings associated with power was noted earlier. At the present level of development such variety is probably beneficial. Because authors invariably specify their meaning of power less confusion is produced by definitional differences than by the tendency to assign different names to identical, or similar, research operations. For instance, the results of having group members rate how much they like each other has been labeled, "attributed power," "attractiveness," "resource ownership," as well as merely "liking." A complete theoretical statement would describe the mapping rules by which the component parts are to be observed and enhance comparability among studies. Movement in this direction might be accelerated by the development of theories with limited scope applied to a well-defined domain, rather than by general theories aiming to intergrate the entire area.

In the absence of theoretical advances specific to power, solutions to problems in allied areas, such as motivation or utility theory, would have an immediate pay-off for power research. The current power formulations quickly lead into the area of need satisfaction or utility judgments. Any progress which is made is such areas as classification of needs, comparisons among different needs, or comparisons among utility judgments, would provide sharper tools with which to conduct power research.

Finally, independent of any particular theoretical formulation, a number of important issues have been delineated. These will certainly generate additional research activity. Although specification of a particular list of issues is a matter of personal taste, the following problem areas have been emphasized in this review: (1) the effectiveness of different power bases, especially in relation to the permanence of changes, (2) the effects of a consumable power base, (3) the conditions leading to the exercise of power and to the development of power strategies, (4) the consequences to the high-power person of exercising his power, and (5) the interpersonal by-products of power relationships. Progress in any of these areas would contribute to the robustness of power research and would help to realize the potential hoped for by many authors, but not yet attained.

References

Aronson, E., and Golden, B. W. (1962). The effect of relevant and irrelevant aspects of communicator credibility on opinion change. *J. Pers.* **30**, 135–146.

Aronson, E., and Mills, J. (1959). The effect of severity of initiation on liking for a group. *J. abnorm. soc. Psychol.* **59**, 177–181.

Atthowe, J. M., Jr. (1961). Interpersonal decision making: the resolution of a dyadic conflict. *J. abnorm. soc. Psychol.* **62**, 114–119.

Back, K. (1951). Influence through social communication. *J. abnorm. soc. Psychol.* **46**, 9–23.

Bandura, A., Ross, Dorothea, and Ross, Sheila, A. (1963). A comparative test of the status envy, social power, and secondary reinforcement theories of identificatory learning. *J. abnorm. soc. Psychol.* **67**, 527–534.

Bavelas, A. (1960). Communication patterns in task-oriented groups. In D. Cartwright and A. Zander (Eds.), *Group dynamics.* (2nd ed.) Evanston, Ill.: Row, Peterson, pp. 669–682.

Berkowitz, L. (1957). Effects of perceived dependency relationships upon conformity to group expectations. *J. abnorm. soc. Psychol.* **55**, 350–354.

Berkowitz, L., and Daniels, Louise R. (1963). Responsibility and dependency. *J. abnorm. soc. Psychol.* **66**, 429–436.

Berkowitz, L., and Daniels, Louise R. (1964). Affecting the salience of the social responsibility norm: effects of past help on the response to dependency relationships. *J. abnorm. soc. Psychol.* **68**, 275–281.

Berkowitz, L., and Macaulay, Jacqueline R. (1961). Some effects of differences in status level and status stability. *Hum. Relat.* **14**, 135–147.

Bettelheim, B. (1943). Individual and mass behavior in extreme conditions. *J. abnorm. soc. Psychol.* **38**, 417–452.

Blau, P. M. (1964). *Exchange and power in social life.* New York: Wiley.

Borah, L. A., Jr. (1963). The effects of threat in bargaining: critical and experimental analysis. *J. abnorm. soc. Psychol.* **66**, 37–44.

Brigante, T. R. (1958). Adolescent evaluations of rewarding, neutral, and punishing power figures. *J. Pers.* **26**, 435–450.

Campbell, D. T. (1961). Conformity in psychology's theories of acquired behavioral dispositions. In I. A. Berg and B. M. Bass (Eds.), *Conformity and deviation.* New York: Harper, pp. 101–142.

Cartwright, D. (1959a). Power: a neglected variable in social psychology. In D. Cartwright (Ed.), *Studies in social power.* Ann Arbor, Mich.: Institute for Social Research, pp. 1–14.

Cartwright, D. (1959b). A field theoretical conception of power. In D. Cartwright (Ed.), *Studies in social power.* Ann Arbor, Mich.: Institute for Social Research, pp. 183–220.

Cartwright, D. (in press). Influence, leadership, control. In J. March (Ed.) *Handbook of Organizations.* Chicago: Rand, McNally.

Cohen, A. R. (1958). Upward communication in experimentally created hierarchies. *Hum. Relat.* **11**, 41–53.

Cohen, A. R. (1959). Situational structure, self-esteem, and threat-oriented reactions to power. In D. Cartwright (Ed.), *Studies in social power.* Ann Arbor, Mich.: Institute for Social Research, pp. 35–52.

Croner, M. D., and Willis, R. H. (1961). Perceived differences in task competence and asymmetry of dyadic influence. *J. abnorm. soc. Psychol.* **62**, 705–708.

Dahl, R. A. (1957). The concept of power. *Behav. Sci.* **2**, 201–218.

Daniels, Louise R., and Berkowitz, L. (1963). Liking and response to dependency relationships. *Hum. Relat.* **16**, 141–148.

Deutsch, M., and Krauss, R. M. (1960). The effect of threat upon interpersonal bargaining. *J. abnorm. soc. Psychol.* **61**, 181–189.

Emerson, R. M. (1962). Power-dependence relations. *Am. sociol. Rev.* **27**, 31–41.

Eskola, A. (1961). *Social influence and power in two-person groups.* Transactions of the Westermarck Society, Vol. VI. Transl. by J. Railo, Munksgaard, Finland: Turun Saromalehti ja Kirjapaino Osakeyhtio.

Festinger, L., Schachter, S., and Back, K. (1950). *Social pressures in informal groups.* New York: Harper.

French, J. R. P., Jr. (1956). A formal theory of social power. *Psychol. Rev.* **63**, 181–194.

French, J. R. P., Jr. (1963). The social environment and mental health. *J. soc. Issues* **19**, 39–56.

French, J. R. P., Jr., and Raven, B. (1959). The bases of social power. In D. Cartwright (Ed.), *Studies in social power.* Ann Arbor, Mich.: Institute for Social Research, pp. 150–167.

French, J. R. P., Jr., Morrison, H. W., and Levinger, G. (1960). Coercive power and forces affecting conformity. *J. abnorm. soc. Psychol.* **61**, 93–101.

Gamson, W. (1964). Experimental studies of coalition formation. In L. Berkowitz (Ed.), *Advances in experimental social psychology.* Vol. 1. New York: Academic Press, pp. 81–110.

Gold, M. (1958). Power in the classroom. *Sociometry* **21**, 50–60.

Harary, F. (1959). A criterion for unanimity in French's theory of social power. In D. Cartwright (Ed.), *Studies in social power.* Ann Arbor, Mich.: Institute for Social Research, pp. 168–182.

Harsanyi, J. C. (1962a). Measurement of social power, opportunity costs, and the theory of two-person bargaining games. *Behav. Sci.* **7**, 67–80.

Harsanyi, J. C. (1962b). Measurement of social power in n-person reciprocal power situations. *Behav. Sci.* **7**, 81–91.

Heider, F. (1958). *The psychology of interpersonal relations.* New York: Wiley.

Herson, L. J. R. (1961). In the footsteps of community power. *Am. Polit. Sci. Rev.* **55**, 817–830.

Hollander, E. P. (1958). Conformity, status, and idiosyncrasy credit. *Psychol. Rev.* **65**, 117–127.

Hollander, E. P. (1961). Some effects of perceived status on responses to innovative behavior. *J. abnorm. soc. Psychol.* **63**, 247–250.

Homans, G. C. (1950). *The human group.* New York: Harcourt, Brace.

Homans, G. C. (1958). Social behavior as exchange. *Amer. J. Sociol.* **63**, 597–606.

Homans, G. C. (1961). *Social behavior: its elementary forms.* New York: Harcourt, Brace.

Horwitz, M. (1958). The veridicality of liking and disliking. In R. Tagiuri and L. Petrullo (Eds.), *Person perception and interpersonal behavior.* Stanford: Stanford Univer. Press, pp. 191–209.

Hurwitz, J. I., Zander, A. F., and Hymovitch, B. (1953). Some effects of power on the relations among group members. In D. Cartwright and A. Zander (Eds.), *Group dynamics: research and theory.* Evanston, Ill.: Row, Peterson, pp. 483–492.

Janda, K. F. (1960). Towards the explication of the concept of leadership in terms of the concept of power. *Hum. Relat.* **13**, 345–363.

Jones, E. E. (1960). Review of D. Cartwright (Ed.) *Studies in social power* (Ann Arbor: Institute for Social Research, 1959), in *Contemp. Psychol.* **5**, 130–131.

Jones, E. E. (1964). *Ingratiation: a social psychological analysis.* New York: Appleton, Century.

Karlsson, G. (1962). Some aspects of power in small groups. In Joan H. Criswell, H. Solomon, and P. Suppes (Eds.), *Mathematical methods in small group processes.* Stanford: Stanford Univer. Press, pp. 193–202.

Kelley, H. H., and Ring, K. (1961). Some effects of "suspicious" versus "trusting" training schedules. *J. abnorm. soc. Psychol.* **63**, 294–301.

Kelley, H. H., Thibaut, J. W., Radloff, R., and Mundy, D. (1963). The development of cooperation in the "minimal social situation." *Psychol. Monogr.* **76,** No. 14 (Whole No. 538).

Kipnis, D. (1958). The effects of leadership style and leadership power upon the inducement of an attitude change. *J. abnorm. soc. Psychol.* **57,** 173–180.

Lane, R. E. (1963). Political science and psychology. In S. Koch (Ed.), *Psychology: a study of a science.* Vol. 6. New York: McGraw-Hill, pp. 583–638.

Levinger, G. (1959). The development of perceptions and behavior in newly formed social power relationships. In D. Cartwright (Ed.), *Studies in social power.* Ann Arbor, Mich.: Institute for Social Research, pp. 83–98.

Lippitt, R., Polansky, N., Redl, F., and Rosen, S. (1952). The dynamics of power: a field study of social influence in groups of children. In G. Swanson, T. Newcomb, and E. Hartley (Eds.), *Readings in social psychology.* (Rev. ed.) New York: Holt, pp. 623–636.

Machiavelli, N. (reprinted 1940). *The prince and the discourses.* Translated by L. Ricci, revised by E. R. P. Vincent. New York: Random House.

March, J. G. (1955). An introduction to the theory and measurement of influence. *Amer. Polit. Sci. Rev.* **49,** 431–451.

March, J. G. (1957). Measurement concepts in the theory of influence. *J. Polit.* **19,** 202–226.

March, J. G. (1963). The power of power. Paper read at Amer. Polit. Sci. Ass., New York, September.

Mulder, M. (1960). The power variable in communication experiments. *Hum. Relat.* **13,** 241–256.

Newcomb, T. M. (1953). An approach to the study of communicative acts. *Psychol. Rev.* **60,** 393–404.

Newcomb, T. M. (1963). Stabilities underlying changes in interpersonal attraction. *J. abnorm. soc. Psychol.* **66,** 376–386.

Nunn, C. Z. (1964). Child control through a "coalition with God." *Child Develpm.* **35,** 417–432.

Pepitone, A. (1950). Motivational effects in social perception. *Hum. Relat.* **3,** 57–76.

Raven, B. H., and French, J. R. P., Jr. (1958a). Group support, legitimate power and social influence. *J. Pers.* **26,** 400–409.

Raven, B. H., and French, J. R. P., Jr. (1958b). Legitimate power, coercive power and observability in social influence. *Sociometry* **21,** 83–97.

Riesman, D. (1954). *Individualism reconsidered.* Glencoe, Ill.: Free Press.

Ring, K., and Kelley, H. H. (1963). A comparison of augmentation and reduction as modes of influence. *J. abnorm. soc. Psychol.* **66,** 95–102.

Rosen, S. (1959). Effects of adjustment on the perception and exertion of social power. In D. Cartwright (Ed.), *Studies in social power.* Ann Arbor, Mich.: Institute for Social Research, pp. 69–82.

Rosen, S., Levinger, G., and Lippitt, R. (1960). Desired changes in self and others as a function of resource ownership. *Hum. Relat.* **13,** 187–193.

Rosen, S., Levinger, G., and Lippitt, R. (1961). Perceived sources of social power. *J. abnorm. soc. Psychol.* **62,** 439–441.

Rotter, J. B. (1954). *Social learning and clinical psychology.* New York: Prentice-Hall.

Russell, B. (1938). *Power: a new social analysis.* New York: Norton.

Schachter, S., Ellertson, N., McBride, Dorothy, and Gregory, Doris (1951). An experimental study of cohesiveness and productivity. *Hum. Relat.* **4,** 229–238.

Schopler, J., and Bateson, N. (1962). A dependence interpretation of the effects of a severe initiation. *J. Pers.* **30**, 633–649.

Schopler, J., and Bateson, N. (1965). The power of dependence. *J. pers. soc. Psychol.* **2**, 247–254.

Sidowski, J. B., Wyckoff, L. B., and Tabery, L. (1956). The influence of reinforcement and punishment in a minimal social situation. *J. abnorm. soc. Psychol.* **52**, 115–119.

Siegel. S., and Fouraker, L. E. (1960). *Bargaining and group decision making.* New York: McGraw-Hill.

Simon, H. A. (1953). Notes on the observation and measurement of political power. *J. Polit.* **15**, 500–516.

Solomon, L. (1960). The influence of some types of power relations and game strategies upon the development of interpersonal trust. *J. abnorm. soc. Psychol.* **61**, 223–230.

Solomon, R. L. (1964). Punishment. *Amer. Psychologist* **19**, 239–253.

Stotland, E. (1959). Peer groups and reactions to power figures. In D. Cartwright (Ed.), *Studies in social power.* Ann Arbor, Mich.: Institute for Social Research, pp. 53–68.

Strodtbeck, F. L. (1951). Husband-wife interaction over revealed differences. *Amer. sociol. Rev.* **16**, 468–473.

Strodtbeck, F. L., James, Rita M., and Hawkins, C. (1958). Social status in jury deliberations. In Eleanor E. Maccoby, T. Newcomb, and E. Hartley (Eds.), *Readings in social psychology.* (3rd. ed.) New York: Holt, Rinehart, & Winston. pp. 379–388.

Tagiuri, R., and Kogan, N. (1960). Personal preference and the attribution of influence in small groups. *J. Pers.* **28**, 257–265.

Tannenbaum, A. S. (1962). An event-structure approach to social power and to the problem of power comparability. *Behav. Sci.* **7**, 315–331.

Thibaut, J. W. (1950). An experimental study of the cohesiveness of underprivileged groups. *Hum. Relat.* **3**, 251–278.

Thibaut, J. W. (1964). The motivational effects of social dependence on a powerful agency of control. In W. Cooper, H. Leavitt, and M. Shelly (Eds.), *New perspectives in organization research.* New York: Wiley, pp. 87–96.

Thibaut, J. W., and Kelley, H. H., (1959). *The social psychology of groups.* New York: Wiley.

Torrance, E. P. (1955). Some consequences of power differences on decision making in permanent and temporary three-man groups. In P. Hare, E. Borgatta, and R. Bales (Eds.), *Small groups,* New York: Knopf, pp. 482–492.

Walster, Elaine, and Festinger, L. (1962). The effectiveness of "overheard" persuasive communications. *J. abnorm. soc. Psychol.* **65**, 395–402.

Wilson, K. V., and Bixenstine, V. E. (1962). Forms of social control in two-person, two-choice games. *Behav. Sci.* **7**, 92–102.

Zander, A., and Cohen, A. R. (1955). Attributed social power and group acceptance: a classroom experimental demonstration. *J. abnorm. soc. Psychol.* **51**, 490–492.

Zander, A., and Curtis, T. (1962). Effects of social power on aspiration setting and striving. *J. abnorm. soc. Psychol.* **64**, 63–74.

Zipf, Sheila G. (1960). Resistance and conformity under reward and punishment. *J. abnorm. soc. Psychol.* **61**, 102–109.

FROM ACTS TO DISPOSITIONS

The Attribution Process in Person Perception[1]

Edward E. Jones   and   **Keith E. Davis**

DEPARTMENT OF PSYCHOLOGY   DEPARTMENT OF PSYCHOLOGY
DUKE UNIVERSITY   UNIVERSITY OF COLORADO
DURHAM, NORTH CAROLINA   BOULDER, COLORADO

Many social psychologists have expressed a central interest in the ties between person perception and interpersonal behavior. The writings of Fritz Heider have exerted a predominant and continuing influence on research designed to illuminate these ties. From his 1944 paper on phenomenal causality to his more recent (1958) book on *The Psychology of Interpersonal Relations,* Heider has persistently concerned himself with the cognitive aspects of social interaction. His writings are especially important for recognizing and identifying the major problems with which

[1] Much of the research reported herein was supported by National Science Foundation Grants 8857 and 21955 to the first author.

219

any theory of person perception must contend: causal attribution, cognition-sentiment relations, taking the other's perspective, and so on. Heider's comments are comprehensive, perceptive, and provocative. His exposition does not lend itself readily, however, to the formulation of interrelated propositional statements. Thus the research which has been done to date is largely demonstrational in significance and dismayingly sparse in quantity. While the studies which we intend to review in this chapter may be seen as islands in the same phenomenological sea, it is not very clear how one navigates between them.

We believe that the kind of systematic, conceptual structure that is needed must involve an analysis of phenomenal causality, or the determinants and consequences of attributing causation for particular actions. In the central portion of this chapter we shall attempt to review, and to some extent reformulate, much of the recent research concerning phenomenal causality and the attribution of intentions. Our first task, however, is to introduce the notion of explaining an action by assigning an intention and to set the stage for the theory of inference which follows.

I. The Naive Explanation of Human Actions: Explanation by Attributing Intentions

At the heart of Heider's analysis of naive or "common sense psychology" is the distinction between personal and impersonal causality. We assume that the person-perceiver's fundamental task is to interpret or infer the causal antecedents of action. The perceiver seeks to find *sufficient reason* why the person acted and why the act took on a particular form. Instead of the potentially infinite regress of cause and effect which characterizes an impersonal, scientific analysis, the perceiver's explanation comes to a stop when an intention or motive is assigned that has the quality of being reason enough. "He eats because he is hungry" would not ordinarily bring a request for further explanation. After all, eating is something one would do if one were hungry.

The cognitive task of establishing sufficient reason for an action involves processing available information about, or making assumptions about, the links between stable individual dispositions and observed action. Let us start with the case in which a perceiver observes an action and at least some of its effects. His basic problem as a perceiver is to decide which of these effects, if any, were intended by the actor. Let us first address ourselves to the problem of "if any." In order to conclude that at least some of the effects achieved by an action were intended, the perceiver must first believe that the actor was aware his action would have the observed effects. Thus a first condition in the inference process is the assumption of knowledge on the part of the actor. Consequences of an action which the actor could not have foreseen do not qualify as candidates for what he was trying to achieve. The condition of knowledge is of critical importance within our legal system where it is customary to distinguish among levels of responsibility for a crime: (1) intentional (P did X to enjoy the immediate effects of X), (2) incidental (P did X as a means of getting to Y), and (3) accidental (X was a consequence of P's action that he neither intended nor expected).

In addition to assumptions about knowledge of consequences, decisions linking intentional attributes to the effects of action are also affected by the perceiver's judgments of the actor's ability to bring about the effects observed. Simply put, an actor cannot achieve his objectives solely by desiring to achieve them. He must have the capacities or skill to move from his present condition of desire to a subsequent condition of attainment and satisfaction. When a person's actions have certain consequences, it is important for the perceiver to determine whether the person was capable of producing these consequences in response to his intentions. Especially in the case where an actor *fails* to produce certain effects that might have been anticipated by the perceiver, there may be ambiguity as to whether the actor did not want to produce the effects, or wanted but was not able to.

Even when effects are achieved, however, the perceiver may have the problem of assessing the relative contribution of luck or chance. When a novice archer hits the bull's eye, we are more apt to attribute this to luck than to skill. There are other occasions when we do not assign intentions to correspond with effects achieved because we do not consider the actor capable of producing those effects at will. A jury is more likely to believe that a killing is accidental if the average person would have lacked the skill (the marksmanship, the strength, etc.) to bring about the crime deliberately. It was quite possible to believe that Oswald intended to kill President Kennedy and not Mrs. Kennedy or a secret service man, because he was known to be an expert marksman. For a further discussion of the problems involved in judging ability relative to difficulty and luck, the reader is referred to Heider (1958).

The perceiver may have certain information about knowledge and ability (he may be informed that Oswald knew the gun was loaded and that Oswald often practiced on a local rifle range), or he may merely assume that knowledge and ability were probably present or probably absent. Whether the perceiver's conclusion about such matters is correct or incorrect, the conclusion obviously will affect his decisions about the actor's intentions in the situation. Knowledge and ability are preconditions for the assignment of intentions. Each plays a similar role in enabling the perceiver to decide whether an effect or consequence of action was accidental. The assignment of intention, in turn, is a precondition for inferences concerning those underlying stable characteristics toward which the perceiver presses in attaching significance to action. As Heider (1958) argued, the perceiver ordinarily strives to discover the invariances which underlie manifest actions in order to stabilize the environment and render it more predictable.

We may attempt to summarize the foregoing remarks by the diagram presented as Fig. 1. It is assumed that the perceiver typically starts with the overt action of another; this is the grist for his cognitive mill. He then makes certain decisions concerning ability and knowledge which will let him cope with the problem of attributing particular intentions to the actor. The attribution of intentions, in turn, is a necessary step in the assignment of more stable characteristics to the actor.

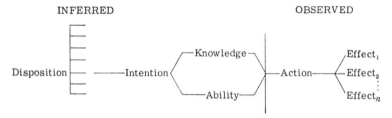

Fig. 1. The action-attribute paradigm.

Fig. 1 attempts to clarify the circumstances under which *any* intentions will be assigned to explain action. But we now seek to extend the analysis in order to account for the attribution of particular intentions and dispositions on the basis of particular actions. We shall here largely ignore the problems involved in imputing knowledge and ability and concentrate on specific linkages between effects achieved and intentions revealed. We assume that those consequences of action obviously neither intended by the actor nor within the range of his capabilities will be considered irrelevant by the perceiver.

II. A Theory of Correspondent Inferences

Our purpose is to construct a theory which systematically accounts for a perceiver's inferences about what an actor was trying to achieve by a particular action. In achieving this purpose we view the action as occurring within a particular situational context which defines, in large part, its meaning for the perceiver. In particular, as we shall attempt to show in greater detail below, the meaning of an action—its intentional significance—derives from some consideration of the alternative action possibilities available to but foregone by the actor. As perceivers of action, we can only begin to understand the motives prompting an act if we view the effects of the act in the framework of effects that other actions could have achieved.

Perhaps an example will further clarify our purpose and approach. Let us imagine ourselves as silent observers of an interaction episode in which A and B are working together on a task. We observe that A gives orders to B, monitors his performance, and shows his displeasure with the quality and quantity of B's work. The inferences about A we would most likely draw from this episode would depend critically on the action alternatives seen to be available to him. If A and B had come together in a free situation, we would be inclined to see A as quite arrogant and domineering. If we were informed that A had been given instructions to take a directive leadership role, we would be less likely to regard his dominating behavior as an indication of his personal qualities: that is, our inferences about dominance from his action would be much less *correspondent*.

Such role-playing instructions presumably limit A's freedom to behave in a "revealing" way, that is, in a way which is characteristic of *him* relative to others. The theory which follows attempts to imbed this consideration of perceived freedom of choice in a systematic framework. We will attempt to extract conceptual commonalities from empirical situations involving different varieties of environmental constraint. Our approach is to cast these "conceptual commonalities" in a form which is amenable to cumulative experimental research.

A. THE CONCEPT OF CORRESPONDENCE

When the perceiver infers personal characteristics as a way of accounting for action, these personal characteristics may vary in the degree to which they correspond with the behavior they are intended to explain. *Correspondence* refers to the extent that the act and the underlying characteristic or attribute are similarly described by the inference. In the example provided in the preceding section, the most correspondent inference is that which assumes with high confidence that domineering behavior is a direct reflection of the person's intention to dominate, which in turn reflects a disposition to be dominant. Thus, to anticipate the broad outlines of the theory to come, correspondence of inference declines as the action to be accounted for appears to be constrained by the setting in which it occurs.

To say that a person is dominant is to say that he is disposed to behave in a dominant fashion in a variety of settings. Of course, the perceiver in the above example would not infer such a dominance disposition if he had not first inferred an intention to dominate. The actor's intention may or may not be conscious and deliberate, but it is marked by some aspect of desire or volition which comes from the person and is not predetermined by environmental forces. Our theory assumes, in using the two concepts of intention and disposition, that correspondence declines as the perceiver moves from inferring intentions to more elaborate inferences about dispositional structures. If the perceiver, having observed a single action, infers intention X with moderate confidence, he cannot be more confident in inferring the underlying disposition X' from the intention X. This would appear to be so because intentions are the data for inferring dispositions, and because an intention may reflect any of several dispositions.

Hopefully, the foregoing discussion has given the reader some general feeling for the meaning of correspondence in the present context. For the sake of theoretical clarity, however, more precise and formal explication is in order. Such an explication may provide a clearer path toward understanding the theory.

All actions have effects on the environment. From the perceiver's point of view, any effect of another person's action is a potential reason why this person had engaged in that action. To infer that the action occurred for X reason is to specify the actor's intention and, indirectly, an underlying disposition. Both intentions and dispositions are attributes of the person. The perception of a link between a particular intention or disposition and a particular action may therefore be called an attribute-effect linkage.

Let us now attempt a more formal definition of correspondence. *Given an attribute-effect linkage which is offered to explain why an act occurred, correspondence increases as the judged value of the attribute departs from the judge's conception of the average person's standing on that attribute.* Turning to the illustration used earlier, the inference that domineering action reflects an underlying trait of dominance is correspondent to the extent that the actor's dominance is seen as greater than that of the average person. This implies, incidentally, that the intention to dominate is out of the ordinary—somehow more intense and noteworthy than we would normally expect.

As a simple example of how the concept of correspondence can be put to use in a research setting, we may provide the perceiver with rating scales designed to measure the strength of the trait attributed to the actor and his confidence in making his rating. The perceiver's certainty that the actor is extreme on a trait which provides sufficient reason for the action's occurrence is, then, the level of correspondence of his inference.

B. ACTS AND THEIR EFFECTS

An act is conceived of as a molar response which reflects some degree of personal choice on the part of the actor (if only between action and inaction, though more typically between alternative courses of action) and which has one or more effects on the environment or the actor himself. *Effects* are distinctive (or potentially distinctive) consequences of action. Stated in the broadest terms, they are discriminable changes in the pre-existing state of affairs that are brought about by action. Delimiting the unit with which we shall be concerned is more a problem in theory than in practice. If we observe that a man leaves his chair, crosses the room, closes the door, and the room becomes less noisy, a correspondent inference would be that he intended to cut down the noise. One might ask whether the inference that the man intended to reach the door is not also a correspondent inference since "reaching the door" is an effect of crossing the room. But the subordinate parts of a meaningful action sequence do not have to be confused with the effects of an action. In this case, the perceiver is likely to "organize" the action in his mind as beginning with the decision to leave the chair and ending with the closing of the door. It is the effects of the terminal act in a meaningful sequence, then, that provide the grist for our theory.

An act may have only one effect, but usually has multiple effects. When the man closes the door this may reduce the draft, reduce the illumination in his office, and make two students talking in the hall feel a little guilty for interrupting his work. Thus, we are usually dealing with *choice areas* rather than single choices. Important implications for the theory are contained in the fact that "the bitter often comes with the sweet"—an action may be performed to achieve effect x, but effects m, p, t, and z are inextricably produced by the act as well. A choice between two choice areas, then, is a choice between two multiple-effect clusters. The multiple effects in one cluster may or may not overlap extensively with the multiple effects in the second cluster. That is, certain effects may be common to the chosen alternative and to the nonchosen alternative.

If the promising young psychologist Dr. Smedley accepts a position at Harvard rather than Yale, the following effects are obviously common to these two areas of choice: being in the Ivy League, living in New England, joining a university with high prestige and good salaries, living near the sea coast, etc. The theory assumes, then, that these common effects could not have been decisive in the choice, and thus do not provide information which could contribute to correspondent inferences. There are also, of course, distinctive differences between the setting at Yale and Harvard—especially if the perceiver were intimately knowledgeable about the psychology departments of the two institutions—and the perceiver's cognitive accounting of these differences would be the critical determinant of whatever inference was made.

For convenience in representing the structure of the situation in which action occurs, we shall from time to time diagram each perceived choice area as a circle within which the effects of the choice expressed as alphabetical letters may be circumscribed. Common effects may then be represented by the appearance of the same alphabetical letters in different "choice circles." Our hypothetical example of Dr. Smedley's dilemma might be diagrammed as in Fig. 2.

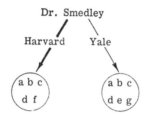

a. Ivy League
b. New England
c. prestige
d. good salary
e. close to New York plays
f. emphasis on interdisciplinary research
g. emphasis on experimental approaches
    to learning, etc.

FIG. 2. Smedley's choice.

C. THE ASSUMED DESIRABILITY OF EFFECTS

As the perceiver considers the multiple effects of action, he will usually assume that some of the effects were more desirable to the actor, and therefore more diagnostic of his intentions than others. In fact, it is almost always the case that some of the effects of the chosen alternative action are assumed to be undesirable to the actor and some of the effects of nonchosen action are assumed to be desirable. The two major effects of a man's buying a car, for example, are the acquisition of an automobile and the incurring of a substantial debt. The average perceiver, given evidence of such a purchase, will probably assume that the individual desired the car so much that he was willing to go into debt for it, not that he was willing to accept the burden of an automobile for the privilege of being a debtor.

These assumptions by the perceiver tend to operate as hypotheses which bias the inference process. Thus upon observing that an action leads to a normally desirable effect, the perceiver usually will believe that most persons, including the present actor, find that effect desirable. The achievement of this effect will therefore be regarded as the actor's most likely intention. The perceiver may, of course, be wrong in his assumptions about people in general. This particular actor may have intended to produce effects in the choice area that most people would be indifferent about or even feel negatively toward. Thus, cultural assumptions or social stereotypes may obscure the true significance of an action.

Let us take a closer look at the consequences for the inference process of assumptions about the desirability of effects. The first step is to distinguish clearly between effects which are assumed to be desirable and those assumed to be undesirable consequences for the average actor. Unless he has evidence to the contrary, the perceiver will assume that the actor has acted in spite of, rather than because of, any negative effects in the choice area. We may go beyond this to assert that any effects in the choice area which are not assumed to be negative will take on greater importance the more negative the remaining effects. Inferences concerning the intention to achieve desirable effects will increase in correspondence to the extent that costs are incurred, pain is endured, or in general, negative outcomes are involved.

Within the range of the supposedly desirable consequences, we still must recognize that effects assumed to be highly desirable are more likely to enter into attribute-effect linkages than effects assumed to be variable or neutral in desirability. However, it is also clear that attribute-effect linkages based on universally desired effects are *not* informative concerning the unique characteristics of the actor. To learn that a man makes the conventional choice is to learn only that he is like most other men. By the definition of correspondence stated above, an inference must characterize the actor's standing as high or low on an attribute relative to the average person, in order to qualify as correspondent. If a choice is explained on the basis of effects in the choice area which anyone would like to produce and enjoy, an attribute inferred to account for that choice will be low in correspondence. In general, we learn more about uniquely identifying intentions and dispositions when the effects of a chosen action are no more universally desired than the effects of a nonchosen action.

D. The Determinants of Correspondence

It may be helpful to divide the inference process into two aspects (which may in fact be seen as stages in the process). Given an act which leads to multiple effects, the perceiver implicitly attaches a probability value to each effect as a candidate for launching the inference process. In other words, the perceiver assumes that certain of the effects achieved are more likely to have been the goal of action than others. In certain cases the probability of all effects but one may be zero, indicating extreme confidence in attributing causation to a particular intention. In other cases, the probability values may be distributed among a range of effects, and since it is possible that the target person acted for more than one reason the probabilities may add up to more than 1.00. The probability value for any given effect should vary directly as a function of the assumed desirability of the effect and inversely as a function of the number of other effects competing for the perceiver's attention. If the perceiver is asked, then, "what was A trying to accomplish?"—his response should reflect this combination of assumed desirability and the number of noncommon effects.

The second aspect or phase is to attach personal significance to the effect or effects singled out as most probable courses of action. In short, what does the action reveal about this particular actor that sets him apart from other actors? By our definition of correspondence, relative extremity of perceiver rating is the crucial measure. Here it seems quite clear that assumed desirability and the number of noncommon effects have conflicting implications. The greater the assumed desirability of the effect in question, the less warrant there is for ratings of relative extremity. The smaller the number of effects in contention, on the other hand, the greater the warrant for extreme ratings. Assumed desirability, then, positively affects the probability of an attribute-effect linkage being chosen to begin the inference process and negatively affects the tendency to assign extreme values to personal characteristics.

The correspondence of an inference, which should directly reflect the amount of information revealed by an action, is thus a function of the two conditions covered by the following explicit formulation: An inference from action to attribute is correspondent *as an inverse function of* (*a*) *the number of noncommon effects following the action, and* (*b*) *the assumed social desirability of these effects.* This relationship may be stated in simpler terms as a near tautology: the more distinctive reasons a person has for an action, and the more these reasons are widely shared in the culture, the less informative that action is concerning the identifying attributes of the person.

It should be reiterated that correspondence has nothing to do, necessarily, with the accuracy of the inference. The actor may have had no intention of producing an effect which is seen by the perceiver as a prominent consequence of his action. Being able to predict the effects of one's own actions is an important precondition for being accurately perceived by others. The theory does not assume, then, that the perceiver and the actor agree on the effects of the latter's action, but focuses on those effects of which the perceiver assumes the actor was aware. The knowledge portion of the attribute-action paradigm (see Fig. 1) is relevant only in determining which effects the perceiver will include in the choice circle (see Fig. 2).

There is an interesting relationship between imputations of knowledge and actions leading to socially undesirable effects. We have already noted that when there are both desirable and undesirable effects of an action, more significance is attached to the desirable effects the more numerous and distasteful the undesirable effects "incurred." In a case where the actor produces solely negative effects, however, the situation

ASSUMED DESIRABILITY

		High	Low
	High	Trivial ambiguity	Intriguing ambiguity
NUMBER OF NONCOMMON EFFECTS	Low	Trivial clarity	High correspondence

FIG. 3. Effect desirability and effect commonality as determinants of correspondence.

is quite different. Here the perceiver has two obvious options: He may decide that the actor is truly a deviant type, that he desires those goals which are shunned by others; or he may decide that the actor was unaware of the effects of his action. It seems reasonable to propose, therefore, that in cases where the action-choice circle contains only effects judged to be socially undesirable, the more undesirable these effects the greater the perceiver's tendency to impute ignorance or lack of awareness to the actor. The possibility of imputing ignorance thus sets a limit on the degree of correspondence predicted when actions lead only to socially undersirable effects. (Note that this is quite different from what one would predict in the case where an action leads to effects which are undesirable *for the perceiver* but recognized by him to serve some purpose of the actor. We shall discuss this latter case below under the heading of Hedonic Relevance.)

It may be helpful in summarizing the theory to consider the joint operation of effect desirability and effect commonality as determinants of correspondence, and to do so in the framework of a fourfold table. Such a table is presented in Fig. 3. As the figure shows, actions which lead to effects deemed highly desirable to most persons cannot help but be trivial from an informational point of view. Also, when the number of noncommon effects is high, the perceiver cannot escape from the ambiguity of his data in making inferences either to common or idiosyncratic personal characteristics. In line with the stated theoretical relationship, the high correspondence cell is that in which assumed desirability and the number of noncommon effects are both low.

E. The Calculation of Commonality

Since the theoretical statement refers to the number of noncommon effects in the chosen alternative, it is important to clarify how effects are identified and their commonality assessed. There are two rather different clusters of problems involved here. One cluster concerns identifying effects and determining whether or not two effects so identified are to be viewed as common. This will simply have to be a matter of cumulative research experience in fractionating and labeling consequences.

The other cluster of problems assumes that we can somehow achieve the necessary identifications and concerns the method of determining how the noncommon effects in the chosen alternative will be sorted out from all others in order to generate reasonably precise predictions. There are essentially three steps involved in sorting out the number of noncommon effects. The first is for the experimenter to lay out (for example, in the graphic manner of Fig. 2) the different action alternatives that the perceiver is likely to envision in the actor's situation. For each of these alternatives there will be a choice area, a circle containing the distinctive effects of that action. Having identified these circles and the effects they circumscribe, the second step is to pool all the effects associated with the nonchosen alternatives and to compare them with the effects in the choice circle of the chosen alternative. Having done this, one follows through on the assumption that effects which appear in both chosen and nonchosen alternatives cannot serve as a basis for inferences about personal dispositions. One is then left with effects which appear only in the chosen alternative and only in the nonchosen alternative(s). The third and final step is to view the noncommon effects in the nonchosen alternatives as effects which the actor may be trying to avoid. They may thus be transposed, with their sign reversed, and regrouped among the noncommon effects of the chosen alternative. The new total of noncommon effects now serves as the basis for making predictions about the level of correspondence.

In order to illustrate these three stages in the calculation of noncommon effects, let us invent a case involving the choice of a marital partner. We are informed that a Miss Adams, who is ripe for matrimony, has received proposals from three suitors, Bagby, Caldwell, and Dexter. All we know about Bagby is that he is wealthy, he has high status in the community, and he is physically attractive. Caldwell is also quite wealthy, he is physically attractive, and he has often expressed his longing for a houseful of his own children. Dexter is physically attractive like

Effects of marriage to be considered:

    a. wealth

    b. social position

    c. sexual enjoyment

    d. children

    e. intellectual stimulation

A. The Choice

Miss Adams

    Bagby   Caldwell   Dexter

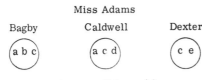

B. Elimination of Common Effects (c)

C. Regrouped Noncommon Effects

If choice is:

    Bagby   b wanted, d and e not important

    Caldwell   d wanted, b and e not important

    Dexter   e wanted, a not wanted, b and d not important

D. Inferences:

If Bagby, Miss Adams is a snob; if Caldwell, Miss Adams is the maternal type; if Dexter, Miss Adams is an intellectual.

FIG. 4. Miss Adams chooses a husband.

the others, and he is very much the intellectual—widely read and conversationally scintillating. These are the only characteristics of these men that we know anything about, and on the basis of this knowledge we may diagram Miss Adam's choice as in Fig. 4A.

    First we lay out those effects presumed to follow from the choice of each man to the exclusion of the other. Then we notice that the three men are physically attractive so we rule out the common effect of sexual enjoyment—we have no information about the importance of this particular characteristic as a determinant of Miss Adams' choice. The remaining effects are regrouped after we receive information about which man has been chosen. The only further distinction is that between effects which are judged to have been wanted by Miss Adams, effects judged to have been unimportant to her, and effects judged to have been *not* wanted or actively avoided. The distinction between lack of importance and undesirability is new; it is based on the commonality of particular effects among the nonchosen alternatives. Thus, if Dexter is chosen, we have no more reason to assume that Miss Adams wanted intellectual stimulation than that she didn't want the responsibilities of wealth. After all, she has avoided two wealthy suitors in favor of one who is not wealthy. Our inference about not wanting wealth, then, would be more correspondent than an inference about not wanting children or not caring about social position. If it were just a matter of not having children, Miss Adams could just as easily have married Bagby. If she was anxious to avoid social position she could have accomplished this by marrying Caldwell. We say these these two effects were not *important* to her to suggest that she is willing to forego them in favor of intellectual stimulation, but our evidence that she wanted to avoid these effects is weaker than in the case of wealth.

A further complexity which must be acknowledged is the fact that some or all of the noncommon effects may be correlated or seen by the perceiver to express the same general purpose. At the present stage of developing the theory of correspondence, no formal provision is made for this possibility. To some extent, our flexibility in deciding what we shall call an effect reduces the magnitude of the problem. Thus, certain combinations of discriminable effects may be treated as a more general, unitary effect if each member of the combination has a common significance for the perceiver. The result would be to increase the correspondence and the generality or importance of the ensuing inference. We shall examine this possibility in greater detail when we consider, below, the contribution of hedonic or affective relevance of effects in the inference process and again when we consider sequences of action choices over time.

F. CONDITIONS AFFECTING DESIRABILITY ASSUMPTIONS

We have remarked that the perceiver's assumptions or hypotheses about which effects of action were most likely desired by the actor play an important role in the inference process. Those effects perceived to have been high in desirability (i.e., commonly desired by all persons or by all members of a particular cultural group) play a smaller role in the determination of correspondence than those effects which are less universally sought. Without going too deeply into the problem, there are a number of variables which might condition the perceiver's assumptions that the actor desires the same effects as most persons. Even if we restrict ourselves to the case in which the perceiver confronts the actor for the first time, there may be cues in the circumstances of their encounter and in the appearance of the actor which affect the likelihood of his being seen as desiring the same things most persons would in a given situation. If the situation is so structured that the actor and the perceiver are working for the same objectives, the perceiver may reflect on his own intentions to draw inferences about the most likely aspirations of the actor. Cues about shared perspectives should thus facilitate the formation of definite hypotheses about the actor's motives and desires. Other cues, perhaps reflected in the features of the actor's appearance, might lead the perceiver to assume similarity of intention and disposition before any action has occurred. Or the perceiver's stereotypes about the members of identifiable classes or cultural groups may be triggered by such appearance cues.

G. INFORMATION GAIN AND THE ROLE OF PRIOR CHOICE

We now come to one of the most frustrating sources of complexity in calculating noncommon effects in the chosen alternative, both for the individual perceiver whose actions the theory concerns and for the theory itself. A person who confronts certain behavior choices has often made previous choices which have brought him to his present decision. There is often a great deal of information contained, then, in knowledge about what alternatives are being considered, above and beyond the information revealed by the actual decision which is made.

Once again, this point can be clarified by an example. Let us consider Miss Adams again, this time caught between the options of going to medical school or to law school. She has been accepted for admission in the two professional schools of comparable universities and the choice is, in that sense, entirely up to her. In comparison, we come upon Mr. Bagby, poised before the choice of going to Duke or to Colorado for graduate study in psychology. Since the Duke and Colorado psychology departments would seem to have much more in common than medical school versus law school, our theory would seem to suggest that any inference we might make about Mr. Bagby after he has chosen would be more correspondent than any comparable inference about Miss Adams. There are many noncommon effects in Adams' chosen alternative, whereas the number of noncommon effects in Bagby's chosen alternative is unquestionably smaller. The hidden factor in this comparison is the fact that considerably more information is contained in the datum that Bagby had already ruled out everything besides psychology, than in the datum that Adams is still struggling with the choice between two basic professions, professions which differ from each other on many different dimensions. The example is thus misleading because Bagby is at a later stage of the choice process than Adams. In order to render them comparable we would have to have more information concerning Bagby's preceding choices, choices which have narrowed the field to psychology.

The example points up the importance of defining correspondence in terms of the information *gained* through the observation of behavior, not in terms of the confidence one has in drawing an inference which may be based on prior information or on knowledge of the culture. If all we know is that Bagby has chosen the Colorado Department of Psychology over the Duke Department of Psychology, we have learned nothing *from the choice itself* concerning the strength of his motivation to become a psychologist. On the other hand, we might be willing to make some rather confident statements about his love of mountains or the degree of his dislike for hot and humid summers. The facts that there are high mountains and low humidity in Colorado are certainly two of the noncommon effects in the Colorado versus Duke choice.

In dealing with cases of complex behavioral choice in the natural environment, the matter of prior choice is destined to create enormous difficulties in the application of the theory to individual cases. However, in the realm of experimental planning, prior choice presents opportunities for empirical exploration rather than disruptive trouble. The probability of imputing prior choice can either be held constant or systematically varied by suitable experimental arrangements. In the former case for example, subject-perceivers, starting from the same baseline of relative ignorance about a stimulus person, may be exposed to a choice made by that stimulus person under conditions which emphasize the stimulus persons's lack of control over the choice presented him.

H. CORRESPONDENCE, CHOICE, AND ROLE ASSIGNMENT

A recent experiment by Jones *et al.* (1961) exemplifies the reasoning which underlies the foregoing theory. It is worth reviewing this study before considering some of the more subtle and tentative extensions of the theory into interaction settings marked by personal involvement. The investigation's central purpose was to demonstrate that behavior which conforms to clearly defined role requirements is seen as uninformative about the individual's personal characteristics, whereas a considerable amount of information may be extracted from out-of-role behavior. In other words, inferences based on out-of-role behavior were predicted to be higher in correspondence than inferences from in-role behavior. The reasons for this will become more apparent after the procedures of the experiment are described.

Male undergraduate subjects were exposed to one of four tape recorded "job interviews" in which the interviewee was instructed (on the tape) to appear very interested in qualifying either as a prospective submariner or as an astronaut. The subjects were aware that the interviewee was being invited to play a role in a fictitious interview situation, but they were not told that the entire interview was carefully written as a prearranged script and was recorded by an experimental accomplice serving as the interviewee.

Those subjects who listened to the recording involving the submariner role, heard the interviewer describe the ideal submariner as obedient, cooperative, friendly, gregarious—in short, as "other directed." The remaining subjects listened to a description of the ideal astronaut as one who does not need other people, who has inner resources—in short, a rather "inner-directed" person. These two interview beginnings were spliced into two different endings, thus creating the four experimental groups. The interviewee either responded with a series of statements indicating extreme other-directedness or he responded with a series of inner-directed statements. On half of the recordings, then, the interviewee-accomplice behaved very much in line with the requirements of the occupational role (astronaut-inner condition, submariner-other condition). On the other half the behavior was distinctly out of line with these requirements (astronaut-other condition, submariner-inner condition).

After listening to these tape recordings, the subjects were asked to rate the interviewee ("what do you think he is *really* like as a person?") and indicate their confidence in the traits they evaluated on their rating scale. The results were striking and unequivocal (see Table I). After the two in-role recordings, the stimulus person was rated as moderately affiliative and moderately independent. In each case the confidence ratings were extremely low. On the other hand, the astronaut-other was seen as very conforming and affiliative, and confidently rated as such. The submariner-inner was seen as very independent and non-affiliative, again with high confidence. Thus the actual responses of the interviewee were clearly evaluated in the context of the structured setting from which they emerged. If other-directedness is called for, an inner-directed response is highly informative. Inner-directedness in the face of a situation which seems to require it, on the other hand, is difficult to interpret. The same kind of contrast applies to other-directedness in the two settings described, providing a replication of the basic hypothesis within the single experiment.

Now we may ask how the results of the Jones *et al.* (1961) experiment are to be explained in terms of the foregoing theoretical statement relating cultural desirability and the number of noncommon effects to the degree of correspondence of an inference about personal dispositions. In-role behavior does not lead to confident, correspondent inferences because such behavior has multiple consequences and many of these are high in cultural desirability. Most people want to avoid embarrassing others by not meeting their expectations, most people want to gain the rewards implicit in approval from authority figures, most people wish to manifest their intelligence by showing that they understand what is required of them, and so on. Each of these effects is a "plausible reason"

TABLE I

PERCEPTIONS OF AFFILIATION AND CONFORMITY[a,b]

| | Astro-other (AO) | Astro-inner (AI) | Sub-other (SO) | Sub-inner (SI) | Comparisons | |
					Direction	t
N:	33	33	31	37		
Affiliation						
$\bar{X}$	15.27	11.12	12.00	8.64	AO > SO	4.02[d]
SD	2.92	3.81	3.53	4.73	AI > SI	2.12[e]
Conformity						
$\bar{X}$	15.91	13.09	12.58	9.41	AO > SO	4.02[d]
SD	3.22	3.42	3.39	4.95	AI > SI	3.65[d]

[a] Data from Jones et al. (1961).

[b] The higher the mean value, the greater the perceived affiliation or conformity. Comparisons between AO and SI are not tabled, but the differences between these conditions would of course be highly significant.

[e] $p < .05$.

[d] $p < .001$.

for in-role behavior in the experiment just described. On the other hand, plausible reasons for out-of-role behavior (i.e., those with a reasonable degree of assumed social desirability) are comparatively scarce. One of the few noncommon effects of behavior at variance with role demands is the satisfaction of expressing one's true nature. This effect is also a possible accompaniment of in-role behavior, but in that case it exists in the choice circle along with many other effects. Since there are fewer noncommon effects in the astronaut-other and submariner-inner choices, the effect of "being oneself" forms the basis of a more correspondent inference in these conditions and the interviewee's behavior tends to be taken at face value.

The implications of this study can probably be extended quite generally to cover behavior which is or is not constrained by a well defined social situation. When certain role requirements are salient, conformity is more rewarding to the actor, more likely to avoid embarrassment and social disapproval, than is nonconformity. The actor may conform for many other reasons as well. Thus, in the case of conformity to role requirements, we do not know the exact reason why the individual behaves the way he does, but there is really no particular mystery in his behavior. This is an example of "trivial ambiguity." On the other hand, behavior which departs from clearly defined role requirements cries for explanation. The fact that the effects of such behavior are presumably low in cultural desirability makes the behavior intriguing to the perceiver. The fact that there are few reasons why a person would behave that way (the action leads to a limited number of noncommon effects) provides the basis for a correspondent inference concerning the intentions and dispositions of the actor.

III. Personal Involvement and Correspondence

In the remaining sections of the chapter, we shall turn to those factors of personal involvement which affect the inference process in person perception. The theory of action implied in the discussion thus far obviously assumes that the actor is concerned with the consequences of his action. It is the very fact that his action choices have motivational significance for *him* that makes these choices informative for the perceiver. But a special and enormously important feature of many person perception settings is that the choice of an actor has significant rewarding or punishing implications for the perceiver. We turn to examine this feature and to consider its implications for our theory of correspondence.

A. THE HEDONIC RELEVANCE OF THE ACTION TO THE PERCEIVER

The actor's behavioral choices may or may not contain effects which have hedonic relevance for the perceiver. The hedonic relevance of an effect is a function of its motivational significance for the perceiver: does the particular action consequence promote or undermine the perceiver's values; does it fulfill or obstruct his purposes? Effects which fulfill a purpose have positive relevance; those which obstruct a purpose have negative relevance. For a *choice* to have relevance means that the algebraic balance of positive and negative effects in the chosen alternative is not equal to the algebraic balance of positive and negative effects in the nonchosen alternative(s). Simply put, the choice proved gratifying or disappointing to the perceiver.

An experiment by Steiner and Field (1960) is conceptually quite similar to the astronaut-submariner study but contains a strong dash of hedonic relevance as an added ingredient. In this study, University of Illinois students met in groups of three to "discuss the desirability of desegregation of public schools and . . . attempt to reach agreement among themselves." The major manipulation varied the extent to which the responsibility for presenting certain points of view was assigned by the experimenter. For half of the groups, a confederate of the experimenter was always assigned the role of "a typical Southern segregationist." In the other groups, subjects were encouraged to take into consideration the viewpoint of an N.A.A.C.P. member, a Northern clergyman, and a Southern segregationist, but no role assignments were made. In both cases, however, the confederate gave an identical, prosegregation performance. From the perceiver's point of view, he apparently chose to express prosegregation beliefs where no role assignment was made, whereas he had little choice *but* to express the same beliefs in the role assignment condition. Since the subjects themselves were all in favor of integration, the expression of prosegregationist beliefs would, we assume, be relevant in the negative direction.

The following results would be expected given the theoretical statement that we have developed thus far: (1) perceivers should attribute more intense prosegregation beliefs to the actor in the choice condition than to the same actor in the assignment condition; (2) perceivers should be more confident of their inferences in the choice condition; and, (3) they should evaluate the chooser less favorably than the actor who had the role assigned to him. The investigators do not report the data bearing on the first hypothesis, but the other data make sense only if it were supported. Hypothesis 2 was strongly supported, and both indices bearing on hypothesis 3 were in the predicted direction, though only one treatment difference was significant. In addition, while the fact is not particularly relevant in the present theoretical context, the subjects were apparently more influenced by the remarks of the actor when he chose the role than when he was assigned to it, even though he was better liked in the latter case.

The results confirm very well the expectation derived from the theory of correspondent inferences, and the subjects show the same uncertainty in the role assignment condition as was observed in the in-role treatments of the astronaut-submariner study. Since there are so many objectives served when the actor in the role assignment condition follows his assignment, and since most of these objectives are quite culturally desirable, the perceiver learns very little from the actor's compliance.

Hedonic relevance is involved because the position taken by the actor is contrary to the view held by all perceivers in the experiment. While the experiment does not manipulate the relevance of the action directly, it does alter the subject's evaluative response to the action by altering his interpretation of the act.

It is not as yet clear, however, precisely how relevance enters into the inference process. At the outset, it may be useful to distinguish between the effects of relevance on correspondence, and the joint effects of relevance and correspondence on evaluation by the perceiver. Let us consider each of these in turn. We propose that as relevance increases there is also an increase in the likelihood that inferences will be correspondent. This is because effects which might appear to have little in common in the eyes of most observers might be functionally equivalent to a particular perceiver. Thus, relevance may provide a potent criterion for grouping and packaging the effects of action, thereby reducing the number of unrelated or noncommon effects in the choice circle. The result is an increase in the correspondence of any inference based on that particular choice. This reasoning does not apply in the event that a nonrelevant effect is seen as the probable goal of the action. However, we may assume that the probability of launching the inference from a relevant effect increases directly as a function of the degree of relevance involved.

In addition to the packaging of effects in terms of their positive or negative significance for the perceiver, the number of noncommon effects may be further reduced by *assimilation to the predominant hedonic value*. When the actor makes a choice which is relevant to the perceiver, there will be a tendency for the remaining more or less neutral effects to take on the sign of other effects in the choice circle. This assimilation should operate in such a way as to increase the differentiation between chosen and nonchosen courses of action. The process may be illustrated by changes in the connotative meaning of attributed dispositions. Let us assume that we have identical information concerning the moderately high risk-taking tendencies of Adams and Bagby. If Adams does something which, on balance, goes against our interests, the assimilation hypothesis proposes that risk-taking proclivity might be construed as recklessness and irresponsibility. If Bagby does something that supports our interests and benefits us, riskiness might take on connotations of creativeness and inventive autonomy. This would seem to be an expression of Heider's (1958) general balance principle: Bad actions come from bad people and good is achieved by the good.

Turning now to the joint effects of relevance and correspondence on evaluation by the perceiver, the following proposition suggests itself: If the consequences of an act are predominantly positive, the perceiver will be more favorably disposed toward the actor, the greater the correspondence value of the action. The converse will be true of actions whose effects are negative. In general, ignoring direction for the moment, the evaluation of an individual will be more extreme as a joint function of increases in relevance and correspondence.

Since relevance increases correspondence, and since relevance and correspondence affect evaluation, it might seem reasonable to link relevance directly to evaluation. However, relevance may well affect only one condition of correspondence—the commonality of effects—and not the other, the cultural desirability of effects. For this reason it is possible to have high relevance and only moderate correspondence. When, for example, the Russian ambassador to the United Nations makes a speech accusing America of imperialistic ambitions, dollar diplomacy, exploitation of the worker, and so on, it is easy for us to put these remarks into a single package under the label of negative hedonic relevance. And yet, we are sufficiently aware of the norms of cultural desirability among Russian public spokesmen to recognize that none of the ambassador's statements departs very far from these norms.

In terms of the fourfold table presented as Fig. 3, we are dealing with a case of trivial clarity. Note that relevance is high—the statements chosen by the ambassador have effects almost all of which are an affront to our values as American perceivers. The number of noncommon effects is low—the disparate remarks may be readily packaged as anti-American; and assumed cultural desirability (for a Russian) is high. But, we would not predict a particularly intense negative evaluation in this case. Since this particular Russian is just saying what any other Russian would say under the same circumstances, it is rather hard to take special umbrage at his "negatively relevant" remarks. The example helps us to see, then, that a combination of relevance and high correspondence is prerequisite for extreme evaluations to occur. Relevance controls the direction of evaluation, but is only one of two contributing determinants of its extremity.

1. Relevance Increases Correspondence: Empirical Support

In order to test the hypothesis that relevance increases correspondence in the inference process, it is necessary to present the same action or series of acts in contexts of differing personal relevance for the perceiver. This was done in an experiment by Jones and deCharms (1957) and in another by Kleiner (1960), the results of which we shall briefly summarize.

Two separate experiments, sharing certain basic procedural features were conducted by Jones and deCharms (1957). In the first experiment a trained accomplice was the only member of a group, including four or five naive subjects, who failed the assigned experimental task. In one condition, *individual fate,* the relevance of this failure was minimized.

The subjects all received the rewards promised them for succeeding and this was in no way contingent on the accomplice's performance. In another condition, *common fate,* the accomplice's failure prevented anyone from reaping the rewards available. This was, then, a condition of negative hedonic relevance for the naive subjects. The subjects rated the accomplice twice; first, prior to the main experimental inductions and again after his failure was established. We would expect to find, in an index of change in ratings of the accomplice, indications of greater correspondence in the negative relevance than in the minimal relevance condition. In line with this prediction, the accomplice was regarded as being less competent, less dependable, and generally judged in less favorable terms in the common fate (negative relevance) than in the individual fate (minimal relevance) condition. Contrary to expectation, no differences in likeability or friendliness occurred as a function of relevance. Perhaps we may cite this pattern of findings to illustrate that relevance may affect certain attributions without necessarily affecting personal evaluation.

A study by Kleiner (1960) varied the positive relevance of constructive member actions by varying the probability of group failure. A previously instructed accomplice then facilitated group goal achievement by solving problems too difficult for the others. We assume that the degree of positive relevance varies directly with the degree of initial threat to the group. Unfortunately for our purposes, Kleiner did not get extensive impression ratings over a variety of traits, but he did get evidence concerning changes in perceived importance of group members. Consistent with the relevance-correspondence hypothesis, the greater the group's need for help, the greater importance attributed to the helpful confederate. Consistent with the second evaluation, the rated likeability of the confederate as both a teammate and as someone to socialize with was positively related to the degree of initial need for help.

While there are no other investigations (to our knowledge) that concern themselves directly with the relevance-correspondence hypothesis, there are several closely related studies which increase our confidence in its validity. These are studies in which conditions of *potential* relevance are created by the anticipation of further interaction, but in which impression ratings are taken before the direction of relevance has been established by final action. The general pattern of findings from these studies has been called "facilitative distortion" of perceived attributes—the stimulus person is assigned attributes that are consistent with the positive outcome hoped for in the interaction.

The classic study was done by Pepitone (1950). Variations in motivation (relevance) were established by having high school students think that their ideas about athletics would be instrumental in obtaining either very desirable championship basketball tickets (high relevance) or much less desirable tickets (low relevance). The three judges who evaluated the students' ideas were again accomplices of the experimenter. They varied their apparent approval of the subject in some conditions, and their apparent power to grant him a ticket in others. On the whole, there was a strong tendency for subjects to view the more favorable judges as more powerful than the less favorable judges, though power was ostensibly equated by instructions and the accomplices' careful attention to their prescribed roles. Similarly, when there was a deliberate attempt to vary the judges' power, the more powerful judges were regarded as more approving. We may only assume that such "facilitative distortion" would not have occurred in a no-relevance control group. It *was* true that the high relevance subjects saw the approving judge as more powerful than the low relevance subjects did, which provides direct support for the relevance-correspondence hypothesis, but the remaining differences which might test the hypothesis were not significant.

A similar pattern of facilitative distortions was found in one phase of Davis' (1962) study. Subjects were given preinformation about an individual with whom they were to engage in a series of either cooperative or competitive interactions. For half of the subjects, this information portrayed an essentially submissive person; for the other half, an essentially ascendant person. When the submissive person was to be a *partner,* she was seen as more active, outgoing, forceful, tough, and as less passive, shy, and uncertain of herself than when she was to be an *opponent.* These differential effects did not approach statistical significance in the condition of ascendant information. Perhaps the constraints of clear information were strong enough to inhibit distortion in the latter case.

Other studies also show both facilitative distortion effects and the absence of such effects, but in no study do "pessimistic" distortions occur. There seems little doubt that relevance may increase distortion by causing increases in correspondence which are not based on added information. What we now need is to determine other parameters which influence the relevance-correspondence relationship and thus affect the perceiver's reliance on the available data he obtains from observed action.

2. Relevance and Correspondence Determine Evaluation: Empirical Support

The second hypothesis concerning relevance was that evaluation is a joint function of the degree of relevance and the level of correspondence. Under a variety of different guises, this hypothesis has received greater empirical attention than the prior hypothesis linking relevance to correspondence. It is not difficult to find ample support for the proposition that people like others who benefit them in some way and dislike others who are harmful. But since we have already argued that relevance increases correspondence, this proposition is not a very precise rendition of the second hypothesis. The second hypothesis requires the demonstration that *both* relevance and correspondence are necessary conditions for evaluation, or at least that evaluation will be more extreme when both are present at a high level. Our reasoning implies that evaluation will become more extreme as a function of increases in either relevance or correspondence, as long as the other variable is held constant at some value greater than zero. If an action is expected to be positively or negatively relevant for a perceiver, for example, the perceiver's evaluations should become more extreme when the conditions of judgment give rise to high correspondence.

As one test of this hypothesis, we may return to the second experiment reported in Jones and deCharms (1957). Cross-cutting the common fate-individual fate variation which characterized both experiments, an additional instructional variation was introduced. Half of the subjects were led to believe that the task was such that failure should be primarily attributed to lack of ability. The remaining subjects were told that failure on the particular problems to be solved could only reflect a lack of motivation, a lack of willingness to try hard. In retrospect, we might now see the ability condition as involving less choice for the actor than the motivation condition. After all, if ability and not motivation is involved, then the subject may try heroically, knowing that others are dependent on him and that doing well is important—but still fail. In the ability condition, therefore, his failure would not provide a basis for correspondent inferences about his attitudes toward the group. The individual must have some degree of choice among action alternatives before one may begin to speak of noncommon effects in the chosen alternative.

The results bear out the prediction quite well. An evaluation change index was composed from the combined ratings of the accomplice made by each naive subject before and after the experimental variables were introduced. The traits involved were deliberately chosen to reflect an evaluative "halo effect": competent, intelligent, conscientious, likeable, dependable, and so on. When the accomplice supposedly had no choice (in the ability conditions), variations in personal relevance for the perceiver did not lead to differential changes in evaluation. Thus the evaluation change scores in the common fate-ability condition were almost identical to the evaluation change scores in the individual fate-ability condition (see Table II). When the accomplice was presumed to have a choice, on the other hand, relevance was a crucial determinant of evaluation. Subjects in the common fate-motivation condition were significantly more negative in their evaluation change scores than subjects in the individual fate-motivation condition.

It should be emphasized, of course, that the actual behavior of the accomplice was as nearly the same in all conditions as careful pre-training and periodic monitoring could make it. In conclusion, then, the accomplice was negatively evaluated if his failing performance prevented the others from obtaining rewards *and* he could have avoided failure by trying harder. Not trying hard in this case may have been equivalent to an attitude of indifference to the group, an attitude which (once inferred) would be resented by the group's members.

TABLE II[a]
CHANGE IN "HALO EFFECT," EXPERIMENT II

	Common fate		Individual fate	
	Motivation	Ability	Motivation	Ability
$\bar{X}^b$	23.0	17.3	14.4	18.9
SD	10.68	6.27	2.12	9.53

Groups heading spans all.

[a] Data from Jones and deCharms (1957).
[b] The greater the mean change, the more negative the "after" evaluation.

Perhaps the most celebrated study linking causal attribution and evaluation is that of Thibaut and Riecken (1955). They conducted two separate experiments to explore the proposition that an act of benevolence which is "internally caused" is more appreciated than one which is the inevitable result of environmental circumstances. We would now view internal causation as another way of talking about the perception of choice alternatives available to the actor. A person "internally causes" certain effects in the environment only when he had the option of causing other effects and did not do so.

In each of the Thibaut-Riecken experiments, an undergraduate subject was introduced to two experimental accomplices or confederates, one of whom was apparently much higher in academic or social status than himself and one of whom was lower in status. The subject soon found himself in the position where he needed the help of at least one of the confederates. The experimenter encouraged him to ask for help and required only that he make an identical request of both the high status and the low status confederate. When both of the confederates eventually complied with his request, the subject was asked to explain the compliance and to evaluate each confederate. Since the differences in experimentally manipulated status were perceived as differences in the ability to resist persuasion, the high status confederate was regarded as having more choice in his decision about compliance. The low status confederate, on the other hand, was more likely to be viewed as complying because he felt "coerced" by the more powerful subject. The norms governing a low status position are such that compliance to those higher in status is often expected. In our terms, then, the behavior of the high status person should lead to more correspondent inferences concerning the intention to help the subject out of a disposition of spontaneous affection or good will.

As our hypothesis would predict, holding relevance constant (the subject is benefitted equally by the two confederates), as correspondence of inference (about spontaneous good will) increases, positive evaluation also increases. The benevolence of the high status confederate earns him a greater increase in attractiveness than does the benevolence of the low status confederate. Relevance in the positive direction, coupled with high correspondence in the form of perceived internal causation, results in more positive evaluation.

Incidental findings from two other studies may be mentioned as well. These findings also bring out the relationship between relevance, correspondence, and evaluation. In the study by Davis (1962) briefly referred to above, control groups were run in which subjects anticipated either cooperative or competitive discussions with each other, but no pre-information about the partners was provided beforehand. Each subject rated the other person prior to the interaction on traits which could be combined into an ascendance-submission index, and on likeability. In the competitive condition, the more ascendant one's opponent, the greater the probability of one's own failure; ascendance has negative hedonic relevance. In the cooperative condition, on the other hand, ascendance has positive relevance since it implies a greater probability of team success. Comparing individual differences in the tendency to assign high first impression ratings on ascendance, we should expect a positive correlation between perceived ascendance and likeability in the cooperative condition and a negative correlation between these two sets of ratings in the competitive condition. The correlational values were actually +.60 and −.18, respectively, reflecting a difference between conditions which is significant.

Finally, in an experiment by Jones and Daugherty (1959), some subjects were led to anticipate interacting with one of two persons about whom a fair amount of information was provided via a tape-recorded interview. Others received the same information about the two persons, but it was clear that no subsequent interaction would take place. One of the two interviewees was presented as a rather intellectual, somewhat diffident person, with moderately strong aesthetic interests. The other was presented as a rather opportunistic and conforming, but obviously sociable person. In the no-anticipation condition, in which we may assume that the characteristics of both persons were of minimal relevance, the diffident esthete was more highly evaluated on a variety of dimensions than was the sociable politician. In contrast, when the subjects were led to anticipate interacting with one of the two, making the relevance of sociability more salient, the subjects' evaluation of the politician markedly and significantly increased. These results, then, suggest that a particular personal attribute (sociability) was assigned approximately the same ratings in the two conditions (varying in the anticipation of interaction) but variations in the relevance of that attribute were associated with shifts in evaluation. If there had been no evidence that the "politician" was sociable, correspondent inferences about him would not have been drawn regarding that disposition and evaluation would not have varied with relevance. It should be emphasized that the obtained differences were not anticipated. However, we view the interpretation as the most plausible one available and are encouraged to think that a replication specifically addressed to the present hypothesis would show the same pattern.

In summary, there seems little question that variations in the relevance of an action to the perceiver have an effect on the process of inferring dispositions which explain the action. Our first hypothesis was that relevance tends to increase correspondence by reducing the number of noncommon effects in the action alternative chosen. We have presented some evidence in favor of this hypothesis, although it is clear that the strength of confirmation depends on other conditions, such as the ambiguity of available information about the actor and the consequent leeway for facilitative distortion. The second hypothesis, which states that personal evaluation varies as a joint function of relevance and correspondence, has received stronger support than the first. Here again, however, much of the evidence is indirect and circumstantial. Hopefully, the present theoretical analysis will point the way toward more precise tests of both hypotheses.

B. Personalism: The Actor's Intention to Benefit or Harm the Perceiver

An act or a choice may be hedonically relevant to the perceiver even though it is quite clear to the latter that the choice was not conditioned by his unique presence. An actor might express opinions which differ radically from the perceiver's without having any knowledge of the latter's views. Such a choice of opinions may have hedonic relevance for the perceiver, but may not have been offered with any intention to gratify or to spite him. The variable of *personalism* is introduced to distinguish between choices which are conceivably affected by the presence of the perceiver and choices which are not conceivably so affected.

It is usually difficult for a perceiver to judge whether a choice was affected by personalistic considerations. He may, in effect, experimentally arrange conditions of his own presence and absence in an attempt to detect differences in the choice made by the stimulus person. This is often done indirectly, as when the perceiver compares reports of choices made in his absence with his own observations of choices made in his presence. We may try, for example, to find out what others say about us and our beliefs behind our backs. When the actions of another person obstruct our interests, it becomes important for us to determine whether the other sets out specifically to make life unpleasant for us or whether we have been disadvantaged as a by-product of actions primarily directed toward other objectives. Similarly, when others go out of their way to help us, we have an interest in establishing whether they did this because of our uniquely attractive personality or because they would have helped almost anyone under the circumstances.

The distinction between relevance and personalism hinges on the perceiver's imputation of a certain kind of knowledge to the actor: the actor's awareness that the interests of the perceiver are positively or negatively affected by his actions. If such knowledge is *not* imputed by the perceiver to the actor, then we are dealing with a case of "impersonal hedonic relevance."

When a hedonically relevant action is produced in the presence of the perceiver, the latter's problem is to decide whether the act was uniquely conditioned by the fact that he was its target. When there is such evidence of a "unique conditioning," the perceiver is likely to draw strong inferences of malevolence or benevolence, stronger than he would as a bystander. He and only he is the target of the other's highly relevant action; therefore, it is assumed that the other has a special interest in making life easy or difficult for him as a person.

Since the perceiver is going to be so vitally concerned with relevant effects that were deliberately produced for his consumption, such effects should clearly play a special role in shaping his inferences about the actor. We propose that action which is both relevant and personal has a direct and dramatic effect on evaluative conclusions about the actor. One reason for this is that personalism clearly implies choice. If an actor benefits a perceiver, this is a personalistic episode only if it reflects the selection of that particular perceiver as a worthy beneficiary in the face of opportunities to select other targets or other actions. The combination of personalism and positive relevance, then, insures a positive evaluation simply by insuring a correspondent inference of focused benevolence. The special significance of such focused benevolence may lie in the fact that it satisfies the perceiver's needs for information about his worthiness, as well as other needs for security, power over others, and so on. In any event, the receipt of focused benefit or focused harm should generate "halo" effects in the inference process which go beyond the assimilation to hedonic value predicted in the case of impersonal hedonic relevance.

Personalism may, of course, be incorrectly assumed by the perceiver. The most extreme form of distortion along these lines may be seen in paranoia, where innocent actions and actions not conditioned by the perceiver's presence, become the data for inferences concerning ulterior malevolent motivation.

Surprisingly, there are few experiments which precisely assess the role of personalism in the inference process. The above proposition implies that hedonically relevant actions which the perceiver judges to be uniquely affected by his presence will give rise to correspondent inferences to all those attributes captured by a positive or negative "halo" effect. In an experiment specifically concerned with variations in personalism, Gergen (1962) arranged to have coeds receive uniformly positive, reinforcing remarks from another coed under personal versus impersonal conditions. Such remarks probably are hedonically relevant and positive as far as the first coed is concerned.

In the personal treatment, the girls had been previously introduced to each other, had engaged in a pleasant and informative interaction, and the reinforcing person (actually an experimental accomplice) had quite a bit to go on in expressing her positive feelings about the subject. In the impersonal treatment, on the other hand, the subjects were informed that the accomplice had been through some intensive training designed to help her establish rapport in a social interaction. In addition, and in clear contrast with the personal treatment, the accomplice never saw the subject, but interacted with her through a microphone-speaker system while the subject observed her through a one-way mirror. Each subject was ultimately asked to record her impression of the accomplice on a series of evaluative scales. From our proposition concerning the role of personalism in producing high correspondence for evaluative characteristics, we would expect a more positive halo effect in the personal than in the impersonal experimental treatment. There were, however, no significant differences between the subjects' evaluative ratings of the accomplice in the two conditions.

There was some evidence that the subjects felt sorry for the accomplice in the impersonal condition, since she had to operate under the rather embarrassing handicap of being seen by the subject without being able to see her. There was also some confusion about whether the subject was to rate the accomplice as she appeared to be or as she "really was." We do not feel, therefore, that the Gergen experiment is a crucial test of the personalism proposition, though some variation of Gergen's procedure would seem to have promise as a fairly direct approach to the problem. It is at least conceivable that the proposition only holds for harmful actions, and that persons are much less sensitive to variations in personalism when positive actions are involved. This may be especially true when these positive actions involve verbal compliments. The reluctance of subjects to assume that a compliment was not intended for them personally is discussed in detail by Jones (1964). In this same source the reader will find a fuller exposition of the Gergen experiment along with results of other dependent variable measures which were more central to his concerns.

1. Factors Mitigating One's Evaluation of an Aggressor

More indirect and yet more promising evidence on the role of personalism comes from experiments concerned with the factors which mitigate one person's reactions to being verbally attacked or insulted by another. The basic paradigm involves comparing perceivers' reactions to the same attacking action when it occurs in different settings. Typically, one setting is designed to bring out reciprocal hostility in the subjects (in the form of highly negative impression ratings) while other settings are arranged to check whether factors which theoretically should mitigate a hostile reaction in fact do. We are especially interested in those studies within this paradigm which exemplify variations in the perceived personalism of the attack.

a. Provocation by the perceiver. An obvious mitigating variable which comes to mind is the extent to which the attack is seen as justified by the target person. If the perceiver believes he has done something to earn attack, insult, or rejection, he will presumably be less inclined to appraise his attacker negatively than if the attack was unreasonable or arbitrary. For example, Deutsch and Solomon (1959) found that subjects who were led to believe they had performed poorly on a task were less negative in appraising a stimulus person who rejected them as future work partners than subjects who were led to believe they had performed well.

A similar point is brought out by the results of an experiment by Strickland *et al.* (1960) on the effects of group support in evaluating an antagonist. Each subject met first with two other subjects who shared his opinions (pro or con) about the role of big-time athletics in university life. He then privately chose a series of five arguments to support his position. These were to be transmitted to a person in the next room who was presumably neither for nor against big-time athletics. After this person had a chance to study the arguments, he was interviewed by the experimenter who probed his feelings about the person who sent the arguments. This interview was broadcast into the subject's room and it contained a strong attack on his intelligence and integrity.

However, prior to his exposure to the broadcast interview (which was actually a standardized tape-recording), the subject learned that his fellow group members would either have chosen the same arguments he did (group support) or would have chosen a very different set (no support). The subject's final ratings of the person in the next room—which tapped into such dispositional characteristics as intelligence, warmth, adjustment, conceit, and likeability—were affected by this variation in group support. These rating differences were corroborated by free response sketches in which each subject expressed his private feelings about the person. Those whose arguments were supported were more negative in their evaluations of the person in the next room than those whose arguments were not supported.

In neither the Deutsch and Solomon (1959) nor the Strickland et al. (1960) study was the potential for perceiver personalism particularly high. In each, regardless of the experimental condition, a very limited sample of the subjects' behavior was the stimulus occasion for attack or rejection. The subject did not, in other words, expose the full range of his personal characteristics as a preface to the attack received. Nevertheless, the attack was directed toward him ostensibly because of behavior for which he must bear at least some of the responsibility.

We now suggest that an attack in the face of good performance (or group support) is more apt to be viewed as an attempt to harm or to disadvantage the subject than an attack in response to poor performance, because after a poor performance (including the sending of arguments defined as inferior by the group), the attacker will be seen as more constrained to respond negatively. The correspondence value of his hostile action, in other words, will be lowered by the presence in the choice area of effects having more to do with fulfillment of task requirements, candor, and realism than with hostility. Since there are fewer reasons for the antagonist's attack in the good performance setting, and one of these is presumably the antagonist's desire to hurt the subject as a person, correspondence and therefore unfavorability of general impression are high in this latter case.

b. *Evidence of chronicity.* Another factor which mitigates a perceiver's evaluation of an antagonist is any evidence concerning the latter's general tendency to be indiscriminately aggressive. If the antagonist is known to be or gives fairly good evidence of being a chronically dyspeptic or uncontrollably negative person, his derogation will have less sting for the target person who bears its brunt.

Two recent experiments by Berkowitz (1960), conducted in quite a different framework from the one we are here proposing, shed some light on the effects of a perceiver's prior knowledge of a particular attack. Since only the first of the Berkowitz studies is particularly relevant to our present concerns, we shall confine ourselves to that.

Pairs of subjects were brought together for a study of first impressions. Through a bogus note exchange, the subject received information first, indicating that the partner was either generally hostile or generally friendly and second, indicating that the partner either liked or disliked the subject personally. The subject recorded his impression of the partner once at the outset of the experiment, once after the general information, and once after the personal evaluation from the partner.

The results showed that if the partner was perceived to be hostile initially, the partner's favorable evaluation of the subject had a decidedly ameliorating effect on the subject's impression, while the unfavorable evaluation changed this impression very little. Similarly, if the subject initially perceived the partner to be friendly, the unfavorable evaluation received from the partner created a striking change of impression in the direction of perceived unfriendliness, while the favorable evaluation resulted in minimal change.

It would appear, then, that the fact of prior knowledge concerning the hostility of the attacker reduces the personal significance of the attack. If we look more closely at the Berkowitz results, however, the point they make is actually rather different from the one we are presently pursuing. If a person who is already seen as generally hostile attacks the perceiver, there will be less of a *decline* (from the second to the third rating) than if a friendly person attacks the perceiver. However, the subject actually ends up liking the hostile attacker less than the friendly attacker, presumably because the evidence concerning the undesirable characteristic, hostility, summates: two hostility indicators are worse than one. The Berkowitz results really do not suggest that the perceiver is less bothered or upset by the attack if he has already decided that the attacker is generally hostile. They merely tell us that the attack is not as unexpected from a hostile person and therefore it contributes less to a change in impression from a point that is more negative to start with. We are dealing here, then, with the attempt on the part of the perceiver-subject to appraise the significance of a particular action choice against background information about different prior choices.

In order to confirm the significance of perceived general hostility as a prior choice factor mitigating the significance of the attack, the results would have to show that the generally hostile attacker is better liked by the recipient of the attack than the friendly attacker. However, such a finding might be difficult to obtain experimentally. After all, the fact that he is hostile does not make the attacker likeable to anybody. It merely means that the attack itself will cause less of a stir.

Evidence from a recent experiment does indicate that someone who starts out being derogatory and continues to act that way is better liked than someone who starts out being favorably disposed to the subject and becomes increasingly derogatory (Aronson and Linder, 1965). In this experiment the subject believed he was over-hearing a series of appraisals referring to him with short episodes of social interaction intervening; he was not the target of openly expressed hostility. This may be a critical difference between the Berkowitz design and the Aronson and Linder design. Another difference that may have been crucial is that the former study asked for an intervening rating (which might have "committed" the subject to a particular rating of the attacker) while the latter study did not.

If we return to the conditions of the Berkowitz experiment, it may be too much to expect the hostile attacker to be better liked than the friendly attacker. What is needed is a comparison between the target of the attack and an "innocent" bystander as regards their impressions of the attacker. Because of the general negative significance attached to being hostile, it does not make sense to predict that either the involved subject or the bystander would like the hostile attacker better than the friendly one. However, a more refined and promising hypothesis, still in the spirit of our earlier remarks on the role of personalism, is that the involved subject will dislike the hostile attacker less than the bystander, relative to the discrepancy between their impressions of the friendly attacker.

c. *Emotional adjustment of the attacker.* Such an experimental comparison has yet to be made, unfortunately, but the results of an earlier experiment by Jones et al. (1959) can be interpreted quite nicely in these terms. The procedures of the study by Jones et al., were roughly as follows. At a given experimental session, a pair of female subjects listened to two female stimulus persons allegedly conversing about one of the subjects in an adjacent room. The conversation was actually a carefully written and skillfully acted tape-recording. The stimulus persons were allegedly enrolled in a "senior course in personality assessment" and it was their duty to observe a designated subject through the one-way mirror for a period of time and then to discuss their impressions of that subject. It was clear to them that their remarks would be overheard by the subjects in the adjacent room. One of the stimulus persons was generally neutral or mildly favorable in her comments, but the other stimulus person ("the derogator") was decidedly hostile and clearly had a low opinion of the subject. The subject whose characteristics were not being discussed was instructed to sit aside as a bystander and to pay close attention to the proceedings.

Prior to the attack, both the involved and bystander subject were given some information about the two students who would be observing them from the next room. It was clear upon reading this information that one of these students was quite maladjusted: She had an unstable home life, inadequate emotional resources, and underlying anxiety. The other student was presented as an effective, well-rounded, insightful undergraduate who had reached her present station from a home life that had been happy and rich with support and affection. For one group of subjects (the *derogator-mal* group), the data sheets presented the stimulus person who did not derogate as well adjusted. For a second group of subjects (the *derogator-well* group), the background information sheets were simply reversed.

After the involved and the bystander subjects listened to the tape-recorded discussion, including the derogatory remarks, they were each instructed to rate the two stimulus persons on a number of items. The items with which we are particularly concerned at the present are two reflecting the perceived likeability of the stimulus person. The subjects were asked to indicate the extent of their agreement with the two statements: "As a person, she is extremely likeable," and "I find it hard to like this person to any extent."

Thus the experimental manipulations created a standard situation in which a subject was derogated by a well-adjusted or a maladjusted person while another subject looked on. The variable of perceived maladjustment was included, in effect, to see whether it would serve as a factor mitigating the subject's response to the derogator. Jones *et al.,* reasoned that the involved subject would be less upset by an attack from a maladjusted person than by an attack from a well-adjusted one. The bystander, on the other hand, was expected to be less concerned in general with the derogation and its implications for inferences about the derogator's personality, and more inclined to prefer the well-adjusted person because she was probably more appealing and talented. The prediction, then, was that there would be a statistical interaction between role (involved versus bystander) and condition of the derogator (maladjusted versus well adjusted).

The data were analyzed in terms of each subject's relative preference for the nonderogator over the derogator, a procedure adopted to reduce that portion of rating variability due to individual differences in scale interpretation or style of responding to the scale items. (Some such device is usually essential in an "after-only" design.) The crucial results are summarized in Table III. It is evident that there is a general dislike for people who are derogatory and a general preference for people who are well adjusted. When these two factors work in the same direction (as in the first column of the table), the discrepancy scores are understandably large. Of greater theoretical interest, when the derogator is well adjusted, the involved subject obviously likes her much less than the bystander subject ($p < .025$). To a slight extent, the average bystander even prefers

TABLE III

JOINT EFFECTS OF DEROGATOR ADJUSTMENT AND SUBJECT INVOLVEMENT
ON "LIKEABILITY"[a,b]

	Condition	
	Derogator-mal	Derogator-well
Involved subjects		
$\bar{X}$	3.92	2.17
SD	(1.78)	(2.29)
Bystander subjects		
$\bar{X}$	4.33	−.57
SD	(3.17)	(3.96)

[a] Based on discrepancy between ratings of derogator and nonderogator. The larger the mean value, the greater the tendency to dislike the derogator *relative to* the nonderogator.
[b] Data from Jones *et al.* (1959).

the well-adjusted derogator to the maladjusted nonderogator (as indicated by the minus sign in that cell). When the derogator is maladjusted, however, the involved subject actually likes her better than the bystander does (though this difference does not approach statistical significance). The predicted interaction effect is minimally significant ($t = 1.877; p < .05$, one-tailed test).

In the context of the present discussion, we would argue that the personalistic significance of the derogation is obviously greater for the involved subject than for the bystander, and that it is greater for the involved subject when the derogator is well adjusted than maladjusted. When the derogator is maladjusted, the involved subject can take comfort in the hypothesis that the attacker's hostility is a symptom of her own problems and she would express similar insults to anyone who came within range. Perceived personalism should be fairly low. When the derogator is well adjusted, the involved subject will be more likely than the bystander to package the insulting remarks into one cluster of highly related hedonic effects, and therefore to assign more correspondent, personalistic meaning to the attack. There is no easy way to escape the inference that the derogator finds the subject personally offensive and is "against her."

The maladjustment treatment in the preceding experiment may be construed in terms of the reduction of freedom to choose which accompanies poor adjustment, and the perception of these restraints on choice by the perceiver. Perhaps the prevailing stereotypes of mental health and mental illness contribute to the tendency to perceive the maladjusted person as not responsible for the trouble he may cause others. Under the proper circumstances, however, he may be seen as *more* responsible for causing trouble than the normal, well-adjusted actor. At least such is the implication of some results from the experiment by Gergen and Jones (1963).

d. Amplification by ambivalence. Gergen and Jones set out to test a set of hypotheses deriving from the assumption that people are ambivalent toward the mentally ill. Many persons expect the mentally ill to have annoying characteristics but inhibit their annoyance because they acknowledge the fact that they are not responsible for their condition and its consequences. Gergen and Jones reasoned that the ambivalence toward a particular mentally ill person would be "split" if a situation were arranged in which his behavior had clear positive or negative consequences for the perceiver. Thus a perceiver should like a benevolent mentally ill person better than a benevolent normal person, and dislike a malevolent mentally ill person more than a malevolent normal person.

In order to test this hypothesis (which was loosely derived from psychoanalytic writings on ambivalence), 64 ambulatory V.A. hospital patients (nonpsychiatric) were given the task of predicting a series of hypothetical consumer choices being made by a patient in the adjoining room. The patient in the next room was alleged to be in the hospital either with a psychiatric illness or with a minor organic ailment. Actually there was no person in the next room, and all the information about him was conveyed by a combination of tape-recorded interviews and feedback through equipment controlled by the experimenter.

The choices of the patient in the adjoining room (hereafter called the stimulus person) were either very hard or very easy to predict. In the *low consequence* (i.e., low relevance) condition, the stimulus person (actually, by a ruse, the experimenter) provided corrective feedback by an informative signal light whenever a prediction error was made. In the *high consequence* condition, prediction errors called forth a raucous buzzer of unpredictable duration. The experimenter also made it clear that he found the buzzer very annoying, implying that it was up to the subject to keep him happy by making the correct predictions. Both before the prediction task and after it was completed, the subject filled out an impression rating scale indicating his current feelings about the stimulus person.

The experimental hypothesis was stated as follows: "Evaluative judgments of a mentally ill stimulus person vary little as a function of predictability unless affective consequences are attached to success and failure of prediction. The role of affective consequences is less important

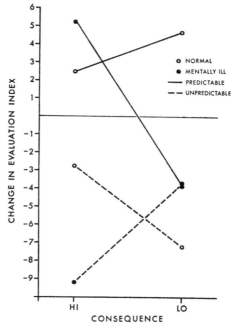

FIG. 5. Changes in evaluation as a function of mental status, predictability, and consequence. (Data from Gergen and Jones, 1963.)

in evaluative judgments of a normal stimulus person. Judgments of the normal should directly reflect variations in predictability, regardless of the consequences of judgment" (Gergen and Jones, 1963, p. 70).

The results presented in Fig. 5 quite strikingly confirm this complicated hypothesis. There is, as implied by the hypothesis, a significant statistical interaction between the three factors of normality, predictability, and consequence. The most striking thing to note is the extent to which consequence determines perceptions of the mentally ill person. When he is in a position to hurt the subject or to spare him pain—in short, when he is either benevolent or malevolent toward the perceiver—the mentally ill stimulus person is judged very favorably or unfavorably. When there are no such personal consequences for the perceiver, the stimulus person's predictability is not a relevant factor in judging him. (There is also an overall effect of predictability such that, across conditions, the predictable person tends to be evaluated more positively than the unpredictable person.)

Furthermore, it may be shown that the perception of benevolent versus malevolent intentions is involved in the subject's judgments of the high consequence-mentally ill person. A variation of the experiment was run in which the stimulus person had supposedly made his consumer choice days before and was not, as alleged in the main experiment, actually in the next room at the time and responding through his own actions to the subject's predictions. In other words, all feedback to the subjects (including the unpleasant buzzer) was openly controlled by the experimenter. The experiment was in all other respects a precise replication of the first version. In this variation, predictability again had a strong effect on average evaluations, but there were no main or interaction differences as a function of consequence or normality. There must, then, be some possibility that the stimulus person is deliberately hurting or sparing the subject for the complex effects noted in the first experiment to occur.

There are many questions raised by the Gergen and Jones experiment. There are also special problems involved in relating these results to the Jones et al. (1959) findings. In interpreting those findings we argued, in effect, that an attack by a maladjusted stimulus person was less devastating than an attack by a well-adjusted stimulus person, because the normal person is perceived to have greater freedom of choice. It is as if evidence concerning maladjustment acts as a damper on the intensity of personal feeling toward the maladjusted person. The Gergen and Jones results, however, seem to show that under certain conditions evidence concerning maladjustment (i.e., mental illness) *amplifies* rather than constricts the intensity of the perceiver's personal feelings. Does this mean that the mentally ill person is assumed to have greater freedom of choice than the normal person in the Gergen and Jones study?

In spite of certain superficial resemblances, the experiments are really quite different in several, crucial respects. In the earlier experiment the very meaning and intensity of the attack is presumably a function of the attacker's adjustment status. To be insulted by a pathetic, perhaps mildly paranoid person is hardly to be insulted at all. In the Gergen and Jones experiment, however, the consequences of the attack are embarrassing, painful, and irritating, regardless of their source. In this case, furthermore, the question of freedom to choose may actually exacerbate rather than mitigate the response to the mentally ill stimulus person.

While the data do not force this interpretation on us, there is at least nothing inconsistent in the rating or the post-experimental questionnaire results with the following speculations: When unpredictability hurts, the "why" of the unpredictability becomes a more important issue to the one who suffers. Two possible effects of "buzzing" the subject in the high consequence condition are especially salient, hurting the subject and being honest to one's true preferences for certain consumer objects. In the replication of the experiment, the first of these effects is ruled out by the change in information about the role of the stimulus person. Perhaps it is the case that when the stimulus person is normal, the most likely hypothesis is that he is making "normal choices" and, therefore, that the subject must take at least some of the blame for not being able to figure these out. When the stimulus person is mentally ill, on the other hand, the abnormal choice becomes an instrument of malevolence. Since the choice is a function of abnormality, it is difficult for the subject to maintain the feelings of sympathy which, in the low consequence condition, are sufficient to keep his impression a fairly neutral one. The impression of malevolence may be heightened by the feeling that since the mentally ill person is confused about his choices anyway, the least he can do is to go along with the subject's predictions and not lean on the error buzzer.

Such speculations are obviously no substitute for clear and compelling data on the role of perceived choice in the assignment of benevolent or malevolent intentions. The preceding review of studies involving the effects of personalism, studies mainly focusing on factors which mitigate a target person's response to being attacked, points up the need for additional research into the cognitive consequences of being singled out for benefit or harm. Those of us who have done research on this problem have lacked the kind of integrating framework which is needed to carry out a series of related studies. Perhaps the theory of correspondent inferences will help to provide a focus for the parametric experiments which are needed in clarifying the basic facts about personalism and its implications.

2. Personalism and Ingratiation

We have defined as personalistic those actions which are relevant to the perceiver's interests and, as far as the perceiver can tell, are deliberately carried out by the actor because of this relevance. The concept of personalism inevitably implies a certain degree of choice on the part of the actor which is not inherent in the concept of relevance. Since the condition of choice increases the likelihood of correspondent inferences, the coexistence of relevance and personalism should produce rather extreme evaluative judgments. It seems intuitively plausible that someone who helps us will be seen as more generous, helpful, friendly, etc., than someone who helps another in our presence. A comparable line of thought applies to the case of malevolent actions when we have been singled out as their target.

In an attempt to provide a more rational basis for this intuition, we suggest the following distinctions and their consequences. There are three basic decisions which lurk in the wings during an interaction episode: whether to approach the person further and open oneself to him, whether to avoid or ignore him, or whether he must be "coped with," i.e., attacked or fended off. When the effects of an action are relevant in the positive direction, the decision is typically made to approach further. Such a decision is likely to be made whether or not the action is personalistic in addition to being relevant. When the effects of an action are negative, however, the imputation of personalism means that coping may be necessary. In other words, if a person's actions happen to offend you, he can merely be avoided—unless he is intent on offending you and will go out of his way to accomplish this objective. To the extent that coping is required, we would expect greater hostility to be aroused toward the threatening person, and those characteristics associated with malevolence should be inferred with higher correspondence. This might be partly a matter of justifying the hostility and partly a matter of keeping it at a high enough level (through self-reminding instigations) to support coping behavior.

On the basis of this reasoning, it would appear that personalism plays a larger role when an action is harmful than when it is beneficial. The examples we have cited, along with most of the relevant experiments in the literature, describe the response of a perceiver to some form of attack or rejection. However, a number of experiments have recently been completed which deal with first impressions in response to beneficial gestures, compliments, and agreements. These studies raise a new set of considerations which we shall discuss in concluding our treatment of the role of personalism.

We have argued that negative actions lead the target person either to avoid the actor or to mobilize cognitive support for the actions involved in coping with him. Positive actions, on the other hand, lead to approach behaviors, personal openness, and reciprocation in kind. But a new and complicated problem arises with respect to positive actions. The perceiver must determine their credibility; to what extent does the beneficial act correspond with the intention really to improve the situation of the perceiver as an end in itself? As Jones (1964) has argued in his extended discussion of *ingratiation,* beneficial actions tend to be much more ambiguous than harmful actions when it comes to deciding on the actor's true intention or his ultimate objectives in the situation. The ambiguity of beneficial actions centers around the extent to which ulterior, manipulative purposes may be served by them.

We may now ask, what implications are contained in the theory of correspondent inferences for predicting the cognitive impressions of someone faced with beneficial action? First of all, it is clear that the ambiguity arises because there are at least two classes of effects following from those actions. Actions such as compliments, agreements, and favors may validate the perceiver's self-concept, reduce his uncertainties, offer support against antagonists. Alternatively, or in addition, such actions may have the effect of obligating the perceiver to benefit the actor in return. If the first class of effects is the most salient, the perceiver will attribute to the actor the intention to express his true feelings. From this starting point, correspondent inferences will be drawn to such dispositions as candor, friendliness, likeability, and generosity. In short, the perceiver's evaluation of the actor who has complimented him or agreed with him will be positive. If, on the other hand, the second effect, creating obligations to benefit, is salient and noncommon, the actor may be seen as manipulative, self-seeking, conforming, lacking in candor, etc.

Whether the inference process is tipped in the first, positive direction or the second, negative direction depends on the perceiver's reconstruction of the action alternatives available to the actor. This cognitive reconstruction will depend, in turn, on the perceiver's own role as one of the components in the actor's situation. Specifically, if the perceiver does not control any resources which are important to the actor, then the circle containing the effects of the chosen alternative will not contain the effect of "obligating the perceiver to benefit the actor in return." Presumably, then, some such effect as "validating the self-concept" will be salient and the perceiver will be seen as intending an honest compliment or expressing his genuine agreement with the perceiver's opinions.

If the perceiver does control resources important to the actor (i.e., if the actor is dependent on him), it will be hard for him to decide whether he is merely the target of an ingratiation attempt or the target of honest compliments. At the very least, the correspondence of inference to favorable dispositions will be reduced as a function of his own position as a dispenser of valuable resources. Depending on the circumstances, the perceiver may infer flattering or manipulative intentions and assign unfavorable dispositions, or he may infer benevolent intentions reflecting favorable dispositions.

Let us now consider three recent experiments which support the conclusions of the above line of reasoning. Jones et al. (1963) conducted an experiment in which upper classmen in a campus R.O.T.C. unit exchanged written messages with freshmen in the same unit. This exchange occurred in response to two different sets of instructions, constituting the major treatments of the experiments. In the *ingratiation* condition, both the high and low status subjects were given instructions concerning the importance of compatibility. The experimenter said he was trying to find a number of highly compatible leader-follower pairs to participate in some crucial studies on leadership later in the year. In the *control* condition, the message exchange was presented as part of a first impression study and the importance of "not misleading your partner" was stressed.

The messages that were sent concerned opinions on a variety of issues and eventually contained ratings by each subject of himself and his partner. These messages were actually intercepted and standard information about each subject was conveyed to his partner. Each found the other agreed with him on a variety of opinion issues, presented a rather modest view of himself, and expressed a complimentary view of his partner, the message recipient. On a post-experimental questionnaire (not to be seen by the partner) he was asked to rate the partner with respect

TABLE IV
PERCEPTION OF FLATTERY[a,b]

	Perceiver group						
	HS			LS			
	M	SD	N	M	SD	N	P_{diff}
Ingratiation	13.05	4.14	19	9.62	3.16	21	.01
Control	11.68	4.46	19	11.85	3.41	20	ns

[a] Mean post-experimental ratings in each condition and differences between them. The higher the mean score, the greater the perceived flattery.

[b] Data from Jones *et al.* (1963).

to the following trait dimensions: completely sincere—on the phony side, trustworthy—unreliable, and brutally frank—flatterer. Each pair of antonyms was separated by a twelve-point scale. By adding a subject's rating on each of the three traits, he could be given a score ranging from 3 to 36 with a "perceived average" value at 19.5.

The results are presented in Table IV. They show that high and low status subjects perceived each other to be equally sincere in the control condition, but that the low status subjects attributed significantly greater sincerity to the highs than the highs did to the lows in the ingratiation condition. Restricting our concern to the ingratiation condition, we would say that the inference concerning sincerity is more correspondent for the low status perceivers than for the highs. Relative to the hypothetical average value of 19.5, the empirical mean of 9.62 is more extreme than the mean of 13.05.

This could have been predicted from the theory of correspondent inferences on the grounds that fewer noncommon effects were involved in the high status person's decisions to compliment the low status person than vice versa. Since the low status person was, presumably, in greater need of approval than the high status person, the latter may have been more apt to include "reciprocation of approval" among the effects serving as grist for the inference process. This could, then, have led to reduced correspondence of inference, i.e., ratings of sincerity which were closer to the mean or, in effect, greater perceived flattery.

Such an interpretation is quite *post hoc* and we offer it to illustrate how the theory might account for such findings rather than as confirmation of the theory. The problem is that other assumptions (which we believe are plausible) must be introduced to account for the fact that low status subjects perceive the highs to be more sincere in the ingratiation than in the control condition.

A study by Jones *et al.* (1963) was more explicitly designed to test the hypothesis that positive, supportive behavior will be taken more at face value as a genuine indication of sincerity and good intentions when the actor is not dependent on the target person. The supportive behavior, in this case, was consistently high agreement with the latter's opinions. Dependence was manipulated in a manner simular to the preceding experiment. Unlike the conditions of that experiment, the subjects were not themselves the targets of agreement, but served in the role of by-standers. Their task was to evaluate a stimulus person who agrees very closely with another person on whom he is obviously very dependent *or* not dependent at all.

In general, when the agreeing person was presented as dependent for approval on the other, he was better liked and was assigned more positive characteristics when he did not agree too closely. When dependence was low, on the other hand, the degree of agreement did not affect the ratings to any significant extent. Once again, the actor's condition of dependence affected the significance attached to highly "ingratiating" behavior. The subjects felt neutral about the high dependent conformist, because they did not know whether he was conforming for strategic advantage or whether his opinion agreement was coincidental. The fact that he was dependent, thus, increased the ambiguity of his behavior by adding the granting of approval to those possible effects of action with which the perceiver had to come to terms in his evaluation.

A study by Hilda Dickoff (discussed in Jones, 1964) also showed quite clearly that an actor who consistently compliments the perceiver is better liked when he is not dependent on the latter. Dependence has no effect when the evaluation received is still positive but contains a few plausible reservations.

The obvious feature of all of these studies is the fact that the same behavior (actions which can be seen as ingratiating in intent) results in quite different inferences depending on the context in which it occurs.

More specifically, the studies on ingratiation which we have cited share a concern with the variable, dependence, as the contextual conditions whose presence or absence affects causal attribution. Our inference that a complimentary or agreeable person really likes us is apt to be stronger if we are unable to think of anything we have that he might covet. In other words, the compliments or expression of opinions will be taken at face value and correspondence will be high when the actor has no apparent reason to choose the compliment other than his belief that it applies to us.

Now let us return to the notion of personalism and note an apparent qualification of our proposition that personalism increases correspondence. It may appear that when we are dealing with actions that are potentially ingratiating, correspondence *declines* as a function of personalism. Compliments to one's face are harder to evaluate than the same positive statements said behind our back. Opinions which agree with our own are more apt to be taken at face value when expressed prior to our opinion avowals than after such avowals.

We would not argue with the above interpretations in these hypothetical cases. We would claim, however, that personalism is involved in quite different ways in the kind of face-to-face confrontation where ingratiation is an issue and in the case of negative or neutral information. In fact, ingratiation only becomes an issue in the absence of indications that personalism is involved. The person who receives a face-to-face compliment must decide whether that compliment was meant for him because of his unique personal qualities, or was meant for anyone who happened to occupy a position as a potential dispenser of resources. The high status person may have a difficult problem arranging conditions to test the reactions of his subordinates to him as a person; it may be hard for him to get certain kinds of self-validating information. The important point is that actions that may be seen as directed toward him as an occupant of a social position may therefore not be personalistic and the correspondence value of inferences derived from such ambiguous actions is apt to be low.

IV. Summary and Conclusions

In the present essay we have attempted to develop a systematic conceptual framework for research on person perception. We have been especially interested in specifying the antecedent conditions for attributing intentions or dispositions, having observed an action. Dispositional attributes are in a general way inferred from the effects of action, but not every effect is equally salient in the inference process. Even if we assume as perceivers that the actor *knew* what the effects of his action would be, we must still engage in the complex analytic process of selectively linking certain effects achieved to certain effects intended. This assignment of intentions can provide sufficient reason for (or explanation of) the action, so that the perceiver may go about his interpersonal business unfettered by a concern with ultimate or infinitely regressive causes.

Our most central assumption in considering the attribution of intentions is that actions are informative to the extent that they have emerged out of a context of choice and reflect a selection of one among plural alternatives. When we pursue the implications of this assumption in some detail, it is apparent that the distinctiveness of the effects achieved and the extent to which they do not represent stereotypic cultural values determine the likelihood that information about the actor will be extracted from an action. We have used the term "correspondence of inference" to refer to variations in this kind of informativeness. To say that an inference is correspondent, then, is to say that a disposition is being rather directly reflected in behavior, and that this disposition is unusual in its strength or intensity. Operationally, correspondence means ratings toward the extremes of trait dimensions which are given with confidence.

Having formulated the inference problem in these terms, an obvious research question arises. What are the factors which control the perceiver's judgment that the actor had a choice? Or, more precisely, what conditions influence his judgment concerning the number and distinctiveness (noncommonness) of effects? It is our hope that cumulative, perhaps even parametric, research will be stimulated by posing the inference problem in these terms. A study in which the stimulus person either went along with or resisted clearly stated role-demands, was presented to exemplify some of the more obvious implications of the theory. The results of the study may be interpreted as showing that a low degree of "psychological" choice is functionally the same thing as having many reasons for making a choice. In-role behavior is supported by too many reasons to be informative about the actor; out-of-role behavior is more informative because the effects of such actions are distinctive (few in number) and not to be dismissed as culturally desirable.

In the latter portions of the present essay we have considered the further complexities associated with perceiver involvement which affect theoretical predictions concerning inferred attributes. Our analysis distinguished between two levels of involvement: hedonic relevance and personalism. An actor's choice is hedonically relevant for the perceiver if, on balance, it promotes or thwarts his purposes. An action is personalistic, in the perceiver's view, if it was uniquely conditioned by the latter's presence: if conditions are such that the perceiver believes he is the intended consumer of the effects produced by the actor.

In discussing the various effects of relevance, we argued that correspondence generally increases with increasing relevance. Evaluation, in turn, is a joint function of both relevance and correspondence. A small number of studies were discussed which seem to shed some light on the impact of relevance. In particular, it was noted that if one holds relevance constant (at some value other than zero) and manipulates the variables alleged to increase correspondence, evaluation becomes more extreme. Similarly, by pegging correspondence at a particular level and increasing relevance, the same increase in evaluation extremity may be observed. It should be emphasized, however, that much of the research cited was only indirectly concerned with variations in relevance. More systematic research is needed to establish the conditions under which relevance calls forth positive or negative evaluations. In addition, we need to know much more about the relations between affective and cognitive processes implied by the linkage between relevance and correspondence.

In the final section on personalism, we discussed a study in which this variable was directly and dramatically manipulated, only to acknowledge that the effects were negligible. It will be important to establish the reasons for this curious result by designing other experiments which directly approach different facets of the complex personalism variable. There is, however, indirect or circumstantial evidence which encourages the conviction that personalism and hedonic relevance are not identical in their effects. Specifically, we discussed several experiments which were concerned with the mitigation versus amplification of hostility toward an attacker. Here it was seen that the intensity of hostile reciprocation was affected by factors in the situation which made it more or less likely that personalism was involved. Such factors as sufficiency of provocation and indiscriminateness of the attack, were shown to affect the recipient's evaluation of the attacker. These conditions could be, and were, discussed in terms of the correspondence-noncommon effect theory. Several experiments on ingratiation and the perception of flattery were also discussed in these terms. The main dilemma of the perceiver, when he becomes the target of actions which may be ingratiating in intent, is to determine whether he is being benefited because of his unique personal qualities or because of the resources which he may control.

This essay, long as it is, could have been much longer if we had hedged our statements with proper qualifications and dealt fully with the problems which remain in our formulation. We have no illusions that we have finally opened the main door on the mysteries of causal attribution. Our formulation has changed considerably since our work on this essay began, and it will undoubtedly change much more with further thought. We trust it is also obvious that the ability to accommodate old findings from complex experiments is an easy hurdle for any theory to jump. We remain optimistic, however, that the present framework encourages systematic thinking about inferring dispositions from actions and suggests some of the major variables that merit initial consideration.

References

Aronson, E. and Linder, D. (1965). Gain and loss of esteem as determinants of interpersonal attractiveness. *J. exp. soc. Psychol.* **1**, 156–172.

Berkowitz, L. (1960). Repeated frustrations and expectations in hostility arousal. *J. abnorm. soc. Psychol.* **60**, 422–429.

Davis, K. E. (1962). Impressions of others and interaction context as determinants of social interaction and perception in two-person discussion groups. Unpublished doctoral dissertation, Duke Univer.

Deutsch, M., and Solomon, L. (1959). Reactions to evaluations by others as influenced by self-evaluations. *Sociometry* **22**, 93–112.

Gergen, K. J. (1962). Interaction goals and personalistic feedback as factors affecting the presentation of the self. Unpublished doctoral dissertation, Duke Univer.

Gergen, K. J., and Jones, E. E. (1963). Mental illness, predictability, and affective consequences as stimulus factors in person perception. *J. abnorm. soc. Psychol.* **67**, 95–104.

Heider, F. (1944). Social perception and phenomenal causality. *Psychol. Rev.* **51**, 358–374.

Heider, F. (1958). *The psychology of interpersonal relations.* New York: Wiley.

Jones, E. E. (1964). *Ingratiation.* Appleton, New York.

Jones, E. E., and Daugherty, B. (1959). Political orientation and the perceptual effects of an anticipated interaction. *J. abnorm. soc. Psychol.* **59**, 340–349.

Jones, E. E., and deCharms, R. (1957). Changes in social perception as a function of the personal relevance of behavior. *Sociometry* **20**, 75–85.

Jones, E. E., Hester, S. L. Farina, A., and Davis, K. E. (1959). Reactions to unfavorable personal evaluations as a function of the evaluator's perceived adjustment. *J. abnorm. soc. Psychol.* **59**, 363–370.

Jones, E. E., Davis, K. E., and Gergen, K. J. (1961). Role playing variations and their informational value for person perception. *J. abnorm. soc. Psychol.* **63**, 302–310.

Jones, E. E., Gergen, K. J., and Jones, R. G. (1963). Tactics of ingratiation among leaders and subordinates in a status hierarchy. *Psychol. Monogr.* **77**, No. 3 (Whole No. 566).

Jones, E. E., Jones, R. G., and Gergen, K. J. (1964). Some conditions affecting the evaluation of a conformist. *J. Pers.* **31**, 270–288.

Jones, E. E., Gergen, K. J., Gumpert, P., and Thibaut, J. W. (1965). Some conditions affecting the use of ingratiation to influence performance evaluation. *J. pers. soc. Psychol.* **1**, 613–626.

Kleiner, R. J. (1960). The effects of threat reduction upon interpersonal attractiveness. *J. Pers.* **28**, 145–156.

Pepitone, A. (1950). Motivational effects in social perception. *Hum. Relat.* **1**, 57–76.

Steiner, I. D., and Field, W. L. (1960). Role assignment and interpersonal influence. *J. abnorm. soc. Psychol.* **61**, 239–246.

Strickland, L. H., Jones, E. E., and Smith, W. P. (1960). Effects of group support on the evaluation of an antagonist. *J. abnorm. soc. Psychol.* **61**, 73–81.

Thibaut, J. W., and Riecken, H. W. (1955). Some determinants and consequences of the perception of social causality. *J. Pers.* **24**, 113–133.

INEQUITY IN SOCIAL EXCHANGE

J. Stacy Adams

BEHAVIORAL RESEARCH SERVICE
GENERAL ELECTRIC COMPANY
CROTONVILLE, NEW YORK

I. Introduction

Philosophers, political scientists, politicians, jurists, and economists traditionally have been the ones concerned with the just distribution of wealth, power, goods, and services in society. Social psychologists and their brethren, with the notable exceptions of Blau (1964), Homans (1961), and Thibaut and Kelley (1959), have displayed remarkably little professional interest in this, despite the fact that the process of exchange is almost continual in human interactions. They have, of course, studied social behavior involving reciprocal, as distinguished from uni-lateral, transactions, but their sights have been focused on the amount and content of communications; attitudinal, affective, motivational, percep-tual, and behavioral changes; changes in group structure, leadership, and so on, rather than on exchange proper. Yet, the process of exchange appears to have characteristics peculiar to itself and to generate affect, motivation, and behavior that cannot be predicted unless exchange proc-esses are understood.

A distinguishing characteristic of exchange processes is that their resultants have the potentiality of being perceived as just or unjust. But what are the consequences of outcomes being perceived as meeting or not meeting the norms of justice? Nearly all the attention given to this question has been to establish a relationship between perceived injustice and dissatisfaction (Homans, 1950, 1953, 1961; Jaques, 1956, 1961a; Patchen, 1959, 1961; Stouffer *et al.,* 1949; Vroom, 1964; Zaleznik *et al.,* 1958). Not surprisingly, this has been accomplished with success. Does a man treated unfairly simply express dissatisfaction? Are there not other consequences of unfair exchanges? What behavior is predictable? These questions and related ones are a principal concern of this paper.

Rather than simply present a theory from which the behavior of persons engaged in a social exchange may be deduced, the plan of this chapter is to present first in chronological order two major concepts relating to the perception of justice and injustice. First is the concept of relative deprivation and the complementary concept of relative gratification, developed by Stouffer and his associates (1949). Homans' highly elaborated concept of distributive justice (1961) will be discussed next. These will then be integrated into a theory of inequity from which it will be possible to specify the antecedents and consequences of injustice in human exchanges.

II. Relative Deprivation

Following World War II, the publication of the first *American Soldier* volume by Stouffer and his colleagues (1949) excited interest among sociologists and social psychologists. The effect was at least in part due to the introduction of a new concept, relative deprivation, used by the authors to explain what were seemingly paradoxical findings. According to Merton and Kitt (1950), the formal status of the concept was that of an intervening variable which explained the observed relationship between an independent variable, such as education level or rate of promotion, and a dependent variable, such as satisfaction with some aspect of Army life.

Relative deprivation was not formally defined by the authors, however, nor by Merton and Kitt (1950), who analyzed in great detail the implication of the concept for sociological theory in general and for reference group theory in particular. The essential meaning of the concept may be inferred from two illustrations of its use by the authors of *The American Soldier.* Despite the objective fact that soldiers with a high school education had better opportunities for advancement in the Army, high school graduates were not as satisfied with their status and jobs as were less educated men. This apparent paradox is explained by assuming that the better-educated men had higher levels of aspiration, partly based on what would be realistic status expectations in civilian life, and that they were, therefore, relatively deprived of status and less satisfied with the status they achieved. It may be noted that the validity of this explanation depends upon showing that level of aspiration is greater than status achieved among high school graduates as contrasted to soldiers with less education. While this is not demonstrated by the authors, it appears to be a credible assumption. It is the relative deprivation, then, that accounts for less satisfaction among better-educated men.

A second illustrative use of relative deprivation is made by the authors of *The American Soldier* in accounting for the puzzling fact that Army Air Corps men were less satisfied with promotion opportunities than were men in the Military Police, even though objective opportunities for mobility were vastly greater in the Air Corps. Relative deprivation is invoked to explain the anomaly as follows: The high promotion rate in the Air Corps induces high expectations of mobility; lower-ranking and low-mobile men, compared to higher-ranking and high-mobile men, feel deprived in the face of their expectations and express dissatisfaction. Among military policemen, on the other hand, expectations of promotion are low, and the fate of most policemen is quite similar: namely, low rank. In sum, there is a discrepancy between expectation and achievement among Air Corps enlisted men and little or no discrepancy between expectation and achievement among men in the Military Police. The discrepancy results in dissatisfaction with mobility. Or more precisely, the assumed existence of a discrepancy between expectation and achievement is held to account for the empirical observation that men were less satisfied in one branch than in the other.

Spector (1956), in an experiment directly related to these findings by Stouffer *et al.,* varied perceived probability of promotion and fulfillment and tested the hypothesis that *"on failing to achieve* an attractive goal, an individual's morale will be higher if the probability of achieving the goal had been perceived to be low than if it had been perceived to be high" (p. 52). He found that the high expectations-nonpromotion group had lower morale and was less satisfied with the promotion system than was the low expectations-nonpromotion group, thus corroborating experimentally the military survey findings. Comparable findings have been made by Gebhard (1949).

The effects of relative deprivation (the unfair violation of expectations) upon sociometric choices are clearly shown in an experiment designed by Thibaut (1950) to learn about the conditions that affect group cohesiveness. Underprivileged boys from camps and settlement houses in the Boston area participated in the experiment in groups of

10 to 12 boys, all of whom had known, played, and lived with one another for some time. After filling out a questionnaire in which they were asked to rank the four· boys they would most like to have on their team to play games if their groups were to be divided, the boys in each group were split into two teams of five or six. Thibaut formed each team so that each boy would have about an equal number of preferred and of nonpreferred partners and so that each team would be composed of approximately the same number of popular, or *central,* and less popular, or *peripheral,* boys in terms of sociometric choices received. Although there were several experimental conditions in his study, only one of them concerns us here. This is the condition in which each set of two teams played four games and one of the pairs was given consistently an inferior, menial, uninteresting, or unpleasant role during the series of games. These were the *low-status* teams (called "unsuccessful low-status" by Thibaut).

Following the last game, each boy answered a questionnaire in which he was again asked to order his preferences for teammates. A general finding was that a boy tended to shift his sociometric choices after the games to boys who had actually been teammates. Of greater interest here is the fact that low-status *central* boys were more likely to display such shifts than were low-status *peripheral* boys. The former were popular boys, presumably aware of their status among their fellows, who were forced to assume low-status roles in violation of the roles they would customarily play. The role of the low-status peripheral boys, on the other hand, were more or less a confirmation of their relatively low popularity among their friends. Compared to the peripheral boys, then, the central boys were relatively deprived, and they manifested their greater dissatisfaction with their fate by shifting to a greater extent their sociometric choices from central boys on the opposing team to boys on their own team. Thibaut also reports evidence that the low-status central boys displayed exceptional hostility to members of the opposing (high-status) teams and that all low-status boys keenly felt the injustice of their fate.

These findings are of especial interest because they cannot be accounted for simply on the hypothesis that abuse or minority group membership will result in withdrawal and increased cohesiveness. Such a hypothesis would have required that low-status peripheral and central boys show the same behavior. But, as noted, central boys were more likely to shift their sociometric choices and to display overt hostility to opponents. They were the ones who suffered the greater relative deprivation.

The studies that have been described form an interesting set. In the data from the surveys by Stouffer *et al.* (1949), there is no empirical evidence of relative deprivation. None of the soldiers or airmen were asked, for example, if specific expectations were violated or, more directly, if they felt relatively deprived with respect to status. Relative deprivation was used, ex post facto, to explain anomalous findings. The concept had no existential character; it was a hypothetical construct—rather than an intervening variable, as Merton and Kitt classified it (1950). The Spector (1956) experiment, by manipulating expectations of promotions and achievement, created a condition of relative deprivation. Thus, operationally, relative deprivation took on the status of a variable, an independent variable, variations in which were related to variations in "morale." In another laboratory experiment, Thibaut (1950) created conditions of relative deprivation, which were not any the less real for having been created unintentionally by his manipulations of group status and group success. In this respect his experiment is analogous to Spector's. But the nature of his experimental task allowed a very broad range of behavior to be displayed spontaneously. As a result there was direct evidence of feelings of injustice in reaction to the manipulation of relative deprivation, as well as of dissatisfaction, hostility, withdrawal, and changes in sociometric choices. Thus, proceeding from the military surveys to the Thibaut experiment, a useful construct emerges, receives experimental support, and its meaning becomes elaborated.

Bearing this and the survey and experimental data described earlier in mind, there emerge certain conclusions. First, it seems that manifest dissatisfaction and other behavior are responses to acutely felt injustice, rather than directly to relative deprivation. Relative deprivation is a condition occurring naturalistically or an experimental manipulation which elicits feelings of injustice. In turn, feelings of injustice trigger expressions of dissatisfaction and, in addition, the kind of behavior exhibited by Thibaut's juvenile subjects. Injustice, then, may be said to mediate the effects of relative deprivation. A second conclusion is that what is just is based upon relatively strong expectations, such as that educational achievement will be correlated with job status achievement and that one will be promoted at about the same rate as one's fellows, or that the role one plays in one situation—in laboratory games—will be in line and with the role one usually assumes—in the settlement house or camp.

Thirdly, it is clear that a comparative process is inherent in the development of expectations and the perception of injustice, as implied by the term relative deprivation. Well-educated men felt unfairly treated in comparison to the treatment they would have received in civilian life or in comparison to the treatment civilians did receive. Injustice was suffered by unpromoted or less-mobile airmen in relation to the general mobility of men in the Air Corps, whereas there was no such felt injustice among low-mobile military policemen when they compared their rate of promotion to the low promotion rate prevalent in the Military Police.

A particularly felicitous additional example of the process of comparison and its importance is provided by Sayles (1958). He notes that ". . . foundries are often hot spots, highly aggressive in seeking fulfillment of their demands where they are part of larger manufacturing organizations. However, when the plant is entirely devoted to the foundry operation, they are relatively weak and inactive" (p. 104). Foundry workers are highly paid to compensate for the unpleasant work conditions and the high physical exertion required and because of a short labor supply in this skill area. Other workers, however, rank foundry operators quite low and look down on them, according to Sayles. Thus, when foundry employees are present for purposes of comparison, other workers feel relatively deprived as regards earnings, and the resulting dissatisfaction may take hostile forms. Conversely, the foundry workers, being the butt of the despisement of others, may react by being unusually assertive and demanding.

Finally, it may be noted, if it is not obvious, that felt injustice is a response to a *discrepancy* between what is perceived to be and what is perceived should be. In the illustrative cases taken from *The American Soldier* and from the Spector and Thibaut experiments, it is a response to a discrepancy between an achievement and an expectation of achievement.

III. Distributive Justice

The existence of relative deprivation necessarily raises the question of distributive justice, or of the fair share-out of rewards; for, as noted earlier, deprivation is perceived relationally. The concept is not new, having been explored by political philosophers and others from the time of Aristotle. In the hands of Homans (1950, 1953, 1961) and of his colleagues (Zaleznik *et al.*, 1958), the concept of distributive justice has taken on the articulated character of what may be more properly called a theory. As fully developed by Homans (1961), it is a theory employing quasi-economic terms. According to him, distributive justice among men who are in an exchange relationship with one another obtains when the profits of each are proportional to their investments. Profit consists of that which is received in the exchange, less cost incurred. A cost is that which is given up in the exchange, such as foregoing the rewards obtainable in another exchange, or a burden assumed as a specific function of the exchange, such as a risk, which would include not only potential real loss but the psychological discomfort of uncertainty as well. Investments in an exchange are the relevant attributes that are brought by a party to the exchange. They include, for example, skill, effort, education, training, experience, age, sex, and ethnic background.

Schematically, for a dyad consisting of A and B, distributive justice between them is realized when:

$$\frac{\text{A's rewards less A's costs}}{\text{A's investments}} = \frac{\text{B's rewards less B's costs}}{\text{B's investments}}$$

When an inequality between the proportions exists, the participants to the exchange will experience a feeling of injustice and one or the other party will experience deprivation. The party specifically experiencing relative deprivation is the one for whom the ratio of profits to investments is the smaller.

Making explicit that it is the relation between *ratios* of profits to investments that results in felt justice or injustice is a distinct contribution that takes us beyond the concept of relative deprivation. To be sure, an individual may feel deprived, but he feels deprived not merely because his rewards or profits are less than he expected or felt was fair. Many men, when comparing their rewards to those of another, will perceive that their rewards are smaller, and yet they will not feel that this state of affairs is unjust. The reason is that persons obtaining the higher rewards are perceived as deserving them. That is, their rewards are greater because their investments are greater. Thus, for example, if being of the male sex is perceived as a higher investment than being of the female sex, a woman operator earning less than a man doing the same work will not feel unjustly treated. The proportionality of profits to investments is comparable for the woman and for the man. Similarly, a young instructor usually does not feel that his rewards, low as they may be, compare unfairly with those of an associate professor in his department. As Homans notes, "Justice is a curious mixture of equality within inequality" (1961, p. 244).

The theory of distributive justice also addresses itself to the case of two or more persons, each of whom receives his rewards from a third party: an employer, for example. In such an instance, each of the persons is in an exchange with the employer, as in the simple dyadic situation discussed; but, in addition, each man will expect that the employer will maintain a fair ratio of rewards to investments between himself and other men. This, of course, is the perennial dilemma of employers, and it almost defies a perfect solution, though it is capable of better solutions that are often developed. One difficulty with finding neat solutions is that A's perception of his rewards, costs, and investments are not necessarily identical with B's perception of A's situation. To complicate matters, two persons, though they might agree as to what their investments are, may disagree as to the weight each investment should be given. Should age count more than sex? Should education be given as much weight as job experience? The psychometrics of this has not yet received much attention.

The relationship of distributive justice to satisfaction is treated only briefly by Homans, but it is nevertheless the subject of a formal theoretical proposition. If a state of injustice exists and it is to a man's disadvantage—that is, the man experiences deprivation—he will "display the emotional behavior we call anger" (Homans, 1961, p. 75). Here Homans is overly influenced by Skinnerian rhetoric. He means, plainly, that dissatisfaction will be felt or expressed. If, on the other hand, distributive justice fails of realization and is, to an observer at least, to a man's advantage, he will feel guilty. This aspect of the proposition is more novel and is substantiated by observations by Jaques (1956, 1961a) and by laboratory experiments by Adams (1963a) that will be discussed later. Homans also implies that the thresholds for displaying dissatisfaction and guilt are different when he remarks that ". . . he (the guilty man) is less apt to make a prominent display of his guilt than of his anger" (1961, p. 76). This suggestion, also made by Adams (1963a) and deducible from observations made by Jaques (1956), implies that distributive justice must fail of realization to a greater extent when it is favorable to an individual before he reacts than when it is to his disadvantage.

Others have stated formal propositions that obviously refer to the same phenomena as encompassed by the theory of distributive justice. The propositions listed by two writers are especially noteworthy because they were expressed in terms similar to those of Homans. Sayles (1958, p. 98), discussing the manifestation of dissatisfaction in industrial work groups, surmised that factory workers "compute" the fairness of their wages as follows:

$$\frac{\text{Our importance in the plant}}{\text{Any other group's importance}} = \frac{\text{Our earnings}}{\text{Their earnings}}$$

When the equality obtains, satisfaction is experienced. An inequality between the ratios causes pressures for redress, accompanied by dissatisfaction. "Importance in the plant" may be taken as equivalent to the perceived investments of group members, including skills and type of work performed, length of service, and such. This is made explicit in his model of the "economic world of the worker in his work group." According to this analysis, men are portrayed as comparing their jobs to other jobs and asking the questions, "Are these higher paying jobs actually more skilled than our own?" and "Do we earn *enough more* than the lower rated jobs to compensate for the skill difference?" (Sayles, 1958, p. 105). The term "earnings" is, of course, comparable to Homans' rewards but is a less comprehensive term, excluding other outcomes such as intrinsic job rewards. It also subsumes less than the concept of profit or net reward, since it makes no provision for negative outcomes or costs, such as unfavorable work conditions or tyrannical supervision. Nevertheless, it is clear that Sayles conceives of justice as being a function of the perceived equality of ratios of investments and of rewards.

Using the terms of Festinger's theory of cognitive dissonance (1957), Patchen postulates that workers making wage comparisons make a cognitive relation of the following type (1961, p. 9):

$$\frac{\text{My pay}}{\text{His (their) pay}} \text{ compared to } \frac{\text{My position on dimensions related to pay}}{\text{His (their) position on dimensions related to pay}}$$

This formulation is similar to Sayles' but more explicit, for dimensions related to pay are specified as being attributes such as skill, education, and seniority. These are clearly the same as Homans' investments. Patchen differs somewhat from Homans in his conceptualization, however, in that he also includes job interest among his "dimensions" related to pay. This is not so much an investment as it is a reward, either with positive or negative valence. When, according to Patchen, an inequality results from the comparison of the two proportions, cognitive dissonance is experienced. In turn, dissatisfaction is manifested. However, dissonance and the attendant dissatisfaction are not necessarily a bad state of affairs from the point of view of the individual. Patchen points this out in an interesting departure from dissonance theory. Although consonant comparisons may be satisfying, they provide no basis for mobility aspirations, whereas dissonant comparisons unfavorable to the person permit a man to think that he is more deserving, that he merits higher pay or status. In effect, then, Patchen suggests that the motivation to attain consonance may be dominated by achievement motivation, and that under these circumstances dissatisfaction resulting from dissonant comparisons may be tolerated. Parenthetically, it may be pointed out that the pitting of these two motivations may partially explain why researchers have been unable to replicate some experiments that offered support for dissonance predictions (see Conlon, 1965, for example).

Relative deprivation and distributive justice, as theoretical concepts, specify some of the conditions that arouse perceptions of injustice and, complementarily, the conditions that lead men to feel that their relations with others are just. But they fail to specify theoretically what are the consequences of felt injustice, other than dissatisfaction. To be sure, Sayles (1958) mentions the use of grievance procedures and strikes to force redress, Homans (1961) cites a study by Clark (1958) in which a female employee reported slowing her pace of work as a means of establishing a more just relation with a co-worker, and Patchen (1961) gives evidence of dissonance reduction when wage comparisons are dissonant. However, these are more or less anecdotal and are not an articulated part of a theory. Men do not simply become dissatisfied with conditions they perceive to be unjust. They usually do something about them. In what follows, then, a theory will be developed that will specify both the antecedents of perceived injustice and its consequences. It is not a new theory. There are already too many "little" theories in social psychology. Rather, it builds upon the work previously described, and, in addition, derives a number of major propositions from Festinger's theory of cognitive dissonance (1957).

IV. Inequity

In what follows it is hoped that a fairly comprehensive theory of inequity will be elaborated. The term *inequity* is used instead of *injustice* first, because the author has used this term before (Adams and Rosenbaum, 1962; Adams, 1963a,b, 1965; Adams and Jacobsen, 1964), second, to avoid the confusion of the many connotative meanings associated with the term *justice,* and third, to emphasize that the primary concern is with the causes and consequences of the absence of equity in human exchange relationships. In developing the theory, major variables affecting perceptions of inequity in an exchange will be described. A formal definition of inequity will then be proposed. From this point the effects of inequity upon behavior and cognitive processes will be discussed and research giving evidence of the effects will be presented. For heuristic purposes employee-employer exchanges will be a focus because such relations are within the experience of almost everyone and constitute a significant aspect of human intercourse. Moreover, much empirical research relating to inequity has been undertaken in business and industrial spheres or in simulated employment situations. It should be evident, however, that the theoretical notions offered are quite as relevant to any social situation in which an exchange takes place, explicitly or implicitly, whether between teammates, teacher and student, lovers, child and parent, patient and therapist, or opponents or even enemies, for between all there are expectations of what is fair exchange.

A. ANTECEDENTS OF INEQUITY

Whenever two individuals exchange anything, there is the possibility that one or both of them will feel that the exchange was inequitable. Such is frequently the case when a man exchanges his services for pay. On the man's side of the exchange are his education, intelligence, experience, training, skill, seniority, age, sex, ethnic background, social status, and, of course, the effort he expends on the job. Under special circumstances other attributes will be relevant. These may be personal appearance or attractiveness, health, possession of certain tools, the characteristics of one's spouse, and so on. They are what a man perceives as his contributions to the exchange, for which he expects a just return. As noted earlier, these are the same as Homans' (1961) investments. A man brings them into an exchange, and henceforth they will be referred to as his *inputs*. These inputs, let us emphasize, are *as perceived by their contributor* and are not necessarily isomorphic with those perceived by the other party to the exchange. This suggests two conceptually distinct characteristics of inputs, *recognition* and *relevance*.

The possessor of an attribute, or the other party to the exchange, or both, may recognize the existence of the attribute in the possessor. If either the possessor or both members of the exchange recognize its existence, the attribute has the potentiality of being an input. If only the nonpossessor recognizes its existence, it cannot be considered psychologically an input so far as the possessor is concerned. Whether or not an attribute having the potential of being an input is in fact an input is contingent upon the possessor's perception of its relevance to the exchange. If he perceives it to be relevant, if he expects a just return for it, it is an input. Problems of inequity arise if only the possessor of the attribute considers it relevant to the exchange, or if the other party to the exchange considers it irrelevant and acts accordingly. Thus, unless prohibited from doing so by contract terms, an employer may consider seniority irrelevant in granting promotions, thinking it wiser to consider merit alone, whereas the employee may believe that seniority is highly relevant. In consequence, the employee may feel that injustice has been done. Conversely, the employer who is compelled to use seniority rather than merit as a promotion criterion may well feel that he has been forced into an inequitable exchange. In a personal communication Crozier (1960) made a relevant observation. Paris-born bank clerks worked side by side with clerks who did identical work and earned identical wages but who were born in the provinces. The Parisians were dissatisfied with their wages, for they considered that a Parisian upbringing was an input deserving recognition. The bank management, although recognizing that place of birth distinguished the two groups, did not, of course, consider birthplace relevant in the exchange of services for pay.

The principal inputs that have been listed vary in type and in their degree of relationship to one another. Some variables such as age are clearly continuous; others, such as sex and ethnicity, are not. Some are intercorrelated: seniority and age, for example. Sex, on the other hand, is largely independent of the other variables, with the possible exception of education and some kinds of effort. Although these intercorrelations, or the lack of them, exist in a state of nature, it is probable that the individual cognitively treats all input variables as independent. Thus, for example, if he were assessing the sum of his inputs, he might well "score" age and seniority separately. It is as if he thought, "I am older and have been with Acme longer than Joe," without taking account of the fact that the two attributes are correlated. This excursion into the "black box" should not imply, as Homans (1961) seems to imply, that men assess various components of an exchange on an ordinal scale. If the work of Jaques on equitable payment (1956, 1961a) is taken at face value, there is reason to believe in this respect that men employ interval and ratio scales, or that, at the very least, they are capable of making quite fine ordinal discriminations.

On the other side of an exchange are an individual's receipts. These *outcomes,* as they will be termed, include in an employee-employer exchange pay, rewards intrinsic to the job, satisfying supervision, seniority benefits, fringe benefits, job status and status symbols, and a variety of formally and informally sanctioned perquisites, such as the right of a higher-status person to park his car in a privileged location. These are examples of positively valent outcomes. But outcomes may have negative valence. Poor working conditions, monotony, fate uncertainty, and the many "dissatisfiers" listed by Herzberg *et al.* (1959) are no less "received" than, say, wages and are negatively valent. They would be avoided, rather than approached, if it were possible. As in the case of job inputs, job outcomes are often intercorrelated. For example, greater pay and higher job status are likely to go hand-in-hand.

In other than employee-employer exchanges, though they are not precluded from these exchanges, relevant positive outcomes for one or both parties may consist of affection, love, formal courtesies, expressions of friendship, fair value (as in merchandise), and reliability (as part of the purchase of a service). Insult, rudeness, and rejection are the other side of the coin. It may be noted that in a vast array of social relations reciprocity is a functional element of the relation. What is in fact referred to by reciprocity is equality of exchange. The infinitive "to reciprocate" is commonly used to denote an obligation to give someone equal, positively valent outcomes in return for outcomes received. When a housewife says, "John, we must have the Browns over, to reciprocate," she means to maintain a social relationship by reestablishing a parity in the outcomes of the two families. In this connection, it can be observed that reciprocation is usually "in kind." That is, there is a deliberate effort to match outcomes, to give equal value for value received. People who undershoot or overshoot the mark are called "cheapskates" or "uppish" and pretentious, respectively.

In a manner analogous to inputs, outcomes are *as perceived,* and, again, they should be characterized in terms of recognition and relevance. If the recipient or both the recipient and giver of an outcome in an exchange recognize its existence, it has the potentiality of being an outcome psychologically. If the recipient considers it relevant to the exchange and it has some marginal utility for him, it *is* an outcome. Not infrequently the giver may give or yield something which, though of some cost to him, is either irrelevant or of no marginal utility to the recipient. An employer may give an employee a carpet for his office in lieu, say, of a salary increment and find that the employee is dissatisfied, perhaps because in the subculture of that office a rug has no meaning, no psychological utility. Conversely, a salary increment may be inadequate, if formalized status recognition was what was wanted and what had greater utility. Or, in another context, the gift of a toy to a child may be effectively irrelevant as reciprocation for a demonstration of affection on his part is he seeks affection. Fortunately, in the process of socialization, through the reinforcing behavior of others and of the "verbal community" (Skinner, 1957), the human organism learns not only what is appropriate reciprocation, but he learns also to assess the marginal utility of a variety of outcomes to others. In the absence of this ability, interpersonal relations would be chaotic, if not impossible. An idea of the problems that would exist may be had by observing travelers in a foreign culture. Appropriate or relevant reciprocation of outcomes is difficult, even in such mundane exchanges as tipping for services.

In classifying some variables as inputs and others as outcomes, it is not implied that they are independent, except conceptually. Inputs and outcomes are, in fact, intercorrelated, but imperfectly so. Indeed, it is because they are imperfectly correlated that there need be concern with inequity. There exist normative expectations of what constitute "fair" correlations between inputs and outcomes. The expectations are formed—learned—during the process of socialization, at home, at school, at work. They are based by observation of the correlations obtaining for a reference person or group—a co-worker or a colleague, a relative or neighbor, a group of co-workers, a craft group, an industry-wide pattern. A bank clerk, for example, may determine whether her outcomes and inputs are fairly correlated, in balance so to speak, by comparing them with the ratio of the outcomes to the inputs of other female clerks in her section. The sole punch-press operator in a manufacturing plant may base his judgment on what he believes are the inputs and outcomes of other operators in the community or region. For a particular professor the relevant reference group may be professors in the same discipline and of the same academic "vintage." While it is clearly important to be able to specify theoretically the appropriate reference person or group, this will not be done here, as the task is beyond the scope of the paper and is discussed by others (e.g., Festinger, 1954; Hyman, 1942; Merton and Kitt, 1950; Patchen, 1961). For present purposes, it will be assumed that the reference person or group will be one comparable to the comparer on one or more attributes. This is usually a co-worker in industrial situations, according to Livernash (1953), but, as Sayles (1958) points out, this generalization requires verification, as plausible as it may appear.

When the normative expectations of the person making social comparisons are violated, when he finds that his outcomes and inputs are not in balance in relation to those of others, feelings of inequity result. But before a formal definition of inequity is offered, two terms of reference will be introduced to facilitate later discussion, *Person* and *Other*. *Person* is any individual for whom equity or inequity exists. *Other* is any individual with whom Person is in an exchange relationship, or with whom Person compares himself when both he and Other are in an exchange relationship with a third party, such as an employer, or with third parties who are considered by Person as being comparable, such as employers in a particular industry or geographic location. Other is usually a different individual, but may be Person in another job or in another social role. Thus, Other might be Person in a job he held previously, in which case he might compare his present and past outcomes and inputs and determine whether or not the exchange with his employer, present or past, was equitable. The terms Person and Other may also refer to groups rather than to individuals, as when a class of jobs (e.g., toolmakers) is out of line with another class (e.g., lathe operators), or when the circumstances of one ethnic group are incongruous with those of another. In such cases, it is convenient to deal with the class as a whole rather than with individual members of the class.

B. DEFINITION OF INEQUITY

Inequity exists for Person whenever he perceives that the ratio of his outcomes to inputs and the ratio of Other's outcomes to Other's inputs are unequal. This may happen either (a) when he and Other are in a direct exchange relationship or (b) when both are in an exchange relationship with a third party and Person compares himself to Other. The values of outcomes and inputs are, of course, as perceived by Person. Schematically, inequality is experienced when either

$$\frac{O_p}{I_p} < \frac{O_a}{I_a}$$

or

$$\frac{O_p}{I_p} > \frac{O_a}{I_a}$$

where $O = \Sigma_{o_i}$, $I = \Sigma_{o_i}$ and p and a are subscripts denoting Person and Other, respectively. A condition of equity exists when

$$\frac{O_p}{I_p} = \frac{O_a}{I_a}$$

The outcomes and inputs in each of the ratios are conceived as being the sum of such outcomes and inputs as are perceived to be relevant to a particular exchange. Furthermore, each sum is conceived of as a weighted sum, on the assumption that individuals probably do not weight elemental outcomes or inputs equally. The work of Herzberg *et al.* (1959) on job "satisfiers" and "dissatisfiers" implies strongly that different outcomes, as they are labeled here, have widely varying utilities, negative as well as positive. It also appears reasonable to assume that inputs as diverse as seniority, skill, effort, and sex are not weighted equally. Zaleznik *et al.* (1958), in attempting to test some predictions from distributive justice theory in an industrial corporation, gave equal weight to five factors which correspond to inputs as defined here—age, seniority, education, ethnicity, and sex—but were unable to sustain their hypotheses. In retrospect, they believe (Zaleznik *et al.*, 1958) that weighting these inputs equally may have represented an inadequate assumption of the manner in which their respondents summed their inputs.

From the definition of inequity it follows that inequity results for Person not only when he is, so to speak, relatively underpaid, but also when he is relatively overpaid. Person, will, for example, feel inequity exists not only when his effort is high and his pay low, while Other's effort and pay are high, but also when his effort is low and his pay high, while Other's effort and pay are low. This proposition receives direct support from experiments by Adams and Rosenbaum (1962), Adams (1963a), and Adams and Jacobsen (1964) in which subjects were inequitably overpaid. It receives some support also from an observation by Thibaut (1950) that subjects in whose favor the experimenter discriminated displayed "guilty smirks" and "sheepishness." The magnitude of the inequity experienced will be a monotomically increasing function of the size of the discrepancy between the ratios of outcomes to inputs. The discrepancy will be zero, and equity will exist, under two circumstances: first, when Person's and Other's outcomes are equal and their inputs are equal. This would be the case, for example, when Person perceived that Other's wages, job, and working conditions were the same as his and that Other was equal to him on such relevant dimensions as sex, skill, seniority, education, age, effort expended, physical fitness, and risk incurred (risk of personal injury, of being fired for errors committed, for instance). Secondly, the ratios will be equal when Person perceives that Other's outcomes are higher (or lower) than his and that Other's inputs are correspondingly higher (or lower). A subordinate who compares himself to his supervisor or work group leader typically does not feel that he is unjustly treated by the company that employs them both, because the supervisor's greater monetary compensation, better working conditions, and more interesting, more varied job are matched on the input side of the ratio by more education, wider range of skills, greater responsibility and personal risk, more maturity and experience, and longer service.

Although there is no direct, reliable evidence on this point, it is probable, as Homans (1961) conjectured, that the thresholds for inequity are different (in absolute terms from a base of equity) in cases of under- and overreward. The threshold would be higher presumably in cases of overreward, for a certain amount of incongruity in these cases can be acceptably rationalized as "good fortune" without attendant discomfort. In his work on pay differentials, Jaques (1961b) notes that in instances of undercompensation, British workers paid 10% less than the equitable level show "an active sense of grievance, complaints or the desire to complain, and, if no redress is given, an active desire to change jobs, or to take action . . ." (p. 26). In cases of overcompensation, he observes that at the 10 to 15% level above equity "there is a strong sense of receiving preferential treatment, which may harden into bravado, with underlying feelings of unease . . ." (p. 26). He states further, "The results suggest that it is not necessarily the case that each one is simply out to get as much as he can for his work. There appear to be equally strong desires that each one should earn the right amount—a fair and reasonable amount relative to others" (p. 26).

In the preceding discussion, Person has been the focus of attention. It should be clear, however, that when Person and Other are in an exchange interaction, Other will suffer inequity if Person does, but the nature of his experience will be opposite to that of Person. If the outcome-input ratio discrepancy is unfavorable to Person, it will be favorable to Other, and vice versa. This will hold provided Person's and Other's perceptions of outcomes and inputs are equivalent and provided that the outcome-input ratio discrepancy attains threshold level. When Person and Other are not engaged in an exchange with one another but stand in an exchange relationship with a third party, Other may or may not experience inequity when Person does. Given the prerequisites mentioned above, he will experience inequity if he compares himself to Person with respect to the same question as induces Person to use Other as a referent (e.g., "Am I being paid fairly?").

C. CONSEQUENCES OF INEQUITY

Although there can be little doubt that inequity results in dissatisfaction, in an unpleasant emotional state, be it anger or guilt, there will be other effects. A major purpose of this paper is to specify these in terms that permit specific predictions to be made. Before turning to this task, two general postulates are presented, closely following propositions from cognitive dissonance theory (Festinger, 1957). First, the presence of inequity in Person creates tension in him. The tension is proportional to the magnitude of inequity present. Second, the tension created in Person will motivate him to eliminate or reduce it. The strength of the motivation is proportional to the tension created. In short, the presence of inequity will motivate Person to achieve equity or to reduce inequity, and the strength of motivation to do so will vary directly with the magnitude of inequity experienced. From these postulates and from the theory of cognitive dissonance (Festinger, 1957; Brehm and Cohen, 1962), means of reducing inequity will be derived and presented. As each method of reduction is discussed, evidence demonstrating usage of the method will be presented. Some of the evidence is experimental; some of it is the result of field studies, either of a survey or observational character.

1. Person Altering his Inputs

Person may vary his inputs, either increasing them or decreasing them, depending on whether the inequity is advantageous or disadvantageous. Increasing inputs will reduce felt inequity, if

$$\frac{O_p}{I_p} > \frac{O_a}{I_a}$$

conversely, decreasing inputs will be effective, if

$$\frac{O_p}{I_p} < \frac{O_a}{I_a}$$

In the former instance, Person might increase either his productivity or the quality of his work, provided that it is possible, which is not always the case. In the second instance, Person might engage in "production restriction," for example. Whether Person does, or can, reduce inequity by altering his inputs is partially contingent upon whether relevant inputs are susceptible to change. Sex, age, seniority, and ethnicity are not modifiable. Education and skill are more easily altered, but changing these requires time. Varying inputs will also be a function of Person's perception

of the principal "cause" of the inequity. If the discrepancy between outcome-input ratios is primarily a function of his inputs being at variance
with those of Other, Person is more likely to alter them than if the
discrepancy is largely a result of differences in outcomes. Additionally,
it is postulated that given equal opportunity to alter inputs and outcomes,
Person will be more likely to lower his inputs when

$$\frac{O_p}{I_p} < \frac{O_a}{I_a}$$

than he is to increase his inputs when

$$\frac{O_p}{I_p} > \frac{O_a}{I_a}$$

This is derived from two assumptions: first, the assumption stated earlier
that the threshold for the perception of inequity is higher when Person
is overrewarded than when he is underrewarded; secondly, the assumption
that Person is motivated to minimize his costs and to maximize his gains.
By the second assumption, Person will reduce inequity, insofar as possible,
in a manner that will yield him the largest outcomes.

Altering certain inputs has the corollary effect of altering the outcomes of Other. A change in the quality and amount of work performed,
for instance, will usually affect the outcomes of Other. When this is
the case, the effect of both changes will operate in the same direction
in the service of inequity reduction. It follows, therefore, that *less*
a change in inputs is required to eliminate inequity than if the change
had no effect on Other's outcomes. Inputs, a change in which would
have no or very little impact on Other's outcomes, are attributes such
as education, age, and seniority—at least to the extent that they are
uncorrelated with performance.

Several experiments have been conducted specifically to test the
hypothesis that Person will reduce inequity by altering his inputs (Adams
and Rosenbaum, 1962; Adams, 1963a; Adams and Jacobsen, 1964).
The most recent of these will be described in detail here. In this experiment
the hypothesis tested was that if Person perceives that he is overpaid
in an exchange with his employer because his inputs are inadequate,
he will experience inequity and attempt to reduce it by increasing relevant
inputs.

Students hired to proofread galley pages were exposed to one of
three conditions of inequity. In a *high inequity* condition (H), they were
induced to perceive that they were unqualified to earn the standard proof-
reader's rate of 30 cents per page and were told that they would, nevertheless, be hired and paid that rate. Another group of subjects were in

the *reduced inequity* condition (R), in which an identical perception was induced, but in which the piece rate was reduced to 20 cents by reason of the subjects' lack of qualifications. In this condition, in effect, the low inputs of subjects were matched by low outcomes. Thus, if the basic model of inequity was valid, subjects in this condition should suffer no greater feelings of inequity than subjects in the third, *low inequity* condition (L), in which persons hired were made to believe that they were fully qualified to earn the standard rate of 30 cents per page. The task consisted of correcting errors in simulated galley proof pages from a manuscript on human relations in industry. Proofreading required that each page be read, that each error detected be underlined in the text, and that a checkmark be placed in the margin at the level of the error. Each galley page contained a standard number of words, and a set number of errors were introduced systematically on each page. The errors were misspellings, grammatical mistakes, incorrect punctuation, and typographical errors, such as transpositions of letters. Productivity was measured by the number of pages proofed in one hour; work quality was measured by the mean number of errors detected per page proofed.

Since they could not alter their outcomes, it was predicted that H subjects would attempt to reduce inequity by investing high inputs, which, in this situation, they could also perceive as increasing the outcomes of the employer. More specifically, it was hypothesized that the work quality would be higher among H subjects than among R and L subjects, and that it would not vary significantly between the R and L conditions. The prediction that input differences would be on the dimension of work quality was based on the consideration that the only other relevant input subjects could vary was productivity; but since an increase in productivity would result in increased outcomes, due to the piece-rate payments, inequity could not be reduced in this manner. Doing better quality work *on each piece,* however, would effectively serve to reduce inequity. Following this reasoning, a second hypothesis could be formulated: Productivity among H subjects would be lower than among R and L subjects, since more careful work would require additional time to complete each page.

The results supported the hypothesis. Subjects in the H condition performed significantly better work, as measured by the number of introduced errors detected per page, and produced significantly less in one hour than subjects in the R and L conditions. The latter did not differ from each other with respect to either quality of work or productivity. An unexpected finding was that significantly more nonerrors were classified as errors by subjects in the H condition than in the other conditions. Generally, these misclassified nonerrors were of a type that permitted minimal or no basis for being perceived as errors. For example, the word "conceive" was underlined as an error by several subjects, although it was correctly spelled. This gives some indication of the strength of motivation underlying the behavior. A somewhat analogous finding was made by Arrowood (1961). He paid his subjects in advance for three hours of work and found that those who perceived their pay as too great tended to work more than three hours.

In similar experiments (Adams and Rosenbaum, 1962; Adams, 1963a), subjects were paid by the hour. In these it was predicted that in the high inequity conditions subjects would alter their productivity inputs. The data bore this out. In one of these experiments subjects performed identical tasks under hourly and piece-rate wage conditions. Under a high inequity induction, productivity was higher with hourly pay and lower with piecework pay than under a low inequity induction. These results give support to the earlier suggestion that there exists a tendency to reduce inequity in a manner that yields the largest outcomes. Hourly paid workers could have reduced inequity by improving the quality of their work, but this would have lowered their outcomes. On the other hand, pieceworkers had no choice but to reduce inequity by increasing work quality, with consequent loss of income. Considering the fact that subjects in this experiment, as in others, needed their earnings, the results also suggest that the need to establish equity was a more potent motivation that the motivation to maximize monetary gains.

In the experiments described above, inequities potentially advantageous to Person were the focus because, if the hypotheses were sustained, the evidence would be more striking. There is, of course, also evidence that Person will reduce his inputs when he suffers the disadvantages of inequity, when the discrepancy of outcome-input ratios is unfavorable to him. This is apparent in a field study by Clark (1958), which investigated supermarket checkout counters manned by a "ringer" (cashier) and a "bundler." These two were not involved in a direct exchange with one another; rather, both were in an exchange with the employer and expected him to see to it that their outcome-input ratios were not incongruous. Under normal conditions, ringing was a higher-status, better-paid job, handled by a permanent, full-time employee. Bundling was of lower status and lower pay, and was usually done by part-time employees, frequently youngsters. Furthermore, psychologically, bundlers were perceived as working *for* ringers.

Because customer flow in supermarkets varies markedly from day to day, a preponderance of employees were part-timers. This same fact required that many employees be assigned to checkout counters during rush hours. When this occurred, many ringer-bundler teams were formed, and it is this that resulted in inequities, for employees differed considerably in a number of input variables, notably sex, age, and education. Not infrequently, a bundler would be directed to work for a ringer whose status (determined by sex, age, and education) was lower. For example, a college male 21 years of age would be ordered to work for a high school girl ringer of 17. Or a college girl would be assigned as a bundler for an older woman with only a grade school education. The resulting inequities may be described as follows in theoretical terms: A bundler with higher inputs than a ringer had lower outcomes—i.e., working *for* someone of lower status, which is assumed to be invidious and psychologically negatively valent, as well as receiving lower wages.

When interviewed by the investigator, the store employees were quite explicit about the inequities that existed. It appeared that the principal means used by the bundlers to reduce inequities were to decrease the rate at which they filled shopping bags—i.e., by reducing their inputs, which would have effectively decreased inequity since some of their other inputs were too high relative to their own outcomes and to the inputs of the ringers. One girl explicitly stated to the investigator that when she was ordered to bundle for a ringer of lower status than herself, she deliberately slowed up bundling.

Interestingly, this behavior is nicely reflected in the financial operation of the stores. A substantial part of the total labor cost of operating a supermarket is the cost of manning checkout counters. It follows, therefore, that one should be able to observe a correlation between the incidence of inequities among ringer-bundler teams and the cost of store operations, since the inequity reduction took the form of lowered productivity. This is indeed what was found. When the eight supermarkets were ranked on labor efficiency (number of man-hours per $100 of sales) and "social ease" (an index of the proportion of ringer-bundler pairs whose outcome-input ratios were discrepant), the two measures correlated almost perfectly: the greater the inequity, the greater the cost of operating the stores. To give an example, one of the two stores studied most intensively ranked high in inequity and had labor efficiency of only 3.85, whereas the other which ranked low in inequity, had a labor efficiency of 3.04. Thus, it cost approximately 27% more to operate the store in which inequities were more frequent.

A further finding of Clark's is worth reporting, for it gives one confidence that the relative inefficiency of the one store was indeed due to the presence of relatively more inequity. This store went through a period of considerable labor turnover (perhaps as a result of employees leaving the field to reduce inequity), and associated with this was an increase in labor efficiency and an increase in the "social ease" index. There is, therefore, quasi-experimental evidence that when inequities are reduced, individual productivity increases (i.e., production restriction is lowered), with the result that operating costs decrease.

2. Person Altering his Outcomes

Person may vary his outcomes, either decreasing or increasing them, depending on whether the inequity is advantageous or disadvantageous to him. Increasing outcomes will reduce inequity, if

$$\frac{O_p}{I_p} < \frac{O_a}{I_a}$$

conversely, decreasing outcomes will serve the same function, if

$$\frac{O_p}{I_p} > \frac{O_a}{I_a}$$

Of these two possibilities, the second is far less likely, and there is no good evidence of the use of this means of reducing inequity, though some may be available in the clinical literature. There are, however, data bearing on attempts to increase outcomes, data other than those related to wage increase demands in union-management negotiations, probably only a part of which are directly traceable to wage inequities.

In the experiment by Thibaut (1950), to which reference was made earlier, teams of 5 or 6 boys made up of approximately equal numbers of popular and unpopular boys were assigned either high- or low-status roles in playing a series of four games. The low-status teams were unfairly treated in that, although they were comparable in their characteristics (i.e., their inputs) to the high-status teams, they were forced to adopt an inferior, unpleasant role vis-a-vis the other team. For example, in one game they formed a human chain against which the other team bucked; in another, they held the target and retrieved thrown bean bags. Thus, since their inputs were equal to, and their outcomes lower than, those of the high-status teams, they were clearly suffering the disadvantages of inequity. From Thibaut's report of the behavior of the low-status teams, it is evident that at least four means of reducing the inequity were used by them: lowering the high-status team members' outcomes by fighting with them and displaying other forms of hostility; lowering their inputs by not playing the games as required, which would also have had the effect of lowering the outcomes of the high-status team members; by leaving the field, that is, withdrawing and crying; and by trying to interchange roles with the high-status teams. The latter is the relevant one for purposes of discussion here.

Thibaut (1950) reports that about halfway through the second game the participants had come to understand the experimenter's intention, i.e., that the status differentiation was to be permanent. At this stage of the experiment low-status subjects began to express mobility aspirations, asking the experimenter that the roles of the two teams be reversed. This may be interpreted as an attempt to establish equity by increasing outcomes, since assumption of high status would have been accompanied by pleasurable activities. Interestingly, though the report is not entirely clear on this point, there is the suggestion that, when the attempt of low-status subjects to increase their outcomes was rejected by the experimenter, they desisted and, instead, engaged more in withdrawal.

Also giving evidence that increasing outcomes will serve to reduce inequity is a study of unfair wages among clerical workers by Homans (1953). Two groups of female clerical workers in a utilities company, cash posters and ledger clerks, worked in the same, large room. Cash posting consisted of recording daily the amounts customers paid on their bills, and management insisted that posting be precisely up to date. It required that cash posters pull customer cards from the many files and make appropriate entries on them. The job was highly repetitive and comparatively monotonous, and required little thought but a good deal of walking about. Ledger clerks, in contrast, performed a variety of tasks on customer accounts, such as recording address changes, making breakdowns of over- and underpayments, and supplying information on accounts to customers and others on the telephone. In addition, toward the end of the day, they were required by their supervisor to assist with "cleaning up" cash posting in order that it be current. Compared to the cash posters, ledger clerks performed a number of nonrepetitive clerical jobs requiring some thought; they had a more *responsible* job; they were considered to be of higher status, since promotion took place from cash poster to ledger clerk; and they were older and had more seniority and experience. Their weekly pay, however, was identical.

Summarizing in the terms of the inequity model, cash posters had distinctly lower inputs than ledger clerks (i.e., they were younger, and had less experience, less seniority, and less responsibility). With respect to outcomes they received equal wages, but their jobs were somewhat more monotonous and less interesting. On the other hand, the ledger clerks' inputs were superior with respect to age, experience, seniority, skill, responsibility, and versatility (they were required to know and do cash posting in addition to their own jobs). Their earnings were equal to the cash posters', but they were required to "clean up" (note connotation) posting each day, an activity that would deflate self-esteem and would, therefore, be a negative outcome. In the balance, then, the net outcomes of ledger clerks and cash posters were approximately of the same magnitude, but the inputs of the clerks were definitely greater.

From this it would be predicted that the ledger clerks felt unfairly treated and that they would try to increase their outcomes.

The evidence reported by Homans (1953) is that the ledger clerks felt the inequity and that they felt they ought to get a few dollars more per week to show that their jobs were more important—that their greater inputs ought to be matched by greater outcomes. On the whole, these clerks seemed not to have done much to reduce inequity, though a few complained to their union representative, with, apparently, little effect. However, the workers in this division voted to abandon their independent union for the CIO, and Homans intimates that the reason may have been the independent union's inability to force a resolution of the inequity.

The field studies of dissatisfaction with status and promotions by Stouffer et al. (1949) and the experiments by Spector (1956), in which expectation of promotion and morale, which were described in Section II, may also be interpreted as cases of inequity in which dissatisfactions were expressions of attempts by Persons to increase their outcomes.

3. Person Distorting his Inputs and Outcomes Cognitively

Person may cognitively distort his inputs and outcomes, the direction of the distortion being the same as if he had actually altered his inputs and outcomes, as discussed above. Since most individuals are heavily influenced by reality, substantial distortion is generally difficult. It is pretty difficult to distort to oneself, to change one's cognitions about the fact, for example, that one has a BA degree, that one has been an accountant for seven years, and that one's salary is $700 per month. However, it is possible, within limits, to alter the utility of these. For example, State College is a small, backwoods school with no reputation, or, alternatively, State College has one of the best business schools in the state and the dean is an adviser to the Bureau of the Budget. Or, one can consider the fact that $700 per month will buy all of the essential things of life and a few luxuries, or, conversely, that it will never permit one to purchase a Wyeth oil painting or an Aston Martin DB5. There is ample evidence in the psychological literature, especially that related to cognitive dissonance theory, that individuals do modify or rearrange their cognitions in an effort to reduce perceived incongruities (for a review, see Brehm and Cohen, 1962). Since it has been postulated that the experience of inequity is equivalent to the experience of dissonance, it is reasonable to believe that cognitive distortion may be adopted as a means of reducing inequity. In a variety of work situations, for example in paced production line jobs, actually altering one's inputs and outcomes may be difficult; as a consequence these may be cognitively changed in relatively subtle ways.

Although not a cognitive change in inputs and outcomes per se, related methods of reducing inequity are for Person to alter the *importance* and the *relevance* of his inputs and outcomes. If, for example, age were a relevant input, its relative importance could be changed to bring about less perceived inequity. Person could convince himself that age was either more or less important than he thought originally. In terms of the statement made earlier that net inputs (and outcomes) were a weighted sum of inputs, changing the importance of inputs would be equivalent to changing the weights associated with them. Altering the relevance of inputs and outcomes is conceived of as more of an all-or-none process: Present ones are made irrelevant or new ones are made relevant. For instance, if Person perceived that the discrepancy between his and Other's outcome-input ratios were principally a result of his outcomes being too low, he might become "aware" of one or more outcomes he had not recognized as being relevant before, perhaps that his job had variety absent from Other's job. Obviously, importance and relevance of inputs and outcomes are not completely independent. An outcome suddenly perceived as being relevant automatically assumes some importance; conversely, one that is made irrelevant in the service of inequity reduction assumes an importance of zero. Nevertheless, the psychological processes appear to be different and it is useful, therefore, to keep them conceptually distinct.

Evidence of cognitive distortion to reduce inequity is not very impressive. In a study by Leventhal *et al.* (1964), subjects were hired to participate in an experiment to taste pleasant and unpleasant liquids. At the end of the task one-third of the subjects were told they would receive a payment of 60 cents in lieu of the promised $1.25, one-third were informed they would be paid $1.90 in lieu of $1.25, and to the remaining one-third it was stated they would be paid the promised $1.25. According to the inequity model, the first two groups presumably felt unfairly rewarded. When asked under what circumstances they felt subjects should be paid for their services, these two groups were significantly less likely to assert that they should always be paid than were subjects who were paid the full amount promised. Considering first only the underpaid subjects, this can be taken as an indication that they revised either the judgment of their inputs, by lowering it, or their estimate of fair outcomes, by lowering it. They could, in effect, have been saying, "What I did wasn't much," or "Sixty cents is about the right amount for this kind of task." Alternatively, they could have adduced a new, relevant outcome, such as the satisfaction of contributing to science. An equally plausible explanation which is unrelated to the reduction of inequity is offered by Leventhal and his associates, namely, that the decreased payment induced a low expectancy set with respect to payment in experiments.

The lower expectancy of the overpaid subjects does not manifest inequity reduction by cognitive distortion. More likely, as Leventhal *et al.* suggest, this indicates a desire to rectify the inequity by accepting lower payment in subsequent experiments, that is, to increase the experimenter's outcomes on a later occasion.

An experiment by Weick (1964) suggests that subjects, some of whose outcomes are unjustly low, may increase their net total outcomes by "task enhancement," that is, by distorting their evaluation of the task. Weick found that subjects working for an inconsiderate experimenter who had lured them to work for no credit, evaluated their task more highly than subjects who worked for normal course credits. Specifically, it appeared that the subjects who were short-changed by the experimenter distorted their outcomes by coming to believe that the experiment was relatively quite interesting and important.

4. Person Leaving the Field

Leaving the field may take any of several ways of severing social relationships. Quitting a job, obtaining a transfer, and absenteeism are common forms of leaving the field in an employment situation. These are fairly radical means of coping with inequity. The probability of using them is assumed to increase with magnitude of inequity and to decrease with the availability of other means.

Data substantiating the occurrence of leaving the field as a mode of reducing inequity is sparse. In the aforementioned study by Thibaut (1950), it was observed that low-status team members withdrew from the games as it became increasingly clear what their fate was and as, it must be presumed, the felt injustice mounted. In a study by Patchen (1959) it was observed that men who said their pay should be higher had more absences than men who said the pay for their jobs was fair. This relationship between perceived fairness of pay and absenteeism was independent of actual wage level. That absenteeism in this study was a form of withdrawal is strongly supported by the fact that men with high absence rates were significantly more likely than men with low rates to say that they would not go on working at their job, if they should chance to inherit enough money to live comfortably without working.

5. Person Acting on Other

In the face of injustice, Person may attempt to alter or cognitively distort Other's inputs and outcomes, or try to force Other to leave the field. These means of reducing inequity vary in the ease of their use. Getting Other to accept greater outcomes, which was a possible interpretation of some of the findings by Leventhal *et al.* (1964), would obviously be easier than the opposite. Similarly, inducing Other to lower his inputs may be easier than the reverse. For example, all other things being equal, such as work group cohesiveness and the needs and ability of an individual worker, it is probably easier to induce a "rate buster" to lower his inputs than to get a laggard to increase them. The direction of the change attempted in the inputs and outcomes of Other is the reverse of the change that Person would make in his own inputs and outcomes, whether the change be actual or cognitive. By way of illustration, if Person experienced feelings of inequity because he lacked job experience compared to Other, he could try to induce Other to decrease a relevant input instead of increasing his own inputs.

Cognitive distortion of Other's inputs and outcomes may be somewhat less difficult than distortion of one's own, since cognitions about Other are probably less well anchored than are those concerning oneself. This assumption is consistent with the finding that "where alternatives to change in central attitudes are possible, they will be selected" (Pilisuk, 1962, p. 102). Acceptable evidence that inequity, as such, is reduced by cognitive distortion of Other's inputs or outcomes is nonexistent, although there is ample evidence that cognitive dissonance may be reduced by perceptual distortion (e.g., Bramel, 1962; Brehm and Cohen, 1962; Steiner and Peters, 1958). An observation made while pretesting procedures for an unpublished study by Adams (1961) is little better than anecdotal. To test some hypotheses from inequity theory, he paired a subject and a stooge at a "partner's desk." Each performed sequentially one part of the preparation of a personnel payroll. In one condition the subject was paid $1.40 per hour and performed the relatively complex task of looking in various tables for standard and overtime rates, looking up in other tables the products of pay rates and hours worked, and recording the products on a payroll form. The stooge, whose pay was announced as being $2.10 per hour, performed the presumably much easier task of summing products on a machine and recording the totals on the form the subject passed to him across the desk. In addition, the stooge was programmed to be slightly ahead of the subject in his work, so that his task appeared fairly easy. It was hoped that these conditions would lead the subject to perceive that, compared to the stooge, he had higher inputs and lower outcomes. Nothing of the sort happened. Most subjects pretested felt that the relationship was equitable, and this appeared to result from the fact that they distorted cognitively the stooge's inputs in an upward direction. Specifically, they convinced themselves that the stooge was performing a "mathematical task." Simple *adding* on a machine became *mathematics*.

Forcing Other to leave the field, while theoretically possible, is probably difficult of realization and would, no doubt, be accompanied by anxiety
about potential consequences or simply by the discomfort of having done
something socially unpleasant. This aspect makes it costly to Person;
it lowers his outcomes to some extent. Firing an individual in an em-
ployer-employee exchange and some divorces and separations are common
examples of this means put to use. Somewhat though barely more subtle
is the practice of creating an inequity by withholding expected outcomes
(e.g., salarly increases, promotions) to the point where an individual
leaves the field "voluntarily."

6. Person Changing the Object of His Comparison

Person may change Other with whom he compares himself when
he experiences inequity and he and Other stand in an exchange relationship
with a third party. This mode is limited to the relationship specified;
it is not applicable when Person and Other are in a direct exchange.
Changing the object of comparison in the latter situation would reduce
to severing the relationship.

The resolution of inequity by changing comparison object is undoubtedly difficult of accomplishment, particularly if Person has been
comparing himself to Other for some time. Person would need to be
able to make himself noncomparable to Other on one or more dimensions.
For instance, if Other, whose outcome-input ratio was previously equal
to Person's received a salary increase without any apparent increment
in inputs, Person could try to reduce the resulting feeling of inequity
by conceiving of Other as belonging now to a different organizational
level. But this would likely meet with little success, at least in this culture.
A cognitive change of this sort would be extremely unstable, unless it
were accompanied by changes in the perception of Other's inputs: for
instance, that Other had assumed greater responsibility when his salary
was increased. But this involves a process of inequity reduction already
referred to.

In the initial stages of comparison processes, as when a man first
comes on the job, it probably is relatively easy to choose as comparison
Others individuals who provide the most equitable comparisons. This
does not necessarily entail making comparisons with men whose outcomes
and inputs are the same as one's own; it is sufficient that their outcome-input ratio be equal to one's own. In a study of the choice of
wage comparisons. Patchen (1961) asked oil refinery workers to name
someone whose yearly earnings were *different* from theirs and then proceeded to ask them questions about the resulting wage comparisons and
about their satisfaction with them. Of the workers who named someone

earning *more* than they, 60% indicated satisfaction with the comparison and only 17.6% reported dissatisfaction. Among those who were satisfied, 44.6% stated they were satisfied because they had financial or other advantages, i.e., compensating outcomes, and 55.8% indicated satisfaction with the upward comparison because the person with higher earnings had more education, skill, experience, seniority and the like, i.e., higher inputs. Patchen's data may be recast and reanalyzed to make a different point. Among the men who chose comparison persons whose outcome-input ratios seemingly were equal to theirs, approximately 85% were satisfied with the comparison and only about 4% were dissatisfied. While Patchen's study does not bear directly either on what wage comparisons men actually make in their day-to-day relations with others or on changes in comparison persons when inequity arises, it gives clear evidence that comparisons are made on the basis of the equality of the outcome-input ratios of the comparer and comparison person and that such comparisons prove satisfying, i.e., are, at least, judged to be not inequitable.

7. *Choice among Modes of Inequity Reduction*

Although reference has been made previously to conditions that may affect the use of one or another method of reducing inequity, there is need for a general statement of conditions that will govern the adoption of one method over another. Given the existence of inequity, any of the means of reduction described earlier are potentially available to Person. He may alter or attempt to alter any of the four terms in the inequality formula or change his cognitions about any of them, or he may leave the field and change his comparison Other, but it is improbable that each of the methods are equally available to him *psychologically* (no reference is made to environmental constraints that may affect the availability of methods), as the work of Steiner and his colleagues on alternative methods of dissonance reduction suggests (Steiner, 1960; Steiner and Johnson, 1964; Steiner and Peters, 1958; Steiner and Rogers, 1963).

Set forth below are some propositions about conditions determining the choice of modes by person. As will be noted, the propositions are not all independent of one another, and each should be prefaced by the condition, *ceteris paribus.*

(*a*) Person will maximize positively valent outcomes and the valence of outcomes.

(*b*) He will minimize increasing inputs that are effortful and costly to change.

(*c*) He will resist real and cognitive changes in inputs that are central to his self-concept and to his self-esteem. To the extent that any of Person's outcomes are related to his self-concept and to his self-esteem, this proposition is extended to cover his outcomes.

(*d*) He will be more resistant to changing cognitions about his own outcomes and inputs than to changing his cognitions about Other's outcomes and inputs.

(*e*) Leaving the field will be resorted to only when the magnitude of inequity experienced is high and other means of reducing it are unavailable. Partial withdrawal, such as absenteeism, will occur more frequently and under conditions of lower inequity.

(*f*) Person will be highly resistant to changing the object of his comparisons, Other, once it has stabilized over time and, in effect, has become an anchor.

These propositions are, admittedly, fairly crude, but they permit, nevertheless, a degree of prediction not available otherwise. In the resolution of a particular injustice, two or more of the processes proposed may be pitted one against the other. To propose which would be dominant is not possible at this stage of the development of the theory. One might propose that protection of self-esteem would dominate maximization of outcomes, but it would be conjecture in the absence of evidence.

V. Conclusion

Dissatisfaction is both so commonplace and such an irritant, particularly in industrial and other large organizations, that it has been the subject of widespread research (see Vroom, 1964, for a recent, thorough review). Despite prima facie evidence that feelings of injustice underlay a significant proportion of cases of dissatisfaction, thorough behavioral analyses of injustice were not made until recently. In the classic Hawthorne studies (Roethlisberger and Dickson, 1939), there was ample evidence that much of the dissatisfaction observed among Western Electric Company employees was precipitated by felt injustice. Describing complaints, the authors referred frequently to reports by workers that wages were not in keeping with seniority, that rates were too low, that ability was not rewarded, and the like, as distinguished from reports that, for example, equipment was not working and that the workshop was hot. They stated that "no physical or logical operations exist which can be agreed upon as defining them" (p. 259), and they sought "personal or social situations" (p. 269) that would explain the complaints parsimoniously. Yet, the notion of injustice was not advanced as an explanatory concept.

It is not contended here, of course, that all dissatisfaction and low morale are related to a person's suffering injustice in social exchanges. But it should be clear from the research described that a significant portion of cases can be usefully explained by invoking injustice as an explanatory concept. More importantly, much more than dissatisfaction may be predicted once the concept of injustice is analyzed theoretically.

In the theory of inequity that has been developed in this chapter, both the antecedents and consequences of perceived injustice have been stated in terms that permit quite specific predictions to be made about the behavior of persons entering social exchanges. On the whole, empirical support for the theory is gratifying, but it falls short of what is desirable. More research is required. This is particularly so because some of the support comes from data leading to the formulation of parts of the theory. Needed are direct tests of propositions made in the theory, as well as empirical tests of novel derivations from the theory. Some research filling these needs is under way. Being tested, for example, is the hypothesis that overpaid workers for whom an increase in inputs is impossible will reduce inequity by decreasing their outcomes, specifically by developing unfavorable attitudes toward their employer, their working conditions, the pay rates, and so on.

In order for more refined predictions to be made from the theory, theoretical, methodological, and empirical work are also required in at least two areas related to it. First, additional thought must be given to social comparison processes. The works of Festinger (1954), Hyman (1942), Merton and Kitt (1950), Newcomb (1943), and Patchen (1961) are signal contributions but still do not allow sufficiently fine predictions to be made about whom Person will choose as a comparison Other when both are in an exchange relationship with a third party. For example, as a function of what variables will one man compare himself to a person on the basis of age similarities and another man compare himself on the basis of attitude similarities? Second, psychometric research is needed to determine how individuals aggregate there own outcomes and inputs and those of others. Is the assumptive model that net outcomes are the algebraic sum of elemental outcomes weighted by their importance a valid one?

The need for much additional research notwithstanding, the theoretical analyses that have been made of injustice in social exchanges should result not only in a better general understanding of the phenomenon, but should lead to a degree of social control not previously possible. The experience of injustice need not be an accepted fact of life.

REFERENCES

Adams, J. S. (1961). Wage inequities in a clerical task. Unpublished study. General Electric Company, New York.

Adams, J. S. (1963a). Toward an understanding of inequity. *J. abnorm. soc. Psychol.* **67**, 422–436.

Adams, J. S. (1963b). Wage inequities, productivity, and work quality. *Industr. Relat.* **3**, 9–16.

Adams, J. S. (1965). Etudes expérimentales en matière d'inégalités de salaires, de productivité et de qualité du travail. *Synopsis* **7**, 25–34.

Adams, J. S., and Jacobsen, Patricia R. (1964). Effects of wage inequities on work quality. *J. abnorm. soc. Psychol.* **69**, 19–25.

Adams, J. S., and Rosenbaum, W. B. (1962). The relationship of worker productivity to cognitive dissonance about wage inequities. *J. appl. Psychol.* **46,** 161–164.

Arrowood, A. J. (1961). Some effects on productivity of justified and unjustified levels of reward under public and private conditions. Unpublished doctoral dissertation (Dep. Psychol.), Univer. of Minnesota.

Blau, P. (1964). *Exchange and power in social life.* New York: Wiley.

Bramel, D. (1962). A dissonance theory approach to defensive projection. *J. abnorm. soc. Psychol.* **64,** 121–129.

Brehm, J. W., and Cohen, A. R. (1962). *Explorations in cognitive dissonance.* New York: Wiley.

Clark, J. V. (1958). A preliminary investigation of some unconscious assumptions affecting labor efficiency in eight supermarkets. Unpublished doctoral dissertation (Grad. Sch. Business Admin.), Harvard Univer.

Conlon, Elizabeth T. (1965). Performance as determined by expectation of success and failure. Unpublished doctoral dissertation (Dep. Social Psychol.), Columbia Univer.

Crozier, M. (1960). Personal communication to the author.

Festinger, L. (1954). A theory of social comparison processes. *Hum. Relat.* **7,** 117–140.

Festinger, L. (1957). *A theory of cognitive dissonance.* Evanston, Ill.: Row, Peterson.

Gebhard, Mildred E. (1949). Changes in the attractiveness of activities: the effect of expectation preceding performance. *J. exp. Psychol.* **39,** 404–413.

Herzberg, F., Mausner, B., and Snyderman, Barbara B. (1959). *The motivation to work.* New York: Wiley.

Homans, G. C. (1950). *The human group.* New York: Harcourt, Brace.

Homans, G. C. (1963). Status among clerical workers. *Hum. Organiz.* **12,** 5–10.

Homans, G. C. (1961). *Social behavior: its elementary forms.* New York: Harcourt, Brace.

Hyman, H. (1942). The psychology of status. *Arch. Psychol.* **38,** No. 269.

Jaques, E. (1956). *Measurement of responsibility.* London: Tavistock.

Jaques, E. (1961a). *Equitable payment.* New York: Wiley.

Jaques, E. (1961b). An objective approach to pay differentials. *Time Motion Study* **10,** 25–28.

Leventhal, G., Reilly, Ellen, and Lehrer, P. (1964). Change in reward as a determinant of satisfaction and reward expectancy. Paper read at West. Psychol. Assoc. Portland, Ore.

Livernash, E. R. (1953). Job evaluation. In W. S. Woytinsky *et al.* (Eds.), *Employment and wages in the United States.* New York: Twentieth Century Fund, pp. 427–435.

Merton, R. K., and Kitt, Alice S. (1950). Contributions to the theory of reference group behavior. In *Continuities in social research.* R. K. Merton and P. F. Lazarsfeld (Eds.), Glencoe, Ill.: Free Press, pp. 40–105.

Newcomb, T. M. (1943). *Personality and social change: attitude formation in a student community.* New York: Dryden.

Patchen, M. (1959). Study of work and life satisfaction, Report No. II: absences and attitudes toward work experience. Inst. for Social Res., Ann Arbor, Mich.

Patchen, M. (1961). *The choice of wage comparisons.* Englewood Cliffs, N.J.: Prentice-Hall.

Pilisuk, M. (1962). Cognitive balance and self-relevant attitudes. *J. abnorm. soc. Psychol.* **65,** 95–103.

Roethlisberger, F. J., and Dickson, W. J. (1939). *Management and the worker.* Cambridge, Mass.: Harvard Univer. Press.

Sayles, L. R. (1958). *Behavior of industrial work groups: prediction and control.* New York: Wiley.

Skinner, B. F. (1957). *Verbal behavior.* New York: Appleton.

Spector, A. J. (1956). Expectations, fulfillment, and morale. *J. abnorm. soc. Psychol.* **52,** 51–56.

Steiner, I. D. (1960). Sex differences in the resolution of A-B-X conflicts. *J. Pers.* **28,** 118–128.

Steiner, I. D., and Johnson, H. H. (1964). Relationships among dissonance reducing responses. *J. abnorm. soc. Psychol.* **68,** 38–44.

Steiner, I. D., and Peters, S. C. (1958). Conformity and the A-B-X model. *J. Pers.* **26,** 229–242.

Steiner, I. D., and Rogers, E. D. (1963). Alternative responses to dissonance. *J. abnorm. soc. Psychol.* **66,** 128–136.

Stouffer, S. A., Suchman, E. A., DeVinney, L. C., Starr, Shirley A., and Williams, R. M., Jr. (1949). *The American soldier: adjustment during army life.* Vol. 1. Princeton, N.J.: Princeton Univer. Press.

Thibaut, J. (1950). An experimental study of the cohesiveness of underprivileged groups. *Hum. Relat.* **3,** 251–278.

Thibaut, J. W., and Kelley, H. H. (1959). *The social psychology of groups.* New York: Wiley.

Vroom, V. H. (1964). *Work and motivation.* New York: Wiley.

Weick, K. E. (1964). Reduction of cognitive dissonance through task enhancement and effort expenditure. *J. abnorm. soc. Psychol.* **66,** 533–539.

Zaleznik, A., Christensen, C. R., and Roethlisberger, F. J. (1958). The motivation, productivity, and satisfaction of workers. A prediction study (Grad. Sch. Business Admin.) Harvard Univer.

THE CONCEPT OF AGGRESSIVE DRIVE: SOME ADDITIONAL CONSIDERATIONS[1]

Leonard Berkowitz

DEPARTMENT OF PSYCHOLOGY
UNIVERSITY OF WISCONSIN
MADISON, WISCONSIN

I. Introduction

There is a ferment today in the study of motivation. Old concepts are being reshaped; old ideas long accepted as a matter of course are now increasingly being confronted by searching re-examination and challenge (Bindra, 1959; Cofer and Appley, 1964). Much of this turmoil has centered around the notion of "drive," and especially about the question of whether the concept should refer to both the directionality and

[1] This paper was written while the author was on a research leave at the University of Oxford under a grant from the National Science Foundation.

vigor of behavior or only one of these two aspects. Thus, as an illustration, Hebb, in common with such writers as P. T. Young (1961), at one time argued that the chief problem of motivation "is not arousal of activity but its patterning and direction" (1949, p. 172). But in a paper published six years later (1955), he drastically altered his position. Separating cue and arousal, he now gave more thought to arousal as a general drive state which energized but did not guide behavior. This two factor conception has not conquered all, however. Estes (1958) insisted that there is no really good evidence for the notion of a general energizing or arousal factor as employed by the Hullians, and attempted to interpret motivational phenomena in terms of stimulus-response relationships essentially similar to all other stimulus connections.

Perhaps as a reflection of the conceptual turmoil in the general field of motivation, there has been considerable controversy in recent years as to just what is the source of aggressive behavior (Bandura and Walters, 1963a,b; Berkowitz, 1962; Buss, 1961; Feshbach, 1964). I will try here to review some of these theoretical positions briefly, elaborating and extending my earlier discussions of aggression (1962, 1964, 1965a). Hopefully, by highlighting and sharpening the issues dividing the various theorists, scientific progress in this area can be accelerated. In presenting this analysis, furthermore, I will outline what I believe to be parallels between my line of reasoning and recent developments in other areas.

Instrumental aggression, or actions carried out in the pursuit of nonaggressive aims, will be minimized in this discussion, and I will not deal with situations in which a person is trained to act aggressively. Putting aside this problem of learning, attention will be focused, first, on the relation between frustration and aggression, and then, on the nature and operation of the instigation to aggression, however it is acquired.

Aggression is defined in this discussion as behavior whose goal is the injury of some person or object (cf. Dollard et al., 1939). The use of the term "goal" in this definition is quite deliberate. Some writers have argued that the notion of an aggressive goal should be avoided as should any implication of purpose. I will try to show that we must consider aggressive intent if we are fully to understand aggressive behavior.

II. Instinct, Frustration, and Learning

A. SOME COMMENTS ABOUT THE INSTINCT CONCEPTION IN ORTHODOX PSYCHOANALYSIS

While it is not my purpose to review the various ways in which aggression has been interpreted as instinctive behavior [cf. Berkowitz

(1962) for a more complete discussion], psychoanalysis' great popularity demands that some attention should be given to the instinct doctrine in this body of thought. Since psychoanalysis purports to be rooted in biological processes, observations reported by biologists will be our main concern in this section.

The psychoanalytic literature gives considerable attention to the question of whether aggressive behavior is the product of an instinctual drive or is an ego-defensive reaction. Some orthodox theorists, such as Hartmann et al. (1949) and Anna Freud (1949), taking what is regarded as the instinctual position, posited a somatically rooted source of aggressive urges. They maintained that aggressive energy is constantly being generated (in some unknown and unspecified manner) within the body. Unless this energy can be neutralized or discharged in some socially acceptable action (e.g., muscular activity), the pent-up urge presumably would inevitably lead to destructive attacks upon the self or other people. According to Hartmann et al., aggression is similar to the sex drive in many respects. Both instigations are supposedly the product of a "constant driving force." Further, in both cases the object was said to become attached to the drive only because of the satisfactions it has provided.

The opposing analytic formulation stresses the role of aggressive behavior in ego functioning. Some theorists, such as Beata Rank, did not conceive of aggression as an unmodifiable innate destructive force. They "surmise that aggressive behavior means adaptation to the surrounding reality, hence is a part of ego-organization" (Rank, 1949, pp. 43–48).

Both of these conceptions are somewhat one-sided for the present writer. Aggressive actions undoubtedly are sometimes carried out to achieve certain purposes, as the ego formulation maintains. Yet it is also apparent that automatic processes, unaffected by ego controls, also occasionally govern the magnitude of aggression displayed in a given situation. These automatic processes, however, do not reflect the operation of an exclusively internally based destructive drive. A major flaw in the Hartmann et al. instinct view, and indeed in most orthodox psychoanalytic discussions of instinctive behavior, is the neglect of situationally determined stimulus conditions.

In contrast to the orthodox psychoanalytic position, which employs an hydraulic model with notions of the accumulation and discharge of internal somatic energy, contemporary biologists typically place greater weight on the role of external stimulus conditions. These stimulus conditions control the activation and termination of species-specific behavior patterns (Bowlby, 1957; Thorpe, 1957). An animal's instinctive action in any given situation, then, is a function of both internal conditions and externally influenced stimuli.

This can be seen in what ethologists term "displacement activities." Such behavior patterns usually occur when one or more motives seem to be strong, but still cannot find expression in action: as if an overflow of the pent-up motive energy from its usual neural channels into other neural centers thereby set off the presumably irrelevant actions. When a chaffinch appears to be in conflict between approaching and avoiding a food, for example, it may display preening behavior. This had been explained by assuming that the motive energy blocked by the conflict had "sparked over" into the displacement activity, the preening. We now know, however, that this hydraulic energy interpretation is incomplete. Recent findings indicate that "those factors which elicit the behavior in its normal functional context are also present when it appears as a displacement activity" (Hinde, 1960).

Ethologists often employ the concept of "releaser" in dealing with eliciting stimuli. A releaser, or sign stimulus, is a cue in the external environment which produces a given reaction from an organism ready to make this response. There is an interaction between the organism's internal condition and the external stimulation. Research shows that a strong releaser is necessary to elicit a reaction if the animal is under a low arousal condition, while a weak releaser is sufficient if the animal is in a stronger motivational state (Hess, 1962).

Some well-known ethological observations point to how specific stimuli can elicit aggressive behavior in lower organisms. The male stickleback fish (Tinbergen, 1951) will display an aggressive reaction in response to a red spot on the belly of a rival male. The red stimulus evoking the attack is highly specific; aggression does not occur if the red is on the rival's back. The sign stimulus alone has little effect, however, if the organism is not in a suitable condition. In the case of stickleback aggression the necessary prerequisite apparently is the presence of the hormones associated with reproduction. Given the appropriate internal state, the sign stimulus releases behavior the organism is ready to exhibit.

My chief quarrel with the orthodox psychoanalytic instinct conception, therefore, is not that reference is made to instincts—although this "explanation" undoubtedly is used too frequently and too readily. Rather, I would suggest that the psychoanalytic model, assuming a constant, internal, driving force, does not pay sufficient attention to the role of specific external stimulation. "Instinctive behavior . . . is evoked in response to only a few of the stimuli in an animal's environment" (Hess, 1962).

B. The Frustration-Aggression Hypothesis

To say there is no constantly operative, biologically rooted drive to destruction in man does not mean there are no innate components in human aggressive behavior. Indeed, those writers who have explained aggression as a reaction to some frustration have either implicitly or explicitly based their account upon an inborn, biological process. Since American psychology like Russian is generally predisposed to deny or minimize the role of "built-in" factors in human behavior, many of the objections to the frustration-aggression hypothesis appear to stem from this prejudice rather than from research findings. Let us examine some of the criticisms of this formulation, especially of the version published by Dollard *et al.* (1939).

Briefly, these psychologists proposed that a frustration, defined as "an interference with the occurrence of an instigated goal response at its proper time in the behavior sequence" aroused an instigation to aggression. They did not claim that frustration had no consequences other than aggression, and Miller later (1941) made it clear that a thwarting will produce instigations to many different kinds of responses. Some of these other response tendencies may be stronger than the instigation to aggression, so that aggression is not revealed openly. One part of their formulation is undoubtedly incorrect. Although they held that all aggressive actions presuppose the existence of frustration, we know today that a person does not have to be frustrated in order to engage in aggressive actions. He can, for example, learn to behave aggressively by watching other people (Bandura and Walters, 1963b). A contemporary revision of the frustration-aggression hypothesis must be less sweeping and all-explanatory than the original version.

The hypothesis does not have to be discarded altogether, however, as a number of writers have insisted (e.g., Bandura and Walters, 1963a,b; Buss, 1961). Putting aside some of the criticism (cf. Berkowitz, 1962 for a more complete discussion), several of the arguments against this thesis can be answered.

1. Do Only Some Frustrations Produce Aggression?

Several critics have maintained that only certain kinds of frustrations give rise to hostile reactions. Threats or attacks upon the ego produce aggressive tendencies, they say, but mere deprivations supposedly lead to other consequences. In answering this type of objection, two points can be made. First, recent evidence indicates that the frustration need not be a direct attack on the self in order to produce aggression. Buss (1963) demonstrated that college students who were prevented by a peer from attaining a desirable goal (such as a money prize) tended to display more intense open aggression toward him than did a nonfrustrated control group. The thwarting was not an arbitrary one, and the allowable aggression was not instrumental to the attainment of other ends, but there was a definite aggressive reaction, if only a weak one. Similarly, Hartup and

Himeno (1959) found that social isolation was frustrating for young children and led to an increase in aggression in doll-play.

The second point has to do with the matter of deprivations and arbitrary frustrations. For Dollard and his colleagues, a frustration is the blocking of some *on-going*, goal-directed activity. A person thoroughly engrossed in his work is not frustrated just because he has been without food for a number of hours. He may be deprived of food, but there are no ongoing eating response sequences either in his thoughts or his overt activity that are prevented from reaching completion. His failure to eat at his regular meal time will therefore not produce an aggressive reaction. But what if some individual expects to be paid and wants to be paid at a certain time, but finds that the money is not forthcoming? Here we would expect the person to become angry. Where some would say he has now experienced an arbitrary frustration, I maintain that this latter individual was frustrated, while the former person was not. Only in the latter case is an ongoing response sequence prevented from reaching completion at its anticipated time.

2. Other Reactions to Frustration

Some opposition to the frustration-aggressive hypothesis rests on the observation of nonaggressive reactions to thwartings. Research has shown, for example, that frustrations can intensify the strength of the responses following immediately afterward. Thus, in one study (Haner and Brown, 1955) children were given the task of placing marbles in holes in a board. At the end of each trial the experimenter sounded a buzzer (signifying a failure) which the youngsters were then to turn off by pressing a plunger. The closer the subjects were to completing the task when they were failed, the more vigorously did they press the plunger. The thwarting had led to an increased pressure, as if an "irrelevant drive" had been created which added to the pressure response. This type of effect comes about in both animals and humans, whether the frustration is the omission of an anticipated reward or an interference with a consummatory response, and even when the post-frustration act is not an intrinsic component of the thwarted behavior (Cofer and Appley, 1964).

Going on from such observations, Bandura and Walters (1963a,b) argued that social judgments are primarily responsible for the classification of many post-frustration responses as aggressive actions. People have learned to categorize an individual's vigorous behaviors following a thwarting as aggressive even when the frustrated person does not intend to commit injury. Consistent with this "high-magnitude theory of aggression," Walters and Brown (1964) demonstrated that when children were trained to make intense responses on a nonaggressive lever-pressing task, their subsequent play behavior was more likely to be judged as "aggressive" by naive observers than when they earlier had been trained to make less intense lever presses.

The last-mentioned findings are interesting, but they do not explain how the social judgments have arisen. One possibility, of course, is that the judgment is an inference based upon past experience. People could have learned that vigorous responses made in certain kinds of situations often do have the goal of inflicting injury upon someone. Extrapolating from these prior experiences, then, the observers in the Walters-Brown experiment might have defined the vigorously acting children as behaving aggressively.

Many kinds of reactions can follow frustrations. This has already been acknowledged and, we have seen, does not necessarily contradict the frustration-aggression hypothesis (cf. Miller, 1941; Berkowitz, 1962). This formulation is not grounded on post-hoc explanations, however. As worked out by Dollard and his colleagues, the hypothesis does specify conditions which heighten the likelihood of an aggressive reaction to thwartings.

3. The Innate Nature of the Aggressive Reaction

Critics of the use of instinctive mechanisms in accounting for human aggressive behavior often also cite evidence regarding the influence of prior learning experiences. Animals and humans can be trained to respond nonaggressively to situations that ordinarily produce hostile responses. They can also learn to act aggressively where formerly they had displayed little violence. In an experiment with school children, for example, Davitz (1952) rewarded one group of youngsters for acting aggressively and competitively and another group for acting cooperatively and constructively. After several training sessions the experimenter frustrated all of the children by stopping a movie they were seeing and, at the same time, taking away their candy. Observations showed that the aggressively trained group exhibited more aggression in free play immediately afterwards and that the constructively trained youngsters reacted more constructively to the thwarting. After reviewing several such experiments which had obtained essentially similar results, some writers have concluded that aggression was the product of previous learning.

Yet the experiments just mentioned do not really invalidate the frustration-aggression hypothesis. They demonstrate that previous experience can enhance or reduce the likelihood of aggressive behavior, but they do not prove that aggression will not occur under suitable conditions in the absence of any aggression training. Indeed, several experiments indicate that animals reared in isolation, who had not previously learned to be aggressive, can react aggressively to arousing stimuli. But even disregarding these latter investigations, the criticism ultimately rests upon faulty logic. The presence of learning does not exclude the possibility of an innate predisposition. Miller and Dollard (1941) raised this possibility in suggesting that anger (the emotional reaction to a thwarting) is a *learnable* drive. The exact nature and mode of operation of this "drive" is unimportant for the moment. What is important is that we recognize the likelihood that certain kinds of stimulation such as a frustration, may instinctively heighten the probability that a given class of responses (e.g., aggression) will occur. For too long too many American social scientists have regarded learning and instinct as mutually opposed, at least in man, where they may actually co-exist. As Neal Miller said recently:

> It seems highly probable that . . . innate patterns exist, that they play an important role in the development of human social behavior, and that these instinctual patterns are modifiable enough so that they tend to be disguised by learning although they may play crucial roles in motivating, facilitating, and shaping socially learned behavior (1964, p. 160).

C. A REVISED FRUSTRATION-AGGRESSION HYPOTHESIS

As indicated earlier, I do not mean to say that the analysis published by the Yale psychologists can withstand all attacks and that the hypothesis should remain just as it was in 1939. From my point of view (cf. Berkowitz, 1962), the original version should be altered in at least three ways. First, I would contend that the emotional reaction (let us call this "anger") resulting from a frustration (defined as before) creates only a *readiness* for aggressive acts. Previously acquired aggressiveness habits can also establish this readiness. Second, making explicit what was only implicit in the Yale papers, we should recognize that aggressive responses will not occur, even given this readiness, unless there are suitable cues, stimuli associated with the present or previous anger instigators. Objects having some connection with aggression generally may also have this cue property. Whatever their exact origin, these cues evoke aggressive responses from the organism that is "primed" to make them. The strength of the aggressive response made to the appropriate cue is presumably a function of (1) the aggressive cue value of this stimulus—the strength of the association between the eliciting stimulus and the past or present determinants of aggression—and (2) the degree of aggression readiness—anger intensity or strength of the aggressiveness habits.

Finally, as mentioned before, we must restrict the extent to which thwartings are employed as an explanation of aggression. Instead of postulating that all aggression "presupposes the existence of frustration," as

Dollard and his colleagues did, we now know that suitable cues may lead to aggressive behavior by arousing previously learned but latent aggressiveness habits. Furthermore, these habits can probably be formed without the learner being frustrated. He can, for example, learn by observing the behavior of some aggressive model (Bandura and Walters, 1963b).

Before proceeding to examine this revised formulation in more detail, I would like to point out one implication of this analysis. Some critics of the frustration-aggression hypothesis have flogged the hypothesis with experiments which apparently did not obtain aggressive reactions to a thwarting (cf. Bandura and Walters, 1963a, p. 397). Perhaps these reactions did not occur, we can now say, because there were no suitable stimuli in the situation which were sufficiently capable of "pulling" aggression from the thwarted subjects.

III. The Drive Concept

A. External Stimuli in "Biological" Drives

The formulation presented here differs in important respects from the classic drive model accepted by most motivational theories. Since this classic model must raise some doubts about the analysis outlined above, it would be helpful to look at the present status of the drive concept in experimental psychology.

When the term was first introduced into psychology by Robert Woodworth in 1918, "drive" referred to an internal state of excitement or energy which impelled the organism to action. This general energy was distinguished from the organism's habits or the external stimuli which guided behavior in one direction or another. But other writers then began to posit more specific drives, such as hunger, thirst and sex, supposedly having definite goals as their aim. The organism was now often said to be driven by specific classes of internal excitation toward or away from specific categories of objects or events. Motivational thinking since World War II has generally fluctuated between these two extremes, and there has been considerable debate as to how much weight should be given to a general drive state and how much to more specific instigations. The general drive notion, at least in the extreme form that talks about general arousal or activation, assumes that the directionality of behavior is supposedly due to the operation of specific, environmentally induced stimuli rather than different kinds of internal excitation.

To be more concrete, let us consider briefly the supposedly basic biological drives of hunger and sex.[2] The classic drive model is based on the notion of homeostatic mechanisms. Prolonged periods of food or

[2] Much of the material included in this section is taken from the excellent survey published by Cofer and Appley (1964).

sexual deprivation supposedly disturb the body's homeostatic equilibrium and give rise to an internal excitatory state. This internal excitation or drive automatically impels the organism to activity until a suitable food or a sexual object can be obtained. Then with the performance of the goal or consummatory responses, the internal excitation subsides and the organism's activity decreases or even disappears altogether.

Early physiological research appeared to provide overwhelming support for this model. Richter and his colleagues reported, as an example, that the activity level of animals increased when they were forced to be without water or food for some time. They would then cross obstructions in order to reach the goal objects needed to abolish the bodily deficit. Cannon suggested that the heightened activity level was caused by deprivation-produced peripheral stimulation such as stomach contractions. While all theorists following the classic model do not place this much emphasis upon peripheral stimulation (and, indeed, it is now known that the central nervous system plays a very important role in hunger-related behavior—cf. Cofer and Appley, 1964, Chs. 5 and 6), all maintain that the organism's behavior is an automatic response to deficit-induced, internal stimulation which pushed the animal into action.

(Orthodox psychoanalysis has an essentially similar motivational conception. Freud and his adherents also maintained that deprivations resulted in increased internal excitation, although this was said to be a tension accumulation produced by the failure to discharge sufficient instinctive energy. Like the classic drive theorists, furthermore, the psychoanalysts also viewed behavior as being carried out, ultimately, in order to reduce the internal excitatory state.)

But although the standard drive model has been widely and long accepted, there is increasing dissatisfaction with it. All of the model's shortcomings cannot be listed here (see Cofer and Appley, 1964 for a complete and up-to-date discussion), but it is pertinent to note its characteristic indifference to the role of response-eliciting, environmental stimuli. Again this can be seen in the case of food deprivation. More recent investigations show that Richter's observations regarding the relation between food deprivation and activity are misleadingly oversimplified. Deprivation per se does not necessarily lead to increased activity. Instead, the behavioral increments apparently arise only when the deprived animal has learned to anticipate the coming of food (Cofer and Appley, 1964, pp. 819–822). What this suggests, then, is that the food-deprived animal's heightened activity is caused by environmentally related cues—stimuli associated with food which are first provided by external environment and then, through learning, become introduced internally in the form of anticipations.

Bodily conditions, such as those caused by organic deprivations, may be quite important in motivated behavior. Some specific internal states could create a *readiness* for certain specific classes of responses. Nevertheless, appropriate cues are necessary if the responses are actually to occur. Such may be the case, for example, in sexual behavior. According to Cofer and Appley:

> . . . stimulation is necessary to [elicit] sexual behavior in an organism that is hormonally "ready" for it. In other words, sexual behavior depends upon two conditions: adequate hormonal levels *and* adequate direct stimulation. (In the human, symbolic stimuli may replace direct stimulation.) . . . In accounting for this, Beach suggests . . . that the hormonal state sensitizes the animal selectively with respect to stimuli. Thus the hormonally ready male rat is more likely to respond and be aroused by the receptive female than he would be if not hormonally ready or than he would be if the stimuli were nonsexual (1964, p. 823).

Much the same analysis can be offered for other kinds of motivation. Thus, McClelland, Atkinson, *et al.* (cf. Atkinson, 1958) regard an individual's achievement motivation as a disposition which must be activated by appropriate situational cues before it is manifested in behavior. Further research is obviously necessary, however, before this type of formulation can be extended with any confidence

B. The Problem of Aggressive Drive

1. Freefloating Aggression and Hostility Displacement

As I indicated earlier, writers influenced by orthodox psychoanalytic theory have typically interpreted aggressive behavior in a manner consistent with the classic drive model. Whether they posit an instinctual drive to destruction that is continually being generated within the organism or view aggression as a reaction to past frustrations, many social scientists assume that an internal, aggressive drive state accumulates somehow and finally goads the animal into making aggresssive responses. Following this vein, as an illustration, Kluckhohn (1945) once suggested that "freefloating aggression" existed in every society because of the thwartings to which people are inevitably subjected in the course of living. This pent-up aggressive force supposedly is drained off in some societies through periodic wars, but in other cultures is safely channeled into more constructive paths such as public works.

Some of my earlier writings (Berkowitz, 1962; Berkowitz and Green, 1962) attempted to show that many discussions of the scapegoat theory of prejudice which are based on the psychoanalytic version of the classic drive model are seriously incomplete. The scapegoat notion, as it is most frequently presented, applies the old-line frustration-aggression hypothesis to many cases of prejudice and intergroup hostility. It contends that a thwarted person is unable or unwilling to discharge his hostility in attacks upon the frustrating source and consequently aggresses against safe and visible targets, minority groups such as Negroes and Jews. His hostile drive has "pushed out" the aggression toward the minority groups. In accord with several other critics, I argued that this doctrine does not adequately account for the selection of particular groups as victims for the displaced aggression (1962, p. 149). More than just an internal drive must be postulated. There are any number of minority groups who may safely be attacked, but aggression is directed against only some of them, and the victim is not always the one who is least to be feared (1962, pp. 139 and 149). We must also consider the stimulus characteristics of the possible targets. Some groups are capable of eliciting strong hostility where others are not.

2. Aggressiveness Habits and the Drive Model

This failure to give sufficient attention to eliciting cues also applies to a number of psychologists who are themselves somewhat uncomfortable with classic drive theorizing. Basing their reasoning on the operation of habits rather than energy notions, they too envision organisms as being propelled by constant internal action tendencies (habits) and only steered by external stimuli. Bandura and Walters (1963b) manifest this type of analysis, for example, in their discussion of the effects of filmed violence. They prefer to emphasize two processes in explaining why movie and TV aggression often leads to heightened aggressive responses by audience members: (a) imitative learning and (b) inhibitory and disinhibitory effects (cf. p. 60). By watching the actions of another person, they state, "the observer may require new responses that did not previously exist in his repertory." In addition, the observed model's behavior may also either arouse or weaken the audience's inhibitions against particular actions. Thus, witnessed hostility presumably gives rise to a persistent action tendency, a readiness to display aggression toward *anyone*. If certain persons are attacked rather than other people, the former supposedly have produced a disinhibition against aggression. As an example, they may somehow remind the observer that hostility toward these people is permissible.

3. Anger and the Drive Model

Skipping to another proponent of the standard model, Feshbach (1964) has argued for a distinction between two different kinds of instigations: (a) a drive to "hit," i.e., to express aggression, presumably arising innately from a preceding frustration, and (b) a drive to hurt someone which is said to be due to learning. But while these response tendencies are differentiated, Feshbach clearly sees both expressive aggression and deliberate injury attempts as impelled solely by internal stimulation. (According to Feshbach, the goal of the first-mentioned instigation is to discharge emotional excitation only through performing anger-expressive motor responses; attacks on anything or anyone presumably will do for this performance. I will return to this point later.)

While Feshbach's view of anger as pushing out at least certain kinds of aggressive responses is fairly typical, other psychologists besides myself have suggested deviations from this theoretical model. In a book published before my own text on this subject, Buss (1961) contended that anger only lowered the "threshold for the occurrence of aggressive responses," and "energized" these responses, but that the hostile actions themselves were habitual modes of responding to particular stimuli. Thus, contrary to my formulation, Buss does not seem to regard anger as a biologically determined, predisposing state, requiring the presence of some cue functioning as a releaser if the aggressive behavior is actually to occur.

The above represents only a sampling of recent interpretations of the instigation to aggression. Rather than attempt to summarize each of the published formulations, I have selected only a few conceptions in order to sharpen some of the theoretical issues. From my point of view the major issue revolves around the role of external cues. Is aggressive behavior primarily a response to some internal state, whether it be called "drive" or "habit," that is only guided by external conditions, or is the action evoked by external cues (which, however, may at times be represented within the organism)?

C. Cues Evoking Aggressive Responses

1. Effects of Movie Aggression

Some of the writer's recent experiments on filmed violence demonstrate how aggressive responses can be elicited by external cues. These investigations sought to test a line of reasoning that differed somewhat from the Bandura-Walters thesis outlined earlier. Where Bandura-Walters suggested that observed aggression would result in a heightened likelihood of attacks upon anyone, assuming inhibitions were low, my research predicted that specific targets would evoke the greatest volume of aggression (cf. Berkowitz, 1962, Ch. 9). Observed aggression supposedly activated the audience's previously acquired aggressiveness habits to the extent that the observed scene was associated with the prior conditions that had instigated aggression by the audience members. But this association is generally relatively weak, and so the activated habits do not necessarily lead to overt behavior even when inhibitions are low. If the audience members were then to encounter an appropriate stimulus having a strong cue value for aggression, the activation would intensify and the stimulus object would evoke fairly strong, aggressive responses. According to this formulation, a stimulus' cue value is a direct function of its association with (a) the observed violence, and/or (b) previous aggression instigators.

Three experiments to be reported here sought to vary a stimulus person's aggressive cue value by means of verbal labels. These labels either connected the person directly with the violent scene or did not associate him with the witnessed event. In all three experiments, further, essentially the same procedure was followed. When each subject, a male university student, entered the experimental room, he was introduced to another student, ostensibly another subject but actually the experimenter's paid confederate. The accomplice then either angered the subject or treated him in a neutral fashion. Following this, a seven-minute film clip was then shown, either a prize fight scene from the movie "Champion" or a nonaggressive, neutral film. The prize fight scene, it should be noted, was always introduced with a story summary which serves to lower restraints against aggression (Berkowitz and Rawlings, 1963; Berkowitz et al., 1963). Immediately after the movie each subject was provided with a socially sanctioned opportunity to administer electric shocks to the confederate who was then in another room.

The confederate's aggressive cue value was varied in the first experiment (Berkowitz, 1965b) by means of information regarding his role at the University. In one condition (Boxer Role) he was said to be a physical education major who was interested in college boxing, while in the other cases he supposedly was majoring in the Speech Department (Speech Major Role). For those people witnessing the prize fight film, the information that the confederate was a college boxer presumably would associate him with the observed violence and, therefore, should enhance the extent to which he would elicit electric shocks from the angered subjects. Or so we predicted.

Table I shows the mean number of shocks and the mean total duration of the shocks administered in each of the eight experimental conditions. As expected, the angered men who had seen the prize fight film sent a reliably higher volume of aggression toward the confederate when he was in the Boxer Role rather than the Speech Major Role. However, while this finding is consistent with the theorizing on which the study was based, other condition differences also shown in the table cast some doubt on the specific hypothesis. Holding constant the nature of the film, we can see that the subjects generally directed stronger aggression toward the Boxer than toward the Speech Major. This difference was statistically significant for the Nonangered Subjects when the measure was total shock duration. Why should the Boxer draw more and longer shocks, regardless of the nature of the witnessed scene and the confederate's degree of association with it, when the boxer had not provoked the men (to any noticeable extent at least)? One possibility, of course, is that his role had produced a disinhibition; the subjects could have been more willing

TABLE I
MEAN NUMBER AND DURATION OF SHOCKS[a]

	Angered subjects				Nonangered subjects			
	Boxer role		Speech major role		Boxer role		Speech major role	
	Agg. film	Neut. film	Agg. film	Neut. film	Agg. film	Neut. film	Agg. alm	Neut. film
Number of shocks	5.35_d	4.94_c	4.90_c	4.78_c	4.42_{abc}	4.37_{abc}	3.92_a	4.16_{ab}
Duration of shocks	16.56_d	11.47_c	11.90_c	11.16_{bc}	10.15_{bc}	12.04_c	6.67_a	8.15_{ab}

[a] Data from Berkowitz (1965b).
NOTE: Before analyzing the shock data an $\sqrt{X} + \sqrt{X + 1}$ transformation was employed. Separate analyses of variance were conducted for each measure. Cells having a subscript in common are not significantly different at the .05 level by Duncan Multiple Range test. Each mean is based on 11 cases.

to attack a person they believed to be a boxer. My preference, however, is to suggest that the label applied to the confederate governed the extent to which he could evoke aggressive responses from the subjects. Boxers could have elicited strong aggression either because they were disliked by these students or because of their connection with fighting.

A second experiment was then conducted (Berkowitz and Geen, 1966) which used another means of varying the confederate's association with the observed aggressive scene. This method capitalized on the fact that the well-known actor, Kirk Douglas, played the part of the character who received a fairly bad beating in the filmed prize fight. For half of the subjects the confederate was introduced at the start of the session as *Kirk* Anderson, while his name was given as *Bob* Anderson to the remaining people. We assumed that the subjects would associate Kirk, the confederate, with the prize fight scene because he had the same name as the film protagonist. One other change was made which should also be mentioned. The nonaggressive film clip used in this second experiment depicted a fairly exciting track race between the first two men to run a mile in less than four minutes. By contrast, the neutral film used in the earlier investigation was a less exciting excerpt from a movie about English canal boats.

The major findings obtained in this experiment are given in Table II. Here we can see much clearer evidence for the eliciting-cue hypothesis. Although the men who had been angered by Kirk reported feeling slightly

TABLE II

RATINGS OF FELT ANGER AND NUMBER OF SHOCKS GIVEN TO CONFEDERATE[a]

	Aggressive film				Track film			
	Angered		Nonangered		Angered		Nonangered	
	Kirk	Bob	Kirk	Bob	Kirk	Bob	Kirk	Bob
Felt anger	7.36_a	6.00_a	11.27_b	12.09_b	7.27_a	7.27_a	10.55_b	11.27_b
Number of shocks	6.09_a	4.55_b	1.73_c	1.45_c	4.18_b	4.00_b	1.54_c	1.64_c

[a] Data from Berkowitz and Geen (1966).

NOTE: For the "Felt anger" ratings, the *lower* the score the greater the anger. Each measure was analyzed separately, and in each case cells having a subscript in common are not significantly different at the .05 level by Duncan Multiple Range Test. There are 11 men in each condition.

less angry than the subjects who had been similarly provoked by Bob, the former people gave the confederate a reliably greater number of shocks than the latter group and also significantly greater than the Kirk-angered men shown the track film. The label applied to the frustrating confederate in this study resulted in the highest volume of aggression being directed toward him only when it associated this person with the violent scene. There were no differences between the "Kirk" and "Bob" conditions when the men had witnessed the nonaggressive event having no obvious connection with the confederate.

These findings, while not conclusive in themselves, strongly suggest that the designation of the confederate as a "boxer" in Experiment One had produced an eliciting rather than a disinhibiting effect. There is no reason to believe that the name Kirk had lowered restraints against aggression in the present study. Indeed, a supplementary investigation demonstrated that the students in this population tended to be relatively neutral in their feelings toward both the name "Kirk" and the actor Kirk Douglas.

A third experiment, by Geen and Berkowitz (1966), confirms and extends the earlier Berkowitz-Geen findings regarding label-mediated associations. In this investigation all of the subjects were led to become angry with a peer, the experimenter's confederate. Then again following our standard procedure, each subject was shown either the usual prize fight scene or the exciting track race, after which he was provided with the opportunity to give electric shocks to the confederate. And as before, the confederate's association with the aggressive event was varied by means of the name with which he was introduced to the subject at the start of the experimental session. But this time different names were used. Kirk Douglas

TABLE III

MEAN NUMBER OF SHOCKS ADMINISTERED TO ANGER-AROUSING CONFEDERATE[a]

Confederate's name	Boxing film	Track film
Kelly	5.40$_a$	3.60$_b$
Dunne	4.15$_b$	3.87$_b$
Riley	4.40$_b$	4.00$_b$

[a] Data from Geen and Berkowitz (1966.)

NOTE: Cells having a subscript in common are not significantly different at the .05 level by Duncan Multiple Range Test. There are 15 subjects in each condition.

played the part of a fighter named Midge Kelly, so one-third of the subjects in both movie conditions were told the confederate's name was Bob *Kelly*. His challenger in the filmed fight, and the person who gave the protagonist the bad beating, was a man called Dunne; for another third of the men, therefore, the confederate was introduced as Bob *Dunne*. Finally, in the case of the remaining subjects in both film groups, the frustrating confederate's name was given as Bob *Riley*, a name which does not occur at all in the boxing scene.

As Table III reveals, the results are entirely in accord with our theoretical expectations. The anger-arousing confederate had received significantly more shocks after the men had witnessed the prize fight film when he was called Kelly than when his name was Dunne or Riley. His name did not make a difference, however, when the subjects saw the track race, perhaps because the confederate was not connected with this film and/or the scene was nonaggressive in nature. (We might also note that the men in the Aggressive Movie condition as a whole gave significantly more shocks than the people in the combined Nonaggressive Movie groups, but only the "Kelly"-Aggressive Movie group differed reliably from each of the Nonaggressive Movie conditions considered separately.)

The confederate's aggressive cue value apparently varied directly with his association with the victim rather than the giver of the observed aggression; Kelly received stronger attacks than Dunne. (However, since the film character Dunne had a minor part in the scene, the confederate's degree of association with the event may not have been too great when he had the same name as this minor role.) But consistent with our associationistic theory, the confederate was also the recipient of relatively intense hostility when his name, like the movie protagonist's, was also obviously Irish, Riley. A generalization gradient evidently existed varying in association with the victim: Kelly-Riley-Dunne, and it was the target's location on this gradient that determined the extent to which he could evoke aggression from the angered subjects.

2. Dislike for Stimulus Person

The writer has also proposed (1962, pp. 152–160) that dislike for a stimulus object enhances its cue value for aggressive responses. The dislike presumably associates the object with other people who have aroused anger or, perhaps more generally, have instigated aggression. Several experiments have yielded findings consistent with this proposition. In one of the first of these (Berkowitz and Holmes, 1960), for example, we sought to determine whether the anger aroused by the experimenter would affect the aggression directed toward liked and less-liked people. College women were made to have either high or low liking for a peer and then were either deliberately frustrated or treated in a neutral manner by the experimenter. They were given three socially sanctioned opportunities to administer electric shocks to this peer: after the initial attitude toward the peer was inculcated but prior to the interaction with the experimenter, and then twice more following this interaction. Changes in the number of shocks sent to the peer from the first (baseline) period to the later occasions were employed as a measure of the extent to which the anger generated by the experimenter had influenced the strength of the aggressive responses directed toward the peer.

The results were as we had predicted. The girls who had been thwarted by the experimenter and who then had an opportunity to attack a disliked person exhibited a greater increase in the number of shocks given to their peer than did the subjects in any other condition. Contrary to a simple anger-drive notion, the experimenter's treatment of the women did not reliably affect the number of shocks sent to the peer when she was not disliked. The increased arousal state resulting from the experimenter's provocation had not led to strengthened attacks upon just anyone. It was primarily the disliked people who elicited a high volume of aggression from the strongly angered subjects.

But there is another possible explanation as well; the condition differences might be due simply to an accumulation of frustration effects. We created the negative attitude toward the peer by leading some women to believe that their peer had insulted them. Thus, some of the subjects had been insulted twice, by the peer and by the experimenter, and these two provocations acting together could perhaps have led to the strong attacks upon the only target available. Another experiment (Berkowitz and Green, 1962) was then conducted in which two people were available for attack. In this study, employing male college students, each subject was introduced to two other people, one a paid confederate and the other another actual subject. He rated his first impressions of these two men on an adjective checklist and then, as in the earlier experiment, was induced to have either high or lower liking for the confederate, and then was either deliberately provoked or given a kindlier treatment by the experimenter. Following this, each man worked with the confederate and the other person on a brief task after which he again rated both people on the adjective checklist. The hostility measure used in this investigation was the change in the favorableness of the ratings given to each of the other two people from the start to the end of the session.

Analyses of these changes again revealed results consistent with our expectations. The experimenter's provocation had increased the level of hostility expressed toward the disliked peer much more than toward the other, neutral person. While there were indications of a hostility displacement toward this neutral "bystander" (perhaps because, being in the experiment, he was associated with the thwarting researcher), the disliked stimulus person evoked stronger aggressive responses than he did. Thus, the comparatively intense resentment expressed toward the unpleasant stimulus person in both experiments is not merely due to the accumulation of frustration effects; some of the available targets received stronger attacks than did other possible victims. This difference in received hostility, further, is evidently not necessarily the result of differences in inhibitions against aggression that are aroused by each of the potential targets. If "Kirk" could draw stronger aggression from the angered men than could "Bob" in the Berkowitz-Geen study cited above, it is altogether possible that the disliked confederate could similarly evoke stronger aggression in the present investigation.

D. Some Results of Brain Stimulation Studies

The use of the classic drive model is by no means confined to those investigators who are concerned solely with animal or human behavior. Many students of internal physiological and neurological processes have been guided by essentially the same type of conception. Like the drive theorists, they have interpreted behavior as being the outcome of some particular pattern of internal events without giving sufficient attention to external stimulus conditions. Yet an increasing body of physiological research has demonstrated the importance of these external factors.

I have discussed one of these studies elsewhere (1962, 1964). Von Holst and von Saint Paul (1962) stimulated specific regions of chicken brains and found that specific situational cues were necessary to evoke recognizable aggressive responses from the fowls. The electrically induced arousal did not lead to attacks upon any available object. Organized aggressive behaviors were exhibited primarily when relevant cues ("an enemy, real or artificial") were present, while "only motor restlessness" was shown when "all substitutes for an enemy" were lacking.

Other relevant findings were reported by Roberts and Kiess (1964). Reviewing several investigations in which electrical stimulation was delivered to regions in the hypothalamus of cats, they noted that overt aggressive responses (such as hissing, growling and piloerection, as well as striking with claws) "were directed toward appropriate objects in the environment" but did not appear when the animals were in an empty area (p. 187). In their experiment hypothalamic stimulation caused normally nonaggressive cats to attack rats, but evidence was also obtained for a stimulus specificity. When various objects were presented separately to the stimulated animals in another phase of the study, 100% of the cats attacked either a live or dead rat, 89% a small stuffed dog, 33% a "hollow red rubber rat," 11% a "rat-sized wood block covered with white terrycloth," and none of the animals attacked "a rat-sized wood block" (W. W. Roberts, personal communication). Roberts also pointed out that several researchers have made similar observations. Wasman and Flynn, for example, mentioned in their paper (cited by Roberts and Kiess) that "the predatory attack was weaker to a dead rat than a live rat, and still weaker to a stuffed dog." In general, Roberts concluded "that the stimulation elicited a readiness for attack that was only performed (or perhaps 'released') when a relatively narrow range of objects was present."

One other observation made by Roberts and Kiess should be discussed here. The brain stimulation did not create a general arousal state which merely intensified whatever response sequence happened to be underway at the time. If the cats were eating when the stimulation was turned on, they would turn to attack a nearby rat rather than consume their food with increased vigor. This stimulation at least had a somewhat selective rather than general effect, and it may be that other types of arousal also increase the probability of certain response classes rather than making all actions equally likely.

E. IMPLICATIONS FOR OTHER CONCEPTIONS

The studies summarized so far have important implications bearing upon various conceptions of aggressive behavior. But in the interest of brevity we will single out only Feshbach's (1964) analysis of aggression, mentioned earlier, and also Schachter's (1964) theory of emotion.

According to Feshbach, expressive aggression must be differentiated from deliberate attempts to injure people. A frustrated person becomes angry and is then instigated "to hit rather than to hurt." Nothing is said about hitting particular objects. Indeed, the nature of the attacked object is theoretically unimportant in comparison to the "desire for a particular form of responding." Satisfaction is obtained through expressing the angry emotion rather than through injury to some person or object (p. 262). The view taken in the present paper, by contrast, is that the available objects help determine whether the aggressive responses will actually occur following the emotional arousal and, as we have seen, research findings document the importance of these objects. Consider the brain stimulation experiments just cited. These investigations created an arousal state that should have lead to just those forms of expressive aggression that Feshbach had in mind. Roberts and Kiess (1964) stated that the "rage" reaction exhibited by the electrically-stimulated cats "resembles the normal behavior of cats in conflict with animals of equal or larger size" (p. 187). Yet, many of the components of this "rage," such as striking with claws—perhaps equivalent to the "hitting" in the Feshbach scheme—were typically not performed unless appropriate objects were present. The nature of the available targets is important in this type of behavior.

It is conceivable, of course, that the electrical stimulation aroused only the second type of instigation discussed by Feshbach: the desire to hurt. Since the cats were not frustrated (in the technical sense of this term), perhaps they did not display a true rage reaction. But would we have predicted beforehand that the stimulation would give rise to the presumed desire to hurt and not to the expressive aggression? At any rate, why should we postulate two different instigations if available evidence can be accommodated under only one theoretical concept?

Schachter (1964) has published an important and provocative conception of emotions that gives special attention to the individual's environment, or at least to his understanding of it. Pointing out that "a general pattern of sympathetic discharge is characteristic of emotional states," Schachter maintained that any specific emotion is a function both of this physiological arousal and the individual's understanding of the events that produced the excitation. This cognition presumably "exerts a steering function." Two people may be similarly aroused physiologically, but one person may understand the precipitating situation as a happy event while the other individual regards it as unfortunate or bad. Because of these differing cognitions, the former person will act in a happy, elated manner and the second may exhibit depression or sadness.

An experiment conducted by Schachter and Singer (see Schachter, 1964) supports this reasoning. Subjects were aroused by giving them an injection of epinephrine and then were exposed to the actions of a peer. In some cases this other person (actually the experimenter's confederate) behaved in a euphoric if not manic manner, while for other people he acted as if he were very angry. Since we are here concerned with aggression, let us look at those subjects who watched the "angry" confederate. The experimenters predicted that those persons who did not have an appropriate explanation for the physiological sensations created by the drug (because they had been misinformed about the drug and its effects) would interpret their feelings in a manner consistent with the confederate's behavior. ("If he is angry, my feelings must mean that I am angry also.") In comparison to a nonaroused control group, they would then be more likely to rate themselves as feeling angry and would be more likely to exhibit aggressive actions. Where other people would understand their feelings differently, and therefore, would act differently, these subjects thought they were angry and then behaved in a manner consistent with this interpretation. By and large, the researchers' expectations were confirmed.

Walters and Parke (1964), however, advanced an explanation that is somewhat different from Schachter's and which is in accord with the present writer's own view of the Schachter-Singer study. According to Walters and Parke, the other investigators did not give sufficient attention to the actual sequence of events in their experiment. The physiologically aroused subjects may have acted aggressively and *then* interpreted their feelings as anger because of what they had done (p. 267). Phrasing this type of argument somewhat differently, I would also suggest that the subjects' cognitions had served to inhibit all but those actions which were consistent with their understanding of their sensations. Cues in the situation, such as the confederate's aggressive and perhaps unpleasant behavior, could have evoked aggressive responses from the physiologically aroused people. Becoming aware of these aggressive responses, they could have interpreted their feelings as "anger." This knowledge, which was perhaps also considerably influenced by the confederate's behavior, could have prevented various nonaggressive actions from appearing.

IV. Purpose in Aggressive Behavior

We now come to another of the controversies in the study of aggression: To what extent is intentionality important in defining an action as aggressive? The man on the street would have little trouble with such a question; he probably would distinguish readily between accidental and purposive injuries, saying that an individual was not being aggressive unless he had wanted to hurt some one. A number of psychologists, however, have questioned the scientific respectability of such a definition. Adherents of an old-fashioned behavioristic orthodoxy which condemned all theoretical reference to thought processes, they would cast out all inferences about goals, purpose, or intentions in behavior. Thus, Buss (1961) attempted to define aggression without considering intentionality, preferring to think of aggressive actions only as responses delivering noxious stimuli to other objects. How successful this attempt has been is open to question (Bandura and Walters, 1963b, pp. 112–115).

A. The Completion Tendency

But without debating the merits of orthodox behaviorism, there is ample reason to insist upon the inclusion of purpose in any theory of aggression. A number of recent investigations suggest that the activation of an aggressive response sequence establishes an aggressive goal. The organism possessing such an ongoing sequence seeks to inflict injury and is frustrated when this cannot be done. His intent or purpose, we might say, is to hurt someone. In discussing this phenomenon elsewhere (Berkowitz, 1962, 1964), I employed the concept of "completion tendency," maintaining that the infliction of harm is the goal "completing" an activated chain of aggressive responses. This notion assumes, in accord with writers as varied as Kurt Lewin and Fred Sheffield, that organisms have a general tendency to continue an activity until the activity goal is reached. Preventing them from reaching this goal and completing the activity is a frustration which leads to a heightened arousal state. In turn, the increased arousal (a) is felt as an unpleasant tension, and (b) strengthens the ongoing but blocked aggressive response sequence.

An experiment with mice (Lagerspetz, 1964, pp. 101–108) points to this completion tendency in animal aggression. A submissive or aggressive opponent was placed in the goal box either at the start of the experimental trials or after a fight had begun, while for a third set of animals the goal box was empty. The investigator then recorded the number of trials in which the mice crossed a charged electric grid to reach the goal box and the length of time taken to do this (i.e., the latency of the response). She found that the animals given a submissive opponent—and who therefore had not been severely punished for their aggression—crossed the charged grid most often and most quickly in order to reach this opponent if they had been interrupted in the middle of a fight. The obstruction crossings were fewest and slowest in this submissive-opponent condition when the goal box was empty. The fight had set an implicit aggressive response sequence into motion, so to speak. Interrupted combat (assuming it had not led to painful injuries), gave rise to an increased arousal, which then led to the more frequent and more rapid crossing of the obstruction. The mice apparently sought sufficient completion of the ongoing aggressive response chain operating within them. In a very real sense they had a goal or purpose.

The completion of the activated aggressive response sequence can also be rewarding and thus facilitate the learning process. Roberts and Kiess (1964) demonstrated this in their previously cited research with brain-stimulated cats. Not only did the hypothalamic stimulation cause the cats to attack rats, but the animals also learned to run a maze in order to get at their victims. This learning then deteriorated when the stimulation was omitted and no more attacks were made. As the experimenters concluded, the overt performance of the aggressive responses was evidently positively reinforcing. Worchel (1957) has obtained somewhat similar findings with college students. Here we assume that the tension resulting from the inability to complete the activated response chain is disturbing. People who aggressed against a frustrater, either directly to him or to another person, did reliably better on a digit-symbol test than similarly provoked subjects not given this aggressive opportunity.

If the ongoing aggressive response chain is not completed, according to Berkowitz (1964), this frustration results in a heightened arousal state. But in predicting the occurrence of such a frustration we must remember that the infliction of injury is the goal of an *ongoing or activated* aggressive response sequence. An angry person or someone with a "highly aggressive" personality is not necessarily frustrated if he does not have a target to attack. The anger in itself or the previous learning creates only a readiness for aggression; appropriate cues must also be present in order to set the response sequence into operation. Once such aggressive responses are put into motion, even if only implicitly in the person's thoughts, then an individual will not attain completion until the goal object has been aggressively injured. The writer has reported findings consistent with this formulation (cf. Berkowitz, 1962, 1964, for a more complete discussion). Deliberately angered men who had been prevented from attacking their frustrater immediately displayed a significantly stronger volume of aggression soon afterwards than did a nonprovoked control group—but only when they had initially expected to make the immediate attacks.

As I have argued elsewhere, explaining these findings by saying there was a frustrated "expectancy" or "set" is insufficient. What is an expectancy or set? Invoking these concepts as an explanation is only word magic. I would prefer to say that the men who expected to be able to attack their tormenter had provided themselves with cues activating implicit aggressive responses. They may have thought, for example, how they were going to get the person who had insulted them. These implicit symbolic cues had set into motion the aggressive responses their anger had primed them to make. When the aggressive expectancy was not fulfilled, the instigated aggressive responses operating within them were not completed; injury was not inflicted. As a consequence, the men were frustrated still more and a heightened arousal state resulted, strengthening the ongoing internal aggressive responses.

B. The Equivalence of Targets and Actions

Psychoanalytic and psychological discussions of hostility catharsis have given considerable attention to the problem of the equivalence of the various targets and actions (see Berkowitz, 1962, especially Chap. 8). Can *any kind* of attack upon *any object* produce a "catharsis"— or in my terms, serve as a completion of the instigated aggressive response chain? The view presented here suggests that only a relatively narrow range of possible substitute targets will yield completion but that there can be a fairly wide range of satisfactory aggressive actions.

Remember that aggressive responses are presumably set into motion by specific aggressive cues. These cues are generally particular objects, such as a frustrating person, or stimuli associated with these objects. It may well be that completion is attained only when the objects serving as or connected with the aggression-eliciting cues are deliberately injured. But because of man's conceptual abilities, the specific manner in which this injury is inflicted may not be too important; the aggressive individual may be satisfied by almost any kind of aggressive action—as long as it is the action that he has initially set out to perform.

There are two types of experiments which test the substitutability of various targets once an aggressive sequence has been activated. Some studies, those that are less appropriate, deal with the effects of filmed violence. They ask whether a person who has been angered by, say, Individual A, is less likely to aggress against this individual after witnessing a scene in which Individual B is severely beaten. If we assume that the completion of the activated aggressive response sequence results in a decreased probability of further aggression, these investigations determine whether viewing attacks upon one target can complete an aggressive sequence that had been initiated by another person. Available evidence indicates that this observation does not produce a substitute completion (cf. Berkowitz, 1962, Ch. 9). Thus, Berkowitz et al. (1963) found that deliberately provoked male college students expressed stronger—rather than weaker—hostility toward their frustrater after seeing a filmed villain being beaten than after witnessing a neutral, nonaggressive scene. The difficulty with such research, of course, is that observing aggression may not be sufficient for completion; there is still a possibility that direct attacks upon one person can substitute for aggression against another.

A more appropriate experiment, and the only one to my knowledge that really bears directly upon the present problem, was conducted by Hokanson et al. (1963). This study makes use of a finding obtained by Hokanson in other research. Systolic blood pressure rises in those people who are deliberately angered (and, perhaps, who cannot complete their activated, aggressive response sequences right away), and then tends to drop back to the baseline level after aggressive actions are taken. As I have suggested elsewhere (1962, p. 223), the high systolic pressure may be indicative of a high level of physiological tension resulting, in part at least, from the inability to complete the activated response chain. At any rate, the experimenters reported that frustrated college students exhibited a reduction in blood pressure level after attacking their tormenter, but that a similarly angered control group did not show as much of a decline in systolic pressure when they could aggress against only substitute objects such as the frustrater's assistant. Completion apparently is most readily achieved through attacks upon the aggression instigator.

A variety of investigations, on the other hand, point to the equivalence of different aggressive actions. The previously cited Worchel (1957) experiment, for example, suggests that indirect aggression in the form of complaints given to a person other than the frustrater had the same presumed tension-reducing effects as verbal aggression sent directly to the anger instigater. While the injury to the frustrater had to be mediated through another person in this study, the subjects probably believed that their tormentor would somehow be hurt by complaining to this other person.

More direct evidence of this equivalence of aggressive actions was obtained, however, by Hokanson and Burgess (1962). Half of the subjects, male and female college students, were deliberately angered and half were not. Several experimental conditions were then established immediately after this. One group of people could aggress against their tormenter right away by means of electric shocks. Another set of subjects was required to make exactly the same motor responses, i.e., press a button, but these actions would only flash a light and would not inflict injury. Two remaining conditions had to do with verbal behaviors. In one of these the people could aggress against the frustrater; they could rate him on a questionnaire. The other group, on the other hand, was asked only to create a story in response to a TAT card. Systolic blood pressure changes demonstrated again that there was a significant, physiological arousal following the provocation. But when the subjects attacked their frustrater, either physically (by the electric shocks) or verbally (through the questionnaire ratings), systolic pressure declined to the level of the nonangered groups. The physiological tension remained high in the other insulted groups even though they had carried out the same motor actions. Thus, it is evidently the belief that the aggression instigator has been injured that produces the presumed completion, not the form of the aggression in itself.

Perhaps we can say that the person in whom an aggressive response sequence has been activated has the goal of attaining this particular cognition. He wants to know that a certain object has been hurt. Perhaps, feeling the operating aggressive responses within him, and aware of the object that had set the response chain in motion (either by itself or through associated cues), his intent is to harm this object. He then may become frustrated if this goal is not achieved.

REFERENCES

Atkinson, J. W. (1958). *Motives in fantasy, action and society.* Princeton, N. J.: Van Nostrand.

Bandura, A., and Walters, R. H. (1963a). Aggression. In *Child psychology: the 62 yearbook of the National Society for the Study of Education,* Part 1. Chicago: The National Society for the Study of Education.

Bandura, A., and Walters, R. H. (1963b). *Social learning and personality development.* New York: Holt.

Berkowitz, L. (1962). *Aggression: a social psychological analysis.* New York: McGraw-Hill.

Berkowitz, L. (1964). Aggressive cues in aggressive behavior and hostility catharsis. *Psychol. Rev.* **71,** 104–122.

Berkowitz, L. (1965a). Aggression. In *International Encyclopedia of the Social Sciences* (in press).

Berkowitz, L. (1965b). Some aspects of observed aggression. *J. Pers. social Psychol.* **2,** 359–369.

Berkowitz, L., and Geen, R. G. (1966). Film violence and the cue properties of available targets. *J. Pers. social Psychol. (in press).*

Berkowitz, L., and Green, J. A. (1962). The stimulus qualities of the scape-goat. *J. abnorm. soc. Psychol.* **64,** 293–301.

Berkowitz, L., and Holmes, D. S. (1960). A further investigation of hostility generalization to disliked objects. *J. Pers.* **28,** 427–442.

Berkowitz, L., and Rawlings, E. (1963). Effects of film violence on inhibitions against subsequent aggression. *J. abnorm. soc. Psychol.* **66**, 405–412.

Berkowitz, L., Corwin, R., and Heironimus, M. (1963). *Public Opinion Quart.* **27**, 217–229.

Bindra, D. (1959). *Motivation: a systematic reinterpretation.* New York: Ronald Press.

Bowlby, J. (1957). An ethological approach to research in child development. *Brit. J. medical Psychol.* **30**, 230–240.

Buss, A. H. (1961). *The psychology of aggression.* New York: Wiley.

Buss, A. H. (1963). Physical aggression in relation to different frustrations. *J. abnorm. soc. Psychol.* **67**, 1–7.

Cofer, C. N., and Appley, M. H. (1964). *Motivation: theory and research.* New York: Wiley.

Davitz, J. R. (1952). The effects of previous training on postfrustration behavior. *J. abnorm. soc. Psychol.* **47**, 309–315.

Dollard, J., Doob, L., Miller, N., Mowrer, O., and Sears, R. (1939). *Frustration and aggression.* New Haven, Conn.: Yale Univer. Press.

Estes, W. K. (1958). Stimulus-response theory of drive. In M. R. Jones (Ed.), *Nebraska symposium on motivation, 1958.* Lincoln, Nebr.: Univer. Nebraska Press.

Feshbach, S. (1964). The function of aggression and the regulation of aggressive drive. *Psychol. Rev.* **71**, 257–272.

Freud, A. (1949). Aggression in relation to emotional development. *Psychoanal. Study Child* **3–4**, 37–41.

Geen, R. G., and Berkowitz, L. (1966). Name-mediated aggressive cue properties (in preparation).

Haner, C. F., and Brown, P. A. (1955). Clarification of the instigation to action concept in the frustration-aggression hypothesis. *J. abnorm. soc. Psychol.* **51**, 204–206.

Hartmann, H., Kris, E., and Loewenstein, R. M. (1949). Notes on the theory of aggression. *Psychoanal. Study Child* **3–4**, 9–36.

Hartup, W. W., and Himeno, Y. (1959). Social isolation vs. interaction with adults in relation to aggression in preschool children. *J. abnorm. soc. Psychol.* **59**, 17–22.

Hebb, D. O. (1949). *The organization of behavior.* New York: Wiley.

Hebb, D. O. (1955). Drives and C.N.S. (conceptual nervous system). *Psychol. Rev.* **62**, 243–254.

Hess, E. H. (1962). Ethology. In R. Brown *et al.* (Eds.), *New directions in psychology.* New York: Holt.

Hinde, R. A. (1960). Energy models of motivation. *Symp. Soc. exp. Biol.* **14**, 199–213.

Hokanson, J. E., and Burgess, M. (1962). The effects of three types of aggression on vascular processes. *J. abnorm. soc. Psychol.* **64**, 446–449.

Hokanson, J. E., Burgess, M., and Cohen, M. F. (1963). Effects of displaced aggression on systolic blood pressure. *J. abnorm. soc. Psychol.* **67**, 214–218.

Kluckhohn, C. (1945). Group tensions: analysis of a case history. In L. Bryson *et al.* (Eds.), *Approaches to national unity.* New York: Harper.

Lagerspetz, K. (1964). *Studies on the aggressive behavior of mice.* Helsinki: Suomalainen Tiedeakatemia.

Miller, N. E. (1941). The frustration-aggression hypothesis. *Psychol. Rev.* **48**, 337–342.

Miller, N. (1964). Some implications of modern behavior theory for personality change and psychotherapy. In P. Worchel and D. Byrne (Eds.), *Personality change*. New York: Wiley.

Miller, N., and Dollard, J. (1941). *Social learning and imitation*. New Haven: Yale Univ. Press.

Rank, B. (1949). Aggression. *Psychoanal. Study Child* **3–4,** 43–48.

Roberts, W. W., and Kiess, H. O. (1964). Motivational properties of hypothalamic aggression in cats. *J. comp. physiol. Psychol.* **58,** 187–193.

Schachter, S. (1964). The interaction of cognitive and physiological determinants of emotional state. *Adv. exp. soc. Psychol.* **1,** 49–80.

Thorpe, W. H. (1957). *Learning and instinct in animals*. London: Methuen.

Tinbergen, N. (1951). *The study of instinct*. London: Oxford Univer. Press.

von Holst, E., and von Saint Paul. U. (1962). Electrically controlled behavior. *Sci. American* **206,** 50–59.

Walters, R. H., and Brown, M. (1964). A test of the high-magnitude theory of aggression. *J. exp. Child Psychol.* **1,** 376–387.

Walters, R. H., and Parke, R. D. (1964). Social motivation, dependency, and susceptibility to social influence. *Adv. exp. soc. Psychol.* **1,** 231–276.

Worchel, P. (1957). Catharsis and the relief of hostility. *J. abnorm. soc. Psychol.* **55,** 238–243.

Young, P. T. (1961). *Motivation and emotion*. New York: Wiley.

AUTHOR INDEX

Numbers in italics refer to pages on which the complete references are listed.

SUBJECT INDEX

A

Ability,
  conformity and, 164–166
  inference and, 221–222
  perceived, 103
  problem solving and, 110–112
Acquisition, 6–8, 7, 11–20
Action(s),
  ambiguity of, 259–263
  effects of, 225–226
  equivalence of, 326–327
  hedonic relevance of, 237–246
Activity level, 309–311
Adrenalin,
  aversive conditioning and, 39
Affective arousal, *see* Emotional arousal
Aggression, 23–25, 26
  brain stimulation and, 319–321
  completion tendency and, 323–325
  cues and, 22–25, 308–309, 313–319
  disinhibition and, 21
  dislike for stimulus person and, 318–319
  emotion and, 23–28, 321–322
  equivalence of targets and actions and, 325–327
  expectancy and, 325
  expressive, 321
  "freefloating," 311
  frustration-aggression hypothesis and, 304–309
  movie, 313–318
  observational learning and, 14–16, 20, 21–28
  psychoanalytic theory and, 302–304
  purpose in, 323–327
  releaser and, 25, 304
  vicarious participation in, 21–28
Aggressive drive, 311–313
Aggressive reaction,
  innate nature of, 307–308
Aggressive response,
  strength of, 308

Aggressor,
  evaluation of, 249–258
Ambivalence, 255–258
Anger,
  aggression and, 23–28
  drive and, 312–313
Animal(s),
  emotional arousal in, 36–37
  observational learning in, 16–18, 33
Anticonformity, 134–135
Arousal, 27–28, 34–35
  brain stimulation and, 320–321
  completion tendency and, 323–325
  drive and, 309–310
  emotional, *see* Emotional arousal
Aspiration(s),
  power and, 198–199
Association,
  label-mediated, 315–318
Associative theory,
  reponse acquisition and, 3–4
Attentional shifts, 28
Attitude,
  group influence and, 144
  leader and, 120
Attitude change,
  power and, 184, 199–200, 203–205
  prejudice and, 201
Attribute-effect linkage, 224
Attribution of intentions, *see* Inference
Autokinetic effect,
  social influence and, 140–142
Autonomic responses,
  vicarious emotional arousal and, 34–35
Avoidance-conditioning, 36–37

B

Behavior,
  conforming, *see* Conformity
  effects of exposure to modeling stimuli on, 14–34
Behavior control, 191–192